Developing ActiveX Web Controls

Al Williams

THE CORIOLIS GROUP

Publisher	Keith Weiskamp
Project Editor	Scott Palmer
Cover Artist	Gary Smith/Performance Design
Cover Design	Anthony Stock
Layout Design	Bradley O. Grannis
Layout Production	April Nielsen
Copy Editor	Patrick J. Vincent, Scott Palmer
Proofreader	Marisa Peña
Indexer	Lenity Mauhar

Trademarks: Any brand names and product names included in this book are trademarks, registered trademarks, or trade names of their respective holders.

Text copyright © 1996 Coriolis Group, Inc. All rights under copyright reserved. No part of this book may be reproduced, stored, or transmitted by any means, mechanical, electronic, or otherwise, without the express written consent of the publisher.

Copyright © 1996 by The Coriolis Group, Inc.

All rights reserved.

Reproduction or translation of any part of this work beyond that permitted by section 107 or 108 of the 1976 United States Copyright Act without the written permission of the copyright owner is unlawful. Requests for permission or further information should be addressed to The Coriolis Group, 7339 E. Acoma Drive, Suite 7, Scottsdale, Arizona 85260.

The Coriolis Group, Inc.
7339 E. Acoma Drive, Suite 7
Scottsdale, AZ 85260
Phone: (602) 483-0192
Fax: (602) 483-0193
Web address: http://www.coriolis.com

1-57610-002-2: $39.99

Printed in the United States of America

10 9 8 7 6 5 4 3 2 1

For my mother, Bea, and, of course, always for Pat.

Acknowledgments

One of the best things about working on a book is all the great people you get to impose upon. For all the impositions, they get a crummy mention at the front of the book. Kind of like one of those shirts that says, "Someone went to Hawaii, and all I got was this lousy shirt." Except, someone probably reads the shirt. Nevertheless, to me, this is the most important page in this book. I hope you'll take a moment to find out why. I'm sure I can't remember everyone who deserves a pat on the back, but here goes, anyway.

My thanks to the Coriolis folks including: Jeff Duntemann for all of his encouragement over the years and for saving me from driving perpetually through the Arizona desert; Keith Weiskamp for turning me on to what a big deal ActiveX really is; and–not least–Scott Palmer for having to put up with my schedule and running interference for me.

Thanks, too, to Jon Erickson of *Dr. Dobb's Journal* for many things, the least of which was allowing me to reuse the TCONTROL example which appeared in a different form in that magazine.

Another fellow who deserves special recognition is my old friend Beau Senyard. I owe Beau for plenty of things, but especially for loaning me a laptop when mine decided to die about month before this book was due to go to press.

Normand and Yvette Damien–our local movie experts–cross checked my cinema references which helped keep me honest. Next time we are at the movies, I guess I'll have to buy the popcorn.

Thanks to William Shakespeare for the quotes. Or thanks to Sir Francis Bacon. It depends on your opinion.

As always, I am greatly indebted to my lovely wife, Pat, and our kids (Jerid, Amy, and Patrick) for putting up with my lunacy when the deadlines draw near. Nothing I do would be possible without Pat's help and support. Thanks for some great years!

No thanks, I'm afraid, can go to Madison, our spoiled Dachshund, whose contribution to this book was limited to forcing me to get up every few minutes to let her in or out of the house.

—Al Williams

Contents

Introduction xv

Part 1 ActiveX Fundamentals 1

Chapter 1 The Future Of Windows, The Web, And Everything 3

A Peek Over The Shoulder 4
What About Us? 5
    WinInet 7
    Local Caching 8
    Browsing 8
    ActiveX Controls And Containers 8
    ActiveX Categories 9
    Monikers: URL And Asynchronous 9
    ISAPI 10
    Scripting 11
    Security 11
Summary 12

Chapter 2 One Mile Up 13

The Structure Of An
  ActiveX Object 14
Definitions 14
That's An Object? 16
Code Reuse 17
Polymorphism 19
A Few Miscellaneous
  ActiveX Oddities 20
  HRESULT and SCODE 20
  GUID/UUID/IID 21
About IUnknown 22
Creating Objects And
  Finding Interfaces 23
More About Reference Counts 24
About Aggregation 25
More Oddities 27
  Predefined Interfaces 27
  Type Libraries 27
  Proxies, Stubs, And Marshalling 28
  About Multiple Threads 30
The ActiveX/C++ Connection 30
Why Not Use C++ Directly? 31
Why Not Use Java? 31
Summary 32

Chapter 3 Information, Please 33

Give Up INI Files? 34
The Registry: Up Close
  And Personal 35
Registry Oddities 37

Contents ix

RegEnumValue 37
RegDeleteKey 37
Error Returns 38
Typed Data 38

An Example 38

That's It? 49

Registering Objects 50

Class Installation 52

Using REGEDIT 53

Self-Registration 55
Self-Registering EXEs 56
Self-Registering DLLs 56

Impersonating Objects 56

Type Libraries 57
Where Is The Type Library? 58
Creating Type Libraries 60
Type Library Wrap-Up 63

Summary 63

Part 2   Getting Down And Dirty 65

Chapter 4   Get On With It, Man! 67

Macro Mania 69

Learning Client Basics 70

A Simple Server Design 74
General Server Issues 75
Server Usage 76
Class Factories 76

A Simple Client 76

An EXE Server 78

Contents

    Will That Work? 83
    No Peeking 85
    Marshalling 85
    Writing the Script 86
    Now It Works! 88
    More About The Server 88

A DLL Server 89

Supporting Multiple Interfaces 93

MFC Techniques 94
    An MFC EXE Server 95
    Other Considerations 104

An MFC DLL Server 105

MFC Aggregation 106

Summary 108

Chapter 5   Interface Bestiary 109

IMalloc And IMallocSpy 110

IEnum 111

IStorage And IStream 119
    Streams in Detail 122
    Storages in Detail 124
    Practical Considerations 127
    An Example 127
    The Implementation 129

ILockBytes 141

IPersistFile, IPersistStream, And IPersistStorage 142
    IPersistFile 142
    IPersistStream and IPersistStreamInit 143
    IPersistStorage 144
    Associating CLSIDs with Storage 145

IMoniker And IOleItemContainer 147

IConnectionPoint And IConnectionPointContainer 150

IProvideClassInfo 151
IDispatch 152
BSTR, SAFEARRAY, and VARIANT 154
Back to Invoke 158
Simplifying IDispatch 161
Binding Time and Efficiency 170

IDataObject 171
The End Of The Bestiary 175

Chapter 6   ActiveX Controls   177

Some History 178
The Simplest Web Control 179
Traditional Controls—A User's View 185
Properties 186
Methods 188
Events 188
Extended Controls 188
Stock Properties, Methods, and Events 189
Persistence 190
Runtime State 191
Keyboard Handling 191
Frame Controls 191

Traditional Control Interfaces 191
IOleObject 193
IOleClientSite 196
IOleInPlaceObject 197
IOleInPlaceActiveObject 198
IOleControl 198
IRunnableObject 200
IViewObject and IViewObject2 200
IOleCache and IOleCache2 200
IPropertyPage and IPropertyPage2 201
ISpecifyPropertyPages 203
IPerPropertyBrowsing 203
IExternalConnection 204
Extra Registry Entries 204

Bad News/Good News 205
Getting Started With MFC 206

Using Control Wizard 206
Code You Add 208
Adding Properties 210
Using Ambient Properties 212
Adding Methods 212
Adding Events 213
Adding Property Sheets 215
More Sophisticated Additions 216
Examining the Generated Files 216
Testing and Using the Control 217

A Simple Control 218

A More Useful Control 229

A Subclassed Control 236

Subclassing A Custom Control 243

A Custom Control 244
Subclassing the Control 249
Using the Control 256

Summary 257

Part 3 ActiveXing The Internet 259

Chapter 7 ActiveX And The Internet 261

Building The Browser 268
About CFormView 285

ActiveX And Non-Dialog Views 288

Asynchronous Monikers 298

URL Monikers 302

Code Downloading 303
Writing An INF File 304
Building a CAB File 306

Seeking Components 307
Trust Verification 307
Using Trust Verification 309
Summary 312

Chapter 8 Other Interface Building Techniques 315

About Templates 317

Key Features Of The ActiveX Template Library 320

Drawbacks Of ATL 322

Getting Started With ATL 322

Working With Maps 324

Customizing Interfaces 326

Decreasing Code Size 327

Aggregation And ATL 328

Creating Enumeration Classes 328

Connection Point Containers 329

Tear-off Interfaces 330

Error Handling 330

An ATL Project 331

Next Steps 336

Useful ATL Classes 337

BASECTL: Another Approach 339

Summary 340

Chapter 9 The End? 343

The Future Of The Internet 345

The Future Of Java 345

The Future Of Other Object Standards   346
The Future Of Windows   346
The Future Of Programming   347
Where To Go?   348
End Of The Soapbox   349

Appendix A   ActiveX Thesaurus And Glossary   351

Appendix B   Just Enough HTML   359

What's On The CD-ROM   369

Index   371

Introduction—
What Is ActiveX?

*You shall seek all day ere you find them,
and, when you have them,
they are not worth the search.*

—The Merchant of Venice

EVERY FEW YEARS, the programming community sets out on a new quest. I think the first quest I personally witnessed was the search for modular code: that was when FORTRAN ruled. Later quests sent everyone after structured design methodology, artificial intelligence, neural networks, and object-oriented programming. All of these "holy grails" have one thing in common: upper-management types knew that these technologies would allow them to get rid of those ornery, rude, high-paid, unsociable programmers. Any technology that will allow you to have monkeys turning out high-quality, provably-correct code must be a good thing, right?

Funny, that never seems to happen—and good for us, eh? We all go merrily along writing our programs, using what new techniques are useful and discarding those that are not. In the last few years, you've probably heard about the upcoming software component revolution. Of course, it will allow monkeys and dogs to write software and cure all known ills. Is this just another fad?

This time, I think it's not just another fad. Software components have the potential to revolutionize software development. Don't worry. There won't be any dogs and monkeys, but things will be different (and I think better) for the humans who create computer software.

It's Happened Before!

Before we look at software components and ActiveX, let's talk about an industry where the same transformation occurred a few years ago: the electronics industry. I started in this business, by the way, as a hardware designer. I only got the programming bug when I started working on embedded systems. Even when I was a kid, I loved electronics. I had a ham radio license before I had a driver's license.

When I first became interested in electronics, you did everything with individual transistors, and occasionally with tubes. The electronics magazines of the day had projects you could build: hi-fi amplifiers, light beam communicators, metal detectors, and so on. Lightweight stuff compared to today's high technology. An advanced project might have a dozen or more individual transistors and 50 or more other components.

Suppose that you were a design engineer in those days, and your boss told you to create an electronic ear to listen for fish. You might start with a special crystal that changes sound into electricity. You'd also need a very sensitive amplifier. On your first attempt at building an amplifier, you use four transistors. It works well, but when the device gets hot, the speaker squeals, indicating that you need a way to compensate for temperature. Add two more transistors. A bit later, you discover that if an electric boat motor is operating nearby, you can't hear any fish at all. You need a filter and better common-mode noise rejection (whatever that is). Add five more transistors. If this were a government project to listen for submarines, you could use 11 transistors (or even more). You could spend a year designing the amplifier. However, you boss wants to sell fish finders for $9.95. Emulate the Pentagon, and your employer will quickly scrap both the project *and* you.

The problem isn't that you don't know how to design an amplifier. The problem is that you can only sell 10,000 fish finders for $9.95. That means you can't use 40 transistors and spend two years developing the thing. But what if you could sell 10,000,000?

What revolutionized the electronics industry was the integrated circuit (IC). ICs are little slivers of silicon that hold miniature electronic components. Your CPU and memory chips are ICs. You can also get outstanding amplifier ICs. Today, if your boss wants a fish finder, you'll just grab an amplifier IC and use it. In fact, it will probably be a much better amplifier than you need, but so what? In quantity it will only cost ten cents. The amplifier might contain 40 transistors. It probably took two people a year to design. The IC probably contains four identical amplifiers for a total of 160 transistors! All for ten cents.

There are several reasons this is possible: First, ICs are expensive to design, but cheap to make. It is more expensive to make an IC with 10,000 transistors than it is to make one with 100 transistors, but it isn't 100 times as expensive. Second, with the price so low, and the quality so high, your company will easily buy 10,000. So will your competitors. The big fish finder company will buy 250,000. Companies you haven't even heard of will buy millions. The IC manufacturer will sell many more amplifiers than your company can alone.

Of course, all of this only works because the ICs follow well-documented standards. Packages are standard and the manufacturer makes the connections known via a data sheet. Often identical parts are available from multiple vendors. If an IC is popular, vendors will create enhanced parts that can replace the original but perform even better.

What's this got to do with software? If you think about it, the software business is startlingly similar:

1. All the costs go into design
2. You usually can't afford to over-design software
3. If you can sell lots of software, you can afford to sell it cheap

So?

You might be wondering, "So What?" Imagine if programming could work this way. If you like down and dirty programming, you could create components that might have a wide audience. If you prefer solving problems to programming, you can assemble solutions from well-designed standard components. Even if you are creating components, you might use other components as building blocks to construct part or even all of your creation.

So how does this relate to ActiveX? ActiveX is Microsoft's standard for building binary software components. This standard allows you to deploy components in DLLs, executable files, across different machines over a network or even over the Internet. Because it is a binary standard, you can write components (or programs that use components) in any language–at least in theory.

If you thought Microsoft called this standard OLE, don't feel bad. Microsoft seems to change all the terminology surrounding this technology every few months. At one time or another, Microsoft used the terms OLE controls, OCX (OLE Control Extensions), and COM objects to refer to what is now ActiveX. This is so confusing, you might want to look at the *ActiveX Thesaurus* in Appendix I to get some historical perspective.

Ahead of its Time

Is ActiveX a new technology? Yes and no. The term ActiveX is recent, but the technology is an extension of existing OLE/COM (Component Object Model) specifications. Don't worry too much about ActiveX technology changing as it matures, however. One of the keys to ActiveX is that it is extensible and allows changes to occur without breaking existing code.

The newest parts of ActiveX allow components to store data efficiently when that data must pass over a network like the Internet. If you follow this part of the specification your controls will work with popular web browsers. However, this is just a standard. You can, if you like, design your own protocols for use with ActiveX. Don't expect anyone else to use them, of course, but the capability is there.

As a new technology, ActiveX is likely to change in the short term. However, because ActiveX builds on a more mature, extensible technology, these changes will be minimal. As you learn more about ActiveX, you'll see that the core is very simple–the complex parts are the agreements between providers (servers) and consumers (clients) about how to utilize that core.

Where to Now?

ActiveX (by other names) has been important for programmers interested in compound documents and components for Visual Basic. But now, with the explosive growth of the World Wide Web, ActiveX is emerging as a standard for developing components that can work across the desktop or across the continent.

If you have heard that OLE or ActiveX programming is difficult, put that aside. In the next few chapters, you'll see that the ideas behind ActiveX are quite simple. A Lego block isn't very complicated. Still, kids build some very complex space ships with them. ActiveX is the same way. By itself, it is very simple. If you want to make a tower, that's not very difficult. However–like Legos–you can build ActiveX space ships that are very complex. Any bad reputation that ActiveX has is probably due to the complex protocol involved in creating compound documents—for example, creating a graphic you can embed in a Microsoft Word document. This is a small sliver of the ActiveX picture, and one made of many individual ActiveX Legos. Taken individually, none of these is very difficult. It is the number of Legos and the relationship between them that are sometimes difficult to understand.

In this book, we will only look at ActiveX as it relates to building reusable controls. Although this can have some complex sides to it, it can also be as simple as you want it to be. True, there are some special concerns when you want to operate the controls over a network, including the Internet. Still, if you approach the subject logically, it isn't too difficult. Certainly, learning C++, event driven programming, or the Windows API is at least as tough.

What Should I Have?

Speaking of C++, event driven programming, and the Windows API, you should know these things before you attempt ActiveX development. Truthfully, you don't need an in-depth knowledge of C++. If you understand classes and inheritance, you should have no problem. Don't worry if you haven't delved into type-safe casts, RTTI, and other C++ oddities–you don't have to do anything that complex to work with ActiveX. It is true that you can create ActiveX programs using any language, but we will use C++ and the Microsoft Foundation Classes (MFC) to simplify development in most cases.

If you don't know MFC, don't worry. ActiveX programs are quite a bit different from ordinary Windows programs. If you know how to write regular applications with MFC, it won't hurt, but it won't help all that much, either. The current version of MFC doesn't directly help you write most ActiveX programs, but with a little coaxing it can do most of the work for you.

The examples in this book work with Microsoft Visual C++ version 4.1 (and probably later versions, too). They should also work with other compilers that support MFC. Be sure to check out our World Wide Web page (http://www.coriolis.com) for details about later versions.

Go Get Started

Like most things, the best way to learn about ActiveX is to jump right in and get started. If you are familiar with the general idea of ActiveX (or COM) and you know about the system registry, you might skip ahead to Chapter 4. Otherwise, read on for a peek at the near future and how the times are "a-changing."

PART 1

ActiveX Fundamentals

The Future Of Windows, The Web,
   And Everything   3
One Mile Up   13
Information, Please   33

1

The Future Of Windows, The Web, And Everything

*The undiscovered country from whose bourn
No traveler returns, puzzles the will,
And makes us rather bear those ills we have
Than fly to the others that we know not of.*

—Hamlet

WHAT DOES WWW STAND FOR? Okay, it is supposed to stand for *World Wide Web*. But sometimes when I'm in one of my more cynical moods, I think it stands for *Wow! What a Waste*. On the other hand, when I'm being more charitable, I think it means *Whatever, Whenever, Wherever*. If Microsoft gets its way, however, it will stand for the *Wonderful Windows Workplace* or something like that.

Microsoft's vision of the future (apparently) is to integrate Windows with the Internet as seamlessly as possible. This vision—today known as *AIP* or Active Internet Platform—is really two pieces. The piece the users see looks suspiciously like a Web browser that can browse everything (not just Web pages). The part programmers see is a bit more complicated, but it supports several things you need to successfully integrate Windows, the Internet, and networks in general. It also helps programs browse things (on or off the Net) with a minimum of fuss. ActiveX is an integral part of AIP. AIP uses ActiveX, and you must use ActiveX to fully utilize AIP.

A Peek Over The Shoulder

Suppose in the near future, you are browsing the Web and you wind up on my home page. My latest white paper expounds that the key to programmer productivity is to have an office with a door and one programmer per office. You think this is rubbish (perhaps you sell Herman Miller cubicles) and decide to set me straight. First, you click on the telephone icon at the bottom-right corner of the Web page—you'd like to talk to me directly.

The telephone obligingly rings (complete with an animation of a phone shaking). After a minute, my answering machine page comes on the screen. An AVI file plays a video of me telling you that I'm not in but you can leave a message. You click on the back button to go back to the original page and disconnect the call. You then click on the mailbox icon (next to the telephone) to send me a flaming note.

You are still working in the "Web browser" but now it looks slightly different. The menus and toolbars look suspiciously like Microsoft Word (or whatever your favorite word processor is). A dialog box pops up, prompting you to select one of my "in boxes". Annoyed that you can't start composing your mail, you pick *Complaints* and dismiss the dialog. After the automatically generated mail header, you begin typing your point of view about cubicle workspace synergy.

As you compose your message, you remember that you have a nice chart showing that the ideal number of programmers per cube is three. You click on the *Favorite Places* menu item and open the Charts folder. Nothing changes—you are still in the browser, but it shows you a list of chart documents. You click on one to open it (just a single click) and you copy it to the clipboard. Two clicks on the back button brings you back to your email in progress. You paste the chart in and smugly press *Send* on the toolbar.

The Future Of Windows, The Web, And Everything 5

Satisfied that you have made your point, you decide to pay some bills. Another click on *Favorite Places* brings you to a page that looks very much like Quicken. It isn't Quicken, however. You are still working in the browser. The only difference is that the "page" you are browsing looks like Quicken and the browser's menus and toolbars merge with Quicken's toolbar. The Quicken/browser automatically and securely logs you into your bank over the Internet.

This is AIP's *Page View* (see Figure 1.1). You don't have to use page view. If you prefer, you can still do things the way you do now: open a program or a document and manage multiple windows. However, the page view is quite simple and mimics a Web page in every way. In the above scenario, you can't tell when you are working on a local application, a Web page, or something else. For example, the answering machine application runs on my machine, not yours. The ringing telephone control also belongs to me. The dialog box where you select my mail in-box belongs to me, too. My computer made your copy of Word display it.

What About Us?

That's the user's view. But what does this mean to programmers? Does this mean we just write plug-in modules for Microsoft's Web browser? No. Although the programming part of AIP supports the page view, that's just the tip of the iceberg.

Figure 1.1 Page View in Action.

Here's a list of the major components integral to AIP. They're illustrated in Figure 1.2.

1. WinInet, an API that presents a high-level interface that allows you to easily fetch files (and perform other common operations) from the Internet without bothering with details
2. Local caching of resources over a network
3. A generalized browsing mechanism that keeps track of the navigation portion of a browsing application
4. An ActiveX-enabled browser that allows any ActiveX (OLE) server to reside on a browser page
5. ActiveX controls that know how to display common data types (GIF, JPEG, AVI, and so on)
6. Support for ActiveX controls that reside on remote machines or store data on remote machines; Web pages can automatically download ActiveX controls and install them
7. More efficient ways of communicating information about ActiveX controls in the system registry without creating them (Categories)
8. A method to represent a URL (for example, *http://www.coriolis.com*) at the operating system level (URL Monikers)

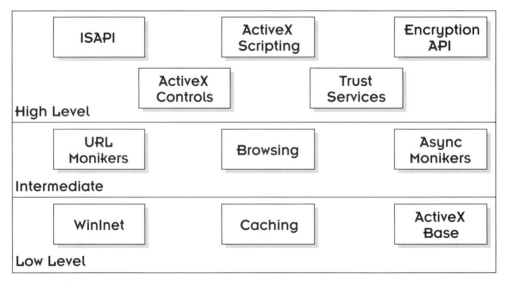

Figure 1.2 AIP Components.

9. A mechanism (Asynchronous Monikers) that allows ActiveX to load large blocks of data over a potentially slow network connection (and using the cache mentioned in item 2, above)
10. A programming API (the Internet Server API or ISAPI) to customize Web server functionality
11. A generalized scripting service that you can use to control Web pages (or any other compatible program, for that matter)
12. Methods to verify that downloaded code is safe, encrypt data, and rate content (similar to rating movies)

Nearly all of the AIP uses ActiveX controls—that's why you need to know how to use ActiveX and how to create your own ActiveX components. This has several advantages. First, ActiveX does a great deal of work to make certain that you don't care much if a component and its user are on the same machine. Also, ActiveX is extensible. Suppose a new graphics format becomes popular on the Web next week (not hard to imagine, eh?). With ActiveX, you only need to install a new component to take advantage of it.

In the following sections, I'll show you what each of the above pieces means to you. Don't worry about the details; I'll get into those in the next few chapters. For now, try to see how each piece is important. The same goes for terms. In this chapter, I'll throw around some terms without rigorously defining them. That, too, will come in later chapters.

WinInet

Since the goal of AIP is to integrate seamlessly with the Internet, it isn't surprising that one of the core AIP technologies is a simple way to work with networks. If you've been frustrated trying to write WinSock programs in the past, then WinInet is for you. As an example of how easy this is, consider the case where you want to read a file from a Web server. You can use simple calls like *InternetOpen*, *InternetOpenUrl*, and *InternetReadFile* to retrieve the file. Similar services make it easy to work with the FTP and Gopher protocols, too.

Before you use the WinInet calls, you always call *InternetOpen*. Like many other API calls, this one returns a handle to you. However, this handle refers to the Internet (it is a hINTERNET). Imagine what you can do with that. WinInet takes care of all the messy details of establishing the connection, negotiating protocols, and those other things that you don't care about.

Local Caching

The Internet isn't necessarily speedy. True, connections are getting faster, but the connection speed usually pales compared to the raw speed of the machine. Even if the network connection is fast, there are many, many users on the Internet (make that many, many, *many*). This makes caching of data very important. Instead of loading a file over and over again, why not load it once, keep a copy of it, and satisfy future requests from the same file?

That is the purpose of the Cache API. It allows programs to associate a file on disk with a URL. You can specify if the cache system will automatically free these associations and files when the cache begins to fill. WinInet calls can also specify that they wish to bypass the cache. You might want to directly reread a file from the Internet if its contents are volatile or you suspect it has changed.

Browsing

Because browsing is so integral to AIP, Microsoft provides two ways you can easily create browsing applications. The first is an ActiveX component that manages browsing. What you browse—URLs, files, database records—isn't important. The browsing component helps you maintain a context where you can move backwards, forwards, and maintain a history regardless of the actual content.

Since some programs don't use ActiveX, there is a simplified API you can use to support browsing. This API is not as powerful as the ActiveX version because it is a simple wrapper around the base ActiveX objects.

ActiveX Controls And Containers

ActiveX is more than just the technology that Microsoft uses to build AIP—it is an integral part of how programmers use and extend AIP. The page view I described above is little more than a Web browser that can contain ActiveX controls and some special ActiveX controls to provide views on a variety of objects.

More importantly, the browser can automatically download ActiveX controls on demand. In the above example, my Web page specified a ringing telephone icon. If your machine didn't already have it, the browser would automatically download it from my computer.

Any ActiveX program can use any ActiveX control. If you want an ActiveX container to display your data or special control, you can write your own ActiveX controls. That's what this book is all about.

ActiveX Categories

OLE controls (the precursor to ActiveX) relied on the registry to alert containers to their presence. However, this didn't tell the container what the control does. Categories allow ActiveX components to notify clients that they are present, and also what they can do. In this way, you can be reasonably certain that it is worthwhile for a container like the browser to create a component (which may take a while).

Consider this example: In an old-style container, you need to create a control that can load a BMP file. First you create a control and ask it if it can load BMPs. If the answer is no, you destroy the control and move on to the next one. This is very inefficient, particularly when the controls may reside on the Internet.

ActiveX components can place entries in the registry (using unique Category IDs or CATIDs) that signify that they can handle certain operations (for example, loading BMP files). A container need only scan the registry to determine which component can load BMP files. Then, if the container creates the component, it is reasonably sure it will do the right things. The user can also associate a default component with a particular CATID. Then containers that want to display BMP files, for example, can use the default component even if several components have that capability.

Categories also allow components to request certain functions from a container. This allows containers to not waste time creating components that they can't use.

Some containers may want to display categories graphically (for instance, in a tool box). To this end, the registry can also contain icons for each type of category.

Monikers: URL And Asynchronous

Writing simple ActiveX controls isn't the entire picture, however. You need to take special care when writing controls that may stretch over a slow data link (like the Internet). AIP deals with this in several ways. For many years, traditional OLE programs have had the notion of a moniker. A moniker is a special ActiveX component that contains the name of some other object. In a simple case, suppose you want to link to a file on your hard disk. The moniker might simply contain the file's name. As a more complex example, what if you were linking just three paragraphs from a document on disk? Then the moniker contains the file name and some way to indicate which three paragraphs you want. You don't need to know what that indication is—you ask the moniker to get the data and it does it. You can think of a moniker as an object-oriented file name—it knows where the data is and how to get it.

Now that AIP encapsulates the Internet, Windows provides a standard moniker for URLs. You know URLs; they are those odd strings you use to identify resources on the Internet. For example: *http://www.coriolis.com* or *ftp://coriolis.com*. Using the moniker, you can get an object or a storage that corresponds to a URL.

There is one other special twist to monikers you'll use with AIP. Suppose you have a URL moniker that points to a 25-megabyte video clip on the Internet. If it were a traditional moniker, when you asked it to give you an object for the video clip, your program would grind to a halt while the 25 megabytes crawled through cyberspace. This isn't a good idea. Instead, you'll use an asynchronous moniker, which allows things to continue while the download proceeds. This is how Web browsers work today. When a large graphic or sound bite loads, you can view text, move on to another page, and generally continue to work as usual.

ISAPI

Web pages that supply simple text and graphics are easy to create. But what about interactive Web pages like search forms or games? These special Web pages require some code to run on the server to handle requests. That's where ISAPI (Internet Server API) comes into play. This special API allows you to write custom code that executes in response to input from a Web page and create new Web content on the fly.

You can also create ISAPI filters to monitor or alter data in conjunction with a server. You might use a filter to encrypt stock market data, for example. Another use for a filter might be to log transactions.

Although ISAPI is part of AIP, it isn't of much use to the casual Web page creator. You don't use ISAPI to create Web pages; you use it to customize an HTTP server.

Scripting

Scripting isn't really new. It's what Microsoft used to call OLE Automation (see the *ActiveX Thesaurus* in Appendix I). Any script-capable program (including the page view browser) can accept commands from generic script languages. The best example of such a script language today is Visual Basic Scripting Edition (similar to the older Visual BASIC for Applications). However, any program that can control ActiveX objects (C++, for example) can participate. There are already a few third-party scripting languages that work the same way, and you can look for more in the near future. Remember: The language doesn't have to be BASIC—as long as it can drive ActiveX objects, it can be a scripting language.

Why should you care about scripting? Scripting is an easy way to control other applications, especially the page view browser. For many Web programmers, scripting can take the place of more complicated techniques like ISAPI or CGI (Common Gateway Interface) programming.

Security

With the increased connectivity afforded by AIP, security is even more of an issue than usual. How do you transmit data securely? If a Web page wants to run an ActiveX component, how can you be sure it isn't a virus? There are several parts of AIP that deal with this problem. In particular, PCT (Private Communication Technology) and the new cryptography API can ensure privacy. The Windows Trust Verification Services system combined with digital signatures allows network administrators to allow (or disallow) certain ActiveX components to run on their network.

Another security issue arises when you set up an *Intranet*. An Intranet is a private network you can set up to work like the Internet (and possibly connect to the Internet as well). For example, suppose your company maintains a Web site for your customers. However, if someone accesses this Web site from the local network (the Intranet), you want some links to appear that go to special pages that are not accessible to the general public. You might have inventory data, private messages, or a time and expense entry form protected this way. AIP allows you to authenticate users—only certain users may have access to specific information on your Intranet.

Summary

Wow! If that seems like a lot of information, that's because it is. AIP is a major architecture change for Windows. There is even more, but these 12 items are the high points. Luckily, if you want to develop Web pages, most of this technology hides in the background. Some of it is mainly used by other parts of AIP. For example, URL monikers use the cache and WinInet to actually do the work. You only need to worry about URL monikers.

This book focuses on ActiveX because it is the core of AIP and it is the part that most programmers will deal with. The ability to run controls over the Internet allows unprecedented control and flexibility for Web programming.

Two issues immediately come to mind, however: Java and portability. Of course, Java targets the same applications as ActiveX. Both attempt to run programs over the Internet. However, Java isn't as robust as ActiveX. Besides, it is a new programming language and not a very powerful one at that. Why not stick with C++ (or whatever language you choose to use to develop ActiveX controls)?

Portability is a bit trickier. Obviously, Microsoft is aiming AIP at Windows platforms. However, they have agreements with other companies to bring ActiveX to multiple platforms. As we examine the architecture of ActiveX, you'll see this isn't as far-fetched as it may sound. Not only can ActiveX components operate easily over a network, but with the automated downloading of ActiveX, you can run your controls on the user's machine. A mechanism exists that allows you to specify different versions of an ActiveX control depending on the user's operating system and CPU type.

No one knows the future. But with Microsoft betting the Windows farm on AIP, you can bet it's going places. And if you want to go those places too, you're going to need to learn ActiveX.

ONE MILE UP 2

Like the one that stands upon a promontory,
And spies a far-off shore where he would tread,
Wishing his foot were equal with his eye.

—King Henry VI

ACTIVEX MIGHT BE THE NEXT BIG THING, but how do you get started? Do you have to write OLE programs? Before you can write ActiveX servers and clients, you need to know about a few other things (like the system registry). In most cases, you don't have to write what most people think of as an OLE program. Traditional OLE programming allows you to embed or link one document inside another. This is a complex process involving many different ActiveX objects. However, writing ordinary ActiveX components isn't hard at all. Writing ActiveX controls is only a bit more difficult.

Wait a minute! What's the difference between a component and a control? This chapter will introduce a few terms and some basic ideas you should become familiar with before you try to tackle the later chapters.

Definitions

In the last chapter, I used several terms without defining them rigorously. Let's define a few of them a little better now:

- **ActiveX Component**   An ActiveX object that other programs can use.
- **ActiveX Control**   A special component that works like a controlwindow.
- **ActiveX Client**   Any program that uses any ActiveX component.
- **ActiveX Container**   A program that can accept ActiveX document objects or controls.
- **ActiveX Server**   A DLL or executable program that provides one or more ActiveX objects.
- **ActiveX Document Object**   A document that you can embed or link into a container (this is the traditional OLE functionality).

Currently, Microsoft calls any ActiveX object a control. Personally, I don't think that's a good idea. I prefer to call any ActiveX object a component. Some components know how to act like traditional windows and those are controls. For example, an ActiveX object that converts names to Internet addresses is just a component. You can't drag it onto a Visual Basic form, for instance. On the other hand, the ringing telephone control from the last chapter is both a component and a control. Controls are similar to the older-style OCX (OLE Control Extensions) or VBX (Visual Basic Extension) controls.

The Structure Of An ActiveX Object

Here is the most startling and important sentence in this book: *To a client program, an ActiveX object is nothing more than a table of function pointers.* That's it. Read it again. When a client accesses an object, it simply calls functions using the pointers in the table (see Figure 2.1). Objects can supply any number of tables for different purposes, but the client works with one at a time. These tables are called *interfaces*. Of course, the client and server must completely agree on the order and form of these functions. The calling convention, parameters, and return value must match both sides' expectations.

Consider this example: You are writing a system that allows users to retrieve stock market data. You create an ActiveX object with functions to validate

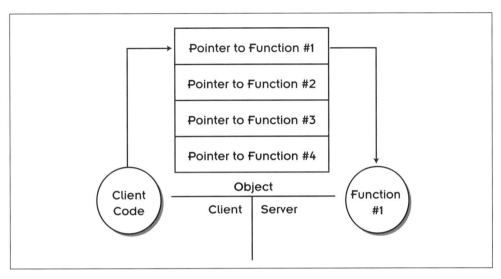

Figure 2.1 An Interface Table.

the user's ID, make an entry in the user's account (so you can charge him for the transaction), and get the data. The object then has three functions, **LogIn()**, **AccountLog()**, and **GetStockData()**. You might use two interface tables; one for the logging and accounting (the **ILog()** interface); another for the data retrieval (**IGetStockInfo()**; see Figure 2.2). Could you use one single table? Yes, you could. However, consider another example.

Your stock market data program is so successful, you branch into providing data for mutual funds, too. You might then create the object in Figure 2.3. Notice that two of the functions are the same and they appear in the same

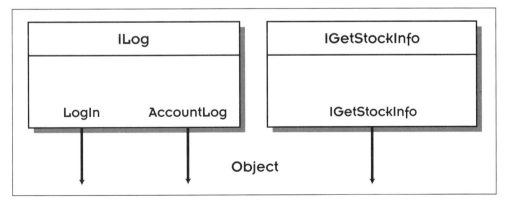

Figure 2.2 The Stock Market Object.

interface. Only the **GetStockData()** function changes. Keep this example in mind. We'll look at it more closely in just a minute. By the way, it is customary (although not mandatory) to specify interface names that begin with **I**, like **IGetStockInfo()** and **ILog()**.

It doesn't matter what language you use to create your object. You can use C, C++, Delphi, or Visual Basic. The only thing that is important is that your language can create the magic table of function pointers. ActiveX servers can reside in DLLs or EXE files and supply objects to other programs. It doesn't matter what language you use to write the client or the server.

That's An Object?

That seems too simple, doesn't it? (In truth, there is a bit more to it than this, but not much more.) If you are familiar with objects from C++, this doesn't seem like the same thing. Well, it isn't exactly the same thing, but if you look closely, it allows you to do the same fundamental operations as C++ objects.

Objects are important for several reasons:

1. Objects hide their implementation of functions. You ask the object to perform, and it does, but you shouldn't have to know how it performs. This is encapsulation and allows you to make major changes in the way an object operates without affecting any other code.

2. Objects allow you to reuse their code to build other objects. In C++, you do this via *derivation*. When you derive one class from another, the derived class inherits all of the code from the base class.

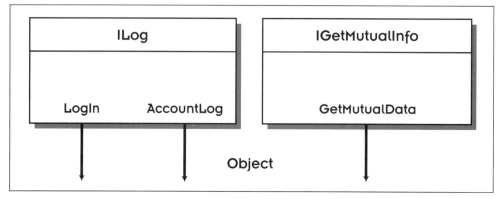

Figure 2.3 The Mutual Fund Object.

3. Objects are *polymorphic*. If you have a base object for vehicles, for example, you can create more specific classes for cars, trucks, and vans. Polymorphism allows you to treat cars, trucks, and vans as vehicles. In other words, you can define a list of vehicles that may contain cars, trucks, and vans without knowing which is which. C++ handles this via derivation, also. If all three classes derive from the vehicle class, you can store pointers to them in a vehicle pointer.

How does ActiveX accomplish these goals? Encapsulation is easy. Since each ActiveX object exposes interfaces (and nothing else), client programs must call using the pointers in those interfaces. You are free to change the object in any way as long as the interface table contains pointers that work the way they originally did. If you agree that Slot 6 in the interface table prints its five-integer arguments, then that's what it has to do. However, exactly how you do that is up to you. You could write the object in C++ or Visual Basic, or you could connect over the Internet to a mainframe and print it there using FORTRAN. The client doesn't know or care.

That still leaves the question of derivation, right? Not exactly. C++ uses derivation to support code reuse and polymorphism. Derivation is not especially important to object orientation. It is simply one way to meet the goals of code reuse and polymorphism. ActiveX uses different mechanisms to provide these features.

Code Reuse

There are two ways ActiveX components can reuse other ActiveX components: containment and aggregation. Aggregation requires a good deal of work and design (which we'll talk about later). Containment, on the other hand, is quite simple. There is no reason why an ActiveX object can't use another ActiveX object in its implementation. The new object can provide the same interfaces as the base object as well as additional interfaces. When the object receives a call to one of the contained interfaces, it can do any of the following:

1. Handle the call itself (this is similar to a C++ override).
2. Call the contained object (this is similar to doing nothing in C++).
3. Execute some code, call the contained object, and—perhaps—execute some more code (this is similar to C++ overrides that call their base class).

 Chapter 2

This allows you to reuse any number of other ActiveX components the same way a C++ derived class reuses its base classes. Look at the advantages to this method:

- You don't need the source code for the base class
- The base class doesn't even have to use the same language
- If the base class changes, the containing class will automatically use the new version without recompiling
- You don't have to expose all the interfaces an object supplies, which allows you to selectively expose interfaces from a base class

Since ActiveX components only expose interface functions (and never variables), you don't have the problems you see in C++, where the derived class depends on some internal state of the base class. The only communication permitted is via the interfaces.

Figure 2.4 shows an example of a contained object. Notice that the outside client has no idea what the contained class is. If the object later decides to use a different object to provide an interface, or provide the entire interface internally, it is free to do so. If the object needs to inherit from multiple base classes, it can simply contain multiple objects.

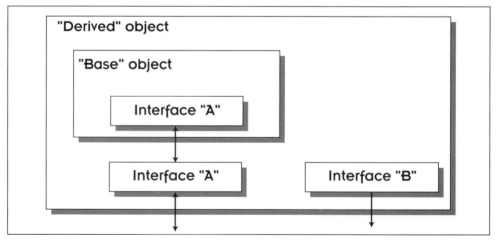

Figure 2.4 Object Containment.

Polymorphism

Because objects can support multiple interfaces, they can be polymorphic. Returning to the vehicle/car/truck/van example, look at Figure 2.5. These three objects are polymorphic because they all support the **IVehicle** interface. A client can treat all of these objects the same by requesting their **IVehicle** interface table. If the client requires more detail, it can get the more specific interface table, too. Notice that if there is an object for vehicles, the other objects can reuse it through containment.

The only problem here is when you want the vehicle class to be abstract. In C++, an abstract base class is one that you can't create. You can only derive from it. If you plan to reuse an ActiveX object via containment, then the "derived" classes must create it. Therefore, anyone else can create it too.

There are some *ad hoc* solutions to this problem. For example, if you don't tell clients about the vehicle class, they can't create it. That isn't a very good answer, however. Usually, the idea of an abstract base class in ActiveX is just that: an idea.

This method of polymorphism has many advantages (some of which are similar to the advantages of containment):

- You can create unrelated objects that are polymorphic with respect to each other
- The objects don't need to be in the same language, nor do you require the other object's source code

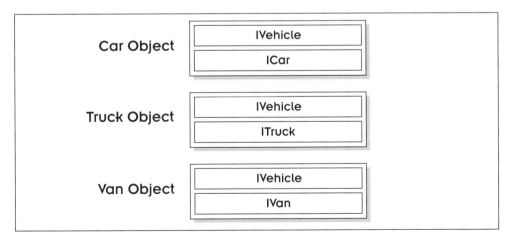

Figure 2.5 Polymorphic Objects.

- Any program can work with your polymorphic objects, regardless of the language or origin of the program

Another example of polymorphism occurs in the stock market/mutual fund example (see Figures 2.2 and 2.3). Here the parts of your code that deal with logging in the user and computing his charges need not change. Regardless of the object in use, the interface remains the same. Only the data interface is special. If you want another object later that has a more complicated data interface, so what? The login interface remains constant.

A Few Miscellaneous ActiveX Oddities

There are a few other oddities that you ought to know about before you start exploring ActiveX. These aren't fundamentally important, but they are peculiar to ActiveX.

HRESULT and SCODE

By convention, many ActiveX functions return a type known as an **HRESULT**. This is simply a 32-bit value that indicates success or failure along with an explanation in either case (see Figure 2.6). The top bit indicates the error status. The next 15 bits identify what system causes the success or failure (the facility code defined by Microsoft). Finally a 16-bit code tells you more information. On 32-bit platforms, an **HRESULT** is the same thing as an **SCODE**.

An **HRESULT** is almost never zero—even when it succeeds—so you can't just test it for being zero or non-zero. While you can break the fields apart manually and test them, it is usually easiest to use the **SUCCEEDED** and **FAILED** macros to test for success or failure.

The ActiveX headers define many codes that you can return as **HRESULT**s. For example, you might return **S_OK** to indicate success or **E_FAIL** to indicate a failure. Other codes are more specific. For example, **E_OUTOFMEMORY**, **E_NOTIMPL**, or **S_FALSE** indicate specific failures. This last code means that the function succeeded, but the answer is **FALSE** (whatever that means for a particular function).

Notice that not all ActiveX functions return **HRESULT**s—they can return any type you want. However, if your functions are to work across process boundaries (or over a network), they must return **HRESULT**s. When an

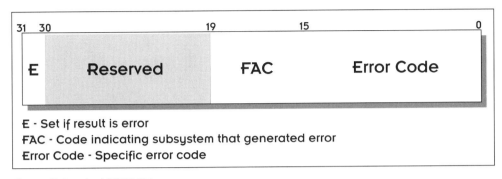

E - Set if result is error
FAC - Code indicating subsystem that generated error
Error Code - Specific error code

Figure 2.6 An HRESULT.

HRESULT indicates failure, you can't assume anything about the state of any output parameters. A function that wants to succeed partially must return some sort of successful **HRESULT**.

GUID/UUID/IID

One of the daunting problems with ActiveX is identifying particular components uniquely—even across the Internet. This problem crops up whenever you have networking considerations. The Open Software Foundation's Distributed Computing Environment defines a Universally Unique Identifier (UUID) that addresses this problem. Microsoft calls UUIDs, GUIDs (for Globally Unique Identifier), and often calls them CLSIDs (Class IDs) or IIDs (Interface IDs) depending on their use. All of these terms refer to the same thing. Which name you use depends on how you are using the UUID.

What's a UUID look like? It is a 128-bit number formed in such a way as to be unique (or at least reasonably so). When you create a UUID, the system builds it using the current date and time and unique information about your machine (for example, a network card's hardware address).

So how do you create a magic UUID? You can call **CoCreateGuid()** if you need one at run-time. More often, you'll run a program named UUIDGEN (this comes with most development tools). UUIDGEN will create as many IDs as you need at random, or in a sequence. For example, consider the following:

```
C:\>UUIDGEN
f6d0f800-992a-11cf-a7b2-444553540000

C:\>UUIDGEN -n3
0c10ba20-992b-11cf-a7b2-444553540000
0c10ba21-992b-11cf-a7b2-444553540000
0c10ba22-992b-11cf-a7b2-444553540000
```

By the way, I ran these two invocations of UUIDGEN about 10 seconds apart. You can also ask UUIDGEN to create C structures (-S) and in a few other formats. Enter UUIDGEN -H to see a list.

Another way to create a UUID is with the Component Gallery (available in Microsoft's Visual C++ 4.0 and later). One of the components there allows you to create a UUID in one of several formats. It then places the UUID on the clipboard so you can paste it into your code (or anywhere else for that matter).

UUIDs usually go in your code, the system registry, and type information files. You'll learn more about the registry and type information in later chapters. When you see text representations of a UUID in places like the registry, they will look like this:

```
{f6d0f800-992a-11cf-a7b2-444553540000}
```

The braces and dashes are not optional, although they serve no good purpose. You also have to be careful not to get extra spaces anywhere in the UUID. This is especially bothersome at the beginning and end of the string where the blank isn't apparent.

Not all objects require a UUID. Only objects you need to identify uniquely to the system require one. It turns out most interesting objects will have a UUID, but you could have private objects that don't have a UUID.

About IUnknown

Does all this sound too easy? How does this simple protocol work so much magic? Well, there is one little thing I forgot to mention. There is one pseudo-interface called **IUnknown**. It isn't a true interface because it is really a part of every interface.

Remember earlier when I said that an interface is a table of function pointers? That's true, but ActiveX reserves the first three slots in the table for the **IUnknown** interface functions. This allows you to treat any interface as an **IUnknown** interface. You never know or care exactly how many functions are in any interface—as long as there are at least as many as you plan on calling. If you think an interface is **IUnknown**, then it is because every interface has the same three functions appearing first in its table.

In C++ jargon, **IUnknown** is the base interface from which all other interfaces derive. What could be so important about three functions that every interface needs them? The **IUnknown** functions (see Table 2.1) are vital. Two of them manage the object's reference count. When you create an object, it has a reference count of 1. Each time you acquire a different interface for the same object, or copy an existing interface pointer, the count should go up by one. That's what **AddRef()** does. When you no longer need an interface, you call **Release()**, which decreases the count. If the count falls to zero, the object can destroy itself. Notice that the reference count is usually per object, not per interface. Interfaces may implement their own **AddRef()** and **Release()** logic, or they may call a common routine to do the work. Either way, they usually manage a single reference count per object.

Creating Objects And Finding Interfaces

The third function that **IUnknown** specifies is **QueryInterface**. You call **QueryInterface** with an IID (remember, that's a UUID that identifies an interface). If the object supports that interface, **QueryInterface** returns a pointer to the appropriate interface table. Let's go back to the stock market and mutual fund data objects in Figures 2.2 and 2.3. Suppose you are in some part of your code that doesn't know which of the two objects it is working with. It only knows it has an **IUnknown** interface. (Note: Figures 2.2 and 2.3 don't explicitly show **IUnknown**, but assume it is there.)

The first thing your code will do is call **QueryInterface()** on the pointer it has, specifying the IID for **ILog**. Of course, the pointer might have been an **ILog** interface already. That's okay. **QueryInterface()** will just return the same pointer. The difference is that now your code knows it is an **ILog** interface. In any case, **QueryInterface()** will search the object, looking for an interface that matches the IID. If it finds it, it returns a pointer to the interface. Otherwise it returns **E_NOINTERFACE** (a standard **HRESULT**).

Table 2.1 IUnknown.

Function	Purpose
AddRef	Adds one to the object's reference count
Release	Decreases the object's reference count; frees the object when count is zero
QueryInterface()	Asks any interface if its underlying object supports another interface and returns the interface's pointer

All this assumes you know how to create an object. There are many ways you might get an initial interface pointer to an object. Here are the four most common ways:

1. Call some function that specifically returns a particular interface pointer to you. This function might be part of ActiveX, or it might be code in a private library.

2. You might call an interface function that belongs to one object to create another object.

3. Someone else might pass you an interface pointer via a function or interface function in your code.

4. Call a function that can create any ActiveX component. Usually, this is **CoCreateInstance()**. You can think of this like the C++ **new** operator. You supply an object ID (a CLSID) and an interface ID (IID). The function creates the object and returns a pointer to the interface you requested (or returns an error if, for any reason, that didn't work).

More About Reference Counts

It seems like a lot of trouble to call **AddRef()** each time you make a copy of an interface pointer, doesn't it? Luckily, you don't have to do it in every case. A little common-sense reasoning will show you that it doesn't always make sense. Consider this pseudo-code:

```
AnInterface *p,*p1;
p=GetTheObject();  // ref count == 1
p1=p;    // make "copy" of pointer to send to function
p1->AddRef();      // ref count == 2
DoSomething(p);
p1->Release();  // ref count == 1
p->Release();// ref count == 0; object destroyed
```

Assuming that **DoSomething** doesn't start a new thread, it is pointless to call **AddRef()** and **Release** a second time. The original **AddRef()** won't **Release()** until the function returns. We really don't care what the value of the reference counter is as long as it won't go to zero until the object is not in use. While the above code would work, it is wasteful.

Consider what could happen if **DoSomething()** started a new thread to work with the interface pointer passed into it. Then you wouldn't code the first **Release()** statement above. Instead, the **DoSomething()** code would call **Release()** at the end of the thread (or when it finished with the interface). You'd need the first **AddRef()** since the final release in the code might occur while the second thread is still using the object. It is very impolite to destroy an object while some other part of your code is using it.

Here are the two most common rules on when you must call **AddRef()**:

1. Any function that returns an interface pointer (like **QueryInterface()** or **CoCreateInstance()** must call **AddRef()** so the object has an initial count of one.

2. Anytime you pass an interface pointer to another thread, you'll need to call **AddRef()** first (as in the above example).

If you think about it, it is usually plain where you'll need to call **AddRef()**. Just make sure the reference count stays above zero until the object is no longer in use.

About Aggregation

Earlier, I told you about two methods you can use to support code reuse: containment and aggregation. Containment is very simple, but aggregation requires you to know about **IUnknown** and reference counting. So armed with that information, we are ready to tackle the idea of aggregation.

The only thing wrong with containment is that you usually have to write little stub functions for the entry points that you want to pass directly to the contained object. This is an advantage for the functions you want to override or alter, but it seems stupid if you just want to directly expose the contained object's interface (contrast Figure 2.7 and Figure 2.4).

You might try this simple solution. What if the main object creates another copy of the subordinate object. Using **QueryInterface**, the main object learns the address of the exposed interface. Then, when the main object receives the correct **QueryInterface** call from a client, it simply returns that address. That sounds good, but there is a slight problem.

What happens if a client gets the exposed interface, and calls **QueryInterface** on it to learn another interface that belongs to the main object? It won't work. The subordinate object doesn't know about the main object. The **AddRef()** and **Release()** calls won't work correctly either because the main object's reference count won't reflect calls made against the subordinate.

The answer is to use special features that ActiveX supplies to support aggregation. Both the main object and the subordinate object must do

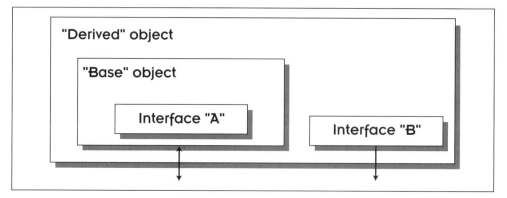

Figure 2.7 First Attempt at Aggregation.

special things, so you may not be able to aggregate just any object. When the main class creates the subordinate one, it passes an address to an **IUnknown** interface (the controlling **IUnknown**). If the subordinate object supports aggregation, it will pass any calls directed at its **IUnknown** to the controlling interface (see Figure 2.8).

The subordinate object still has a private set of **IUnknown** functions, and the main object requests a pointer to them when it creates the object. This allows the main object to call **IUnknown** in cases where that is necessary. If this seems a bit complicated, don't worry. You'll usually use containment to reuse any ActiveX component.

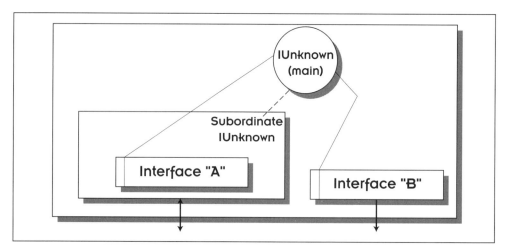

Figure 2.8 Correct Aggregation.

More Oddities

There are a few other things you should be aware of regarding ActiveX, which we'll explore more fully later. For now, you should just know they exist.

Predefined Interfaces

Part of ActiveX is the definitions of many standard interfaces. You'll use some of these (like **IMalloc** to allocate memory), and you'll create others (**IDispatch**). In certain cases, you'll have to supply certain interfaces to work with some other part of the AIP or Windows (for example, the browser).

However, there is nothing to stop you from adding your own interfaces. If you are writing an object that requires three interfaces, there is no reason you can't supply other custom interfaces, too. That's polymorphism again. If certain clients never ask for particular interfaces, who's the wiser?

Of course, you can also design your own objects with whatever interfaces you desire (predefined, custom, or both). The only thing you must support is **IUnknown**, and you need that in every interface. Other than that, you are free to do what you want. The only restrictions come when you want to interact with other ActiveX programs that you don't control (like the browser or Word). Then you have to follow their specific protocols, at least.

Here's a specific example: Suppose you want clients to create your component by calling **CoCreateInstance**. Then you must provide a specific object (a class factory) that has an **IClassFactory** interface. This component knows how to create your component, and **CoCreateInstance()** uses it. However, if you have another method for creating your component and don't care about **CoCreateInstance**, you don't need a class factory object or the **IClassFactory** interface. Don't worry about the specifics of **IClassFactory** just yet. Just realize that to work with certain parts of ActiveX, you need to provide certain interfaces.

Type Libraries

Because you are free to design your own objects and interfaces, how can any program know what to expect? That's where type information comes into play. In brief, a type library contains information about objects and their interfaces in machine-readable format. You can use special function calls to read this information from a database that each component contains. You can also use functions to create the type library (often a TLB file or resource). However, you usually create a text file that describes the type information, which you then pass through a special compiler (MKTYPLIB) to generate the TLB file.

Proxies, Stubs, And Marshalling

One key aspect of the ActiveX object structure is that clients don't know or care where the interface table's function pointers go. If an ActiveX server is in a DLL, then the pointers probably go directly to the proper functions. The DLL loads into the client's address space and the functions run fast and efficiently.

What if the server is in an EXE file? You can't pass pointers across process boundaries. In this case, ActiveX creates a proxy. The proxy is just a simple function that resides in the client's address space and forwards calls to a stub function in the server's address space. Then the stub calls the actual server function. Of course, the functions have to move any data back and forth between the address spaces (see Figure 2.9). ActiveX calls the process of translating data across process boundaries *marshalling*.

Here's an interesting twist on proxies: Why not have a proxy that forwards calls across network boundaries, not just process boundaries? Figure 2.10 shows a typical situation. The proxy receives a call, marshalls the data, and passes the call to a stub on the remote machine. The stub receives the data and makes the call to the server. Neither the server nor the client need ever know they are not on the same machine. The exact mechanism used to pass

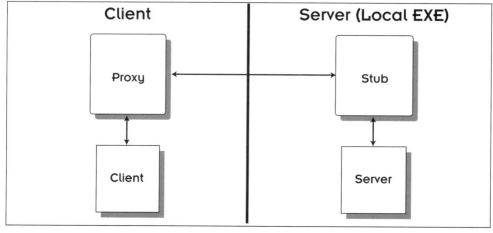

Figure 2.9 Proxy to an EXE.

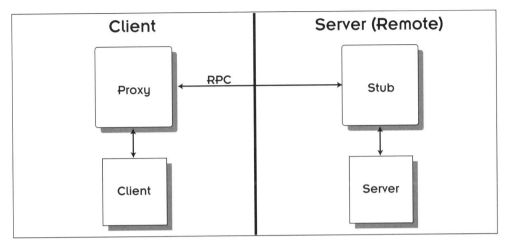

Figure 2.10 A Network Proxy.

the data (named pipes, remote procedure calls, and so on) is unimportant and subject to change. ActiveX hides these details from both the client and the server.

The nice part about proxies and marshalling is that it usually happens automatically—at least for predefined interfaces. There are a few exceptions, but mostly it all happens with no effort on your part. The only problem is when a certain data type can't pass between process boundaries. For example, consider a device context (an HDC). What good would it do to send an HDC to another machine? You can't draw on it or even find out much about it. In cases like this, you'll often have a two-part server. One part (either a DLL or an EXE) can run on the remote machine. The other part (always a DLL) handles functions that must occur on the local machine and passes the other requests to the main server. If the main server is an EXE, this technique also can improve local performance since code in the DLL runs in the client's address space. An EXE server always runs in a different process space and requires marshalling.

If you want your custom interfaces to have marshalling support over networks, that is possible, too. The easiest way to do this is to describe your interface using Microsoft Interface Description Language (MIDL). If you've ever done Remote Procedure Calls (RPC), this will look familiar. You pass a MIDL script through the MIDL compiler and it generates all the marshalling code you need. You'll use that code to build a DLL. Then you'll need to inform ActiveX that it needs to use the DLL for your interface. You'll see how simple this is in Chapter 4. There is no reason you can't support network marshalling with your own personal interfaces.

About Multiple Threads

If all this seems simple, it's because it is. There is one small complication, however. An ActiveX server can contain multiple threads of execution, but clients can also call servers from multiple threads. This can lead to problems. ActiveX supports a threading model known as the Apartment Model. This is just an odd way to say that ActiveX treats each thread in a process as a separate process (or apartment, if you prefer).

This has several ramifications. First, each thread that will make ActiveX calls must initialize the ActiveX library separately. Also, each object belongs to a particular thread. Other threads that access the object must use a form of marshalling—just as if they were in separate processes. This special marshalling isn't to share data—it is to ensure that only one thread modifies the object at any time. If the object uses any shared data (like a reference count), it must take steps to protect that data using a critical section, a mutex, or some other synchronization method. Supporting multiple threads using the apartment model is fairly complex. However, when you use MFC to create servers—and you will in later chapters—MFC will handle these details automatically.

ActiveX will one day support a different threading standard called the Free Threading model, which uses a pool of worker threads that handle each call to an object and requires more synchronization on the part of the object. However, this does not exist today. You can also write servers that are not thread-safe. ActiveX will attempt to load these servers into the main apartment. However, most multithreading clients (for example the Windows 95 shell) will fail if a server is not thread-safe.

The ActiveX/C++ Connection

If you've worked with C++ in detail, you might notice that an interface table looks suspiciously like a C++ VTBL (the table that stores virtual function pointers). Conveniently, most C++ compilers do generate VTBLs in the exact format required by an interface table.

This is a tremendous aid to C++ programmers, as you can express objects easily using C++ (you'll see how in Chapter 4). However, this in no way ties ActiveX to C++. You can write objects in any language. You may have to "manually" create the interface table, but you can do it.

The ActiveX SDK is usually C++ biased, although sometimes it has a slight C flavor to it. For example, the online help often uses the :: notation to indicate an interface function, as in:

```
IUnknown::Addref();
```

On the other hand, some versions of Help show function calls with an extra first parameter that you don't need with C++. The parameter, of course, is the C++ **this** pointer that points to the object. In C, you'd need to specify that parameter directly. This makes Help a little difficult to read because you have to switch gears depending on what you are doing. If you are writing in C, you have to remember to insert the **this** pointer manually (regardless of what Help says to do). If you are writing in C++, you have to ignore any **this** pointer argument that Help specifies.

Why Not Use C++ Directly?

For all this trouble, you might wonder why Microsoft didn't elect to use C++ directly. The key is that Microsoft wanted ActiveX to be a binary standard. You should be able to work with objects without having their source and without recompiling. You should be able to distribute objects without having to give away your source code.

ActiveX meets these goals. Although it may be easier to create ActiveX objects in C++, you can create them in practically any language. You can reuse code at the binary level via containment and aggregation, regardless of the language you use. You can design objects that are polymorphic with other objects, even if you don't have access to the source code for all the objects.

Why Not Use Java?

The biggest competitor to ActiveX is Java (from Sun Microsystems). This is an advanced interpreter that allows you to write code that runs over the Internet. However, Java is a relatively simple C++-like language (though it isn't *exactly* like C++). Switching to Java means losing support for many advanced C++ features. It also means embracing new development tools. With ActiveX, you can continue to write code in whatever language you like. If you like the simplicity of Visual Basic, use it. If you need the power of C++, go ahead and use that.

Of course, Java is much simpler than ActiveX, but class libraries and other tools can make ActiveX relatively easy, too. And the fact that Java is an interpreter means you can expect it to run more slowly than fast, compiled ActiveX code.

The other advantage to ActiveX is that it isn't just for the Internet. There's no such thing as an "ActiveX Internet Control". Any ActiveX control is usable on the Internet, in Microsoft Word, or in Visual Basic. If you design a control with the Internet in mind, you can make it more efficient, but there is nothing about ActiveX that forces it to work with the Internet.

Although Java can make the same claim—you can run Java programs locally—its limited scope prevents you from writing general, large projects with it (at least for now). Also, Java won't easily integrate with other programs like Word and other ActiveX applications from Microsoft and other vendors.

Summary

In their basic form, ActiveX objects are a simple table of function pointers, with three predefined functions and any number of custom ones. More complex objects provide multiple tables (interfaces). That's it. It can't be much simpler than that.

You won't often deal with many of these constructs directly. Instead, you'll use MFC to do most of the dirty work for you. For example, MFC can automatically create a class factory and provide all of the **IUnknown** functions for you. You'll see how soon. But for now, just concentrate on the fact that none of these things is very difficult. The hard part is knowing what objects and interfaces you must supply to integrate with the rest of ActiveX.

Information, Please 3

For many men that stumble at the threshold
Are well foretold that danger lurks within.

—King Henry VI

WHAT DO YOU THINK OF WHEN someone says database? Oracle, Sybase, DB2, and dBase? Sure, those are the traditional database products, but you usually don't use these in ordinary programs. In Windows 3.1, the most common database you might use in a regular application is an INI file. INI files are easy to use—you just need to know a few easy-to-learn API calls.

However, another system-level database exists: the system registry. In the past, only a few types of programs used the registry. With the advent of Windows NT and Windows 95, though, Microsoft recommends using the registry instead of INI files. So, what's that got to do with ActiveX?

In Chapter 2, you saw that servers can reside in DLLs or EXE files. Each object a server can create often has a CLSID (those long 128-bit numbers) that identifies it. How does the system know that a particular CLSID goes with a given server? The registry. There are many other ActiveX-related items found in the registry—not just CLSIDs. To program ActiveX, you'll need to know all about the registry. Luckily, the registry isn't very hard (although it isn't as easy as INI files). The registry database resembles a file system with directories (keys) and

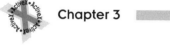

Chapter 3

files (values). You use special APIs to create, manipulate, and destroy these items. In short, if you can navigate the hard disk on your computer, you can learn to use the registry.

Another source of information concerning ActiveX objects is *type libraries*. These ActiveX objects can provide information about the objects a server provides and their interfaces. After you find out more about the registry, you can tackle type libraries.

This chapter will show you how to use the registry to control ActiveX. You'll also learn more about type libraries at a conceptual level. When you start writing components in the next chapter, you'll see how easy it is to make type libraries.

Give Up INI Files?

Giving up INI files causes most programmers to experience a slight panic. INI files are friendly, easy to use, easy to modify, and well understood. However, INI files have a few limitations:

- INI files can't exceed 64K on some platforms
- Adding entries to WIN.INI and SYSTEM.INI quickly clutter those files up and may push them past 64K
- Accessing a large INI file can be slow since Windows performs a linear search for the item
- INI files are not easily protected or remotely administered over a network
- Data in INI files is untyped—you must store the data as a string and convert it in your program

The registry addresses all of these problems. In essence, it is a hierarchical database. You access a key and obtain its values. Keys may have subkeys as well as values. This is very similar to the file system. Think of a key as a directory and values as files. The registry has been around for a while, but most programs didn't use it until recently. Traditionally, only OLE programs and the old program manager used the registry. Now, however, most new Windows features (the advanced shell, ActiveX, and so on) rely on the registry.

Have INI files gone away? No, not at all. You can still use the INI file calls if you like. However, to interact with the shell, get Windows logo compliance, or be a good Win32 citizen, you'll want to use the registry. Since you must

Information, Please   35

use the registry for ActiveX, you might as well store your private profile data there as well. Once you use the registry a few times, you'll find that it is an improvement over INI files.

The Registry: Up Close And Personal

Figure 3.1 shows REGEDIT, the standard Windows 95 registry editor (the equivalent NT program is REGEDT32). As you can see, the registry resembles a file system with folders and files. The root of this pseudo file system contains six items: **HKEY_CLASSES_ROOT**, **HKEY_CURRENT_USER**, **HKEY_LOCAL_MACHINE**, **HKEY_USERS**, **HKEY_CURRENT_CONFIG**, and **HKEY_DYN_DATA**. These items loosely segregate the various entries in broad categories.

Suppose you want to work with a value called **PATH** in the **HKEY_CURRENT_USER\SOFTWARE\AWC\REALFAST\1.0** key. You have several choices. The best plan is to open the **HKEY_CURRENT_USER\SOFTWARE\AWC\REALFAST\1.0** key and then modify the **PATH** subkey. However, you could simply open the **HKEY_CURRENT_USER** key and work with the **SOFTWARE\AWC\REALFAST\1.0** subkey. On Windows NT, you may have security issues with the latter method, so it is best to open the most specific key possible.

You'll use an **HKEY** variable (a key handle) to refer to an open registry key. You can obtain an **HKEY** with **RegOpenKeyEx()** or **RegCreateKeyEx()**

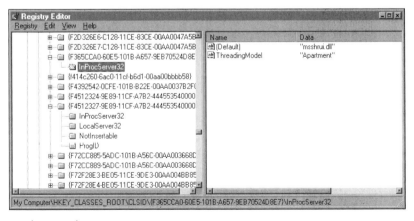

Figure 3.1 The Windows REGEDIT Program.

(see Table 3.1 for a list of registry-related calls). These calls present a chicken-and-egg problem: The first argument required is an **HKEY**. However, you can use a constant to refer to any of the root entries (as mentioned above). For example, you might write:

```
HKEY key;
RegCreateKeyEx(HKEY_CURRENT_USER,
  "SOFTWARE\AWC\REALFAST\1.0",0,
  NULL,REG_OPTION_NON_VOLATILE,
  KEY_ALL_ACCESS,NULL,&key,NULL);
```

Once you have an open key, you can read a value (**RegQueryValueEx()**), change the value (**RegSetValueEx()**), delete the key (**RegDeleteKey()**), or enumerate the subkeys (**RegEnumKeyEx()**). You can also enumerate all of the named values for a given key (**RegQueryValue()**). Once you are done,

Table 3.1 Selected Registry Calls.

Function	Description
RegCloseKey()	Closes an open registry key
RegConnectRegistry()	Connects to a remote registry
RegCreateKeyEx()	Creates a new subkey
RegDeleteKey()	Deletes a key
RegDeleteValue()	Deletes a value
RegEnumKeyEx()	Enumerates subkeys (returns a different key on each call)
RegEnumValue()	Enumerates values (returns a different value on each call)
RegFlushKey()	Flushes (writes) key values (only required if you demand immediate update)
RegLoadKey()	Loads a key from a special file (see RegSaveKey)
RegOpenKeyEx()	Opens a key
RegQueryInfoKey()	Queries key information
RegQueryValueEx()	Reads value
RegReplaceKey()	Replaces a key after system restart
RegSaveKey()	Saves a key to a file
RegSetKeySecurity()	Sets key security
RegSetValueEx()	Sets a value
RegUnloadKey()	Unloads a set of entries

you need to close the open **HKEY** using **RegCloseKey()**. Table 3.1 shows the details of registry-related calls.

The registry has additional features I won't cover. For example, Windows NT includes advanced security features to protect portions of the registry. A particular program may not have access rights to work with every registry key on the system. Also, with Windows NT or Windows 95, you can connect to a remote registry and manipulate it over the network. But these features don't have anything to do with ActiveX. Besides, once you understand the concepts, the remaining features are not difficult.

Registry Oddities

There are a few things about the registry that don't work the way you'd expect. Here, in no particular order, are some of the more unusual things I've noticed.

RegEnumValue

RegEnumValue() has a peculiar property. The documentation says that this function walks through the values for a particular key. If the key only has a default value, the function returns it. However, if the key has non-default values, this function will return them but not the default value. That means if you want to be sure to get all the values, you'll need to get the default value explicitly (**RegQueryValue()**) and then enumerate. If you retrieve the default value during enumeration (it will have an empty string as its name), just discard it.

RegDeleteKey

If you attempt to delete a key that has subkeys under Windows NT, the **RegDeleteKey()** call will fail. Under Windows 95, the call succeeds but wipes out the key and all subkeys! Not surprisingly, this can be very dangerous. In particular, you can get into lots of trouble under Windows 95 with code like the following:

```
char subkey[100];
GetSubKeyName(subkey);  // this fails—subkey is NULL
RegDeleteKey(HKEY_CLASSES_ROOT,subkey);
// if subkey is NULL, the entire HKEY_CLASSES_ROOT
// branch is now gone!
```

Error Returns

Don't depend on **GetLastError()** to check for error values from the registry functions. These functions all return the error code directly. Calling **GetLastError()** will simply return whatever error some other API call generated earlier in your program.

Typed Data

If you browse the help files, you'll see that the registry can contain many exotic data types (see Table 3.2). The system doesn't pay attention to these types in any real way. For example, the **REG_EXPAND_SZ** type is for strings that should have environment variables expanded in-line. Don't think that the registry will do this expansion for you. The flag implies that you should do the expansion yourself (use the Win32 function **ExpandEnvironmentStrings()**).

There are a few exceptions. For example, Windows 95 will add a terminating zero to a **REG_SZ** string if you forget to do it. Windows NT, however, will not add the zero. Neither system adds the extra NULL to **REG_MULTI_SZ** or **REG_EXPAND_SZ** types.

An Example

Figure 3.2 shows a simple MFC program that manipulates the registry (REGDEMO). You can create a new key, delete keys, and view the keys and values that are present. Be careful when deleting keys, especially if you are running Windows 95. When you start the program, it may take a minute to read and sort every key in the registry.

Since this code is just for illustration's sake, I took a few shortcuts with the user interface. You'll notice that each key's default value appears after it (preceded by an equal sign). This can cause strange behavior if a key or value exists that has an equal sign in it already. In practice, this doesn't seem to be a problem. If you want to view a key's values, delete the key, or create a new subkey, just double click on the key you want to alter. A dialog will appear that shows the values and allows you to delete the key or create a new subkey. The program doesn't allow you to alter or add values. That would be easy to add, and a worthwhile exercise if you'd like to try your hand at some registry programming. If you really need to modify the registry, just use REGEDIT or REGEDT32.

Information, Please

Table 3.2 Registry Data Types.

Type	Description
REG_BINARY	Binary data in any form
REG_DWORD	A 32-bit number
REG_DWORD_LITTLE_ENDIAN	A 32-bit number in Intel-style format
REG_DWORD_BIG_ENDIAN	A 32-bit number in Motorola-style format
REG_EXPAND_SZ	A null-terminated string that contains unexpanded references to environment variables (for example, "%PATH%")
REG_LINK	A Unicode symbolic link
REG_MULTI_SZ	An array of null-terminated strings, terminated by two null characters
REG_NONE	No defined value type
REG_RESOURCE_LIST	A device-driver resource list
REG_SZ	A null-terminated string

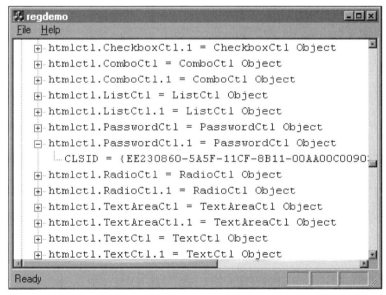

Figure 3.2 REGDEMO.

Chapter 3

The code in Listing 3.1 shows the highlights of the registry manipulation code. Of course, a great deal of code on the companion CD handles the user interface of the program. The functions you'll want to examine are all in RegDemoView.CPP (Listing 3.1). Look closely at **DoUpdateRegView()**. This function opens each top level key, one at a time. It then inserts a text string to represent the key into the tree view. Next, it calls **InsertReg()**. This function recursively adds each subkey to the tree. Finally, the program closes the top-level key before moving on to the next root key. **InsertReg()** examines the key passed in by the caller and enumerates each subkey. It adds the key (and its value) to the tree and then calls itself to add the new key's subkeys.

The only other interesting function (concerning the registry, anyway) is **OnDblClick()**. As you might expect, this function executes when the user double-clicks an entry. Don't be distracted by the **FindFullKey()** function; it simply pulls the names back out of the tree view. The action occurs when the call to **DoModal()** returns. If the user decided to delete or create (you can tell by the **m_cmd** variable), the code takes the appropriate action.

Listing 3.1 REGDEMOVIEW.CPP.

```
// regdemoView.cpp : implementation of the CRegdemoView class
//

#include "stdafx.h"
#include "regdemo.h"
#include "winreg.h"
#include "regdialog.h"
#include "waitdlg.h"
#include "promptdlg.h"

#include "regdemoDoc.h"
#include "regdemoView.h"

#ifdef _DEBUG
#define new DEBUG_NEW
#undef THIS_FILE
static char THIS_FILE[] = __FILE__;
#endif

/////////////////////////////////////////////////////////////////////////////
// CRegdemoView

IMPLEMENT_DYNCREATE(CRegdemoView, CTreeView)

BEGIN_MESSAGE_MAP(CRegdemoView, CTreeView)
    //{{AFX_MSG_MAP(CRegdemoView)
    ON_NOTIFY_REFLECT(NM_DBLCLK, OnDblclk)
```

Information, Please

```
   //}}AFX_MSG_MAP
// Standard printing commands
ON_COMMAND(ID_FILE_PRINT, CTreeView::OnFilePrint)
ON_COMMAND(ID_FILE_PRINT_DIRECT, CTreeView::OnFilePrint)
ON_COMMAND(ID_FILE_PRINT_PREVIEW, CTreeView::OnFilePrintPreview)
END_MESSAGE_MAP()

/////////////////////////////////////
// CRegdemoView construction/destruction

CRegdemoView::CRegdemoView()
   {
   // TODO: add construction code here

   }

CRegdemoView::~CRegdemoView()
   {
   }

BOOL CRegdemoView::PreCreateWindow(CREATESTRUCT& cs)
   {
   // TODO: Modify the Window class or
   //  styles here by modifying the CREATESTRUCT cs

   return CTreeView::PreCreateWindow(cs);
   }

/////////////////////////////////////
// CRegdemoView drawing

void CRegdemoView::OnDraw(CDC* pDC)
   {
   CRegdemoDoc* pDoc = GetDocument();
   ASSERT_VALID(pDoc);

   // TODO: add draw code for native data here
   }

void CRegdemoView::OnInitialUpdate()
   {
   CTreeView::OnInitialUpdate();
   fixedfont.CreatePointFont(100,"Courier New");
   GetTreeCtrl().SetFont(&fixedfont);
   GetTreeCtrl().ModifyStyle(0,
      TVS_HASLINES|TVS_LINESATROOT|TVS_HASBUTTONS,0);
   UpdateRegView();
   }

/////////////////////////////////////
// CRegdemoView printing

BOOL CRegdemoView::OnPreparePrinting(CPrintInfo* pInfo)
   {
```

```
   // default preparation
   return DoPreparePrinting(pInfo);
   }

void CRegdemoView::OnBeginPrinting(CDC*, CPrintInfo*)
   {

   }

void CRegdemoView::OnEndPrinting(CDC*, CPrintInfo*)
   {
   // TODO: add cleanup after printing
   }

/////////////////////////////////////
// CRegdemoView diagnostics

#ifdef _DEBUG
void CRegdemoView::AssertValid() const
   {
   CTreeView::AssertValid();
   }

void CRegdemoView::Dump(CDumpContext& dc) const
   {
   CTreeView::Dump(dc);
   }

// non-debug version is inline
CRegdemoDoc* CRegdemoView::GetDocument()
   {
   ASSERT(m_pDocument->IsKindOf(
      RUNTIME_CLASS(CRegdemoDoc)));
   return (CRegdemoDoc*)m_pDocument;
   }
#endif //_DEBUG

/////////////////////////////////////
// CRegdemoView message handlers

void CRegdemoView::UpdateRegView(LPCSTR s)
   {
   CWaitDlg dlg;
   if (s) dlg.message=s;
   dlg.Create(CWaitDlg::IDD);   // create wait dialog
   DoUpdateRegView();           // update view
   dlg.DestroyWindow();         // kill wait dialog
   }

void CRegdemoView::DoUpdateRegView()
   {
   HKEY root;
   CTreeCtrl &tree=GetTreeCtrl();
```

Information, Please

```
    HTREEITEM parent;
    // Kill everything already there
    tree.DeleteAllItems();

    // Start with HKEY_CLASSES_ROOT
    if (RegOpenKeyEx(HKEY_CLASSES_ROOT,NULL,0,
        KEY_READ,&root)!=ERROR_SUCCESS)
    return;
    // Insert string to represent the root key
    parent=tree.InsertItem("HKEY_CLASSES_ROOT",
       TVI_ROOT,TVI_LAST);
    tree.SetItem(parent,TVIF_PARAM,NULL,0,0,0,0,
        (LPARAM)HKEY_CLASSES_ROOT);

    // Recursively add subkeys
    InsertReg(root,tree,parent,TVI_LAST);
    tree.SortChildren(parent);
    // Finished with key
    RegCloseKey(root);

    // Repeat for other root keys
    if (RegOpenKeyEx(HKEY_CURRENT_USER,NULL,0,
        KEY_READ,&root)!=ERROR_SUCCESS)
    return;
    parent=tree.InsertItem("HKEY_CURRENT_USER",
      TVI_ROOT,TVI_LAST);
    tree.SetItem(parent,TVIF_PARAM,NULL,0,0,0,0,
        (LPARAM)HKEY_CURRENT_USER);
    InsertReg(root,tree,parent,TVI_LAST);
    tree.SortChildren(parent);
    RegCloseKey(root);
    if (RegOpenKeyEx(HKEY_LOCAL_MACHINE,NULL,0,
        KEY_READ,&root)!=ERROR_SUCCESS)
    return;
    parent=tree.InsertItem("HKEY_LOCAL_MACHINE",
      TVI_ROOT,TVI_LAST);
    tree.SetItem(parent,TVIF_PARAM,NULL,0,0,0,0,
        (LPARAM)HKEY_LOCAL_MACHINE);
    InsertReg(root,tree,parent,TVI_LAST);
    tree.SortChildren(parent);
    RegCloseKey(root);
    if (RegOpenKeyEx(HKEY_USERS,NULL,0,
        KEY_READ,&root)!=ERROR_SUCCESS)
    return;
    parent=tree.InsertItem("HKEY_USERS",TVI_ROOT,TVI_LAST);
    tree.SetItem(parent,TVIF_PARAM,NULL,
        0,0,0,0,(LPARAM)HKEY_USERS);
    InsertReg(root,tree,parent,TVI_LAST);
    tree.SortChildren(parent);
    RegCloseKey(root);

}

void CRegdemoView::InsertReg(HKEY key,CTreeCtrl &tree,
```

```
                HTREEITEM parent,HTREEITEM last)
                {
                int i=0;
                char subkeyname[1024];
                HTREEITEM nextparent;
                HKEY nextkey;
                DWORD siz;
                while (1)
                    {
                    // Enumerate each subkey
                    siz=sizeof(subkeyname);
                    if (RegEnumKeyEx(key,i,subkeyname,&siz,NULL,
                       NULL,NULL,NULL)!=ERROR_SUCCESS)
                       break;
                    i++;
                    if (RegOpenKeyEx(key,subkeyname,0,KEY_READ,
                       &nextkey)==ERROR_SUCCESS)
                       {
                       char val[256];
                       DWORD type,siz=sizeof(val);
                       // Ask key for default value
                       if (RegQueryValueEx(nextkey,NULL,NULL,&type,
                          (BYTE *)val,&siz)==ERROR_SUCCESS)
                          {
                          if (siz&&*val)
                             {
                             strcat(subkeyname," = ");
                             // no need to check type because
                             // default key is always string
                             strcat(subkeyname,val);
                             }
                          }
                       nextparent=tree.InsertItem(subkeyname,parent,TVI_LAST);
                       InsertReg(nextkey,tree,nextparent,TVI_LAST);
                       RegCloseKey(nextkey);
                       }
                    }
                }


         void CRegdemoView::OnDblclk(NMHDR* pNMHDR, LRESULT* pResult)
             {
             // Find full name of key
             CString name;
             HTREEITEM sel=GetTreeCtrl().GetSelectedItem();
             HKEY rootkey;
             if (FindFullKey(sel,name,rootkey))
                 {
                 CRegDialog dlg(rootkey,name);

                 if (dlg.DoModal()==IDOK)
                     {
                     CString msg;
                     // Windows 95 will delete no matter what
```

Information, Please

```
            if (dlg.m_cmd==-1)
               {
               if (RegDeleteKey(rootkey,name)==ERROR_SUCCESS)
                  msg="Delete sucessful";
               else
                  msg="Delete failed";
               }
            else // create new subkey
               {
               CPromptDlg pdlg;
               pdlg.Prompt="Enter name of subkey";
               if (pdlg.DoModal()!=IDOK) return;

               msg="Create failed";
               HKEY newroot,newkey;
               if (RegOpenKeyEx(rootkey,name,0,KEY_WRITE,
                 &newroot)==ERROR_SUCCESS)
                   {
                   if (RegCreateKeyEx(newroot,pdlg.Result,0,NULL,
                    0,KEY_READ,NULL,&newkey,NULL)==ERROR_SUCCESS)
                      {
                      RegCloseKey(newkey);
                      msg="Create successful";
                      }
                   RegCloseKey(newroot);
                   }
               }
            UpdateRegView(msg+"\nPlease wait...");
            }
       }

    *pResult = 1;
    }
BOOL CRegdemoView::FindFullKey(HTREEITEM sel,CString &name,
   HKEY &rootkey)
   {
   // This algorithm may break if a
   // key with no value contains an = sign
   CString raw;
   HTREEITEM next;
   CTreeCtrl &tree=GetTreeCtrl();
   TV_ITEM item;
   name="";
   do
      {
      next=tree.GetParentItem(sel);
      if (next)
         {
         int n;
         raw=tree.GetItemText(sel);
         n=raw.ReverseFind('=');
         if (n!=-1)
            name="\\"+raw.Mid(0,n-1)+name;
```

Chapter 3

```
            else
                name="\\"+raw+name;
            sel=next;
            }
        } while (next);
    item.mask=TVIF_PARAM;
    item.hItem=sel;
    tree.GetItem(&item);
    rootkey=(HKEY)item.lParam;
    name=(LPCSTR)name+1;
    return TRUE;
    }
```

You'll also find some code concerning values in Listing 3.2 (RegDialog.CPP). The **OnInitDialog()** call first generates a readable name for the key. Then it opens the key and enumerates each value. This is a good place to use the debugger to see that default values only enumerate if there are no other values present. To prevent confusion, the program itself filters out default values by testing the **val** variable.

Listing 3.2   REGDIALOG.CPP.

```
// RegDialog.cpp : implementation file
//

#include "stdafx.h"
#include "regdemo.h"
#include "winreg.h"
#include "RegDialog.h"

#ifdef _DEBUG
#define new DEBUG_NEW
#undef THIS_FILE
static char THIS_FILE[] = __FILE__;
#endif

/////////////////////////////////////////
// CRegDialog dialog


CRegDialog::CRegDialog(HKEY root,CString &nam,
    CWnd* pParent /*=NULL*/)
: CDialog(CRegDialog::IDD, pParent)
    {
        //{{AFX_DATA_INIT(CRegDialog)
        m_key = _T("");
        //}}AFX_DATA_INIT
    rootkey=root;
    name=nam;
    }
```

Information, Please 47

```
void CRegDialog::DoDataExchange(CDataExchange* pDX)
   {
   CDialog::DoDataExchange(pDX);
      //{{AFX_DATA_MAP(CRegDialog)
      DDX_Control(pDX, IDC_LIST, m_listbox);
      DDX_Text(pDX, IDC_KEY, m_key);
      //}}AFX_DATA_MAP
   }


BEGIN_MESSAGE_MAP(CRegDialog, CDialog)
   //{{AFX_MSG_MAP(CRegDialog)
   ON_BN_CLICKED(IDC_Create, OnCreate)
   //}}AFX_MSG_MAP
END_MESSAGE_MAP()

/////////////////////////////////////
// CRegDialog message handlers


BOOL CRegDialog::OnInitDialog()
   {
   CDialog::OnInitDialog();
   m_key="\\";
   switch ((DWORD)rootkey)
      {
      case (DWORD)HKEY_CLASSES_ROOT:
         m_key+="HKEY_CLASSES_ROOT";
         break;
      case (DWORD)HKEY_LOCAL_MACHINE:
         m_key+="HKEY_LOCAL_MACHINE";
         break;
      case (DWORD)HKEY_CURRENT_USER:
         m_key+="HKEY_CURRENT_USER";
         break;
      case (DWORD)HKEY_USERS:
         m_key+="HKEY_USERS";
         break;
      default:
         m_key+="<<Unknown>>";
         break;
      }
   m_key+="\\";
   m_key+=name;
   UpdateData(FALSE);

   m_listbox.ResetContent();
   m_listbox.SetTabStops(154);

   //Enumerate all values
   HKEY curkey;
   char val[256],data[1024];
   DWORD siz=sizeof(val),datasiz=sizeof(data),type;
```

```
    RegOpenKeyEx(rootkey,name,0,KEY_READ,&curkey);
    for (int i=0;
       RegEnumValue(curkey,i,val,&siz,
         NULL,&type,(BYTE *)data,&datasiz)==ERROR_SUCCESS;
       i++)
       {
       CString lbval;
       CString num;
       if (*val)
          lbval=val;
       else
          continue; // don't show default
       lbval+="\t";
       switch (type)
          {
          case REG_SZ:
             lbval+=data;
             break;
          case REG_DWORD:
             num.Format("0x%08x",*(DWORD *)data);
             lbval+=num;
             break;
          case REG_BINARY:
             lbval+="<Binary data>";
             break;
          default:
             lbval+="<Unknown>";
             break;
          }
       m_listbox.AddString(lbval);
       }
    RegCloseKey(curkey);


    return TRUE;
    }

void CRegDialog::OnOK()
   {
   m_cmd=-1;
   CDialog::OnOK();
   }

void CRegDialog::OnCreate()
   {
   m_cmd=0;
   CDialog::OnOK();
   }
```

Values have a type flag associated with them. This program checks for **REG_SZ** (strings), **REG_DWORD** (32-bit binary), and **REG_BINARY** (series of bytes). There are other types (see Table 3.2), but the system doesn't actually deal with them. They are for your program to interpret. Default values, by the way, are always **REG_SZ**. This dates back to when there was no support for multiple values or multiple data types in the registry.

If you need to get a specific value from the registry, you can use **RegQueryValueEx()** and pass a NULL value name for the default. You can create new values with **RegSetValueEx()** or delete them with **RegDeleteValue()**.

You might be wondering why some of these functions have an "Ex" in their name while others don't. The reason is that Microsoft has changed the registry in many ways since its first release. All the older calls are there, but you should use the "Ex" call when you program under Win32. This allows you to control issues like security, multiple values, value data types, and so on. In some cases, the calls haven't changed, which means you can still use the original call. This is always very confusing when coding late at night.

That's It?

Is that all there is to manipulating the registry? Hmm, yes and no. Physically working with the registry *is* this easy. However, you also need to know what goes where so that other programs (and Windows) can work with the information you provide. The registry API is like an alphabet. Even if you know all the letters, you can't communicate without words.

There are many standard places in the registry that you should use to store data. For example, you can register a file type so that the shell can display custom icons, context menus, and so forth for your files. Another example is profile information (what you used to store in INI files). You should put your profile information in **HKEY_CURRENT_USER\SOFTWARE***company_name**product_name**version_number* if it applies to the current user, or under the **HKEY_LOCAL_MACHINE\SOFTWARE***company_name**product_name**version_number* key if it applies to the machine.

This book doesn't cover the myriad places you can put registry information; only the places that apply to ActiveX. If you want to find more information about the registry's format, you'll find it scattered throughout the Microsoft documentation.

Registering Objects

For the ActiveX programmer, the burning question is: Where do I enter servers (or classes, if you prefer) in the registry? There are several answers to that, depending on what you need to do.

Nearly all of the ActiveX registry entries appear under the **HKEY_CLASSES_ROOT** root key. The first thing you'll need is something to identify the server. You place a key equal to the CLSID (with all the curly braces and dashes) under the **\HKEY_CLASSES_ROOT\CLSID** key. The value of this key is a human readable name that identifies the server. The name can contain any characters you like—it is just for display. Further subkeys identify the location of the server. Consider the following example.

```
HKEY_CLASSES_ROOT
   CLSID
      {73FDDC80-AEA9-101A-98A7-00AA00374959} = Word Pad Document
         LocalServer32=C:\PROGRA~1\ACCESS~1\WORDPAD.EXE
         InprocHandler32=OLE32.DLL
         PROGID=WordPad.Document.1
         Insertable=""
```

This entry, which is part of the one Windows 95 uses for Word Pad, identifies WORDPAD.EXE as the server for this object. It is an EXE server because it uses the **LocalServer32** keyword. If the server were in a DLL (an inproc server), the key would read **InprocServer32** instead. Don't confuse this with the **InprocHandler32** key. This key specifies a DLL that stands in for the local server. The client communicates with the handler, and the handler communicates with the local server. This allows the client to avoid making calls across process boundaries. It also allows the local server to perform operations in the client's address space. You almost always use the default system-supplied handler, OLE32.DLL.

It is permissible to have both types of servers for a single CLSID. Clients can request a particular type of server when they create an object. Inproc DLLs are very efficient because all operations occur in the client's address space. However, users can't start a DLL. What if you were writing a word processor program? You certainly need an EXE file that users can run. However, for better ActiveX performance, you might make a DLL that also serves the word processor objects.

Naturally, if you were dealing with old-style 16-bit OLE objects, you'd omit the "32" suffix from all of the above items. Technically, 16-bit components are not part of the ActiveX standard, but you'll probably run into some older OLE objects if you deal with Win32S or Windows 95.

Information, Please

The **ProgID** key serves as a short (hopefully unique) ID for the object. Some languages that don't support GUIDs will use the ProgID when creating objects. You can use any character in a ProgID, except for spaces. In theory, it doesn't matter what you use for a ProgID because end users should never see it. However, in practice, the ProgID needs to be unique. The convention is to use your company name and a component name together. For example:

```
Coriolis.AutoMail
```

You can also support multiple versions of a component by tacking the version number on at the end, as shown in the following code line.

```
Coriolis.AutoMail.2
```

The ProgID has its own entry under **HKEY_CLASSES_ROOT**.

```
HKEY_CLASSES_ROOT
   Coriolis.AutoMail.2=Coriolis Group Auto Mailer Version 2.0
      CLSID = {c353e4a0-9ce6-11cf-a7b2-444553540000}

   Coriolis.AutoMail=Coriolis Group Auto Mailer
      CurVer = Coriolis.AutoMail.2

   CLSID
      {c353e4a0-9ce6-11cf-a7b2-444553540000} =
                      Coriolis Auto Mailer
         ProgID=Coriolis.AutoMail.2
         VersionIndependentProgID=Coriolis.AutoMail
            .
            .
            .
```

The version-independent ID is for clients that want the current version, regardless of what that is. You can use **ProgIDFromCLSID()** and **CLSIDFromProgID()** to convert back and forth between CLSIDs and ProgIDs. In C++ programs, you won't often use the ProgID, but it is important for many other types of clients.

Notice the single **Insertable** key in the Word Pad example, above. This indicates that the client can display this class in a list of objects to insert. For example, many programs have an Insert Object menu item. When you select this item, a dialog appears that allows you to create a new object (see Figure 3.3). The items on this list all have an **Insertable** key. If you have objects that are not for users to see, simply omit the **Insertable** key.

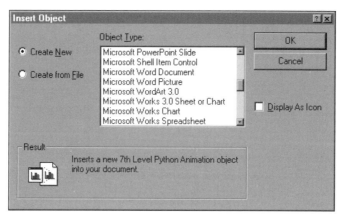

Figure 3.3 The Insert Object Dialog.

Many of the other keys you'll notice in registry entries pertain to specific types of objects. For example, embedded documents may support a **DefaultIcon** key and a **Verb** key. However, for simple ActiveX components, this is all you need. Remember, you don't always need a CLSID and registration for simple objects. Components that require registration include:

- Any object that clients will create with **CoCreateInstance()** (including most objects that other parts of ActiveX will create)
- Objects that want to expose information about themselves to clients before they are created
- Objects that marshal their interfaces

One of the best ways to learn about the registry is to open yours up and browse through it. Many of the entries make sense right away. Others you'll read about later (or, if you can't wait, look them up in your compiler's help). You'll also find a brief summary for many entries in Table 3.3.

Class Installation

Now that you know where to register classes, do you have to write a lot of code to do it? Not necessarily. There are three ways you can inform a machine about your registry entries:

- Write code to manipulate the registry in an installation program
- Write a REG file and call REGEDIT (or REGEDT32) to insert it for you
- Make your servers self-registering by adding code to them

Information, Please 53

Table 3.3 Registry Entries.

Key	Description
LocalServer32	Name of EXE file that contains the server
InprocServer32	Name of DLL file that contains the server
InprocHandler32	Inprocess handler DLL (usually OLE2.DLL)
Insertable	Indicates that server is an insertable object
ProgID	Short name for class (may include version information)
VersionIndependentProgId	Short name for class (independent of version)
TreatAs	Replacement class for this class (see text)
AutoTreatAs	Replacement class for this class (see text)
Interfaces	List of all IIDs that this object may support (optional)

Each of these methods has advantages and disadvantages. The first case is tedious, but not difficult to figure out. Just use the calls outlined in Table 3.1 to put whatever you like in the registry.

Using REGEDIT or REGEDT32 is the easiest way to add entries to the registry. You simply construct an ASCII file (see below) and use **WinExec()** (or any other method) to launch the appropriate program. You pass the file name as a command line argument to the editor, and it provides a dialog box that reports its success or failure. If you don't want the user to see anything, pass a /S argument to REGEDIT and it will remain silent.

Self-registration is a convenient feature that allows servers to automatically register themselves. Of course, servers can reside in DLLs or EXE files, too. As you might expect, the mechanism you use to self-register is different for these two types of servers. Self-registration isn't really a technique in itself. It is just a protocol for the system to ask your server to register itself. When you respond to the request, you'll use one of the other two methods (direct API calls or REGEDIT) to complete the task.

Using REGEDIT

By far, the easiest way to make entries in the registry is by using REGEDIT (or REGEDT32 in Windows NT). You simply create an ASCII text file, which you can install in several different ways:

Chapter 3

- You can import the file using the commands on REGEDIT's menu.
- You can run REGEDIT with the file name to import the file and receive feedback.
- You can run REGEDIT /S with the file name to import the file silently.
- If your system associates REG files with REGEDIT (the default association), you can simply use the shell (or **ShellExec()**) to register the file if it has a REG extension.

Listing 3.3 shows a simple REG file. Notice that it has three main sections. The top line, REGEDIT4, denotes that this is a REG file and what version of REGEDIT it supports.

The next part of the file is a key name surrounded by square brackets. REGEDIT will create as many keys as necessary to generate the full key. For example, if you specify [HKEY_CLASSES_ROOT\X\Y\Z] when there is no X subkey, REGEDIT will create all three subkeys. However, if any (or all) of the keys already exists, REGEDIT will not complain.

After the key name, you specify any values for the key. The default value's name is "@". Other values may have any name you like and may appear up to the next key name. Then the whole process repeats until you have specified all the keys you want.

Listing 3.3 An Example REG File.

```
REGEDIT4
[HKEY_CLASSES_ROOT\CLSID\{F4512327-9E89-11CF-A7B2-444553540000}]

[HKEY_CLASSES_ROOT\CLSID\{F4512327-9E89-11CF-A7B2-444553540000}\LocalServer32]
@="c:\\activex\\aawsound\\debug\\aawsound.exe"
"ExampleValue"="Some string value"

[HKEY_CLASSES_ROOT\CLSID\{F4512327-9E89-11CF-A7B2-444553540000}\ProgID]
@="AAW.Sound"
```

The easiest way to see how to generate a particular REG file is to find a similar entry in the registry and export it using REGEDIT. Then you can modify the file to suit your needs instead of building it from scratch. Programming tools, like MFC's AppWizard, often generate REG files for you with no effort on your part.

Self-Registration

To simplify registration, ActiveX supports an optional means for component servers to register themselves. This self-registration protocol also allows the system to ask a server to remove itself. In most cases, self-registration is optional, but it is handy and not difficult to implement.

There are three basic strategies you might use to implement self registration:

- Use the API calls to directly modify the registry.
- Spawn a copy of REGEDIT to load a REG file.
- Create a temporary file (perhaps from a resource) and run REGEDIT.

Of course to remove entries, you'll always need to use the API calls. The second method, loading an existing REG file, isn't as useful as the other two methods. This is because it requires a separate REG file. If a user forgets to copy the REG file with the component, the registration will fail. The other two methods allow a naïve user to copy your server to another machine and still operate it.

It is optional, but you can indicate your server's ability to self-register by including a special version information string in your resources:

```
VS_VERSION_INFO VERSIONINFO
    .
    .
    .
BEGIN
BLOCK "StringFileInfo"
   BEGIN
   BLOCK "040904B0" // Unicode US English
      BEGIN
         .
         .
         .
      VALUE "OLESelfRegister","\0"
      END
    .
    .
    .
```

When your server self-registers, you'll need to make entries for every single object your server supports. You also need to register type libraries, if you have any. Unregistration should remove all the entries that registration makes.

Self-Registering EXEs

If your server resides in an EXE, you need to look for command line arguments to decide when self-registration should occur. For registration, the command line will contain **/RegServer**. Don't assume anything about the case of the string. Also, the option character may be a dash instead of a forward slash.

Not surprisingly, **/UnregServer** signals that you should remove everything. The same rules apply: The string may be in any case and may use a "-" character instead of the "/".

Self-Registering DLLs

DLLs don't typically process command line arguments. Instead, the system looks for two functions exported by name: **DllRegisterServer()** and **DllUnregisterServer()** (not too imaginative, eh?). These functions take no arguments, and must return an **HRESULT**.

If the routines succeed, they return **S_OK**. If they fail, you can return **SELFREG_E_CLASS**, indicating that class information failed to load, or **SELFREG_E_TYPELIB**, if the type information failed.

Impersonating Objects

There is a different way you can register a class in the registry that allows it to masquerade as a different class. This is handy, for example, if you upgrade to a new server with a different CLSID, but you don't want to break existing code. Another possibility is replacing a competitor's server with your own (which, of course, will be better in every way).

When you replace one server with another, you have to be sure you provide all the same interfaces with identical semantics that the existing server provided. You are free to implement them any way you wish, but the semantics must remain the same. You can also add additional objects and interfaces, as long as the server doesn't require clients to use them. Newer programs will use your "new" CLSID and can request the new objects or new interfaces. The old programs will use the "old" CLSID and will only request objects and interfaces they know about.

The entries required for this emulation might seem odd at first. Suppose we want to replace component **ALPHA** (in ALPHA.DLL) with the **BETA** component (in—surprise—BETA.DLL). The registry might look like this:

```
HKEY_CLASSES_ROOT
   {..Alpha CLSID here..}=The Alpha Component
      TreatAs={..Beta CLSID here}
      AutoTreatAs={Beta CLSID here}
      InprocServer32=ALPHA.DLL
         .
         .
         .
   {..BETA CLSID here..}=The Beta Component
      InprocServer32=BETA.DLL
         .
         .
         .
```

So what's the difference between **TreatAs** and **AutoTreatAs**? When a new server completely replaces an old server, you make entries in both keys. This indicates a permanent replacement. If you are not replacing the existing server, you only make an entry in the **TreatAs** key. That way, when your server unregisters, the old server (either from **InprocServer32** or from **AutoTreatAs**) gains control.

To put it another way, you might use both keys if you were upgrading your existing server with a new version. However, if you install a software package and want to emulate your competitor's server, you only make an entry in **TreatAs**. After all, the user might remove your software and resume using your competitor's (surely not).

ActiveX will automatically manage this process if you call **CoTreatAsClass()** in your registration routines. This function requires two CLSIDs. If the IDs are different, the function creates a **TreatAs** entry in the registry. If the IDs are the same, that indicates that the replacement server is unregistering. Then, the function looks for **AutoTreatAs**. If it finds an entry there, it replaces any existing **TreatAs** key with the value from **AutoTreatAs**. If there is no **AutoTreatAs** key when both arguments are the same, then the **CoTreatAsClass()** function removes the **TreatAs** key.

Type Libraries

ActiveX is very extensible. You can add your own objects and your own interfaces. Your objects can mix predefined interfaces and custom ones. But how can you communicate information about your objects to clients you didn't write?

The answer is type libraries. A type library is a database associated with a server. The library contains type entries. There are five types of elements

Chapter 3

Table 3.4 Type Library Elements.

Element	Description
importlib	Imports another type library
typedef	Defines a new elementary type
interface	Defines an interface
dispinterface	Defines an IDispatch interface
coclass	Description of a component class
module	Describes exported items from a DLL

(see Table 3.4). The library and each of its elements can have attributes (see Table 3.5).

At run-time, the library appears as a set of ActiveX objects you work with using interfaces. You can query for elements or enumerate them, you can set up type libraries to work with different languages, and you can supply different libraries for particular languages.

Where Is The Type Library?

You can distribute a TLB file that contains the type information directly, or you can store it in the DLL or EXE server as a resource. If your application uses ActiveX compound files (as we'll discuss in Chapter 5), you can store it in a special stream.

To identify the type library for an object, you need more entries in the registry. First, you need a **TypeLib** key under the CLSID entry. Each type library has a GUID (which you create like any other). For example:

```
HKEY_CLASSES_ROOT
   {..object CLSID..} = Some Class With TypeInfo
   TypeLib={..TypeLib UUID}
```

Then you also need to define the type library:

```
HKEY_CLASSES_ROOT
   TypeLib
      {..TypeLib UUID..}=TypeInfo for Some Class
         DIR=c:\some_class\bin
         HELPDIR=c:\some_class\help
         1.0
            9
               Win32=English.TLB
            0
               Win32=Any.TLB
```

Table 3.5 Selected Type Attributes.

Attribute	Description
odl	Required on all interface elements
in	Marks argument as an in-parameter
out	Marks argument as an out-parameter
vararg	Indicates that the function takes a variable number of arguments
optional	Marks argument as optional
lcid	Identifies a language for the element
public	Allows external visibility of typedef elements
uuid	Specifies the UUID associated with the element
version	Marks element's version number
appobject	Used with coclass to mark the class as an EXE application
control	Used with coclass to mark the class as an ActiveX control
dllname	Identifies the name of a DLL
entry	Specifies an exported item in a module
helpcontext	Context ID for help
helpfile	Specifies name of help file (no path; see text)
helpstring	Brief help
hidden	Indicates that the object should never appear to the user

Some of these entries deserve some explanation. The **DIR** and **HELPDIR** entries specify the directories that contain the library and the help files, respectively. This is important, because it varies depending on the installation. Help files named in the library must not have an absolute path. Instead, their paths are relative to the directory named in **HELPDIR**.

The next entry is the library version number (1.0 in this case). You can have multiple versions registered, if you like. The numbers below the version are language IDs (a locale). This identifies the library's language. The 9 is generic English, and the 0 is for any language. It is always a good idea to specify at least an entry for language 0. You'll use locales anytime you write programs that support multiple languages. If you want to learn more about locales, see the sidebar *About Locales.*

The **Win32** key, of course, specifies the file that contains the library. This can be a TLB file, an EXE or DLL server, or a compound file.

About Locales

A locale is a 32-bit number that identifies a specific language. Although locales (or LCIDs) are 32 bits wide, only the bottom 16 bits are significant. Windows reserves the top 16 bits, which are always zero.

Of the significant 16 bits, bits 0 through 9 specify the major language. For example, 9 is English and 0x13 is Dutch. The top six bits specify divisions of the major language. Consider English, for instance. What is spoken in London is quite different from what you'll hear in New York. In addition, many words are spelled differently, too (honour vs. honor). Sometimes meanings are even different. For instance, in the U.S., the word "hood" is the part of a car that covers the engine. In the United Kingdom, it is a convertible's top (the engine cover is a bonnet). Also, time and money formats are different. So while 0x0009 is simply English, 0x0409 is U.S. English and 0x0609 is U.K. English.

You can find all the various language bits in WINNT.H. There are language IDs, ranging from Afrikaans to Ukrainian, defined symbolically there. You'll also find macros you can use in your code, like **MAKELANGID**, **PRIMARYLANGID**, and **SUBLANGID**. The first macro builds an LCID from the two IDs. The other two macros extract the parts from an LCID. You can also find definitions for the *neutral* language—that is, the language to use when you just don't care.

Creating Type Libraries

This all begs the question: How do I create a type library? The easiest way to create one is to write an Object Description Language (ODL) script that describes your objects. You compile this file with MKTYPLIB to generate a TLB file. You can then use that file or include it in your server as a resource.

There are three basic things you can describe in an ODL script:

- A module
- Custom data types
- An interface

You can also describe scripting (or automation) classes and interfaces, but that is a special case of interface.

Listing 3.4 shows a typical ODL file. There is a single line at the top that describes the library as a whole. This line contains the library's GUID, its help file, and any attributes (see Table 3.5). It also names the library. Then after the first curly brace, you can use several special keywords, discussed as follows:

IMPORTLIB

The **importlib** statement is similar to a C++ **#include** statement. It reads in another type library. You often use this to read standard types from a common library (such as STDOLE.TLB that contains the predefined types).

TYPEDEF

Use **typedef** to define structures, enumerated types, and unions.

COCLASS

To define an ActiveX component, use the **coclass** keyword. You'll precede this with a **uuid** line to identify the object, its help file, and its attributes. This is the same modifier used in the first line of the script to identify the library as a whole.

Inside the **coclass** braces, you can name interfaces that the object supports. These interface lines consist of an optional attribute (see Table 3.5), the word **interface**, and the name of the interface. To describe the individual functions in the interface, see the **interface** keyword below.

INTERFACE

Not surprisingly, the **interface** keyword describes an interface. You'll precede this with a **uuid** line to identify the interface, its help file, and its attributes. This is the same modifier used in the first line of the script to identify the library as a whole.

MODULE

The **module** keyword describes any exported functions or constants from a DLL. You may precede it with any appropriate attributes (see Table 3.5).

Listing 3.4 An Example ODL File.

```
/*
*EXAMPLE.ODL
* Neutral Language Type Library
*
* "Neutral" language is usually English.
*
*/

[
uuid(5889EE60-AE68-11CF-A7B2-444553540000)
    , helpstring("AAWSound Type Library")
    , lcid(0x0000)
    , version(1.0)
]
   library AAWSoundLibrary
     {
     #ifdef WIN32
     importlib("STDOLE32.TLB");
     #else
     importlib("STDOLE.TLB");
     #endif

/*
 * IID_IAAWSound
 * 'interface' entries must have 'odl' attribute
 */
[
uuid(F4512324-9E89-11CF-A7B2-444553540000)
   , helpstring("Definition of interface IAAWSound")
   , odl
]
interface IAAWSound : IUnknown
   {
   //Methods
   [helpstring("Play the specified sound")]
   HRESULT Play([in] char *file);
   HRESULT GetOptions([out] long *val);
   HRESULT SetOptions([in] long val);
   }


//CLSID
   [
   uuid(F4512327-9E89-11CF-A7B2-444553540000)
   , helpstring("Type information for AAWSound")
   ]
coclass AAWSound
   {
   interface       IAAWSound;
   }
};
```

Type Library Wrap-Up

Some specifics of type libraries will have to wait until we look at other ActiveX details. For now, recognizing that they exist and understanding their basic form is enough. Soon, you'll see how MFC will create starter type libraries for you. You'll only need to maintain those libraries, not create them from scratch.

Summary

If this chapter seems unrelated to ActiveX, don't worry. You really will need to know about the registry when you start writing real ActiveX code in the next chapter. When you do write some code, don't be surprised if it doesn't work and the reason is incorrect registry entries. This sort of problem is maddening because your code looks fine (and it probably is). Sometimes it is the dreaded extra-blank-in-the-registry problem. Maybe you forgot the curly brace in the CLSID. Whatever it is, the registry is one of the first places to look when you can't get an ActiveX program running.

Understanding the Registry is key to ActiveX programming. It is also useful for programming shell extensions, file types, and many other common chores. Time you spend now learning how the registry operates will pay off later down the road.

PART 2

Getting Down And Dirty

Get On With It, Man! 67

Interface Bestiary 109

ActiveX Controls 177

Get On With It, Man! 4

*I see you stand like greyhounds in the slips,
Straining upon the start. The game's afoot...*

—King Henry V

I HAVEN'T ALWAYS BEEN a software jockey. My original association with this business was as a hardware designer (you did read the introduction, didn't you?). Back around 1976 I had just had some exposure to minicomputers about the time MITS announced the Altair (arguably the first personal computer).

I never owned an Altair (it was pretty expensive to get a machine that could do anything), but I followed that whole movement closely. The old original MITS catalog had the 8080 instruction set printed in it (I still have that old catalog, by the way). I pored over it and set out to understand some listings from *Popular Electronics*. With only the instruction set, I couldn't know about odd things like the reversal of the byte order and the implied use of the HL register pair for indexing. I finally figured it out, but because I didn't have a computer, it was all theoretical.

A little later, I built a computer around an RCA 1802—partly from plans in a magazine; partly my own design. I could assemble and disassemble 1802 code just by looking at it. Even today, I still remember most of the instructions. I went on (at work) to design custom systems around 6805s, 6809s, 68000s, and more.

When I finally quit using the 1802 system, I bought a Radio Shack TRS80 model III. Wow! The machine had a built-in monitor and keyboard. It even had BASIC in ROM. I upgraded it to 48K of RAM and put third-party floppy drives in it, though I could never afford the astronomically priced 5MB hard drives.

I learned a lot about computers in those days. I especially learned a lot about programming from the TRS-80. The TRS-80 was the first computer that I owned that a lot of other people owned, too. Wayne Green published a magazine, *80 Micro*, that was full of programs for TRS-80s. You could even buy books about programming these machines. It was great to read about other people's code. Sure, I had read about the Altair, but I didn't have one to try out the things I read about.

This was when floppy disks were expensive and modems were slow. You couldn't get magazine listings in a few minutes online like you can today. Books never had disks with them—the publishers had no idea what those were. The upshot was that I always had to type in the listings from these magazines and books.

Tedious, you say? Perhaps. But it was, and still is, an outstanding way to learn what's going on in someone else's code. You have to examine every line. Unless you are a gifted typist, you'll make some mistakes. Debugging those mistakes is a very valuable experience. This book has a CD-ROM (welcome to the '90s) with all the listings on it. Regardless, I'd encourage you to try typing the examples in this chapter yourself. I've tried to keep them short and to the point. Putting them in yourself will help solidify your understanding. Of course, these are MFC programs, so you can start them with AppWizard—you only want to type the ActiveX parts, right? Refer to the sidebar *About the MFC Examples* for more about creating the examples from scratch.

In this chapter, you'll put the theory you've read about so far to work and actually start constructing some simple ActiveX components. To test them, you'll need a very simple client, too. By the end of this chapter, you'll be writing some fairly sophisticated components using MFC to do much of the work.

About the MFC examples.

Although the examples in this chapter use MFC, they don't use the traditional document-view architecture. To keep things simple, they just bring us a simple dialog box and do the processing there.

If you are at all familiar with MFC, you'll understand this type of program with no difficulty. If you haven't used MFC before, don't worry. So far, the programs don't use any special MFC features. Here are a few tips to help you follow the code:

- Each program has an application object derived from **CWinApp**. This object's **InitInstance** member is the closest thing you'll find to a **WinMain()** in an MFC program. All of the startup code will be in **InitInstance()**.

- There is a specific class that represents the dialog box. Functions with names like **OnInitDialog()** or **OnPaint()** handle the corresponding Windows message (**WM_INIT DIALOG** and **WM_PAINT**). Other functions like **OnPlay** or **OnOK** occur when the user presses a button. In these cases, the corresponding message is **WM_COMMAND** with a particular control ID. Open up Class Wizard to view the mappings between functions and messages.

- Don't worry about the code that paints icons, handles data exchange, and so on. The MFC AppWizard writes all of this code, anyway. The important parts are the portions that appear in the listings.

Macro Mania

Microsoft provides a plethora of macros to—ahem—simplify ActiveX programming. Some of these are part of the basic API. Others are specific to MFC. If you see macros in this chapter like **STDMETHOD** and **STDMETHODIMP_**, just check out the sidebar *ActiveX Support Macros*.

ActiveX support macros.

You'll encounter many odd macros when dealing with ActiveX programming. Here are the most common ones you'll see in both API and MFC programs:

STDMETHOD—Declares a COM interface function that returns an **HRESULT**. Notice that this has an odd syntax. The function name appears as an argument to the macro as in:

```
STDMETHOD(function)(int argument);
```

STDMETHODIMP—Used to implement a COM function that returns an **HRESULT**. This macro has a more ordinary syntax:

```
STDMETHODIMP function(int argument);
```

STDMETHOD_—Declares a COM interface function that returns something other than an **HRESULT**. The syntax, of course, is identical to **STDMETHOD** except that this macro takes a second argument to specify the return type.

STDMETHODIMP_—Implements a COM function that doesn't return an **HRESULT**. (See the **AddRef()** code above for an example of **STDMETHOD_** and **STDMETHODIMP_**).

Why use these macros? Usually, they are a convenience. However, they can also assist you in porting code back and forth between different hardware and operating systems. For example, STDMETHOD expands differently if you are compiling for Windows 3.1, Windows NT, or the Macintosh.

If you want a greater understanding of what these macros do, look up their definitions in the standard header files. None of them are very complex.

Learning Client Basics

The problem with learning about clients and servers is that you can't have one without the other. Instead of trying to plow through both, we will borrow an object from the Windows 95 (or NT 4.0) shell and write a client program that uses it.

The shell exposes an **IShellFolder** interface for each folder (including the desktop). You can obtain the desktop folder's interface by calling **SHGetDesktopFolder**. Armed with this interface, you can manipulate the folder in various ways. The example client in Figure 4.1 asks the desktop to name each item on it and place the names in a list box.

One thing each ActiveX program (client or server) must do is call **CoInitialize** before making other calls. There are cases where you will make a different initialization call that itself calls **CoInitialize()**, but either way, your program must call this at least once. If the call succeeds, you must also call **CoUninitialize()** before your program terminates. These calls are very simple. **CoInitialize()** takes a single **NULL** argument for historical reasons. **CoUninitialize** takes no arguments. You should always check the return value from **CoInitialize**—don't call **CoUninitialize()** unless the initialization succeeds. You may initialize more than once, but you must uninitialize once for each time you call **CoInitialize()**.

Listing 4.1 shows the relevant portion of the simple shell client. Don't get too bogged down in the shell programming portions—focus on the ActiveX components. This program is an MFC dialog-based program. If you are not familiar with this sort of program, see the sidebar *About the MFC Examples*. The program uses three separate interfaces. First, it uses the **IShellFolder** interface to manipulate the desktop. It also requests an enumerator to provide the items the folder contains. Finally, since the enumerator returns a string that the shell wants us to free, the program requires an **IMalloc** interface to free the memory.

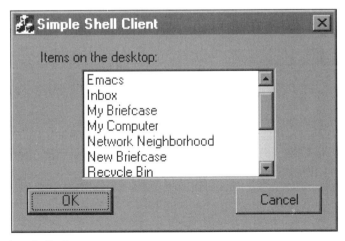

Figure 4.1 The Shell Client in Action.

Listing 4.1 Excerpts from the Shell Client.

```
BOOL CShellClientDlg::OnInitDialog()
  {
  .
  .
  .
  // First initialize ActiveX
  CoInitialize(NULL);
  IMalloc *shmalloc;  // IMalloc interface
  STRRET name;    // A union for returning strings
  HRESULT err;    // ActiveX result
  ITEMIDLIST *list; // List of shell items
  IEnumIDList *idlists;   // Enumerator for shell items
  IShellFolder *desktop;  // Desktop folder
  // We need the shell's allocator so we can free
  // things it gives us
  SHGetMalloc(&shmalloc); // Get IMalloc
  // Get desktop folder
  SHGetDesktopFolder(&desktop);
  // Ask for ActiveX enumerator object
  desktop->EnumObjects(m_hWnd,SHCONTF_FOLDERS|SHCONTF_NONFOLDERS
    ,&idlists);
  // Enumerate until done (S_FALSE) or error
  while ((err=idlists->Next(1,&list,NULL))!=S_FALSE&&SUCCEEDED(err))
    {
    // Ask desktop to translate IDLIST to name
    desktop->GetDisplayNameOf(list,SHGDN_NORMAL,&name);
    // Put it in the box
    if (name.uType==STRRET_CSTR)
      listbox.AddString(name.cStr);
    // Free memory with shell's IMalloc
    shmalloc->Free(list);
    }
  // Release all ActiveX interfaces
  idlists->Release();
  desktop->Release();
  shmalloc->Release();
  // Done with ActiveX library
  CoUninitialize();
  return TRUE;  // return TRUE  unless you set the focus
                // to a control
  }
```

Often, the hard part about ActiveX is not writing custom interfaces, but rather having to puzzle out interfaces that you want to use but didn't create. **IMalloc**, for example, is a standard interface that allows you to allocate and free memory in a thread-safe way (see Table 4.1). You can get the standard ActiveX allocator by calling **CoGetMalloc()**. In this case, we need the shell's allocator (which may or may not be the same) so the program calls **SHGetMalloc()**. Obtaining the **IShellFolder** interface is equally easy. A

Table 4.1 The IMalloc Interface.

Function	Description
Alloc()	Allocates a block of memory (compare to malloc)
Realloc()	Changes the size of an allocated block of memory (compare to realloc)
Free()	Frees memory (compare to free)
GetSize()	Returns the size (in bytes) of a block of memory
DidAlloc()	Determines if this instance of IMalloc was used to allocate the specified block of memory
HeapMinimize()	Releases unused memory to the operating system

Table 4.2 The IShellFolder Interface.

Function	Description
ParseDisplayName()	Translates a display name into an item identifier list
EnumObjects()	Enumerates the objects in the folder
BindToObject()	Retrieves the IShellFolder interface for the specified subfolder
BindToStorage()	Reserved; do not use
CompareIDs()	Compares two item identifier lists
CreateViewObject()	Reserved for use by the shell; do not use
GetAttributesOf()	Retrieves the attributes of the specified file object or subfolder
GetUIObjectOf()	Creates an interface that can be used to carry out operations on a file object or subfolder
GetDisplayNameOf()	Retrieves the display name of a file object or subfolder
SetNameOf()	Sets the display name of the specified file object or subfolder and changes its identifier accordingly

simple call to **SHGetDesktopFolder()** does the trick. Table 4.2 shows the interface functions for **IShellFolder**.

The heart of the program requests an enumerator interface (**IEnumIDList**) from the shell. ActiveX often uses enumerators, which allow you to walk a list of some type (which we'll discuss in Chapter 5). In this case, the list is a list of IDs that the shell uses. Don't worry about what these are—we will pass them back to the desktop folder and it will convert them into regular names.

Table 4.3 The IEnum Pseudo Interface.

Function	Description
Next()	Retrieves a specified number of items
Skip()	Skips over a specified number of items
Reset()	Resets the enumeration sequence to the beginning
Clone()	Creates another enumerator that is at the same point in the sequence

Because enumerators have to deal with different types, you use a different enumerator depending on the situation. In other words, there is no generic **IEnum** interface. However, by convention, enumerator names start with **IEnum** and have the same functions (see Table 4.3). The **Next()** function returns **S_FALSE** if no more items remain, **S_OK** if it returns an item, or an error code if something bad happens.

Once the client gets an ID from the enumerator, it passes it to **desktop>GetDisplayNameOf** to convert the ID to a string. Don't worry about the **STRRET** type—it is a shell peculiarity that allows the shell to return different types of strings. It is just an ordinary union.

The documentation for **IEnumIDList()** clearly states that you have to free the memory returned by the enumerator. That's why the program needs the shell's **IMalloc** interface. A simple call to **Free()** does the trick.

When the enumeration is complete, the program calls **Release()** on each interface. Why are there no corresponding calls to **AddRef()** The **AddRef()** is implied in each call that returns an interface pointer. Any call that creates a pointer (**CoCreateInstance()**, **QueryInterface()**, or **ShGetDesktopFolder()**, for example) must call **AddRef()** for you.

Though this client uses API calls to retrieve different interfaces that it needs, this isn't always possible—or desirable for that matter. The more general way to create an object is via **CoCreateInstance()**. Table 4.4 shows the arguments to **CoCreateInstance()**. In order for this call to succeed, the server must make special entries in the registry and make certain function calls. We'll discuss that more when you write a server later in this chapter.

A Simple Server Design

Before you implement a server, you need to know what it does. Table 4.5 shows the **IAAWSound** interface. This is the single interface to a simple object that plays WAV files. The client doesn't need to know about multime-

Get On With It, Man!

Table 4.4 Arguments to CoCreateInstance.

Argument	Type	Description
rclsid	REFCLSID	CLSID of object to create
pUnkOuter	LPUNKNOWN	Controlling unknown for an aggregate; NULL for normal case
dwClsContext	DWORD	Request for EXE or DLL server
riid	REFIID	Requested IID
ppv	LPVOID *	Returned interface pointer

Table 4.5 The IAAWSound Interface.

Name	Description
Play	Plays specified WAV file (pass file name as argument)
GetOptions	Returns options via single DWORD * argument
SetOptions	Sets options (single DWORD argument)

Note: All functions return an HRESULT

dia, or include any multimedia headers or libraries. It can create an object with an **IAAWSound** interface, call the **Play()** member function, and the sound will play. Of course, a practical object will probably have more functions, but all objects will have the same structure.

Servers can reside in EXE files or DLL files. Usually EXE servers are programs that can do something unrelated to ActiveX. Microsoft Word, for example, can create documents without ever using ActiveX (either as a client or a server). However, when called upon, Word will act as an ActiveX server.

Most servers you want to host on the Internet will reside in DLLs (an in-process or inproc server). This is efficient, especially if the DLL and the client are on the same machine. However, users can't run DLLs to do other work.

General Server Issues

The AAWSound object, could reside in either a DLL or an EXE, so you'll see both implementations in this chapter. If you run the server as an EXE, you can manually enter a WAV file name and play it directly.

Table 4.6 The IClassFactory Interface.

Function	Description
CreateInstance	Creates a new object
LockServer	Locks server in memory

Server Usage

There is one other consideration about servers. How many clients can use a single server? In the case of an AAWSound server, probably only one client can use the server. What does it mean to play two sounds at once? Other servers (Word, for instance) might serve multiple objects at once to a variety of clients.

Servers that are for a single client use the **REGCLS_SINGLEUSE** argument to **CoRegisterClassObject()**. If multiple clients request the server, ActiveX must spawn a new copy for each client. **REGCLS_MULTIPLEUSE** servers, on the other hand, can service any number of clients simultaneously.

Class Factories

If you want clients to create your objects without calling a special function, you must provide another object. This object is a Class Factory and it exposes the **IClassFactory** interface, shown in Table 4.6. (There is also an **IClassFactory2** interface that allows you to control who can create the component based on any security scheme you like.) You have to tell ActiveX about the class factory (exactly how depends on where the server resides). Then the system (or a client) calls your class factory when it wants to create objects that your server provides.

The class factory isn't very difficult to write, and later we will trick MFC into writing it for us. If you provide API-style calls that create objects, you don't need a class factory. You only need a class factory if you want clients to create the server using generic calls.

A Simple Client

Before writing the server, you'll need a simple client for testing. Listing 4.2 shows excerpts from a client that requests a file name, creates an AAWSound object, and calls **Play()**.

Listing 4.2 Portions of the Test Client.

```
// We need to "know" about IAAWSound
#include "iaawsound.h"

void CClientDlg::OnOK()
   {
   DWORD err;
   IAAWSound *play;
   UpdateData(TRUE); // read edit control
   if (FAILED(CoInitialize(NULL)))
      {
      MessageBox("Can't initialize ActiveX!");
      return;
      }
   CLSID clsid;
#if 0 // Use ProgID instead of CLSID
   if (FAILED(CLSIDFromProgID(L"AAW.Sound",&clsid)))
      {
      MessageBox("Can't find AAW.Sound server");
      return;
      }
#else
   clsid=CLSID_AAWSOUND;
#endif
   CLSCTX servertype;

   // Use this line for EXE server
   // servertype=CLSCTX_LOCAL_SERVER;
   // Use this line for DLL server
   // servertype=CLSCTX_INPROC_SERVER;
   // Use this line if you don't care
   servertype=(CLSCTX)CLSCTX_ALL;

#if 0 // Use CoCreateInstance
   err=CoCreateInstance(clsid,NULL,servertype,
      IID_IAAWSOUND,(void **)&play);
#else  // "manual" create instance
   IClassFactory *fac;
   err=CoGetClassObject(clsid,servertype,NULL,
      IID_IClassFactory,(void **)&fac);
   if (SUCCEEDED(err))
      {
      err=fac->CreateInstance(NULL,IID_IAAWSOUND,
         (void **)&play);
      fac->Release();
      }
#endif
   if (SUCCEEDED(err))
      {
      if (FAILED(play->Play(fileName)))
         MessageBox("Server reports failure");
      play->Release();
```

Chapter 4

```
    }
  else
    {
    CString s;
    s.Format("Create failed: 0x%08lx",err);
    MessageBox(s);
    }
  CoUninitialize();
  }
```

Notice that this code listing is similar to the client in Listing 4.1, with a few exceptions. This client is simpler because the object it manipulates is also simpler. Another difference is that it uses **CoCreateInstance** to make the object from a CLSID. You'll also see some inactive code that can create the object from its ProgID or by obtaining its class factory (with **CoGetClassObject()** and using it directly. Remember, the ProgID is a short string that should be unique, but isn't as unique as a UUID. The registry maps the ProgID to the corresponding CLSID. All **CoCreateInstance()** does is obtain a class factory and calls it. Therefore, you might find it more efficient to use the class factory directly if you plan to create multiple instances of a class.

One thing you must specify in a client is what type of server you want. If you don't care, you can use **CLSCTX_ALL**. Alternately, you can use **CLSCTX_LOCALSERVER** to get an EXE server or **CLSCTX_INPROC_SERVER** for a DLL.

Of course, you can't test the client until you build a server. For a first attempt, let's build the server in an EXE file.

An EXE Server

Listing 4.3 shows SERVER.CPP. This file contains the code required to provide the server functions. It could hardly be simpler. However, this isn't all you'll need. You need a class factory (Listing 4.4), as well. An EXE server needs some user interface, too. If you run the server by itself, it will allow the user to enter a WAV file name, press the play button, and hear the sound over the computer's speakers.

Listing 4.3 SERVER.CPP.

```
// Server class

#include "stdafx.h"
#include "Server.h"
#include "resource.h"
```

```
#include <mmsystem.h>


CServer::CServer()
    {
// Initial Conditions
    ref_ct=0;
    options=SND_SYNC|SND_NODEFAULT;
    }

STDMETHODIMP CServer::QueryInterface(REFIID iid, void ** obj)
    {
    *obj=NULL;
    if (IsEqualIID(IID_IUnknown,iid))
       *obj=this;
    else if (IsEqualIID(IID_IAAWSOUND,iid))
       *obj=this;
    else
       return E_NOINTERFACE;
    ((IUnknown *)*obj)->AddRef();
    return S_OK;
    }

STDMETHODIMP_(ULONG) CServer::AddRef(void)
    {
    return ++ref_ct;
    }

STDMETHODIMP_(ULONG) CServer::Release(void)
    {
    if (--ref_ct==0)
       {
       AfxGetMainWnd()->PostMessage(WM_CLOSE);
       delete this;
       }
    return ref_ct;
    }

STDMETHODIMP CServer::Play(char const *file)
    {
    AfxGetMainWnd()->SetDlgItemText(IDC_FILENAME,file);
    AfxGetMainWnd()->UpdateWindow();
    return sndPlaySound(file,options)?S_OK:E_FAIL;
    }
```

Listing 4.4   CLASSFAC.CPP.

```
// Server class factory object

#include "stdafx.h"
#include "classfac.h"
#include "Server.h"
```

```
ClassFac::ClassFac()
   {
   ref_ct=0;
   }

STDMETHODIMP ClassFac::QueryInterface(REFIID iid, void ** obj)
   {
   *obj=NULL;
   if (IsEqualIID(IID_IUnknown,iid)||
       IsEqualIID(IID_IClassFactory,iid))
      *obj=this;
   if (*obj) ((IUnknown *)*obj)->AddRef();
   return *obj?S_OK:E_NOINTERFACE;
   }

STDMETHODIMP_(ULONG) ClassFac::AddRef(void)
   {
   return ++ref_ct;
   }

STDMETHODIMP_(ULONG) ClassFac::Release(void)
   {
   // No need to delete anything since class factory
   // is always static in this example
   return --ref_ct;
   }

STDMETHODIMP ClassFac::CreateInstance(IUnknown * control,
   REFIID id,void **obj)
   {
   CServer *newobj;
   if (control)
      return CLASS_E_NOAGGREGATION;
   if (!IsEqualIID(id,IID_IAAWSOUND)&&
       !IsEqualIID(id,IID_IUnknown))
      return CLASS_E_CLASSNOTAVAILABLE;
   newobj=new CServer;
   if (!newobj)
      return E_OUTOFMEMORY;
   // QueryInterface calls AddRef!
   return newobj->QueryInterface(id,obj);
   }

STDMETHODIMP ClassFac::LockServer(BOOL lock)
   {
   return E_NOTIMPL;
   }

// Local private function -- not accessible to clients
void ClassFac::GetObjID(CLSID *clsid)
   {
   *clsid=CLSID_AAWSOUND;
   }
```

Get On With It, Man! 81

As you can imagine, EXE servers can run in one of two modes: as a standalone program or as an ActiveX server. ActiveX passes /Embedding (or -Embedding) on the server's command line if it is running a server. The command line is always ANSI characters, so be sure to take that into account if you are programming with UNICODE. The main program's **InitInstance** checks for this switch (see Listing 4.5). If it finds the switch, it sets the **embed** variable to **TRUE**.

Listing 4.5   InitInstance for EXE Server.

```
BOOL CAawsoundApp::InitInstance()
   {
   // Standard initialization
#ifdef _AFXDLL
   Enable3dControls();
#else
   Enable3dControlsStatic();
#endif

   CString cmd=m_lpCmdLine;
   cmd.MakeUpper();
   if (cmd.Find("/EMBEDDING")!=-1||cmd.Find("-EMBEDDING")!=-1)
      embed=TRUE;
   else
      embed=FALSE;
   if (cmd.Find("/REGSERVER")!=-1||cmd.Find("-REGSERVER")!=-1)
      {
      char fn[1024];
      GetModuleFileName(NULL,fn,sizeof(fn));
      if (SUCCEEDED(RegisterServer(fn)))
         AfxMessageBox("Registration successful");
      else
         AfxMessageBox("Registration failed");
      return FALSE;
      }
   if (cmd.Find("/UNREGSERVER")!=-1||
     cmd.Find("-UNREGSERVER")!=-1)
      {
      if (SUCCEEDED(UnregisterServer()))
         AfxMessageBox("Unregister sucessful");
      else
         AfxMessageBox("Unregister failed");
      return FALSE;
      }
   CsoundDlg dlg;
   m_pMainWnd = &dlg;
   int nResponse = dlg.DoModal();
   if (nResponse == IDOK)
      {
      // TODO: Place code here to handle when the dialog
      //  is dismissed with OK
```

Chapter 4

```
      }
   else if (nResponse == IDCANCEL)
      {
      // TODO: Place code here to handle when the dialog
      //  is dismissed with Cancel
      }
   return FALSE;
   }
```

The real action occurs in the main dialog's **InitDialog()** function (see Listing 4.6). Here, the code checks for the **embed** flag. If it is **TRUE**, the program does the following:

1. Calls **CoInitialize()** because all ActiveX programs must call this function.
2. Calls the class factory's **GetObjID()** member to learn the main CLSID. Notice that this is a private member function, not part of **IClassFactory**.
3. Calls **CoRegisterClassObject()** to inform ActiveX that it can create the object.
4. Disables the play button and forces the dialog box edit control to read-only. The client, not the user, controls the program in server mode.

Listing 4.6 The OnInitDialog Code.

```
BOOL CsoundDlg::OnInitDialog()
   {
   .
   .
   .
   // Register ActiveX Server here
   if ((((CAawsoundApp *)AfxGetApp())->embed)
      {
      CLSID id;
      if (FAILED(CoInitialize(NULL)))
         {
         MessageBox("Can't start ActiveX");
         AfxAbort();
         }
      factory.GetObjID(&id);
      if (FAILED(CoRegisterClassObject(id,&factory,
         CLSCTX_LOCAL_SERVER,REGCLS_SINGLEUSE,&reg_key)))
      MessageBox("Can't register class");
      GetDlgItem(
              IDC_FILENAME)
              ->SendMessage(
              EM_SETREADONLY,1);
      GetDlgItem(ID_PLAY)->EnableWindow(FALSE);
```

```
    }
  else
    localserver=new CServer;
  return TRUE;
  }
```

If the program isn't in server mode, it creates a private copy of the server and places a pointer to it in the **localserver** variable. This shows an important idea. If you want to use your own server, you don't need to register it with ActiveX or do anything but create the server and use it. In non-server mode, the play button uses the **localserver** object to do the work.

When the dialog box exits (see the implementation of **Release** in SERVER.CPP), the code in the **OnOK()** routine revokes the class object. This is a fancy way to say it is telling ActiveX that the server isn't willing to create any more objects. Then it calls **CoUnInitialize()** to end its ActiveX operations.

Will That Work?

What else do you need to get the server to work? Some registry entries, right? You can find those in Listing 4.7. Notice that the path to the EXE must be correct and that you should double any backslashes in the REG file.

Listing 4.7 The REG File.

```
REGEDIT4

[HKEY_CLASSES_ROOT\CLSID\{F4512327-9E89-11CF-A7B2-444553540000}]

[HKEY_CLASSES_ROOT\CLSID\{F4512327-9E89-11CF-A7B2-444553540000}\LocalServer32]
@="c:\\activex\\aawsound\\debug\\aawsound.exe"

[HKEY_CLASSES_ROOT\CLSID\{F4512327-9E89-11CF-A7B2-444553540000}\ProgID]
@="AAW.Sound"
```

If you build this example and run it in stand-alone mode, it will work fine. However, running it with the client program causes an ActiveX error—error 0x80040150 to be exact. What does that mean?

To find out, look in the system header, WINERROR.H. The first eight simply mean that the high bit is set. When the high bit is set in an **HRESULT**, it indicates an error. The important part of the code is the 40150. Searching WINERROR.H with a grep utility or an editor with a search feature will show you that 0x80040150 is **REGDB_E_READREGDB**. It can't read the registry! This is as misleading an error as you are likely to see.

There are two places you'll want to look to find out what is wrong. First—the obvious suspect—is the registry. The other candidate is the code itself. Try debugging the server to see what is happening (see the Sidebar *Server Debugging Tips* to find out how to get started). Verify that the class factory is working. If you get calls into the server code, you can assume the class factory is at least doing something right. In particular, look at the server's **QueryInterface** (in SERVER.CPP, not CLASSFAC.CPP). Notice how many interfaces ActiveX requests. What can this mean?

Think about what else might be missing. Do you think it really relates to the registry? When you think you know, go ahead and read *No Peeking* below.

Server debugging tips

Debugging a client is simple—just run the program with your debugger. Servers pose more of a problem since you don't execute them directly. There are several possible solutions.

If your server resides in an EXE file, you have two options. The first is to run the server under the debugger. If the server is a single-use server, you'll need to include /Embedding in the command line. First, place any breakpoints you want to examine, then start the client and create an object. The debugger should trigger a breakpoint at the appropriate place.

Another trick you can use is to modify the server's registry entry so that the LocalProc32 entry is the debugger EXE combined with the command line arguments required to start the server. Then ActiveX will start the debugger. If you use this method, you must make sure the server registers its class factory before the time out expires.

Debugging DLLs is even easier. Just start with the DLL visible in the compiler's IDE. Select Build Settings from the menu and click on the Debug tab. Fill in the name of the client you want to run in the field labeled Executable for debug session. When you attempt to run, you may see a warning that the client doesn't have debugging information. That's no problem.

One common **HRESULT** you'll see when working with DLLs is 0x800401F9. This result usually means OLE couldn't find your **DLLGetClassObject** or **DLLCanUnloadNow** functions. Perhaps you forgot to export them, or the names don't match exactly.

No Peeking

OK, so what's wrong with this server? The key is that the server resides in an EXE file. That means it is running in a separate process from the client. ActiveX knows this and asks the object for marshalling interfaces. Remember marshalling? That's the procedure that moves data between process boundaries. Of course, our object doesn't supply marshalling interfaces.

When ActiveX discovers that our object doesn't know how to marshall its data, it looks in the registry under \HKEY_CLASSES_ROOT\INTERFACES for the IID the client wants (**IID_IAAWSound** in this case). Guess what? There is no entry in the registry for this. We didn't make one. This is the cause of the registry-related error message.

If you want to verify this, change the client code to ask for **IUnknown** instead of **IAAWSound**, then manually cast the pointer to an **IID_IAAWSound**. The object creation will then succeed, but the client will crash when you call any members in the object. That's because methods like **Play()** will not cross the process boundary.

Of course, if the server was in a DLL, this wouldn't be a problem. It is worth mentioning that the client can ask for a particular type of server when it calls **CoCreateInstance()**. This client passes **CLSCTX_ALL** to indicate that it doesn't care what type of server it obtains. This is usually the case, since the client interacts with the server in exactly the same way in any case. Of course, DLLs are more efficient since they do not marshall data.

Marshalling

So, you need registry entries for marshalling. The INTERFACES key requires a subkey with the **IID**, and the **IID** key will have two subkeys. The first indicates how many functions the interface provides (**NumMethods**) while the other names a DLL that will marshall the interface (**ProxyStubCLSID32**). Usually, this CLSID is the same as the **IID**. Then you need to register that CLSID under **\HKEY_CLASSES_ROOT\CLSID** and add an **InProcServer32** subkey.

Registering the CLSID isn't hard, but where do you get the marshalling? You could write it, but that is moderately difficult. The easy way is to write an Interface Description Language (IDL) script and compile it with a program named MIDL. MIDL writes three C-language source files that you can compile into a DLL.

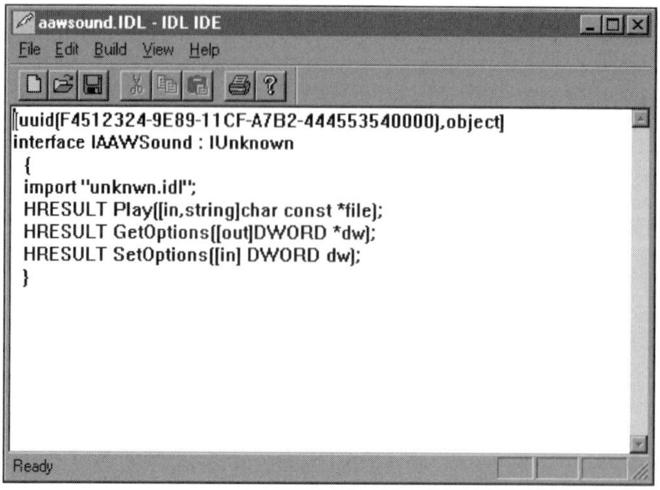

Figure 4.2 The IDL IDE.

In addition to the files that MIDL creates, you'll need RPCPROXY.H and RPCRT4.LIB. You'll usually include UNKWN.IDL in your IDL script (it defines **IUnknown** and it includes **WTYPES.IDL**). To compile, you still need to supply a DEF file and a MAKE file. You also need to register the DLL, which you can do with a REG file.

To make this boring process a little easier, I've included a program named IDLIDE on the companion CD. This program, shown in Figure 4.2, allows you to create IDL files (or load them from disk). You can then select the Build option to run MIDL, and create the DEF, MAKE, and REG files you need automatically. Be sure to read the README.TXT file on the CD to learn more about IDLIDE.

Writing the Script

IDLIDE makes it simple to create the marshalling files, but you still need to know how to write the IDL. IDL isn't unique to ActiveX. It is actually part of the Open Software Foundation's (OSF) Distributed Computing Environment (DCE) specification for Remote Procedure Calls (RPC). Luckily, for ActiveX purposes, you only need a small subset of the entire thing.

Look at Listing 4.8. This is the IDL file required for the sound server. The first line encodes the IID and indicates that it is part of an object. The next line names the interface and indicates that it derives from **IUnknown**.

Listing 4.8 The IDL File.
```
[uuid(F4512324-9E89-11CF-A7B2-444553540000),object]
interface IAAWSound : IUnknown
  {
  import "unknwn.idl";
  HRESULT Play([in,string]char const *file);
  HRESULT GetOptions([out]DWORD *dw);
  HRESULT SetOptions([in] DWORD dw);
  }
```

The lines inside the curly braces are very similar to a C++ structure definition. The script imports UNKNWN.IDL instead of manually defining the functions for **IUnknown**. Following this are three almost ordinary-looking function declarations. The difference is that each parameter has a qualifier in square brackets preceding it. These qualifiers indicate if the parameter is an input, an output, or both. Also, in the case of some ambiguous pointer types, the qualifier tells what the pointer points to. For example, the string qualifier in the line that defines the **Play()** function tells the IDL compiler to generate code to pass a NULL-terminated string.

After you get the DLL working, try removing the string attribute, rebuild the DLL, and see what happens. You won't always use the string attribute with character pointers. Other IDL scripts you write might have different uses for a character pointer. It might point to a fixed-size buffer or even a single character. In this case, however, the string attribute is necessary. Notice that the **DWORD** * argument needs no qualification since it is usually unambiguous. Of course, if it pointed to an array of **DWORD**s, you'd need to indicate that. For example:

```
HRESULT Proc(
    [in] short Length;
    [in, length_is(Length)] DWORD array[10];
```

You can find out about all of the IDL modifiers by looking up IDL in the Help file. When you read Help, remember that the original intent to IDL was for RPC. You'll often read about stubs and proxies. A stub is a piece of code that a client thinks is a server. It calls the stub to do some work. The stub then passes data transparently to the proxy (in a different address space or machine). The proxy reconstitutes the data, and calls the actual server. When the server returns, the proxy packages any output data and passes it back to the stub. The stub reassembles the data and returns it to the client. The net effect is that the client thinks it directly calls the server and the server thinks that the client directly called it. The proxy and the stub are invisible to both processes.

Now It Works!

Once you use IDLIDE to process the IDL script, you can build the DLL using the MAKE file. You'll also need to use REGEDIT to import the REG file. Then the client can call the server with no trouble.

The EXE server is much more complex than a DLL server. First, you need an independent user interface. Second, you need marshalling code to break process boundaries. Also, marshalling is never as efficient as directly passing data to a DLL.

More About The Server

Here are a few not-so-obvious points about the server. First, notice that this server can only handle one client at a time. That's why the call to **CoRegisterClassObject** uses the **REGCLS_SINGLEUSE** flag. This tells ActiveX to run a copy of the server for each client that requires it. Also, this server only creates one type of object. More sophisticated EXE servers will register all of their class objects at once.

Some servers can cope with multiple clients (this might be the case if, for example, if the sound program had an MDI interface—that's "Multiple Document Interface", not, as you might suspect, "Musical Instrument Digital Interface"). Then you'd use **REGCLS_MULTIPLEUSE** instead. However, you'd also need to prevent the server from exiting if the user interacts with it. Suppose a client opens a multiple-use server (like Microsoft Word). The user switches to Word and opens a new document to edit. When the client destroys its object, you don't want to close Word—that would be rude. If a user interacts with the server, it should never shut down unless the user explicitly closes it.

The EXE should also not close down unless its reference count is zero. However, the class factory's reference count isn't important. The EXE is free to close even if the class factory has outstanding references. That's why the class factory interface has the **LockServer()** method—it prevents the EXE from closing even if the object reference count is zero. In the case of this server, we never care about locking it while it is not supplying objects, so the call returns **E_NOTIMPL**.

Since this server only handles a single client per instance, any ActiveX invocation disables the primary user interface. However, more sophisticated servers might need some or all of its user interface active. Notice that a server might detect it is running in an ActiveX context and never even show a window.

One final touch is self-registration. This server finds its location and manually enters or removes the entries required.

A DLL Server

The next logical step is to transform the server into a DLL. It turns out you can almost completely reuse the code in SERVER.CPP (Listing 4.2) and CLASSFAC.CPP (Listing 4.3). However, the DLL version of the AAWSound server doesn't have a user interface, so the new versions delete the lines of code that manipulated the server's window. The only new code is in DLLMAIN.CPP (Listing 4.9). Since this server has no user interface, it doesn't use MFC—it is just a simple C++ DLL.

Listing 4.9 DLLMAIN.CPP.

```
#include <windows.h>
#include "classfac.h"
#include "server.h"
#include <olectl.h>   // Required for SELFREG_E defintions

int in_use=0;
HANDLE inst;

BOOL WINAPI DllMain(HANDLE hInst,
   ULONG reason,
   LPVOID lpReserved)
   {
   if (DLL_PROCESS_DETACH==reason)
      // Could do detach processing here, if desired
      return TRUE;

   if (DLL_PROCESS_ATTACH==reason)
      {
      inst=hInst;
      return TRUE;
      }

   return TRUE;
   }

// You can't use __declspec(dllexport) here!
// Why? STDAPI is the same as EXTERN_C HRESULT
// STDAPICALLTYPE and these functions
// are prototyped in OBJBASE.H as STDAPI.
// STDAPI expands to EXTERN_C HRESULT STDAPICALLTYPE
// However, to use __declspec(dllexport), you would need

// to use: // EXTERN_C __declspec(dllexport) HRESULT STDAPICALLTYPE
// if you try to write that and not use STDAPI it doesn't
// match!
```

Chapter 4

```c
// Therefore, you must have a DEF file to export these
// functions

STDAPI DllGetClassObject(REFCLSID rclsid,REFIID riid,void **ppv)
   {
   HRESULT hr;
   ClassFac *obj;

   if (CLSID_AAWSOUND!=rclsid)
      return E_FAIL;

   obj=new ClassFac();

   if (NULL==obj)
      return E_OUTOFMEMORY;

   hr=obj->QueryInterface(riid, ppv);

   if (FAILED(hr))
      delete obj;

   return hr;
   }

STDAPI DllCanUnloadNow(void)
   {
   return in_use?S_FALSE:S_OK;
   }


static char *ourCLSID="{F4512327-9E89-11CF-A7B2-444553540000}";
static char *prog="AAW.Sound";

HRESULT RegisterServer(void)
   {
   HKEY key,newkey,progkey,svrkey;
   char fn[1024];
   HRESULT err=SELFREG_E_CLASS;
   GetModuleFileName(inst,fn,sizeof(fn));
   if (RegOpenKeyEx(HKEY_CLASSES_ROOT,"CLSID",0,
      KEY_ALL_ACCESS,&key)!=ERROR_SUCCESS)
   return err;
   if (RegCreateKeyEx(key,ourCLSID,0,NULL,0,
      KEY_ALL_ACCESS, NULL, &newkey,NULL)!=ERROR_SUCCESS)
   return err;
   if (RegSetValue(newkey,NULL,REG_SZ,
      "AAWSound Server",16)!=ERROR_SUCCESS)
   return err;
   if (RegCreateKeyEx(newkey,"InProcServer32",0,NULL,0,
      KEY_ALL_ACCESS,NULL,&svrkey,NULL)!=ERROR_SUCCESS)
   return err;
   // Don't forget to add 1 for terminating NULL
   if (RegSetValue(svrkey,NULL,REG_SZ,fn,strlen(fn)+1)
      !=ERROR_SUCCESS)
```

Get On With It, Man!

```
        return err;
    if (RegCreateKeyEx(newkey,"ProgID",0,NULL,0,
        KEY_ALL_ACCESS,NULL,&progkey,NULL)!=ERROR_SUCCESS)
    return err;
    // Don't forget to add 1 for terminating NULL
    if (RegSetValue(progkey,NULL,REG_SZ,prog,strlen(prog)+1)
      !=ERROR_SUCCESS)
        return err;

    RegCloseKey(progkey);
    RegCloseKey(svrkey);
    RegCloseKey(newkey);
    RegCloseKey(key);
    return S_OK;
    }

HRESULT UnregisterServer(void)
    {
    char t[512];
    HRESULT err=S_OK;
    HKEY key;
    if (RegOpenKeyEx(HKEY_CLASSES_ROOT,"CLSID",0,KEY_ALL_ACCESS,
        &key)!=ERROR_SUCCESS) return SELFREG_E_CLASS;
    strcpy(t,ourCLSID);
    strcat(t,"\\InProcServer32");
    if (RegDeleteKey(key,t)!=ERROR_SUCCESS)
        err=SELFREG_E_CLASS;
    strcpy(t,ourCLSID);
    strcat(t,"\\ProgID");
    if (RegDeleteKey(key,t)!=ERROR_SUCCESS)
        err=SELFREG_E_CLASS;
    // Don't overwrite worse error!
    if (RegDeleteKey(key,ourCLSID)!=ERROR_SUCCESS)
        if (err==S_OK) err=S_FALSE;
    RegCloseKey(key);
    return err;
    }


STDAPI DllRegisterServer(void)
    {
    return RegisterServer();
    }


STDAPI DllUnregisterServer(void)
    {
    return UnregisterServer();
    }
```

The code in DLLMAIN.CPP is very simple. The **DllMain()** function is the customary code that executes when the DLL loads or unloads. The other two functions that are in this module are **DllGetClassObject()** and **DllCan-**

UnloadNow(). You must export these functions in a DEF file. Because of their definitions in the system headers, you can't use **__declspec(dllexport)** to export them as you might do for your own functions.

The **DllGetClassObject()** function must create a class factory for the requested CLSID. ActiveX will call the function for each class it wants. Unlike an EXE server, DLLs simply respond to this request. If you support multiple class factories, you only respond with the correct one. Contrast this with an EXE server that registers all of its factories when it starts.

The code verifies that the CLSID is the one expected, creates the class factory with the **new** operator, and uses **QueryInterface()** to return the interface and set the initial reference count.

The **DllCanUnloadNow()** function checks a flag to see if the DLL is in use. When a client creates (or destroys) an object, the server increments (or decrements) this flag. Notice that creating a class factory is not sufficient to hold the DLL. If the client needs to lock the DLL without creating an object, it calls the class factory's **LockServer()** function. This function also manipulates the flag that **DllCanUnloadNow()** uses. When clients want to free memory, they can call **CoFreeUnusedLibraries()**. This causes ActiveX to call **DllCanUnloadNow()** and release any DLLs that reply affirmatively.

Of course, the self-registration portion of the code is different, too. You may wonder how you can execute the self-registration code in a DLL. Microsoft ships a program called REGSVR32.EXE with several products (for example, look in your \MSDEV\BIN directory). You can use this program to register ActiveX DLLs. You'll also find code that performs the registration steps in the CHAP04\DLLREG directory.

Other than these simple changes, the server code is essentially unchanged. Of course, the build process is for a DLL, not an EXE file. Since you can't execute a DLL directly, you'll need to use special techniques to debug it (see the sidebar *Server Debugging Tips* earlier in this chapter).

The most important difference between an EXE server and a DLL server is the address space. A DLL server runs in the client process' address space (that's why it is an inproc server). This means it is much, much faster than an EXE server and easier to write. You don't need any marshalling to make the DLL server work.

Supporting Multiple Interfaces

This example server is simple and only requires a single interface. But what if you have an object that contains multiple interfaces? There are several ways you can supply multiple interfaces. The most straightforward (but not the easiest) way is to supply each interface in a separate C++ object. Then you have to coordinate the ActiveX object behavior (for example, maintaining a common reference count). If you do this, you are responsible for maintaining the cohesion between the ActiveX object and the many C++ objects that implement it.

Another way to support multiple interfaces is via C++ multiple inheritance. Just as the example server object derives from an interface, you can create an object that inherits from all its interfaces. However, this leads to some messy issues, since common elements (like **IUnknown**) become ambiguous. This method doesn't lend itself well to aggregation, either.

Perhaps the best method for creating objects with multiple interfaces is to use nested classes. Consider this piece of pseudo-code:

```
class AnObject
   {
   int class_wide_data_item;
   int ref_count;
   .
   .
   .
   class Interface1 : public IInterface1
      {
      // Interface 1 data and members
      .
      .
      .
      }
   class Interface2 : public IInterface2
      {
      // Interface 2 data and members
      .
      .
      .
      }
   };
```

This method is relatively simple and compact, though there are a few issues you'd normally need to consider. For example, how does code in the **Interface1** object obtain a pointer to the outer **AnObject** pointer so it can access class-wide data objects? One answer is to pass the outer **this** pointer to the nested classes' constructors. In practice, this doesn't matter because MFC will handle this automatically. You'll see how in the next section.

MFC Techniques

MFC can greatly simplify many Windows programs, including ActiveX servers. However, the current version of MFC doesn't directly support building ActiveX servers. It does, however, allow you to build automation servers. An automation server is a special server that implements the **IDispatch** interface (something we have not discussed yet). By starting with an **IDispatch** server, you can easily modify the program to serve any interfaces.

MFC can create DLL or EXE servers. It also generates REG files, ODL files, and handles issues such as multithreading and other thorny problems. If you support multiple interfaces per object, MFC will help you nest classes to support the interfaces. I suppose you could use another method to implement multiple interfaces, but then MFC won't help you.

In MFC, ActiveX objects derive from **CCmdTarget**. **CCmdTarget** contains several useful functions that you can call. There are three calls (**ExternalAddRef()**, **ExternalRelease()**, and **ExternalQueryInterface()** that implement **IUnknown**, for example.

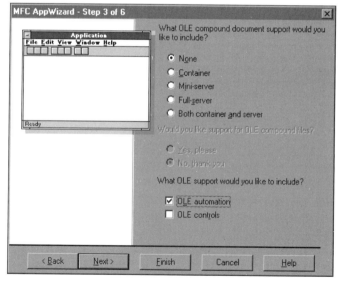

Figure 4.3 Creating an EXE Server with AppWizard.

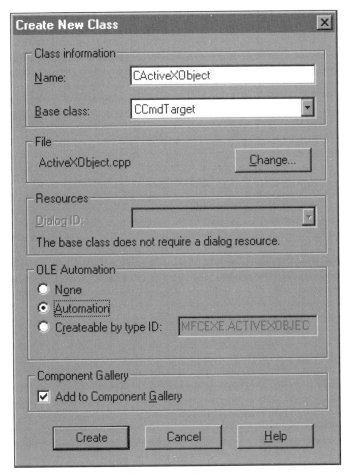

Figure 4.4 Adding a Class with Class Wizard.

An MFC EXE Server

When you ask AppWizard to create an EXE Automation Server, it creates an ActiveX program that implements an **IDispatch** interface. It uses special MFC macros to create nested classes, and maps those nested classes to particular interfaces. You can find more about these macros in the sidebar *MFC ActiveX Macros*.

If looking at these macros seems intimidating, don't worry. AppWizard uses nearly all of these macros and puts them in the right place. In most cases, you'll only need to change some arguments. The process is a simple matter of applying a few steps. You can find an example server in Listings 4.10 through 4.12 with the steps marked. Here is a summary of the steps (the order isn't particularly important after you pass Step 2):

Step 1: Create an EXE with AppWizard

Use AppWizard to create an EXE-based project using any options you like. Just be sure to select *Enable Automation* on page 3 (see Figure 4.3).

Step 2: Create an Object

Use Class Wizard to create an object to represent your ActiveX object. It must derive from **CCmdTarget** and you must select OLE Automation (see Figure 4.4).

Step 3: Remove Automation-specific Code

In the CPP file for the class you created in Step 2, locate and remove the line that calls **EnableAutomation**.

Step 4: Remove Dispatch Map

Only an **IDispatch** interface requires a dispatch map. Remove it from the CPP file and the H file. In the CPP file, you'll need to remove all lines from **BEGIN_DISPATCH_MAP** to **END_DISPATCH_MAP**. In the header file, remove the line that reads **DECLARE_DISPATCH_MAP**.

Step 5: Set Correct UUID

Class Wizard automatically generates a UUID for the **IDispatch** interface to use. If you need an ID for an object or an interface, you can use this one. If you already have an ID you are trying to implement, you can change the generated one to suit you. Look for a definition for a **CLSID** in the CPP file.

Step 6: Correct the Interface Map

The interface map informs MFC that a certain nested class implements a particular interface. The map will have one line for **IDispatch**. You can change this line or delete it and add new lines. The line contains an **INTERFACE_PART** macro that takes three arguments: The main class name, the interface ID, and the nested class name (without the preceding X). Be sure to use the interface ID and not the class ID in this macro in the code.

Step 7: Set Up Class Factory

MFC uses a data-driven class factory. That means that the default class factory automatically knows how to create your classes. To enable this feature, you need to place an **IMPLEMENT_OLECREATE** macro.

You need to inform MFC's class factory that your object exists. You'll need to add the **DECLARE_OLECREATE** macro to the header and the

IMPLEMENT_OLECREATE macro to the CPP file. The **IMPLEMENT_OLECREATE** macro takes three arguments: the main class name, a string (that isn't important in this case), and the class ID. Don't use an interface ID here.

STEP 8: ADD NESTED CLASSES

To add a nested class, you place a **BEGIN_INTERFACE_PART** line in the header file. Then you define each member you want in the class after this line. Finally, you insert an **END_INTERFACE_PART** line. You don't need to declare the **IUnknown** functions (**AddRef()**, **Release()** and **QueryInterface()**. MFC uses internal code for the original **IDispatch** interface, so there isn't any code to delete. You can add as many nested classes as you like. The first argument to **BEGIN_INTERFACE_PART** names the nested class (remember, MFC will prepend an X to the name). The second argument is the interface this class implements.

STEP 9: REMOVE APPLICATION SETUP

In the application's main file (not the object's file), you'll find the definition of the application object. The **InitInstance** member of this class is the closest thing to a **WinMain()** you'll find in an MFC program. One line in this code connects the MFC document template to the automation class. We aren't using automation, so you need to comment out this line. The call is **ConnectTemplate** and you can remove the entire line.

STEP 10: WRITE MEMBER FUNCTIONS FOR NESTED CLASSES

Here's the real meat of the process. You must write functions for all the nested members you defined in Step 8. Remember, you have to put the X in front of each class name (except in the MFC macros). Although MFC declares the **IUnknown** functions automatically, it doesn't write them for you. You must write the functions explicitly.

However, MFC does provide a default implementation for the **IUnknown** functions in **CCmdTarget** (the base class of the outer class). How do you access it? You need the **METHOD_PROLOGUE** macro. This macro takes the outer class name and the nested class name (without the X) and fills in a pointer—**pThis**—with a pointer to the outer class. You don't need to declare the **pThis** variable since the macro declares it for you.

Once you have the **pThis** pointer, you can call **ExternalAddRef()**, **ExternalRelease()**, and **ExternalQueryInterface()** to do all the work required to implement **IUnknown** in a thread-safe fashion. If you browse

Chapter 4

the MFC source, you may notice there are also functions for **InternalAddRef()**, **InternalRelease()**, and **InternalQueryInterface()**. You shouldn't need to call these functions directly. The external calls work when your object stands alone or when it is part of an aggregate. You'll see more about aggregating MFC objects shortly.

You can also use **pThis** to access data or member functions in the outer class. This is a good way to store data and code that apply to the object as a whole from inside each interface class.

Listing 4.10   AAWSOUND.H.

```
// AAWSound.h : header file
//


/////////////////////////////////////////
// CAAWSound command target

class CAAWSound : public CCmdTarget
   {
   DECLARE_DYNCREATE(CAAWSound)
   // Step 7b: Add DECLARE_OLECREATE
   DECLARE_OLECREATE(CAAWSound)

   CAAWSound();

   // Attributes
   public:
      DWORD options;

   // Operations
   public:

      // Overrides
      // ClassWizard generated virtual function overrides
         //{{AFX_VIRTUAL(CAAWSound)
         public:
            virtual void OnFinalRelease();
         //}}AFX_VIRTUAL

      // Implementation
      protected:
         virtual ~CAAWSound();

      // Generated message map functions
         //{{AFX_MSG(CAAWSound)
         // NOTE: The ClassWizard will add and
         // remove member functions here.
         //}}AFX_MSG

      DECLARE_MESSAGE_MAP()
```

Get On With It, Man! 99

```
      // Generated OLE dispatch map functions
      //{{AFX_DISPATCH(CAAWSound)
      // NOTE: The ClassWizard will add and remove
      // member functions here.
      //}}AFX_DISPATCH
  // Step 4b:Remove Dispatch Map
  //      DECLARE_DISPATCH_MAP()
      DECLARE_INTERFACE_MAP()
  // Step 8: Add Interface parts
      BEGIN_INTERFACE_PART(Aaw,IAAWSound)
  // IUnknown added automatically
      STDMETHOD(Play)(char const *file);
      STDMETHOD(GetOptions)(DWORD *opt);
      STDMETHOD(SetOptions)(DWORD opt);
      END_INTERFACE_PART(Aaw)
  };
```

Listing 4.11 AAWSound.CPP.

```
// AAWSound.cpp : implementation file
//

#include "stdafx.h"
#include "mfcexe.h"
#include "IAAWSound.h"
#include "AAWSound.h"
#include "mmsystem.h"
#include "MfcExeDoc.h"
#include "MfcExeView.h"
#include "Mainfrm.h"

#ifdef _DEBUG
#define new DEBUG_NEW
#undef THIS_FILE
static char THIS_FILE[] = __FILE__;
#endif

/////////////////////////////////////
// CAAWSound

IMPLEMENT_DYNCREATE(CAAWSound, CCmdTarget)
// Step 7a: Add IMPLEMENT_OLECREATE
IMPLEMENT_OLECREATE(CAAWSound,"AAW.Sound",
    0xf4512327, 0x9e89, 0x11cf,
    0xa7, 0xb2, 0x44, 0x45,
    0x53, 0x54, 0x0, 0x0);

CAAWSound::CAAWSound()
    {
    // Step 3: Delete this line: EnableAutomation();
    options=SND_NODEFAULT|SND_SYNC;
    CMainFrame *w=(CMainFrame *)AfxGetApp()->m_pMainWnd;
    w->playui=FALSE;
    (((CEdit *)(w->GetActiveView()->GetDlgItem(IDC_FILENAME)))->
```

```
        SetReadOnly(TRUE);
    }

CAAWSound::~CAAWSound()
    {
    }


void CAAWSound::OnFinalRelease()
    {
// When the last reference for an automation object is
// released, OnFinalRelease is called.  The base class
// will automatically delete the object. Add additional
// cleanup required for your object before calling the
// base class.
    CCmdTarget::OnFinalRelease();
    // Here we will close app but if this were a
    // MDI app, you'd need to make sure there were
    // no more open sessions -- especially user
    // initiated windows

    // We are running in an RPC context now, so don't
    // call DestroyWindow, OnFileClose, etc.
    AfxGetApp()->m_pMainWnd->PostMessage(WM_CLOSE);
    }


BEGIN_MESSAGE_MAP(CAAWSound, CCmdTarget)
    //{{AFX_MSG_MAP(CAAWSound)
    // NOTE: The ClassWizard will add and
    // remove mapping macros here.
    //}}AFX_MSG_MAP
END_MESSAGE_MAP()

// Step 4a: Remove dispatch map
//BEGIN_DISPATCH_MAP(CAAWSound, CCmdTarget)
//      //{{AFX_DISPATCH_MAP(CAAWSound)
//
//      //}}AFX_DISPATCH_MAP
//END_DISPATCH_MAP()

// Step 5: Change or remove this ID if you need to
//static const CLSID ID_AAWSound =
//{ 0xf4512327, 0x9e89, 0x11cf, { 0xa7, 0xb2,
// 0x44, 0x45, 0x53, 0x54, 0x0, 0x0 } };


// Step 6: fix up Interface map
BEGIN_INTERFACE_MAP(CAAWSound, CCmdTarget)
  INTERFACE_PART(CAAWSound, IID_IAAWSOUND, Aaw)
END_INTERFACE_MAP()

/////////////////////////////////////
// CAAWSound message handlers
```

```
// Step 10: Write methods
ULONG FAR EXPORT CAAWSound::XAaw::AddRef()
   {
   METHOD_PROLOGUE(CAAWSound, Aaw)
   return pThis->ExternalAddRef();
   }

ULONG FAR EXPORT CAAWSound::XAaw::Release()
   {
   METHOD_PROLOGUE(CAAWSound, Aaw)
   return pThis->ExternalRelease();
   }

HRESULT FAR EXPORT CAAWSound::XAaw::QueryInterface(
   REFIID iid, void FAR* FAR* ppvObj)
   {
   METHOD_PROLOGUE(CAAWSound, Aaw)
   return (HRESULT)pThis->ExternalQueryInterface(&iid, ppvObj);
   }

HRESULT FAR EXPORT CAAWSound::XAaw::Play(char const *file)
   {
   METHOD_PROLOGUE(CAAWSound, Aaw)
   CFrameWnd *w=(CFrameWnd *)AfxGetApp()->m_pMainWnd;
   CMfcexeView *v=(CMfcexeView *)w->GetActiveView();
   v->m_file=file;
   v->UpdateData(FALSE);
   v->UpdateWindow();
   return sndPlaySound(file,pThis->options)?
      S_OK:E_FAIL;
   }

HRESULT FAR EXPORT CAAWSound::XAaw::GetOptions(DWORD *w)
   {
   METHOD_PROLOGUE(CAAWSound, Aaw)
   if (w) *w=pThis->options;
   return w?S_OK:E_FAIL;
   }

HRESULT FAR EXPORT CAAWSound::XAaw::SetOptions(DWORD w)
   {
   METHOD_PROLOGUE(CAAWSound, Aaw)
   pThis->options=w;
   return S_OK;
   }
```

Listing 4.12   InitInstance for MFCEXE.

```
BOOL CMfcexeApp::InitInstance()
   {
   // Initialize OLE libraries
   if (!AfxOleInit())
      {
      AfxMessageBox(IDP_OLE_INIT_FAILED);
```

Chapter 4

```
        return FALSE;
        }

// Standard initialization

#ifdef _AFXDLL
    Enable3dControls();
#else
    Enable3dControlsStatic();
#endif

    LoadStdProfileSettings();
    CSingleDocTemplate* pDocTemplate;
    pDocTemplate = new CSingleDocTemplate(
        IDR_MAINFRAME,
        RUNTIME_CLASS(CMfcexeDoc),
        RUNTIME_CLASS(CMainFrame),
        RUNTIME_CLASS(CMfcexeView));
    AddDocTemplate(pDocTemplate);

// Connect the COleTemplateServer to the document template.
//   The COleTemplateServer creates new documents on
// behalf of requesting OLE containers by using
// information specified in the document template.
// STEP 9: No document template
// m_server.ConnectTemplate(CLSID_AAWSOUND, pDocTemplate,
// TRUE); Note: SDI applications register server objects
// only if /Embedding or /Automation is present on the
// command line.

// Parse command line for standard shell commands
    CCommandLineInfo cmdInfo;
    ParseCommandLine(cmdInfo);

    // Check to see if launched as OLE server
    if (cmdInfo.m_bRunEmbedded || cmdInfo.m_bRunAutomated)
        {
        // Register all OLE server (factories) as
        // running. This enables the  OLE libraries
        // to create objects from other applications.
        COleTemplateServer::RegisterAll();

        // Application was run with /Embedding or
        // /Automation. Don't show the  main window
        // in this case.

        // Disregard the last AppWiz comment
        // In this case, open window
        OnFileNew();
        // should disable UI here!
        return TRUE;
        }
```

```
// When a server application is launched stand-
// alone, it is a good idea to update the system
// registry
// in case it has been damaged.
m_server.UpdateRegistry(OAT_DISPATCH_OBJECT);
COleObjectFactory::UpdateRegistryAll();

// Dispatch commands specified on the command line
if (!ProcessShellCommand(cmdInfo))
   return FALSE;

return TRUE;
}
```

MFC ActiveX macros.

MFC supplies its own set of ActiveX macros. You can still use the others, too. MFC automatically creates a class factory and an **IUnknown::QueryInterface** for you. These macros tell MFC how to implement these things for you.

DECLARE_INTERFACE_MAP—This macro appears in your class' header file and creates an interface map. This map designates which nested class corresponds to a particular COM interface. The built-in **QueryInterface** uses this to return pointers to the correct objects.

BEGIN_INTERFACE_MAP—This macro creates the interface map in the class' CPP file.

BEGIN_INTERFACE_PART—You place this macro inside the object's header file to automatically create a nested class that represents an interface. It automatically writes declarations for the **IUnknown** functions, but you must add declarations for any other functions after this macro. This macro does have an annoying way of handling things. You specify a class name, and the macro automatically prepends an X to the name. If you name the class, CI1, for example, the class name becomes XCI1. You don't need to use the X in other macros (like **INTERFACE_PART**, below), but you do need to use it in other places.

END_INTERFACE_PART—This macro ends the definition of a nested class. Your member function declarations appear between the **BEGIN_INTERFACE_PART** macro and this macro.

INTERFACE_PART—Use this macro after the **INTERFACE_MAP** macro to define the particular map entries. The macro takes three arguments: the main class name, the interface IID, and the nested class name (without the leading X).

END_INTERFACE_MAP—This macro ends the interface map.

DECLARE_OLE_CREATE—Use this macro in your H file to declare a class factory.

IMPLEMENT_OLE_CREATE—This corresponds to **DECLARE_OLE_CREATE** but appears in the CPP file. It takes the class name, an external name, and the object's CLSID.

METHOD_PROLOGUE—This macro appears in member functions of the nested classes that implement each interface. It creates a variable, **pThis**, that points to the main class.

INTERFACE_AGGREGATE—Specifies a variable that contains an interface to aggregate with the object.

Other Considerations

Once you know how to manipulate MFC, it is simple to write an EXE server. Of course, you still have to write your program, too. You also need to write any proxy DLLs and register them. Speaking of the registry, MFC creates a REG file for your server, but you may need to modify it to reflect your choice of CLSID and your proxy DLL. You'll also need to change the ODL file if you want to create a type library. However, if you don't need a type library, you can just delete the file from the project and ignore it.

In the example's case, you don't need a type library. You also can reuse the proxy library built earlier in this chapter. The proxy library isn't in MFC, but since the MIDL compiler builds it automatically, who cares?

Another issue with EXE servers is what to do when a client starts your program. The example program notes that /Embedded appears in the command line while processing **InitInstance()**. The automatically generated comments indicate that you should avoid showing the main window in this case. That's true for an automation server, but may or may not be true for your server. It depends on what you want to happen. The example code calls **OnFileNew** to show its user interface, ignoring the automatically generated comments.

The actual user interface implementation is trivial. Notice that the user interface changes when the EXE file is acting as a server. This is similar to the logic in the original EXE server, just redone for MFC.

Not every ActiveX object requires a CLSID. If yours doesn't, you can omit Step 7. You can also delete the ID in Step 5 if you don't need it. You'll see some objects that don't require CLSIDs in the next chapter. Of course, you can't use **CoCreateInstance()** to generate objects without a CLSID.

Even using this roundabout method, MFC makes server construction more manageable. The library simplifies things by providing an **IUnknown** implementation, registering classes, automatically creating a class factory, and setting the basic structure of the server.

An MFC DLL Server

Writing a DLL server using MFC could hardly be simpler. Just ask AppWizard to create a DLL and make sure the OLE Automation box is checked. MFC will create all the required global functions, along with the same type of skeletal automation object that it created for the EXE file.

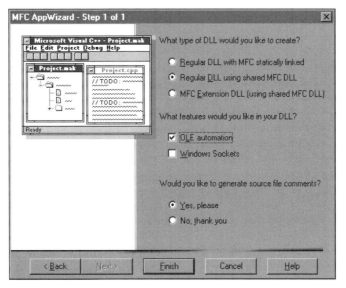

Figure 4.5 Creating a DLL Server with AppWizard.

Again, it is a matter of a few simple steps to convert the specialized automation server into a general-purpose ActiveX server. The steps are very similar to the ones required for an EXE server. You'll find the code on the companion CD. Here are the steps:

1. Use AppWizard to create an OLE automation DLL (see Figure 4.5).
2. Use Class Wizard to derive a class from **CCmdTarget** that uses OLE automation (see Figure 4.4).
3. Delete the call to **EnableAutomation()** in the constructor.
4. Delete the lines that relate to the dispatch map from the new class.
5. Change the automatically generated CLSID, if you want.
6. Fix the interface map, changing the **INTERFACE_PART** macro and adding any others that you require.
7. Remove the **BEGIN_INTERFACE_PART** macro that defines the **IDispatch** interface. Replace it with as many **BEGIN_INTERFACE_PART** macros as you need to define all the interfaces you want to create.
8. Add **DECLARE_OLECREATE** and **IMPLEMENT_OLECREATE** macros to the H and CPP files (unless your class doesn't require a class factory).
9. Write the interface functions you need (including, the **IUnknown** functions).

This is, of course, very similar to the steps you need for the EXE server. Better still, the example code uses the same ActiveX object as the EXE server except for the code that manipulates the user interface. You will need to manually write the REG file for a DLL server.

MFC Aggregation

Remember aggregation? That is the process that allows an object to expose interfaces from a contained object. MFC objects can easily aggregate another object or allow other objects to aggregate its interfaces.

Allowing aggregation is simple. The first step is to call **EnableAutomation** during the object's construction. The only other thing to remember is to call **ExternalQueryInterface()**, **ExternalAddRef()**, and **ExternalRelease()** instead of the internal versions. You can always call the external versions, and you should rarely—if ever—call the internal versions.

Aggregating another interface isn't very difficult either. In your interface map, add an **INTERFACE_AGGREGATE** line. This macro takes two arguments: the main class name and the name of a variable in the main class that points to the aggregated interface. Obviously, this variable has to point to an **IUnknown** or something derived from an **IUnknown**. You initialize the variable during your override of the **OnCreateAggregates()** function. When you create the aggregated object, you'll need to pass it a pointer to the controlling **IUnknown**. You can get this pointer by calling **GetControllingUnknown()**.

Listing 4.13 shows a partial example of aggregating an interface from a different object.

Listing 4.13   Aggregating an interface.

```
class CMain : public CCmdTarget
{
public:
    CMain();

protected:
    LPUNKNOWN m_aggregated;
    virtual BOOL OnCreateAggregates();

    DECLARE_INTERFACE_MAP()
  .
  .
  .
};

CMain::CMain()
{
    m_aggregated = NULL;
}

BOOL CMain::OnCreateAggregates()
{
    // Create new object with our controlling ID
    m_lpAggrInner = CoCreateInstance(CLSID_aggobject,
        GetControllingUnknown(), CLSCTX_INPROC_SERVER,
        IID_IUnknown, (LPVOID*)&m_aggregated);
    if (!m_aggregated)
        return FALSE;
  .
  .
  .
return TRUE;
}

BEGIN_INTERFACE_MAP(CMain, CCmdTarget)
```

```
    .
    .
    .
    INTERFACE_AGGREGATE(CAggrExample, m_aggregated)
END_INTERFACE_MAP()
```

Summary

The mechanics of writing clients and servers are just that—mechanics. The real work is understanding the subtleties of interfaces and objects you didn't design so that you can use them or implement them yourself.

If you use a tool kit like MFC, you can further reduce the chore of writing ActiveX programs. I would not be surprised to see more simplifying tools for ActiveX in the near future.

Either way, you have little choice. Many new APIs use ActiveX. If you want to interact with the shell or take advantage of other new technologies, you have no choice but to embrace ActiveX.

Interface Bestiary

Here comes a pair of very strange beasts,
which in all tongues are called fools.

—As You Like It

THERE'S AN OLD JOKE ABOUT a man who lives in the woods. He goes into town and the dry goods salesman talks him into buying a chain saw. "If it doesn't work out, just bring it back and there's no charge," the salesman says. "You'll be able to do a week's worth of cutting in a single day."

A few days later the man returns to the store. "This thing's no good," he drawled. "I've been cutting down the same tree for three days and I'm only half way done!"

The salesman couldn't believe it. He said, "Let me see that thing. There must be something wrong with it."

The man handed the saw over. The salesman threw the choke, pulled the cord, and started the saw up. The startled man looked up and asked, "What's that awful noise?"

Okay, so you've heard that one before. Pretend you haven't heard it, so that I don't tell another one. The point is that what we've learned about ActiveX so far is just a tool. What do we do with it? Sure, you can define any number of custom objects and interfaces. ActiveX is a good protocol for defining objects.

The real power in ActiveX, however, lies in its ability to write objects that interact with the system (or other programs) via predefined interfaces. Remember, if an object contains an interface, it is polymorphic with all other objects that also expose the same interface. ActiveX provides several objects that you'll use. If you want to interact with ActiveX, you must provide certain interfaces in your objects, too.

A bestiary, by the way, is an old type of book that contained descriptions of animals. Although billed as scientific fact, many of the animals in a bestiary were mythical. This bestiary contains interfaces. Some, you'll find inside ActiveX. Others are almost mythical–you'll have to write them yourself.

IMalloc and IMallocSpy

IMALLOC is an interface that ActiveX provides for you. You can use it to allocate memory that is thread safe. You don't have to stop using **malloc** or **new** for memory that you use within your own program. Why should you? However, sometimes when you need to pass data around to another process, you'll have to use **IMalloc**.

You should never have occasion to write your own implementation of **IMalloc**. Instead, you obtain a pointer to the built-in one by calling **CoGetMalloc**. Table 5.1 shows the functions you can call via **IMalloc**. When you no longer need the interface, be sure to call its **Release** function.

If you need to debug allocation, you can call **CoRegisterMallocSpy** and **CoRevokeMallocSpy**. To use these functions, you have to create an object that exposes **IMallocSpy** (see Table 5.2). When you pass a pointer to this interface to **CoRegisterMallocSpy**, the default **IMalloc** will call your spy functions at key points in the allocation process. What you do with this information is up to you.

A few other entities might supply an **IMalloc** interface. The new-style shell is a good example of this. You can find some code that uses the shell's **IMalloc** in Listing 4.1 (see Chapter 4).

Interface Bestiary

Table 5.1 The IMalloc interface.

Function	Description
Alloc	Allocates a block of memory
Realloc	Changes the size of a block of memory
Free	Frees a block of memory
GetSize	Returns the size in bytes of a memory block
DidAlloc	Determines if this instance of IMalloc allocated a particular memory block
HeapMinimize	Minimizes the heap by releasing unused memory to the operating system

Table 5.2 The IMallocSpy interface.

Function	Description
PreAlloc	Called before invoking IMalloc::Alloc; this function may extend or modify the allocation's size in order to store debug information
PostAlloc	Called after invoking IMalloc::Alloc
PreFree	Called before invoking IMalloc::Free
PostFree	Called after invoking IMalloc::Free
PreRealloc	Called before invoking IMalloc::Realloc
PostRealloc	Called after invoking IMalloc::Realloc
PreGetSize	Called before invoking IMalloc::GetSize
PostGetSize	Called after invoking IMalloc::GetSize
PreDidAlloc	Called before invoking IMalloc::DidAlloc
PostDidAlloc	Called after invoking IMalloc::DidAlloc
PreHeapMinimize	Called before invoking IMalloc::DidAlloc
PostHeapMinimize	Called after invoking IMalloc::HeapMinimize

IEnum

IEnum is an abstract interface that allows you to walk over a list of items. You might remember using **IEnumIDList** in Chapter 4. There is no actual **IEnum** interface. Instead, there are different types of enumerators (like **IEnumIDList**) that enumerate different types.

Table 5.3 The IEnum pseudo-interface.

Function	Description
Clone	Creates a new enumerator having the same contents and state (see text)
Next	Retrieves one or more items in the enumeration
Reset	Resets the current position within the enumerator
Skip	Skips over one or more items in the enumeration

You can find the functions that all **IEnum** interfaces support in Table 5.3. The only thing unusual is that the **Next** function takes different parameters depending on the type of data the enumerator returns.

Sometimes, you'll use an enumerator (like **IEnumIDList**). Other times, you'll have to provide an enumerator for a particular list inside an object you create. Luckily, many types of enumerators have built-in support. You can simply delegate calls to an Active-X provided function or ask ActiveX to create the enumerator for you. For example, you can ask ActiveX to create an **IEnumOLEVERB** enumerator from your registry information by calling **OleRegEnumVerbs**. You'll find a list of common enumeration interfaces in Table 5.4. Typically, an enumeration object will expose only one of these interfaces.

Normally, you'll think of an enumerator as walking over some list of items. However, the list can be abstract. Consider the example in Listings 5.1 and 5.2. This enumerator lists Fibonacci numbers. (You get the next number in the Fibonacci sequence by adding the previous two integers in the sequence: 1, 1, 2, 3, 5, 8 . . .)

Here, the list isn't a physical entity that you can point to. Instead, it is a logical sequence that the enumerator walks over. The example program that exercises this enumerator (Listing 5.3) is very straightforward. However, it does do one interesting trick. The enumerator doesn't have a CLSID or a class factory. That means the test program can't create it using **CoCreateInstance**. That's OK, because it can just make the C++ object using **new**. The problem is, **new** returns a pointer to a **CCmdTarget**-derived class. You need a pointer to the nested class that implements the enumerator.

Interface Bestiary 113

Table 5.4 Common enumerator interfaces.

Object	Enumerates
IEnumFORMATETC	An array of FORMATETC structures
IEnumMoniker	The components of a moniker, or the monikers in a table (discussed later)
IEnumOLEVERB	The different verbs available for an object, in order of ascending verb number
IEnumSTATDATA	An array of STATDATA structures which contain advisory connection information for a data object
IEnumSTATSTG	An array of STATSTG structures, which contain information about a storage, stream, or ILockBytes object (discussed later)
IEnumString	Strings
IEnumUnknown	Enumerates IUnknown interface pointers
IEnumVARIANT	A collection of VARIANT structures (discussed later)

The trick is to call the new class' **ExternalQueryInterface** function to obtain the initial interface. Armed with that interface, you can proceed as usual, calling **QueryInterface** if you need more pointers. Here's the code:

```
CFibEnum *obj=new CFibEnum;
obj->ExternalQueryInterface(&IID_IEnumFib,
    (void **)&enumerator);
```

The only slippery part of implementing an ordinary enumerator is the **Clone** function. For the example enumerator, this isn't a problem because the list is fixed–it never changes. Think about an enumerator that emits a list of users on a network. Suppose there is a list somewhere, maintained by the operating system, that provides the information. You'd think you could simply return elements from that list. You can't do that because of the semantics of the **Clone** function.

Suppose there are three users logged on: Al, Jon, and Jeff. Your enumerator points to Jon as the current item in the list. The client asks the enumerator to clone itself, so you make a copy of the enumerator with an index of 1 (assume zero-based indexing). Meanwhile, Jon logs off and Keith logs in. When you go to use the cloned copy, the list contains Al, Jeff, and Keith. The enumerators are no longer clones of one another. In practice, this means you must snapshot any data that is subject to change. Of course, the Fibonacci numbers have been the same since Leonardo

Fibonacci dreamed them up in the 13th century, so the example code doesn't have this problem.

Listing 5.1 The Fibonocci Enumerator.

```
// FibEnum.cpp : implementation file
//

#include "stdafx.h"
#include "fib.h"
#include "FibEnum.h"

#ifdef _DEBUG
#define new DEBUG_NEW
#undef THIS_FILE
static char THIS_FILE[] = __FILE__;
#endif

/////////////////////////////////////
// CFibEnum

IMPLEMENT_DYNCREATE(CFibEnum, CCmdTarget)

BEGIN_INTERFACE_MAP(CFibEnum, CCmdTarget)
INTERFACE_PART(CFibEnum, IID_IEnumFib, Fib)
END_INTERFACE_MAP()


CFibEnum::CFibEnum(int last_,int current_)
    {
    last=last_;
    current=current_;
    }

CFibEnum::~CFibEnum()
    {
    }


void CFibEnum::OnFinalRelease()
    {
    // When the last reference for an automation object
    // is released OnFinalRelease is called.
    // The base class will automatically
    // delete the object.  Add additional cleanup
    // required for your object before calling
    // the base class.

    CCmdTarget::OnFinalRelease();
    }
```

Interface Bestiary

```
BEGIN_MESSAGE_MAP(CFibEnum, CCmdTarget)
   //{{AFX_MSG_MAP(CFibEnum)
   //}}AFX_MSG_MAP
END_MESSAGE_MAP()



/////////////////////////////////
// CFibEnum message handlers
ULONG FAR EXPORT CFibEnum::XFib::AddRef(void)
   {
   METHOD_PROLOGUE(CFibEnum,Fib);
   return pThis->ExternalAddRef();
   }

ULONG FAR EXPORT CFibEnum::XFib::Release(void)
   {
   METHOD_PROLOGUE(CFibEnum,Fib);
   return pThis->ExternalRelease();
   }

HRESULT FAR EXPORT CFibEnum::XFib::QueryInterface(
   REFIID iid, void FAR* FAR* ppvObj)
   {
   METHOD_PROLOGUE(CFibEnum, Fib)
   return
     (HRESULT)pThis->ExternalQueryInterface(&iid, ppvObj);
   }

STDMETHODIMP CFibEnum::XFib::Next(ULONG elct,int *ret_ary,
   ULONG *ctout)
   {
   METHOD_PROLOGUE(CFibEnum,Fib)
   if (ctout) *ctout=elct; // we always do them all
      while (elct—)
         {
         *ret_ary=pThis->last+pThis->current;
         pThis->last=pThis->current;
         pThis->current=*ret_ary++;
         }
   return S_OK;
   }

STDMETHODIMP CFibEnum::XFib::Skip(ULONG count)
   {
   METHOD_PROLOGUE(CFibEnum,Fib)
   while (count—)
      {
      int t=pThis->last+pThis->current;
      pThis->last=pThis->current;
      pThis->current=t;
      }
   return S_OK;
   }
```

```
STDMETHODIMP CFibEnum::XFib::Reset(void)
    {
    METHOD_PROLOGUE(CFibEnum,Fib)
    pThis->last=0;
    pThis->current=1;
    return S_OK;
    }

STDMETHODIMP CFibEnum::XFib::Clone(IEnumFib **clone)
    {
    METHOD_PROLOGUE(CFibEnum,Fib)
    if (!clone) return E_INVALIDARG;
    *clone=(IEnumFib *)new CFibEnum(pThis->last,
        pThis->current);
    if (!*clone) return E_OUTOFMEMORY;
    return S_OK;
    }
```

Listing 5.2 Enumerator header.

```
// FibEnum.h : header file
//
/////////////////////////////////////
// CFibEnum command target

#include "objbase.h"
#include "afxdisp.h"

const IID IID_IEnumFib =
   { 0xf4512324, 0x9e89, 0x11cf, { 0xa7, 0xb2, 0x44,
     0x45, 0x53, 0x54, 0x0, 0x0 } };

class IEnumFib : public IUnknown
  {
  public:
  STDMETHOD(Next)(ULONG elct,int *ret_ary,
    ULONG *ctout) PURE;
  STDMETHOD(Skip)(ULONG count) PURE;
  STDMETHOD(Reset)(void) PURE;
  STDMETHOD(Clone)(IEnumFib **clone) PURE;
  };

class CFibEnum : public CCmdTarget
  {
  DECLARE_DYNCREATE(CFibEnum)
// protected constructor used by dynamic creation
  CFibEnum(int last_=0,int current_=1);

// Attributes
  public:
  int last;
  int current;
```

```
// Operations
  public:
// Overrides
// ClassWizard generated virtual function overrides
    //{{AFX_VIRTUAL(CFibEnum)
    public:
    virtual void OnFinalRelease();
    //}}AFX_VIRTUAL

// Implementation
    protected:
    virtual ~CFibEnum();

// Generated message map functions
    //{{AFX_MSG(CFibEnum)
    //}}AFX_MSG

    DECLARE_MESSAGE_MAP()
    DECLARE_INTERFACE_MAP()
    BEGIN_INTERFACE_PART(Fib,IEnumFib)
    STDMETHOD(Next)(ULONG elct,int *ret_ary,ULONG *ctout);
    STDMETHOD(Skip)(ULONG count);
    STDMETHOD(Reset)(void);
    STDMETHOD(Clone)(IEnumFib **clone);
    END_INTERFACE_PART(Fib)
    };

//////////////////////////////////////
```

Listing 5.3 Code that uses the Enumerator.

```
// fibView.cpp : implementation of the CFibView class
//

#include "stdafx.h"
#include "fib.h"

#include "fibDoc.h"
#include "fibenum.h"
#include "fibView.h"


#ifdef _DEBUG
#define new DEBUG_NEW
#undef THIS_FILE
static char THIS_FILE[] = __FILE__;
#endif

//////////////////////////////////////
// CFibView

IMPLEMENT_DYNCREATE(CFibView, CFormView)
```

Chapter 5

```
BEGIN_MESSAGE_MAP(CFibView, CFormView)
    //{{AFX_MSG_MAP(CFibView)
    ON_BN_CLICKED(IDC_NEXT, OnNext)
    ON_BN_CLICKED(IDC_RESET, OnReset)
    //}}AFX_MSG_MAP
END_MESSAGE_MAP()

/////////////////////////////////////
// CFibView construction/destruction

CFibView::CFibView()
: CFormView(CFibView::IDD)
    {
        //{{AFX_DATA_INIT(CFibView)
        m_number = 0;
        //}}AFX_DATA_INIT
    // TODO: add construction code here

    }

CFibView::~CFibView()
    {
    }

void CFibView::DoDataExchange(CDataExchange* pDX)
    {
    CFormView::DoDataExchange(pDX);
        //{{AFX_DATA_MAP(CFibView)
        DDX_Text(pDX, IDC_NUMBER, m_number);
        //}}AFX_DATA_MAP
    }

BOOL CFibView::PreCreateWindow(CREATESTRUCT& cs)
    {
    // TODO: Modify the Window class or styles here by modifying
    //   the CREATESTRUCT cs

    return CFormView::PreCreateWindow(cs);
    }

/////////////////////////////////////
// CFibView diagnostics

#ifdef _DEBUG
void CFibView::AssertValid() const
    {
    CFormView::AssertValid();
    }

void CFibView::Dump(CDumpContext& dc) const
    {
    CFormView::Dump(dc);
    }
```

Interface Bestiary 119

```
CFibDoc* CFibView::GetDocument() // non-debug version is inline
    {
    ASSERT(m_pDocument->IsKindOf(RUNTIME_CLASS(CFibDoc)));
    return (CFibDoc*)m_pDocument;
    }
#endif //_DEBUG

/////////////////////////////////////
// CFibView message handlers

void CFibView::OnNext()
    {
    if (FAILED(enumerator->Next(1,&m_number,NULL)))
       MessageBox("Enumeration failure!");
    else
       UpdateData(FALSE);
    }

void CFibView::OnInitialUpdate()
    {
    CFibEnum *obj=new CFibEnum; // direct create
    // trick to find interface pointer
    obj->ExternalQueryInterface(&IID_IEnumFib,
      (void **)&enumerator);
    CFormView::OnInitialUpdate();
    OnNext();
    }

void CFibView::OnReset()
    {
    enumerator->Reset();
    OnNext();
    }

BOOL CFibView::DestroyWindow()
    {
    if (enumerator) enumerator->Release();
    return CFormView::DestroyWindow();
    }
```

IStorage And IStream

ActiveX provides two interfaces that create a pseudo-file system for storing data in some underlying medium (like a file, for example). You can think of a storage (**IStorage**) as a directory and a stream (**IStream)** as a file. As you might expect, a storage can contain any number of streams. A storage can also contain substorages (similar to a sub-directories). That's really all there is to it. You can find the **IStorage** and **IStream** interfaces in Tables 5.5 and 5.6.

Table 5.5 The IStorage interface.

Function	Description
CreateStream	Creates and opens a stream object with the specified name
OpenStream	Opens an existing stream object
CreateStorage	Creates and opens a new storage object
OpenStorage	Opens an existing storage object
CopyTo	Copies the entire contents of this open storage into another storage
MoveElementTo	Copies or moves a substorage or stream from this storage to another
Commit	Reflects changes for a transacted storage to the parent level
Revert	Discards all changes that have been made to the storage object since the last commit
EnumElements	Returns an enumerator for all storage and stream objects contained within this storage
DestroyElement	Removes the specified element
RenameElement	Renames the specified element
SetElementTimes	Sets the modification, access, and creation times of the storage element, if supported by the underlying file system
SetClass	Assigns the specified CLSID to this storage
SetStateBits	Associates up to 32 bits of state information for this storage; currently, Microsoft defines no state bits and reserves them all
Stat	Returns the STATSTG structure for this open storage (see Table 5.9)

Don't get too carried away with the storage/stream/file system analogy. A main storage is often a single file. Inside that file is data that corresponds to individual substorages and streams. From the user's point of view, there is one operating system file that contains all the data. However, you can construct storages and streams in other ways. For example, it is easy to create a stream in memory. You could also create a stream in a database field, if you needed to do that. The point is that **IStorage** and **IStream** are simply interfaces to objects that store data. Where the objects store the data is up to them.

ActiveX provides code (the compound file system) that can expose **IStorage** and **IStream**. This default implementation stores everything inside one operating system file. To create a compound file, you call **StgCreateDocfile** (see Table 5.7). This call uses the archaic name *Docfile* instead of the more

Interface Bestiary

Table 5.6 The IStream interface.

Function	Description
Read	Reads from stream to memory starting at the current position
Write	Writes from memory to stream starting at the current position
Seek	Changes the current position
SetSize	Changes the size of the stream; useful to truncate or preallocate space
CopyTo	Copies bytes from the current position in the stream to the current position in another stream
Commit	Ensures that any changes made to the stream are reflected in the parent storage (not supported for compound files)
Revert	Discards all changes made to a transacted stream since the last Commit call (no effect for compound files)
LockRegion	Restricts access to a specified range of bytes in the stream (not supported for compound files)
UnlockRegion	Removes the access restriction on a range of bytes previously restricted with LockRegion (not supported for compound files)
Stat	Retrieves the STATSTG structure for this stream
Clone	Creates a new stream that is identical to the current stream but has a separate current position

Table 5.7 Arguments to StgCreateDocfile.

Parameter	Type	Description
pwcsName	WCHAR	Unicode path name
grfMode	DWORD	Access mode (see Table 5.10)
reserved	DWORD	Not used
ppstgOpen	IStorage **	Pointer to created IStorage

modern term, compound file. If you want to open an existing compound file, call **StgOpenStorage** (see Table 5.8). In either case, you pass a Unicode file name and an access mode. The calls return an **IStorage** pointer. You use this pointer to create substorages and streams within the storage. It is noteworthy that, regardless of some versions of the online help, **StgOpenStorage** can *not* open an ordinary directory or an ordinary file.

Table 5.8 Arguments to StgOpenStorage.

Parameter	Type	Description
pwcsName	WCHAR	Unicode pathname
pstgPriority	IStorage *	Storage to reopen in priority mode (used instead of pwcsName)
grfMode	DWORD	Access mode (see Table 5.10)
snbExclude	SNB	List of elements to exclude
reserved	DWORD	Not used
ppstgOpen	IStorage **	Pointer to created IStorage

You can also create a stream on a block of memory by calling **CreateStreamOnHGlobal**. You pass this function a handle to memory, along with a flag. If the flag is set, the system will free the memory block when you release the underlying object. The function passes you an **IStream** pointer that you can use.

Streams In Detail

As you can see from Table 5.6, streams do pretty much what you'd expect them to do. The only functions that deserve special comment are **Stat** and **Clone**. **Stat** fills in a **STATSTG** structure for the stream (see Table 5.9). You can find out a great deal about the stream by examining this structure. The name of the stream appears in the **pwcsName** field. You are responsible for freeing the memory this points to by using the **IMalloc** interface you obtain by calling **CoGetMalloc**. The code usually looks something like this:

```
STGSTAT stat;
IStream *str;
.
.
.
if (FAILED(CoGetMalloc(1,&mal))) return;
str->Stat(&stat,STATFLAG_DEFAULT);
.
.
.
mal->Free(stat.pwcsName);
mal->Release();
```

If you pass **STATFLAG_NONAME** to the **Stat** call, the stream doesn't return its name, and you don't have to free the memory in that case.

Interface Bestiary

Table 5.9 Members of the STATSTG structure.

Member	Type	Description
pwcsName	LPWSTR	Name of stream or storage
type	DWORD	Type of item (STGTY_STORAGE or STGTY_STREAM; see the STGTY enumeration)
cbSize	ULARGE_INTEGER	Size of item (64 bits); 0 for storage items
mtime	FILETIME	Last modification time
ctime	FILETIME	Time item was created
atime	FILETIME	Time of last access
grfMode	DWORD	Access mode
grfLocksSupported	DWORD	Type of stream locking allowed (see LOCKTYPES enumeration); not applicable to storage items
clsid	CLSID	ActiveX object associated with a storage (not valid for streams)
grfStateBits	DWORD	Current state bits (only valid for storages); currently, Microsoft defines no state bits and reserves them all
dwStgFmt	DWORD	Storage format (see STGFMT enumeration)

There are a few other things you should know about the **STATSTG** structure. This structure is valid for streams and storages. The **atime, clsid, ctime, mtime, clsid, dwStgFmt,** and **grfStateBits** fields are only valid for storages. The **grfLocksSupported** field is only for streams.

The **Clone** function duplicates a stream, but not the stream's data. That is to say, the duplicate refers to the same file (or other, underlying data storage). However, it has a separate seek pointer. This allows you to easily copy data from one point in the stream to another point in the same stream. You can even use the **CopyTo** function to accomplish this. For example:

```
IStream *str,*copy;
   .
   .
   .
// Copy 10 bytes from beginning to offset 10000
str->Clone(&copy);
str->Seek(0,STREAM_SEEK_SET,NULL);
copy->Seek(10000,STREAM_SEEK_SET,NULL);
```

```
str->CopyTo(copy,10,NULL,NULL);
copy->Release();
```

Stream names can contain up to 32 Unicode characters. All characters are legal except for '/', '\', ':', and '!'. ActiveX reserves names that begin with characters '\x00' to '\x1F'.

Storages In Detail

Storages come in two flavors: root storages, and substorages. For the purposes of compound files, a root storage always corresponds to an operating system file. That means it suffers from the same name limitations as an operating system file. A root storage can contain streams and substorages. Of course, substorages may also contain other substorages and streams.

Given a storage interface, you can use member functions to create, delete, copy, move, enumerate, or open elements (that is, substorages or streams). You can call **Stat** to fill in a **STATSTG** structure to learn about the storage. When you want to enumerate the storage's elements, you call **EnumElements**. This returns an **IEnumSTATSTG** interface (this is an **IEnum** interface). Then, when you call **Next** on the enumerator, it will fill in a **STATSTG** structure.

You can open a storage in several modes (see Table 5.10). Most of these are common-sense. Keep in mind that you may select, at most, one flag from each group. For example, you can't mix the **STGM_DIRECT** and **STGM_TRANSACTED** flags because they are from the same group. If you don't specify any Group I flags, the default (**STGM_DIRECT**) takes effect.

The sharing flags operate as you might expect. The **STGM_FAILIFTHERE** flag only works when creating a storage. This prevents you from creating a new storage on top of an old one. If you want to create a new empty storage, even at the expense of an existing storage, specify **STGM_CREATE**.

The **STGM_TRANSACTED** mode allows you to open a storage, modify it, and then elect to commit the changes or roll them back. If you call **Commit**, your changes become permanent. If you call **Revert** (or **Release** the object without calling **Commit**), you lose all changes. The default mode, **STGM_DIRECT**, works more like an ordinary file. Changes are always permanent. **STGM_TRANSACTED** files can greatly simplify undo commands and revert to saved commands.

Interface Bestiary 125

Table 5.10 Storage modes.

Group I: Type

Name	Description
STGM_DIRECT*	Allows changes to the item to take effect immediately
STGM_TRANSACTED	Prevents changes from taking effect until a commit call
STGM_SIMPLE	Limited, more efficient mode (see online help); must combine with STGM_CREATE, STGM_READWRITE, and STGM_SHAREEXCLUSIVE

Group II: Access Mode

Name	Description
STGM_READ*	Opens for reading only
STGM_WRITE	Opens for writing only
STGM_READWRITE	Opens for reading and writing

Group III: Share Mode

Name	Description
STGM_SHARE_DENY_NONE	Allow others to open object
STGM_SHARE_DENY_READ	Allows others to open object for writing
STGM_SHARE_DENY_WRITE	Allows others to open object for reading
STGM_SHARE_EXCLUSIVE	Disallows others from opening object

Group IV: Disposition

Name	Description
STGM_CREATE	Always creates a new, empty item
STGM_CONVERT	Creates a new item while preserving the old contents in a stream named CONTENTS; useful for converting old file structures to compound files
STGM_FAILIFTHERE*	Fails if item already exists

Group V: Miscellaneous

Name	Description
STGM_NOSCRATCH	For Windows 95 only; allows transacted storages to use dead space in the storage instead of a separate scratch file
STGM_PRIORITY	Opens for semi-exclusive access (others can't commit changes); must combine with STGM_DIRECT and STGM_READ
STGM_DELETEONRELEASE	Instructs the system to delete the item after its final release

You may select only one flag from each group except Group V. You may use any number of flags from Group V. You may also omit any group's flag, in which case the system uses the default value.

*Indicates default value

Table 5.11 Commit options.

Option	Description
STGC_DEFAULT	No options
STGC_OVERWRITE	Allow commit to overwrite existing data–this may lead to data loss if the operation fails
STGC_ONLYIFCURRENT	Prevents commits if other users of the storage have outstanding changes
STGC_DANGEROUSLY COMMITMERELYTODISK CACHE	This commits changes only to the file system cache, which presumably will write the changes to disk some time in the future

When you call **Commit**, you have several options (see Table 5.11). Usually, you'll use the **STGC_DEFAULT** option. However, if you have special requirements, there are other choices available. For example, if you share elements between processes or threads, you can specify **STGC_ONLYIFCURRENT**. This forces an error (**STG_E_NOTCURRENT**) if another process or thread already committed the element. Then your program has to reconcile the changes and commit again without this flag. If you are low on memory, you might specify **STGC_OVERWRITE**. This uses less memory, but can be risky since the operation destroys some old data before the new data is in place.

Another special mode is the **STGM_CONVERT**. This mode allows you to open a normal file as a root storage (using **StgOpenStorage**). The storage will have a single stream named **CONTENTS**. This stream will contain all the bytes of the original file. The conversion rewrites the file, so you must include **STGM_WRITE** with this mode. If you don't want the conversion to be permanent, you'll want to open the file with the **STGM_TRANSACTED** flag, too. That way, you can revert the file to its original state before you exit.

The **STGM_PRIORITY** mode allows you to quickly open a direct, read-only storage or stream. You won't often use this mode, because it bypasses nearly all buffering and also locks out other users. However, it does allow for rapid "save as" operations.

Remember, the root storage of a compound file always corresponds to an operating system file. If you want to know if a file is a compound file root storage, call **StgIsStorageFile**. You can also set the element times of the root storage by calling **StgSetTimes**. This is similar to calling **SetElementTimes**, except you don't need to open the storage.

Practical Considerations

The compound file implementation has several limitations. These aren't limits inherent in arbitrary **IStorage** and **IStream** interfaces. They are limits to the internal code ActiveX provides for compound files. Other implementations of **IStorage** and **IStream** may not have these same limitations.

1. Compound files can only contain four gigabytes of data (the interface specification allows 2^{64} bytes).
2. Streams don't support transactioning. Streams inside a transactioned storage work as you expect, but you can't transaction a single stream.
3. Streams grow in increments of 512 bytes.
4. **IStorage::SetStateBits** doesn't do anything.
5. Some operations (*e.g.,* backward seeking, **IStorage::EnumElements**, etc.) may not perform very rapidly.
6. You can't lock stream objects.
7. **STGM_PRIORITY** mode is only available for root storages.
8. You may not open one storage multiple times via the same parent storage.

Be particularly careful of the 512-byte granularity for streams. It would be a bad idea, for example, to create 100 streams that each contain two integers. That would use 5,120 bytes to store 800 bytes of information. It is better to try to group small data elements together.

Another concern is the performance of **EnumElements**. Microsoft recommends that you avoid enumerating a storage's elements where possible. This usually means maintaining a stream that contains the names of the other streams you create in a storage. Then you can open the directory stream and read from it instead of enumerating the elements directly.

An Example

To explore compound files, consider a simplified version control program. The version control system (AVC for Another Version Controller) is very simplistic. The program is primarily a command-line-driven console application. However, if you don't supply enough arguments, the program will display a dialog box to collect the remaining arguments (see Figure 5.1).

AVC uses one single archive file to store all versions of all files in a project. This archive is a compound file. It contains a single primary stream for each file in the project. This primary stream does not contain the file's data.

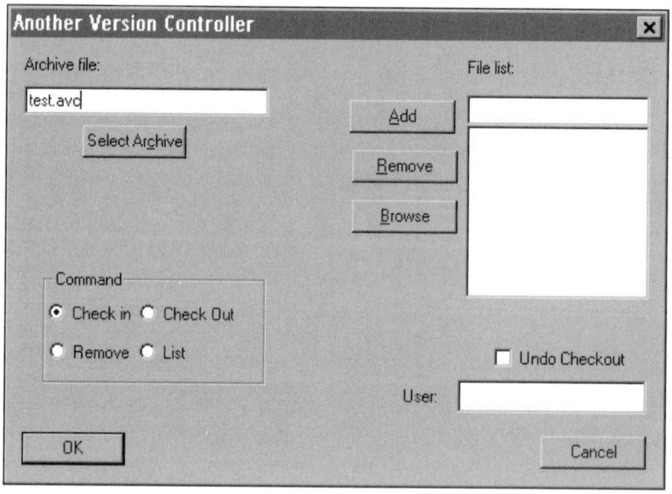

Figure 5.1 The AVC dialog box.

Instead, it contains information about the file's status and the number of versions available. The actual file contents are in a different stream. This stream has the same name as the primary stream followed by a tab character and the version number (in decimal).

Although there is a structured storage function to make a storage enumerate its elements, Microsoft warns that it might not be efficient for compound files. Instead, AVC stores another special stream always named $\tDIR$. This stream just contains a list of the primary file names. For simplicity's sake, AVC doesn't store any path information with the file names.

The command line has a simple structure. The first argument is always the name of the archive file you wish to use. If you want to use a particular user name, you add a comma to the file name and follow it with your user name (no spaces allowed). The second argument is the command you want to execute. Finally, you can specify a list of files to use. The commands are simple:

- **CHECKIN.** Add files to the archive, or create new versions of them. This command will create a new archive if you specify a name that doesn't exist. If you just want to mark a file as checked in without creating a new version, precede its name with an asterisk.
- **CHECKOUT.** Check out files from the archive by copying it to the ordinary file system. This prevents anyone else from checking out the file. It also reserves the file using your user name if you provided one. If

Interface Bestiary

you want a specific version of the file, follow the name with a comma and the version number. By default, the program checks out the most recent version.

- **REMOVE.** Removes files (or particular versions) from the archive. You can specify versions in the same way you would for the CHECKOUT command.
- **LIST.** This command ignores the file list and displays the contents of the archive.

In each case, you can specify a full path in the file list. However, AVC only uses the base file name internally. The CHECKIN command, for example, will copy a file from **\files\file1** into an internal stream named **file1**. The CHECKOUT command might later specify **\new\file1** to retrieve the same file to the **new** directory.

Since compound files allow transactioning, AVC takes advantage of it. If a REMOVE or CHECKIN command doesn't complete successfully, the entire operation fails. In other words, suppose you issue the command:

```
AVC test.avc REMOVE f1.txt f2.txt f3.ttx
```

If **f3.ttx** doesn't exist, AVC removes nothing from the archive.

The Implementation

Once you know how to use structured storage, the implementation of AVC is almost trivial (see Listing 5.4). Here are four important points:

1. The application is a console application–no window classes, message loop, or other Windows stuff. Just a good old-fashioned **main** function and lots of C++-style I/O.
2. By calling **GetModuleHandle**, the program learns its instance handle. Armed with that, it is easy to create a dialog box in the **DialogParms** routine. Just because this is a console application, doesn't mean it can't have resources or make API calls. The dialog callback is unremarkable.
3. Since this is a Win32 program, there is no reason you shouldn't use the usual **fopen/fread** calls to do file I/O. Although you might opt to use the API **ReadFile** and related calls, you don't have to do that.
4. If you don't commit the root storage, none of the changes in it become permanent. That means it doesn't matter if the program

opens and closes the directory or prime streams. Without a commit, it is all temporary. Note that this is only because the root storage is in the transacted mode.

Because this is a simple program, it uses several global variables to keep track of important information. The **cmd**, **filename**, **user**, and **filelist** variables track the command line information. The **archive** variable holds the **IStorage** that AVC uses for storage.

Since the storage calls expect Unicode names, AVC uses a small helper function, **ucode**, to convert an arbitrary string of characters into the correct type. Constant strings don't need the overhead of **ucode**; instead, they have an **L** prefix to mark them as Unicode constants (for example: **L"$\tDIR$"**).

Listing 5.4   The AVC application.

```
// Another Version Control System
// Uses structured storage to perform version control
#include <iostream.h>
#include <stdio.h>
#include <windows.h>
#include <string.h>
#include "avc.h"
#include "dialog.h"


// Global variables
CMD cmd;                    // current cmd
char filename[1024];        // archive file name
char user[33];              // current user (if any)
int listlen;                // length of input list
char **filelist;            // input list
IStorage *archive;          // archive
int dirlen;                 // length of directory
char **dir;                 // directory
HANDLE hInst;               // our hInstance


// Helper to convert ANSI string to unicode
wchar_t *ucode(char *p)
   {
   static wchar_t cvt[1024];
   MultiByteToWideChar(CP_ACP,MB_PRECOMPOSED,
   p,-1,cvt,sizeof(cvt)/sizeof(wchar_t));
   return cvt;
   }

// Open archive
BOOL OpenArchive()
   {
   IStream *dirstream;
```

```
    HRESULT r;
    if (FAILED(r=StgOpenStorage(ucode(filename),NULL,
        STGM_READWRITE|STGM_SHARE_EXCLUSIVE|STGM_TRANSACTED,
        NULL,0,&archive)))
        {
        // if checking in, archive need not
        //    exist, create it
        if (r==STG_E_FILENOTFOUND)
            if (cmd!=CHECKIN||
                FAILED(StgCreateDocfile(ucode(filename),
                STGM_READWRITE|STGM_SHARE_EXCLUSIVE|
                STGM_TRANSACTED,0,&archive)))
            {
            cerr<<"Can't open "<<filename<<"\n";
            return FALSE;
            }
        }
    // Open dir stream
    r=archive->OpenStream(L"$\tDIR$",NULL,
        STGM_READWRITE|STGM_SHARE_EXCLUSIVE,0,&dirstream);
    if (FAILED(r))   // create if not present
        {
        if (FAILED(archive->CreateStream(L"$\tDIR$",
            STGM_READWRITE|STGM_SHARE_EXCLUSIVE,
            0,0,&dirstream)))
            {
            archive->Release();
            return FALSE;
            }
        dirlen=0;
        // must use malloc so we can use realloc
        dir=(char **)malloc(sizeof(char *));
        *dir=NULL;
        dirstream->Release();
        return TRUE;
        }
    dirstream->Read((void *)&dirlen,sizeof(int),NULL);
    // must use malloc so we can use realloc
    dir=(char **)malloc(sizeof(char *)*(dirlen+1));
    for (int i=0;i<dirlen;i++)
        {
        char fn[1024];
        int len;
        dirstream->Read((void *)&len,sizeof(int),NULL);
        dirstream->Read((void *)fn,len,NULL);
        fn[len]='\0';
        dir[i]=strdup(fn);
        }
    dir[dirlen]=NULL;
    dirstream->Release();
    return TRUE;
    }

// Close archive w/o commit
```

```
void CloseArchive()
   {
   archive->Release();
   }

// Write out dir
BOOL WriteDir()
   {
   IStream *dirstream;
   // Use create instead of open so
   // we get an empty stream
   archive->CreateStream(L"$\tDIR$",STGM_WRITE|
     STGM_SHARE_EXCLUSIVE|STGM_CREATE,0,0,&dirstream);
   dirstream->Write((void *)&dirlen,sizeof(int),NULL);
   for (int i=0;i<dirlen;i++)
      {
      int len=strlen(dir[i]);
      dirstream->Write((void *)&len,sizeof(int),NULL);
      dirstream->Write((void *)dir[i],len,NULL);
      }
   dirstream->Release();
   return TRUE;
   }

// Process command line arguments
// Argument string looks like:
// avc archive[,user_name] command [file...]
// command is CHECKIN, CHECKOUT, LIST,
// or REMOVE (any case)
int process_args(int argc, char *argv[])
   {
   char *p;
   cmd=UNKNOWN;
   if (argc==1) return 0;
   p=strchr(argv[1],',');
   if (p)
      {
      *p='\0';
      strcpy(user,p+1);
      }
   strcpy(filename,argv[1]);
   if (argc==2) return 1;
   strupr(argv[2]);
   if (!strcmp(argv[2],"CHECKIN")) cmd=CHECKIN;
   else if (!strcmp(argv[2],"CHECKOUT")) cmd=CHECKOUT;
   else if (!strcmp(argv[2],"LIST")) cmd=LIST;
   else if (!strcmp(argv[2],"REMOVE")) cmd=REMOVE;
   if (argc==3) return 2;
   filelist=argv+3;
   listlen=argc-3;
   return 3;
   }
```

```c
// This routine brings up a dialog if you don't issue
// enough command line arguments
BOOL DialogArg()
   {
   if (DialogBox(hInst,MAKEINTRESOURCE(IDD_OPTIONS),NULL,
      (DLGPROC)dlgcb)==-1)
      return FALSE;
   else
      return TRUE;
   }

// Check in files
// If not successful, rollback
void checkin()
   {
   BOOL success=TRUE;
   char buf[1024];
   int siz;
   IStream *prime=NULL;
   IStream *file;
   LARGE_INTEGER off={0,0};
   int v=0;
   char ckout='Y';
   char puser[33];
   BOOL dirchange=FALSE;
   // for each file in input list
   for (int i=0;i<listlen;i++)
      {
      if (!success) break;
      BOOL found=FALSE;
      char *basename;
      // if file name begins with * then just undo checkout
      strcpy(buf,filelist[i]+(filelist[i][0]=='*'));
      FILE *f;
      // find base name (no directory)
      basename=strrchr(buf,'\\');
      if (basename)
         basename++;
      else
         basename=buf;
      if (filelist[i][0]!='*')
         {
         f=fopen(buf,"r");   // open file
         if (!f)
            {
            cerr<<"Can't open "<<buf<<"\n";
            success=FALSE;
            continue;
            }
         }
      // is filelist[i] in dir string?
      for (int j=0;j<dirlen;j++)
      if (!stricmp(basename,dir[j]))
```

```
                {
                found=TRUE;
                break;
                }

            v=0;
            ckout='Y';
            *puser='\0';

            if (found)
                {
                // read prime storage
                archive->OpenStream(ucode(basename),NULL,
                    STGM_READWRITE|STGM_SHARE_EXCLUSIVE,0,&prime);
                prime->Read((void *)&v,sizeof(int),NULL);
                prime->Read((void *)&ckout,sizeof(char),NULL);
                prime->Read((void *)puser,sizeof(puser),NULL);
                prime->Seek(off,STREAM_SEEK_SET,NULL);
                }
            else if (filelist[i][0]!='*')
                {
                // create prime storage
                archive->CreateStream(ucode(basename),
                    STGM_READWRITE|STGM_SHARE_EXCLUSIVE,0,0,&prime);
                // (v=0, ckout=y, user="")

                *puser='\0';
                prime->Write((void *)&v,sizeof(int),NULL);
                prime->Write((void *)&ckout,sizeof(char),NULL);
                prime->Write((void *)puser,sizeof(puser),NULL);
                prime->Seek(off,STREAM_SEEK_SET,NULL);
                dir=(char **)realloc(dir,++dirlen*
                    sizeof(char *));
                dir[dirlen-1]=strdup(basename);
                // check for out of memory here would be smart
                dirchange=TRUE;
                }
            else   // can't undo checkout if not there
                {
                cerr<<"Can't find "<<basename<<"\n";
                success=FALSE;
                continue;
                }
            // make sure checked out to this user (or no user)
            if (ckout!='Y')
                {
                cerr<<basename<<" is not checked out.\n";
                success=FALSE;
                continue;
                }
            if (*user && stricmp(user,puser))
                {
```

Interface Bestiary

```
            cerr<<basename<<" is not checked out to you.\n";
            success=FALSE;
            continue;
            }
        // increment version
        if (filelist[i][0]!='*')
            {
            v++;
            // write storage for this version
            char fname[1030];
            wsprintf(fname,"%s\t%d",basename,v);
            archive->CreateStream(ucode(fname),
                STGM_READWRITE|STGM_SHARE_EXCLUSIVE,
                0,0,&file);
            do
                {
                siz=sizeof(buf);
                siz=fread(buf,1,siz,f);
                if (siz)
                    {
                    file->Write((void *)buf,siz,NULL);
                    }
                } while (siz);
            fclose(f);
            file->Release();
            }
        // mark prime storage as checked in
        ckout='N';
        *puser='\0';
        prime->Write((void *)&v,sizeof(int),NULL);
        prime->Write((void *)&ckout,sizeof(char),NULL);
        prime->Write((void *)puser,sizeof(user),NULL);
        if (dirchange) WriteDir();
        }
    // if no failure, commit
    if (success)
        archive->Commit(0);
    if (prime) prime->Release();
    }


// Check out files
// (use file,version for specific version)
void checkout()
    {
    for (int i=0;i<listlen;i++)
        {
        BOOL found=FALSE;
        char buf[1024];
        unsigned long siz;
        IStream *prime=NULL;
        IStream *file;
        LARGE_INTEGER off={0,0};
        int v=0,v0=-1;
```

```
      char ckout='Y';
      char puser[33];
      char *p;
      char *basename;
      strcpy(buf,filelist[i]);
      p=strchr(buf,',');   // specific version?
      if (p)
         {
         v0=atoi(p+1);
         *p='\0';
         }
      // find base name (no directory)
      basename=strrchr(buf,'\\');
      if (basename)
         basename++;
      else
         basename=buf;
      // is filelist[i] in dir string?
      for (int j=0;j<dirlen;j++)
      if (!stricmp(basename,dir[j]))
         {
         found=TRUE;
         break;
         }
      // if not, error and continue
      if (!found)
         {
         cerr<<"Can't find "<<basename<<"\n";
         continue;
         }
      // read prime storage
      archive->OpenStream(ucode(basename),NULL,
         STGM_READWRITE|STGM_SHARE_EXCLUSIVE,0,&prime);
      prime->Read((void *)&v,sizeof(int),NULL);
      prime->Read((void *)&ckout,sizeof(char),NULL);
      prime->Read((void *)puser,sizeof(puser),NULL);
      prime->Seek(off,STREAM_SEEK_SET,NULL);
      // if v0>v then must be an error!
      if (v0>v)
         {
         cerr<<basename<<" only contains "<<v
             <<" versions\n";
         prime->Release();
         continue;
         }
      // if file is checked out, error and continue
      if (ckout=='Y')
         {
         cerr<<basename<<" is already checked out\n";
         prime->Release();
         continue;
         }
      // copy file to output file
```

Interface Bestiary

```
            char fname[1030];
            FILE *f;
            f=fopen(buf,"w");
            if (!f)
                {
                cerr<<"Can't open "<<buf<<" for writing\n";
                prime->Release();
                continue;
                }
            wsprintf(fname,"%s\t%d",basename,v0==-1?v:v0);
            if (FAILED(archive->OpenStream(ucode(fname),NULL,
               STGM_READWRITE|STGM_SHARE_EXCLUSIVE,0,&file)))
                {
                cerr<<"Can't locate "<<basename<<","
                    <<(v0==-1?v:v0)<<"\n";
                prime->Release();
                continue;
                }
            do
                {
                file->Read((void *)buf,sizeof(buf),&siz);
                if (siz) fwrite(buf,1,siz,f);
                } while (siz);
            fclose(f);
            file->Release();

            // mark as check out
            ckout='Y';
            strcpy(puser,user);
            prime->Write((void *)&v,sizeof(int),NULL);
            prime->Write((void *)&ckout,sizeof(char),NULL);
            prime->Write((void *)user,sizeof(user),NULL);
            prime->Release();
            }
      archive->Commit(0);
      }

// Directory list
void list()
    {
    // headers
    cout<<"file\t\t\t\tvers.\tckout?\tuser\tsize\n";
    cout<<
  "———————————————————————————————————\n";
    // work through directory
    for (int i=0;i<dirlen;i++)
        {
        char fn[1033];
        IStream *prime, *file;
        int v;
        char ckout;
        char puser[33];
        STATSTG fstatus;
```

```
        // open prime storage
        archive->OpenStream(ucode(dir[i]),NULL,
            STGM_READWRITE|STGM_SHARE_EXCLUSIVE,0,&prime);
        prime->Read((void *)&v,sizeof(int),NULL);
        prime->Read((void *)&ckout,sizeof(char),NULL);
        prime->Read((void *)puser,sizeof(puser),NULL);
        prime->Release();
        // open current version to learn size
        wsprintf(fn,"%s\t%d",dir[i],v);
        archive->OpenStream(ucode(fn),NULL,
            STGM_READWRITE|STGM_SHARE_EXCLUSIVE,0,&file);
        file->Stat(&fstatus,STATFLAG_NONAME);
        // print name, version, ckout, user, size
        cout<<dir[i]<<"\t";
        int l=strlen(dir[i]);
        // logic to tab over to column 32
        if (l<24) cout<<"\t";
        if (l<16) cout<<"\t";
        if (l<8) cout<<"\t";
        cout<<v<<"\t"<<ckout<<"\t"<<puser<<"\t"
            <<fstatus.cbSize.LowPart<<"\n";
        file->Release();
        }
    cout<<
    "———————————————————\n";
    cout<<dirlen<<(dirlen==1?" file\n":" files\n");
    }


// remove files (use file,version for specific version)
void rm()
    {
    for (int i=0;i<listlen;i++)
        {
        BOOL found=FALSE;
        char buf[1024],fn[1024];
        IStream *prime=NULL;
        LARGE_INTEGER off={0,0};
        int v=0,v0=-1;
        char ckout='Y';
        char puser[33];
        char *p;
        strcpy(buf,filelist[i]);
        p=strchr(buf,',');  // specific version?
        if (p)
            {
            v0=atoi(p+1);
            *p='\0';
            }
        // is filelist[i] in dir string?
        for (int j=0;j<dirlen;j++)
        if (!stricmp(buf,dir[j]))
            {
            found=TRUE;
```

Interface Bestiary 139

```
        break;
        }
// if not, error and roll back
if (!found)
    {
    cerr<<"Can't find "<<buf<<"\n";
    return;
    }
// read prime storage
archive->OpenStream(ucode(buf),NULL,
    STGM_READWRITE|STGM_SHARE_EXCLUSIVE,0,&prime);
prime->Read((void *)&v,sizeof(int),NULL);
prime->Read((void *)&ckout,sizeof(char),NULL);
prime->Read((void *)puser,sizeof(puser),NULL);
prime->Seek(off,STREAM_SEEK_SET,NULL);
// if v0>v then must be an error!
if (v0>v)
    {
    cerr<<buf<<" only contains "<<v<<" versions\n";
    prime->Release();
    return;
    }
// if file is checked out, error and roll back
if (ckout=='Y')
    {
    cerr<<buf<<" is already checked out\n";
    prime->Release();
    return;
    }
if (v0!=-1&&(v0!=1||v0!=v))
    {
    // delete specific version
    // unless only 1 version
    wsprintf(fn,"%s\t%d",buf,v0);
    if FAILED(archive->DestroyElement(ucode(fn)))
        {
        cerr<<"Can't remove "<<filelist[i]<<"\n";
        prime->Release;
        return;
        }
    if (v0==v) v--;
    // rewrite Prime
    prime->Write((void *)&v,sizeof(int),NULL);
    prime->Write((void *)&ckout,sizeof(char),NULL);
    prime->Write((void *)user,sizeof(user),NULL);
    prime->Release();
    }
else
    {
    // delete all versions
    for (int k=1;k<=v;k++)
        {
        wsprintf(fn,"%s\t%d",buf,k);
```

```
                archive->DestroyElement(ucode(fn));
            }
        prime->Release();
        // Delete prime storage
        archive->DestroyElement(ucode(buf));
        // remove from dir string
        free(dir[j]);
        for (k=j;k<dirlen;k++)
        dir[k]=dir[k+1];
        dirlen--;
        // write Dir
        WriteDir();
        }
    }
    archive->Commit(0);
}

void main(int argc, char *argv[])
    {
    // Our console app might need its inst. handle
    hInst=(HINSTANCE)GetModuleHandle(NULL);
    // if not enough arguments, call for dialog
    if (process_args(argc,argv)<2)
        if (!DialogArg()) return;
    // Open archive for all commands
    if (!OpenArchive()) return;
    switch (cmd)
        {
        case CHECKIN:
            checkin();
        break;
        case CHECKOUT:
            checkout();
        break;
        case LIST:
            list();
        break;
        case REMOVE:
            rm();
        break;
        default:
            cerr<<"Unknown command\n";
        }
    CloseArchive();         // close archive (no commit)
    }
```

Take a few minutes to examine the AVC code. This is a good example of using the structured storage system. Examine each part that manipulates the archive storage. Pay particular attention to the simplicity of using the virtual file system. The only complex calls create storages and streams. The other calls are no more complex then the corresponding file I/O calls from the standard C library.

ILockBytes

What happens if you want a structured storage to exist on a non-file medium? For example, you might want to store data in a database instead of a file. Or perhaps you need to allow structured storage to coexist in a file with an existing format. The answer to these problems is to implement an object with the **ILockBytes** interface that knows how to manage your storage needs.

ILockBytes is a simple interface that knows how to read from and write to some array of bytes. Where that array resides is strictly up to you. Table 5.12 shows the handful of functions **ILockBytes** requires. You usually won't create your own **ILockBytes** interface since ActiveX provides perfectly good implementations for files and for managing a block of memory. If you do provide your own, you'll probably want to add marshalling to your object, since the system doesn't automatically know how to marshall your objects.

If you want to manage a block of memory as a structured storage, you can call **CreateILockBytesOnHGlobal** to return an **ILockBytes** on a global memory handle. Once you have any **ILockBytes** interface, you can create or open a storage in it by calling **StgCreateDocfileOnILockBytes** or **StgOpenStorageOnILockBytes**.

Why would you need a block of memory to look like structured storage? Consider the case where some external object wants to save its state in a structured storage. However, you want to incorporate the object's storage in your own file format. You could create an **ILockBytes** interface to manage your file format, but that's a lot of work. Instead, you might allocate some

Table 5.12 The ILockBytes interface.

Function Description

ReadAt	Reads a specified number of bytes starting at a given offset
WriteAt	Writes a specified number of bytes to a given offset
Flush	Writes any buffers that the ILockBytes implementation may maintain
SetSize	Changes the size of the object
LockRegion	Restricts access to a specified range of bytes
UnlockRegion	Removes the access restriction on a range of bytes
Stat	Retrieves a STATSTG structure for this object (see Table 5.9)

memory, create an **ILockBytes** interface on it, and create a storage on the **ILockBytes** interface. Then you pass the new storage to the object, it saves itself, and you can copy the memory to your file format. Reading it back is essentially the opposite: read the memory in, convert it to a storage, and pass the storage to the external object.

There is no guarantee that ActiveX won't change your memory handle in certain cases. Therefore, if you need the memory handle after you create the **ILockBytes** object, call the **GetHGlobalFromILockBytes** function to recover the memory handle. Don't use the same handle you passed into **CreateILockBytesOnHGlobal**.

IPersistFile, IPersistStream, And IPersistStorage

If you have some ActiveX object and you want it to save its state to a storage, stream, or file, how do you proceed? All objects that have persistent state support one or more persistence interfaces. For example: **IPersistFile** (Table 5.13), **IPersistStream**, **IPersistStreamInit** (Table 5.14), and **IPersistStorage** (Table 5.15). Each interface supports persistence on different media.

These interfaces share their first four functions. The first three are, of course, the **IUnknown** functions. The fourth function is **GetClassID**. You'll often hear these four functions called the **IPersist** interface (although no objects expose just an **IPersist** interface). Of course, you can treat any of the persistence interfaces as an **IPersist**, interface. There are also some specialized variations on **IPersist** such as **IPersistMemory** or **IPersistPropertyBag**. However, for the most part, you'll deal with persistent files, streams, and storages.

IPersistFile

An **IPersistFile** interface (Table 5.13) allows you to work with an ordinary file of indeterminate format. The file may or may not be structured. You don't know. The functions, as you'd expect, are simple. You can find out if the object requires saving (**IsDirty**), save or load the object (with **Save** or **Load**), or learn the file's full path (**GetCurFile**).

Loading the file is straightforward. The **Load** function informs the object of its file name. The object may leave the file open and write to it if it wishes. In other words, when the load completes, there is no assurance that the object is finished with the file–only that the object is ready.

Table 5.13 The IPersistFile interface.

Function	Description
GetClassID	Returns the CLSID for the server that handles this file
IsDirty	Checks an object for changes since it was last saved to its current file
Load	Opens the specified file and initializes the object from the contents of the file
Save	Saves the object into the specified file
SaveCompleted	Notifies the object that saving is complete (see text)
GetCurFile	Gets the current file name

Saving a file is a bit more complex than it might appear. The **Save** function takes a file name and a flag named **fSameAsLoad**. If the file name is **NULL**, then the save operation saves the object to the current file (presumably passed in the **Load** function or a prior **Save**). Then the object ignores the **fSameAsLoad** flag and clears its dirty bit (the bit that **IsDirty** returns). However, if the file name is not **NULL**, the object can't determine if you are renaming the existing file or just copying it.

The **fSameAsLoad** flag allows the object to differentiate between these cases. If the flag is **TRUE**, the object is free to keep the file open and alter it. The object clears the dirty flag and considers the new file name to be the current file. If the flag is **FALSE**, however, the object must completely write the entire file. Then it must close the file until it receives a **SaveCompleted** call. This allows the object's user to manipulate the file without fear of sharing violations or other interference.

IPersistStream And IPersistStreamInit

The **IPersistStream** interface allows you to save an object to a structured storage stream. **IPersistStreamInit** is identical to **IPersistStream** except for one additional member function (**InitNew**). The functions (see Table 5.14) are as you would expect with two exceptions: **GetSizeMax** and **InitNew**.

It is possible that an object's user may need to preallocate storage for the object (in a database field, for example). Therefore, **GetSizeMax** must return the absolute maximum number of bytes the object might need to save itself. This is especially important if an object's user wants to store several objects in the same stream.

Table 5.14 The IPersistStream and IPersistStreamInit interfaces.

Function	Description
GetClassID	Returns the CLSID for the server that handles this object
IsDirty	Checks the object for changes since it was last saved
Load	Reads the stream into the object
Save	Saves the object to a stream
GetSizeMax	Returns the maximum number of bytes required to save (see text)
InitNew	Initializes an object to a default state (IPersistStreamInit only)

Because it is possible for multiple objects to coexist in a single stream, the object must not hold the stream open. When the object receives a **Load** or **Save** call, it can use the stream pointer provided until it returns from the function. After that, it must not access the stream. It also must start using the stream at the current seek position and not use more bytes than **GetSizeMax** returns.

Some objects may have significant initialization to perform when you first create them. If the first thing you call is **Load** to restore the state from a stream, then performing the initialization is a waste. That's where the **IPersistStreamInit** interface comes into play. This interface is identical to **IPersistStream** except that a client can call **InitNew** to cue the object to initialize a new object.

If you write an object that provides **IPersistStreamInit**, you may be able to use the same interface to handle **IPersistStream**. Just make your **QueryInterface** implementation recognize that these interfaces are the same. If a client requests **IPersistStream**, the fact that there is an extra function is unimportant. Of course, this assumes that you don't need special initialization semantics that differ between the interfaces.

IPersistStorage

The **IPersistStorage** interface (Table 5.15) is the most powerful (and most difficult) of the persistence interfaces. An object that exposes **IPersistStorage** can save itself to a storage object. Within that storage, it can create new substorages and streams at its whim. This effectively gives an object its own private file system for storing its persistent state.

Table 5.15 The IPersistStorage interface.

Function	Description
GetClassID	Returns the CLSID for this object
IsDirty	Indicates whether the object has changed since it was last saved to its current storage
InitNew	Initializes a new storage object
Load	Reads the storage into the object
Save	Saves the object and any nested objects that it contains into the specified storage object
SaveCompleted	Notifies the object that a save operation is finished (see text)
HandsOffStorage	Instructs object to close all open elements (see text)

The functions for **IPersistStorage** are similar to the other persistence interfaces. As usual, the protocol for saving a file is the most complex. When you open or initialize an object that uses **IPersistStorage**, you call **Load** or **InitNew**. In either case, the object is free to hold a pointer to the storage and use it during normal operations. This is a good idea, because you should be able to save even if memory is low. If memory is low, you might not be able to reopen the storage or any elements you need opened. Most objects open everything first and then hold them open.

When the client wants to save the object, it calls **Save**. This is similar to the case for **IPersistFile**. The only difference is that the object need not release any open elements it is using. However, it can't write to the storage after the save. The object can only resume writing to storage after a call to **SaveCompleted**. If the client requires the object to release the storage (so it can rename the storage, for example), then it must call **HandsOffStorage** in between the **Save** and **SaveCompleted** calls.

Notice that the object must not call **Commit** on the main storage managed through **IPersistStorage**. The client decides when and if to make that call.

Associating CLSIDs With Storage

The only unique function in **IPersist** (the effective base class for all persistence interfaces) is **GetClassID**. As you might suspect, this function returns the CLSID of an ActiveX server that knows how to interpret the file or storage. The **WriteClassStg** function writes this value into a storage, and the **WriteClassStm** function writes it into a stream. You can then use the corresponding read functions to recover the CLSID. That means that to read a compound file, you can learn its associated CLSID, call **CoCreateInstance** to create the object (which presumably supports an **IPersist**-derived interface), and call the interface's **Load** function.

If you are using a transacted storage, you can often call **OleSave** to keep from doing so much work. Here's what **OleSave** does:

1. Calls the **IPersistStorage::GetClassID** method to get the object's CLSID
2. Writes the CLSID to the storage object using the **WriteClassStg** function
3. Calls the **IPersistStorage::Save** method to save the object
4. Calls the **IStorage::Commit** method to commit the changes if there were no errors

As you might expect, there is a corresponding **OleLoad** function. Here's what it does:

1. If necessary, performs an automatic conversion of the object. That is, it uses the **OleDoAutoConvert** function to interpret the **TreatAs** and **AutoTreatAs** registry entries (see Chapter 3).
2. Gets the CLSID from the open storage object by calling the **IStorage::Stat** method.
3. Calls the **CoCreateInstance** function to create an instance of the handler.
4. Calls the **IOleObject::SetClientSite** method with the *pClientSite* parameter to inform the object of its client site.
5. Calls the **QueryInterface** method for the **IPersistStorage** interface. If successful, the **IPersistStorage::Load** method is invoked for the object.
6. Queries and returns the desired interface pointer.

Wait a minute! What's this **SetClientSite** function in the **IOleObject** interface? It turns out that this function is for traditional object linking and embedding. Certain ActiveX controls also use it (see Chapter 6). These objects always have an **IOleObject** interface. Because the objects in this chapter don't have **IOleObject** interfaces, you can't use **OleLoad** with them. Still, it is interesting to see what **OleLoad** does. You can easily perform steps as they pertain to your situation.

IMoniker And IOleItemContainer

File names, in the traditional sense, are not very object-oriented. A file name has no meaning in and of itself. The functions that manipulate it (**fopen**, perhaps) have to have explicit knowledge of what to do with a file name. This causes grief when file name formats change (for example, long file names or UNC file names) and the functions don't change along with them.

An object-oriented file name would not only include the file's name, but the operations that you might want to perform on it (open, for one). Imagine this C++ object:

```
class SmartFileName
  {
  char name[MAX_PATH];
  public:
  FILE *open(char *mode) { return fopen(name,mode); };
   .
   .
   .
  };
```

As long as **SmartFileName** (or its subclasses) knows how to return a **FILE** pointer, no one cares what actions it takes. That's the idea behind a moniker. It returns an open storage or stream that refers to some object. What object? Who knows? Who cares? If you have a moniker that refers to, say, a document file, just ask it for the corresponding storage. If you have a moniker that refers to a section of a drawing object, you can open that, too. Monikers can refer to things as generic as files or as specific as a word inside a word processing document. Monikers can also refer to Internet URLs–a type of moniker you'll examine later.

You'll rarely, if ever, need to create monikers from scratch (although you can). Instead you'll build monikers using predefined moniker types. There are four atomic moniker types. They all expose the **IMoniker** interface (selected portions of this interface appear in Table 5.16). You can use these to build composite monikers. A composite moniker is simply a moniker made up of different types of atomic monikers.

Table 5.17 shows the four atomic monikers and the functions you use to create them. Only file and pointer monikers have any usefulness by themselves. Item and anti monikers are only useful inside composite monikers.

As you might expect, a file moniker encapsulates a file name. When you ask the moniker to open its contents (binding the moniker, in ActiveX par-

Table 5.16 Selected IMoniker member functions.

Function	Description
BindToObject	Binds to the object named by the moniker
BindToStorage	Binds to the object's storage
Reduce	Reduces the moniker to simplest form
ComposeWith	Composes with another moniker
Enum	Enumerates component monikers
IsEqual	Compares with another moniker
IsRunning	Checks whether object is running
GetTimeOfLastChange	Returns time the object was last changed
Inverse	Returns the inverse of the moniker
CommonPrefixWith	Finds the prefix that the moniker has in common with another moniker
RelativePathTo	Constructs a relative moniker between the moniker and another
GetDisplayName	Returns the display name
ParseDisplayName	Converts a display name into a moniker
IsSystemMoniker	Checks whether this moniker is one of the system-supplied types

Table 5.17 Atomic monikers.

Moniker	Usage
File	Refers to a file
Item	Refers to an item which is just a string that the server interprets (see text)
Pointer	Refers to an object
Anti	Destroys the previous component moniker in a composite

lance), it finds a CLSID associated with the file, creates an object of that class, finds the object's **IPersistFile** interface, and calls **IPersistFile::Load**. Pointer monikers are convenient because they allow you to treat an existing ActiveX object just as you would a file that uses that object.

Item monikers are only useful inside a composite. You specify a delimiter character (usually an exclamation point) and a string. This string has no intrinsic meaning to the moniker. Hopefully, the string means something to the target object. The string must not contain the delimiter character. Suppose we have an ActiveX object that manages a database that resides in a file. A client might form a composite moniker that contains a file moniker (for the database file), an item moniker to specify the record key, and another item moniker to specify a field.

When it is time to bind this composite moniker, the moniker code will create an instance of our ActiveX server to load the database file (our CLSID is in the file). Our server must support **IOleItemContainer** (see Table 5.18). Next, the system will call **IOleItemContainer::GetObject** or **IOleItemContainer::GetObjectStorage** to convert the item string in the first item moniker to another **IOleItemContainer** (representing the database record). The record **IOleItemContainer** then resolves the second item string to produce whatever interface is necessary to represent the database fields. You'll usually see this type of moniker written with the delimiter (often the exclamation point) between the atomic monikers. For example:

```
file!record!field
```

You'll often hear this called the moniker's display name. Monikers know how to parse a display name and create a display name for their contents.

Anti monikers destroy the previous moniker in a composite. Adding an anti moniker to the above example (file!record!field), would result in a moniker that refers to the file and record. Adding two anti monikers would result in just a file moniker.

You create a composite moniker one piece at a time by calling **CreateGenericComposite**. This function takes two **IMoniker** pointers and returns a third pointer. In effect, this function merges the two input

Table 5.18 The IOleItemContainer interface.

Function	Description
ParseDisplayName	Parses object's display name to form a moniker
EnumObjects	Enumerates objects in this container
LockContainer	Keeps container running until explicitly released
GetObject	Returns a pointer to a specified object
GetObjectStorage	Returns a pointer to an object's storage
IsRunning	Checks whether an object is running

monikers to form the output. If you need more pieces, you simply call the function again using the output from the first call as one of the inputs. You can repeat this until the entire moniker is complete.

IMoniker is derived from **IPersistStream**. As you might guess, file monikers store their file names and item monikers store their strings. The other atomic monikers have no persistent state. A composite moniker's state is a stream that contains the state of each constituent moniker.

IConnectionPoint And IConnectionPointContainer

Some ActiveX objects need to notify another object of an event. To put it another way, a server may ask a client to support a particular interface that the server will call when something interesting happens. This is contrary to the usual model of a client calling a server.

Some older ActiveX interfaces hardwire the logic to do this into the server. Part of the protocol for using a certain server might be to provide a "sink" interface to the server. Then, when the server wants to call the client, it calls prearranged functions in the sink interface.

This works well when there is a one to one relationship between client and server. However, it is inflexible and not a very general method. To fix these problems, Microsoft introduced the concept of connectable objects. A connectable object is one that provides the **IConnectionPointContainer** (see Table 5.19). The two functions in this interface allow you to query an object to see if it supports a particular sink interface or enumerate all supported sink interfaces. Note that these are not interfaces the server implements (you'd find those with **QueryInterface**), but rather interfaces the client must supply.

If you call **IConnectionPointContainer::FindConnectionPoint**, it returns an **IConnectionPoint** interface pointer you can use to register your sink interface (see Table 5.20). Here's some typical pseudo-code that registers a fictitious **IID_OurSinkInterface** sink:

```
if (QueryInterface on server fails for IID_IConnectionPoint)
   error("No connections");
if (FindConnectionPoint for IID_OurSinkInterface fails)
   error("Server doesn't support our sink interface");
   call the connection point's Advise function passing our interface pointer-
   this call returns a 32-bit magic number that identifies the connection;
```

Interface Bestiary

When the client no longer wants to use the sink, call Unadvise, passing the 32-bit magic number from the Advise call.

From the server's point of view, you maintain a list of connections. You add pointers to the list during **Advise** and remove them during **Unadvise**. When you want to call a particular sink function, you walk through the list, calling the function on each sink interface in the list. This allows one server to successfully service multiple clients.

IProvideClassInfo

Objects that expose the **IProvideClassInfo** interface can return their type library information (see Chapter 3 for more on type libraries). This interface is very simple because it only contains a single (non-**IUnknown**) function that is easy to implement. This function is the **GetClassInfo** function.

This function is easy to implement because you can just load your type information from the TLB library (using **LoadRegTypeLib** or **LoadTypeLib**)

Table 5.19   The IConnectionPointContainer interface.

Function	Description
EnumConnectionPoints	Returns an enumerator for all the connection points associated with this object
FindConnectionPoint	Returns a pointer to the IConnectionPoint interface for a specified connection point

Table 5.20   The IConnectionPoint interface.

Function	Description
GetConnectionInterface	Returns the IID of the sink interface managed by this connection point
GetConnectionPointContainer	Returns the parent object's IConnectionPointContainer interface pointer
Advise	Creates a connection between a connection point and a client's sink where the sink implements the outgoing interface supported by this connection point
Unadvise	Terminates a notification previously set up with Advise
EnumConnections	Returns an enumerator for the current connections maintained by this connection point

Chapter 5

and then call the type library's **GetTypeInforOfGuid** function to get the **ITypeInfo** interface that **IProvideClassInfo::GetClassInfo** returns. Here's an example implementation of this function:

```
STDMETHODIMP CMyObject::GetClassInfo(
  ITypeInfo **typeinfo)
  {
  ITypeLib *tlib;
  if (!typeinfo) return E_POINTER;
  if (FAILED(LoadRegTypeLib(LIBID_OurTypeLibrary,
      1,0,LANG_NEUTRAL,&tlib)))
    {
    if (FAILED(LoadTypeLib(_T"OURTYPE.TLB"),&tlib)))
        return FALSE;
    tlib->GetTypeInfoOfGuid(CLSID_OurCLSID,typeinfo);
    if (*typeinfo) *typeinfo->AddRef();
    tlib->Release();
    return *typeinfo?S_OK:E_FAIL;
    }
```

IDispatch

The **IDispatch** interface is arguably one of the most powerful ActiveX interfaces around. Yet it only contains 4 unique functions (see Table 5.21). These functions allow objects to expose variables and functions to other objects—even those from different programs.

Like all other ActiveX technologies, the **IDispatch** interface has to have obscure names. Instead of exposing variables, **IDispatch**-aware objects expose properties. These may be actual variables, or the object may execute code to store and retrieve the property value. Either way, the object's user accesses properties as if they were simple variables.

Table 5.21 The IDispatch interface.

Function	Description
Invoke	Provides access to properties and methods exposed by the object
GetIDsOfNames	Converts a single member name and an optional set of argument names to a set of integer DISPIDs
GetTypeInfo	Retrieves the type information for an object
GetTypeInfoCount	Returns 0 if GetTypeInfo is not supported; 1 if the object can provide type information

IDispatch-aware objects also don't have functions, they have methods. These are simple function calls.

You may recall that in previous chapters, you asked MFC to create an automation server and then stripped out all the automation code to create ActiveX objects. An object that provides an **IDispatch** interface is an automation server (you can also say that the object supports ActiveX scripting).

If you allow MFC to create your **IDispatch**-aware objects, you'll find it quite easy. You can use Class Wizard to add members and properties with little difficulty. MFC also manages your **IDispatch** functions with no effort on your part. Class Wizard also allows you to add events, but these are only for ActiveX controls (see Chapter 6).

The key to the **IDispatch** interface is the **Invoke** function. This function allows ActiveX objects to select, at run time, what variable (property) you want to access or what function (method) you want to call. Each property and method has a unique ID (a **DISPID**). This ID is just an integer that serves to distinguish the various methods and properties from each other. Microsoft predefines **DISPID**s of zero or less (see Table 5.22). You won't always use any of these predefined **DISPID**s.

When you want to call a method or access a property, you call **IDispatch::Invoke**, passing it a **DISPID**, some control flags, an array of arguments, a locale ID, a place to store any return result, and places to store error information. Before you look at these arguments in detail, you need to learn about some special types ActiveX defines.

Table 5.22 Predefined DISPIDs.

DISPID	Value	Description
DISPID_VALUE	0	The default member
DISPID_NEWENUM	-4	Returns an enumerator object that supports IEnumVariant and should have the restricted attribute specified in the ODL script
DISPID_EVALUATE	-5	The Evaluate method
DISPID_PROPERTYPUT	-3	The parameter that receives the value of an assignment in a property put
DISPID_CONSTRUCTOR	-6	The C++ constructor function for the object
DISPID_DESTRUCTOR	-7	The C++ destructor function for the object
DISPID_UNKNOWN	-1	Value returned by IDispatch::GetIDsOfNames to indicate that it could not resolve a name

BSTR, SAFEARRAY, And VARIANT

ActiveX defines three unique data types that you can use in a variety of situations. The simplest of these is the **BSTR**. As the name suggests, this data type is for character strings. A **BSTR** pointer is just like a C string pointer because it points to an array of characters that end with a **NULL** byte. The only difference is that the four bytes *preceding* the contents of the **BSTR** contain the count of characters in the string (not counting the **NULL** byte). You can see the string "ActiveX" in a **BSTR** in Figure 5.2. ActiveX provides several functions to manipulate **BSTR**s (see Table 5.23). If you are an MFC programmer, you can convert a **CString** into a **BSTR** by calling **CString::AllocSysString**.

A **SAFEARRAY** is a simple structure (see Figure 5.3) that contains information about the size and shape of an array, along with a memory handle (and possibly a pointer) that contains the data in the array. ActiveX provides several API functions to manipulate **SAFEARRAY**s (see Table 5.24). A **SAFEARRAY** can contain **BSTR**s, **IDispatch** pointers, **IUnknown** pointers, or **VARIANT**s (see Figure 5.3).

The **VARIANT** (or **VARIANTARG**) union can hold almost anything. In essence, it is just a union and a variable that indicates what kind of data is in the union at any given time (see Tables 5.25 and 5.26). When a client passes a **VARIANT** to a server, you might expect it to be a simple matter to just read the value from the proper field in the union. But, what if the client didn't pass the type of data you expected? ActiveX has two functions that can convert (or coerce) a **VARIANT** that contains one data type into a **VARIANT** that contains a different type (if the conversion is possible). The

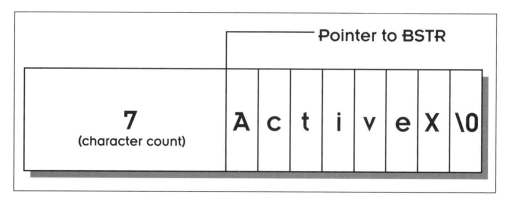

Figure 5.2 A BSTR that contains the text "ActiveX".

Table 5.23 BSTR functions.

Function	Description
SysAllocString	Converts an ordinary string into a BSTR
SysAllocStringByteLen	Converts a byte buffer (which may contain NULL bytes) into a BSTR
SysAllocStringLen	Converts a character buffer (which may contain NULL bytes) into a BSTR
SysFreeString	Deallocates a BSTR
SysReAllocString	Similar to SysAllocString except it uses an existing BSTR
SysReAllocStringByteLen	Similar to SysAllocStringByteLen except it uses an existing BSTR
SysReAllocStringLen	Similar to SysAllocStringLen except it uses an existing BSTR
SysStringLen	Determines the length of the BSTR by reading the embedded length (this may be different from strlen if the BSTR contains NULL bytes)

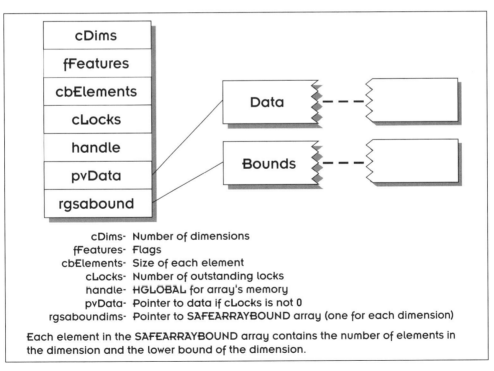

cDims- Number of dimensions
fFeatures- Flags
cbElements- Size of each element
cLocks- Number of outstanding locks
handle- HGLOBAL for array's memory
pvData- Pointer to data if cLocks is not 0
rgsaboundims- Pointer to SAFEARRAYBOUND array (one for each dimension)

Each element in the SAFEARRAYBOUND array contains the number of elements in the dimension and the lower bound of the dimension.

Figure 5.3 A SAFEARRAY.

Table 5.24 SAFEARRAY functions.

Function	Description
SafeArrayAccessData	Locks the array and sets the array's pointer
SafeArrayLock	Locks the array and sets the array's pointer
SafeArrayUnaccessData	Unlocks the array
SafeArrayUnlock	Unlocks the array
SafeArrayCreate	Creates an array of a given type and size
SafeArrayAllocDescriptor	Builds a descriptor of a SAFEARRAY that may be of any type
SafeArrayAllocData	Creates a SAFEARRAY based on a descriptor (see SafeArrayAllocDescriptor)
SafeArrayGetElement	Returns a single element from the array
SafeArrayPutElement	Assigns a single element in the array
SafeArrayPtrOfIndex	Returns a pointer to an element in the array
SafeArrayRedim	Resizes an array
SafeArrayCopy	Creates a copy of the array
SafeArrayDestroy	Destroys the array and its data
SafeArrayDestroyData	Destroys data in the array
SafeArrayDestroyDescriptor	Destroys the array descriptor (no data)
SafeArrayGetDim	Returns the number of dimensions in the array
SafeArrayGetElemsize	Returns the size of the array's elements in bytes
SafeArrayGetLBound	Returns the lower bound for a particular dimension in the array
SafeArrayGetUBound	Returns the upper bound for a particular dimension in the array

Table 5.25 The VARIANT data structure.

Field	Type	Comments
vt	VARENUM	Type of data in VARIANT (see Table 5.26)
iVal	short	Short integer
lVal	long	Long integer
fltVal	float	Four byte real
dblVal	double	Eight byte real
bool	VARIANT_BOOL	Boolean
scode	SCODE	Error code
cyVal	CY	Currency
date	DATE	Date
bstrVal	BSTR	A BSTR
punkVal	IUnknown *	Note that this means IUnknown pointer, not an unknown data type
pdispVal	IDispatch *	Pointer to a dispatch interface
parray	SAFEARRAY *	An array
piVal	short *	Pointer to short
plVal	long *	Pointer to long
pfltVal	float *	Pointer to float
pdblVal	double *	Pointer to double
pbool	VARIANT_BOOL *	Pointer to Boolean
pscode	SCODE *	Pointer to error code
pcyVal	CY *	Pointer to currency
pdate	DATE *	Pointer to date
pbstrVal	BSTR *	Pointer to BSTR
ppunkVal	IUnknown **	Pointer to an IUnknown pointer
ppdispVal	IDispatch **	Pointer to a dispatch interface pointer
pvarVal	VARIANT *	Pointer to a VARIANT
byref	void *	Any pointer

Table 5.26 VARIANT types.

Type	Meaning	Ordinary Field	ByRef Field
VT_EMPTY	No data present	N/A	N/A
VT_NULL	NULL value	N/A	N/A
VT_I2	2-byte integer (signed)	iVal	piVal
VT_I4	4-byte integer (signed)	lVal	plVal
VT_R4	4-byte real value	fltVal	pfltVal
VT_R8	8-byte real value	dblVal	pdblVal
VT_CY	Currency	cyVal	pcyVal
VT_DATE	Date	date	pdate
VT_BSTR	BSTR	bstrVal	pbstrVal
VT_DISPATCH	IDispatch	pdispVal	ppdispVal
VT_ERROR	Error code	scode	pscode
VT_BOOL	Boolean	bool	pbool
VT_VARIANT	VARIANT	N/A	pvarVal
VT_UNKNOWN	IUnknown	punkVal	ppunkVal
VT_UI1	Unsigned character	iVal	iVal
VT_ARRAY	SAFEARRAY	parray	N/A
VT_BYREF	Adds with other VT_ types to indicate passing by reference	N/A	N/A

functions are **VariantChangeType** and **VariantChangeTypeEx**. These functions are very similar in form, but the **Ex**-flavor function understands language concerns (important for date and currency formats). Don't attempt to convert a **VARIANT** in place with these functions–provide a separate output **VARIANT** union.

ActiveX also provides some more mundane macros to simplify **VARIANT** manipulation (see Table 5.27). In most cases, you can use these instead of directly manipulating the **VARIANT** structure.

Back To Invoke

Armed with information about **BSTR**s, **SAFEARRAY**s, and **VARIANT**s, we can return to examining **IDispatch::Invoke**. The **Invoke** method requires 8 parameters:

Table 5.27 VARIANT macros.

Macro	Meaning
VariantClear	Clears the VARIANT and sets the type to VT_EMPTY; attempts to free the existing contents (unless the original type is VT_VARIANT)
VariantCopy	Copies one VARIANT to another; the code first clears the destination VARIANT (see VariantClear, above)
VariantCopyInd	Copies a VT_BYREF VARIANT to an ordinary VARIANT
VariantInit	Sets vt to VT_EMPTY and zeros all reserved fields

1. A **DISPID** that identifies the method or property the client wants to use
2. A **GUID** that has no meaning; always use **IID_NULL**
3. A locale ID to specify the current language in use
4. A flag that specifies the operation (see Table 5.28)
5. A pointer to a **DISPPARAMS** structure (Table 5.29) that identifies the arguments for this call
6. A pointer to a **VARIANT** that will receive the result, if any (may be **NULL**)
7. A pointer to a structure that receives error information in the event that a **DISP_E_EXCEPTION** error occurs
8. A pointer to an unsigned integer that receives the index of the parameter that caused a **DISP_E_TYPEMISMATCH** or **DISP_E_PARAMNOTFOUND** error

The **DISPPARAMS** structure requires a little explanation. This structure identifies all of the arguments for the call. Of course, to read a simple property, you don't need any arguments. However, to set a simple property requires one argument. An indexed property access may need many arguments. A method call may not require any arguments, or it may need several.

Table 5.28 Operationflags.

Flag	Meaning
DISPATCH_METHOD	Perform a function call
DISPATCH_PROPERTYGET	Read a property
DISPATCH_PROPERTYPUT	Set a property
DISPATCH_PROPERTYPUTREF	Set a property by reference

Table 5.29 The DISPPARAMS structure.

Field	Meaning
rgvarg	Pointer to array of VARIANTS
rgdispidNamedArgs	Named argument DISPIDs (see text)
cArgs	Number of total arguments
cNamedArgs	Number of named arguments

The first field in the **DISPPARAMS** structure points to an array of **VARIANTS** (the **rgvarg** field). This is the argument list. There are three kinds of arguments you may encounter: positional arguments, named arguments, and optional arguments. Although some arguments are optional, the **Invoke** function always receives the entire set of arguments. If the client wishes to omit an optional parameter, the corresponding **VARIANT** will have a type of **VT_ERROR** or **VT_EMPTY**. If the client uses **VT_ERROR**, (the preferred method) it also sets the **scode** field to **DISP_E_PARAMNOTFOUND**.

Named arguments each have a unique **DISPID** (from the type information). The client sets the **DISPPARAMS** structure's **rgdispidNamedArgs** field to point to an array that contains the named argument's **DISPID**s (if any). The length of the array (and therefore, the number of named arguments) appears in the **cNamedArgs** field. If that value is zero, there are no named arguments.

If there are any named arguments, they appear first (in a random order) in the **rgvarg** array. The positional arguments follow in reverse order. Consider the following call (from a Visual Basic program):

```
rv=ActiveXObject.Go(p1=30, p2="RESET", 14, "Command")
```

This call has two named arguments (named **p1** and **p2**) and 2 positional arguments. Figure 5.4 shows how the **rgvarg** array will look for this call.

You can easily parse arguments out of the **DISPPARAMS** structure by calling the **DispGetParam** functions. This function accepts the **DISPPARAMS** structure, a proper index (that is, zero is the first argument, not the last), and a type you want that argument to be. The function automatically pulls the correct parameter from the **rgvarg** array and coerces it to the proper type. Since your type information knows about argument types, you can also call **ITypeInfo::Invoke** to magically coerce all of the **VARIANT**s in the argument list. You can also get a similar effect by calling the global function **DispInvoke**.

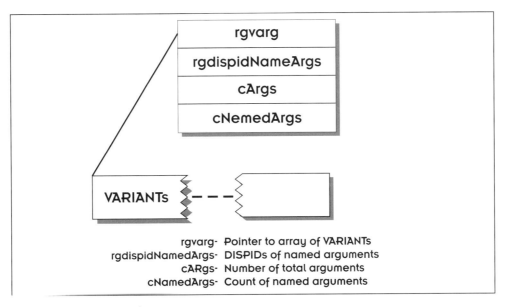

Figure 5.4 An example rgvarg array.

From the client's point of view, it is often more convenient to work with names instead of **DISPID**s for properties, methods, and named parameters. That's why the **IDispatch::GetIDsOfNames** function exists. Using this function, the client can convert the simple names of things into **DISPID**s.

Simplifying IDispatch

Remember, ActiveX doesn't really do much for **IDispatch**. It is a protocol that you implement on the server side of your code and use on the client side. If you do a good job, other programs that provide or understand **IDispatch** will work with your code.

One way to create an **IDispatch** interface easily is to allow ActiveX to aggregate your object with a standard dispatcher. All you need to do is load your type information (see the example under **IProvideClassInfo**) and call **CreateStdDispatch**.

However, there is an easier way. MFC has good support for creating objects that support **IDispatch**. If you want to create such an object, run App Wizard, and make sure to select the OLE Automation check box (OLE Automation is an older term for ActiveX scripting, which means objects that support **IDispatch**).

If you are creating an EXE program, you can add **IDispatch** to your document object. Usually, you'll be creating a DLL. In that case, you need to create an object derived from **CCmdTarget**. This object will serve as the **IDispatch**-aware object. Select Add Class from the Class Wizard dialog to add a new class. In the dialog that appears, derive a new class from **CCmdTarget**. Be sure to check the OLE Automation radio button (see Figure 5.5).

Once you have an object, select Class Wizard's OLE Automation tab (see Figure 5.6). This tab will allow you to add methods or properties. MFC supports the idea of common properties (like background color) for ActiveX controls (see Chapter 6). These are stock properties and have predefined names and semantics. However, in a general-purpose automation object, there are no stock properties.

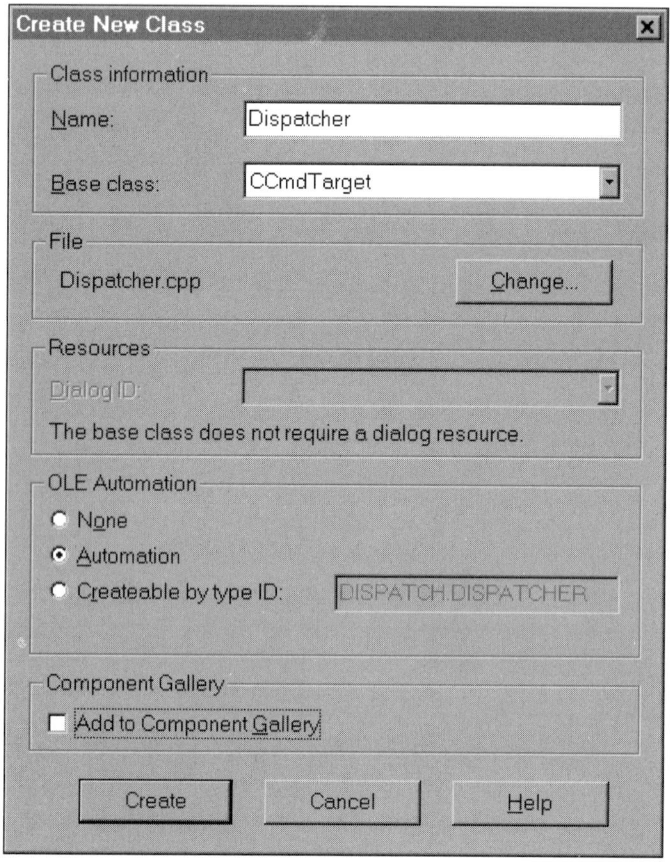

Figure 5.5 Creating an Automation object.

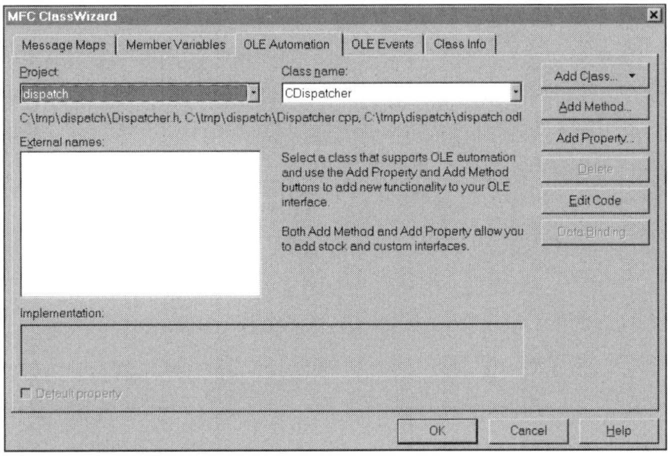

Interface Bestiary 163

Figure 5.6 Adding methods and properties.

To define a property, fill in its name and type (see Figure 5.7). If you want to map this property to a variable in your code, make sure the Member Variable radio button is on and provide the name of the variable in the Variable Name field. Class Wizard will automatically add this variable to your class. If you like, you can add a function in the Notification Function field that MFC will call any time another program changes your property.

Some properties don't map directly to variables. For example, suppose you want a property in centimeters, but you represent it internally in pixels. Then you might elect to select the Get/Set Methods radio button instead of

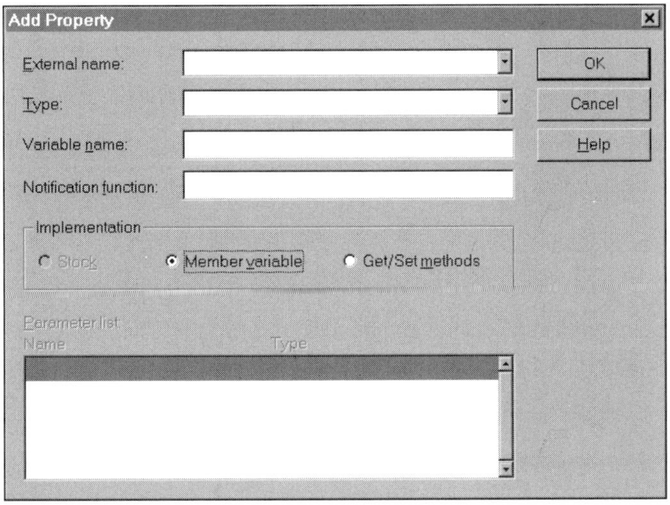

Figure 5.7 Creating a property.

the Member Variable button. This allows you to specify functions that MFC will call when a program attempts to read or write the property. You can take whatever action you require in these functions. If you need a variable, in this case, you'll have to define it yourself. If you want a read-only property, don't supply a write function. If you want a write-only property (as odd as that sounds), don't supply a read function.

MFC's implementation of **GetIDsOfNames** uses the name of the property. If you use MFC, you don't need to care about the **DISPID**. You supply the names, and MFC will automatically assign and convert appropriate **DISPID**s.

Adding methods is very similar. The Class Wizard dialog (see Figure 5.8) allows you to select an external name (used in **GetIDsOfNames**) and an internal name (the name of your function). These names may be the same, if you like. You also select a return type and any arguments you want the method to accept (up to 16 arguments are possible). Again, Class Wizard knows about stock methods, but this is only legal for ActiveX controls (see Chapter 6).

The other related tab in Class Wizard is the OLE Events tab. This is only useful for ActiveX controls (see Chapter 6).

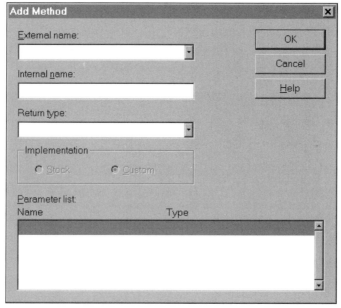

Figure 5.8 Adding a method.

Interface Bestiary 165

As you can see, building an **IDispatch** object with MFC is almost trivial. You use Class Wizard to do all the work. MFC provides a class factory and an implementation of **IDispatch** based on your input to Class Wizard. Better still, the MFC's code is quite efficient. You can read more about MFC's **IDispatch** implementation in the MFC technotes (specifically, look at notes 38 and 39).

Just to illustrate how simple this is with MFC, look at Listings 5.5 and 5.6. These show a simple **IDispatch** object that has a property and a method. The property selects a type of beep (the default is -1) and the method beeps using the selected type (by calling **MessageBeep** from the standard API).

It is amazing how little of this code did not come from MFC. I added a single line to the constructor to set the property variable to -1. I also wrote the **Beep** function (although Class Wizard already had a stub in place for me). I also had to add the **DECLARE_OLECREATE** line in the header and the **IMPLEMENT_OLECREATE** line in the CPP file. That's it. The rest of the code is from App Wizard or Class Wizard.

If you register the class appropriately (see Listing 5.7), you can easily use this object from Visual Basic or any other language that can act as an automation controller or ActiveX script language. You can also use Visual C++ and MFC to write controllers. Simply ask Class Wizard to add a class from a type library and select the automation object's DLL, EXE, or TLB file. This will cause Class Wizard to create a class that stands in for the automation object. It writes simple functions that call **Invoke** with the correct arguments for each case.

Listing 5.5 An IDispatch example.

```
// Dispatcher.cpp : implementation file
//

#include "stdafx.h"
#include "dispatch.h"
#include "Dispatcher.h"

#ifdef _DEBUG
#define new DEBUG_NEW
#undef THIS_FILE
static char THIS_FILE[] = __FILE__;
#endif

/////////////////////////////////////
// CDispatcher
```

```cpp
IMPLEMENT_DYNCREATE(CDispatcher, CCmdTarget)
// Add to Class Factory
IMPLEMENT_OLECREATE(CDispatcher,"Beeper",
   0x8755aa4, 0xd365,0x11cf, 0xa7, 0xb2, 0x44,
   0x45, 0x53,0x54, 0x0, 0x0)

CDispatcher::CDispatcher()
   {
   EnableAutomation();
   m_beepType=-1;   // default
   }

CDispatcher::~CDispatcher()
   {
   }


void CDispatcher::OnFinalRelease()
   {
   CCmdTarget::OnFinalRelease();
   }


BEGIN_MESSAGE_MAP(CDispatcher, CCmdTarget)
   //{{AFX_MSG_MAP(CDispatcher)
   //}}AFX_MSG_MAP
END_MESSAGE_MAP()

BEGIN_DISPATCH_MAP(CDispatcher, CCmdTarget)
//{{AFX_DISPATCH_MAP(CDispatcher)
DISP_PROPERTY(CDispatcher,"BeepType", m_beepType, VT_I4)
DISP_FUNCTION(CDispatcher,"Beep", Beep, VT_EMPTY, VTS_NONE)
//}}AFX_DISPATCH_MAP
END_DISPATCH_MAP()

// {08755AA4-D365-11CF-A7B2-444553540000}
static const IID IID_IDispatcher =
   { 0x8755aa4, 0xd365, 0x11cf, { 0xa7,
     0xb2, 0x44, 0x45, 0x53, 0x54, 0x0, 0x0 } };

BEGIN_INTERFACE_MAP(CDispatcher, CCmdTarget)
INTERFACE_PART(CDispatcher, IID_IDispatcher, Dispatch)
END_INTERFACE_MAP()

/////////////////////////////////////
// CDispatcher message handlers

void CDispatcher::Beep()
  {
  MessageBeep(m_beepType);
  }
```

Listing 5.6 The Dispatch object header.

```
// dispatch.h : main header file for the DISPATCH DLL
//

#ifndef __AFXWIN_H__
#error include 'stdafx.h' before including this file
#endif

#include "resource.h"        // main symbols

/////////////////////////////////////////
// CDispatchApp
// See dispatch.cpp for the implementation of this class
//

class CDispatchApp : public CWinApp
   {
   public:
      CDispatchApp();

   // Overrides
   // ClassWizard generated virtual function overrides
      //{{AFX_VIRTUAL(CDispatchApp)
      public:
         virtual BOOL InitInstance();
      //}}AFX_VIRTUAL

      //{{AFX_MSG(CDispatchApp)
      //}}AFX_MSG
   DECLARE_MESSAGE_MAP()
   };


/////////////////////////////////////////
```

Listing 5.7 Registry entries.

```
REGEDIT4

[HKEY_CLASSES_ROOT\CLSID\{08755AA4-D365-11CF-A7B2-444553540000}]

[HKEY_CLASSES_ROOT\CLSID\{08755AA4-D365-11CF-A7B2-444553540000}\InProcServer32]
@="c:\\activex\\dispatch\\debug\\dispatch.dll"

[HKEY_CLASSES_ROOT\CLSID\{08755AA4-D365-11CF-A7B2-444553540000}\ProgID]
@="Beeper"

[HKEY_CLASSES_ROOT\Beeper\CLSID]
@="{08755AA4-D365-11CF-A7B2-444553540000}"
```

You'll find the code that Class Wizard creates for the sample dispatch class in Listing 5.8. Notice how each stub identifies the argument types and uses a **DISPID**.

Listing 5.8 Class Wizard-generated code.

```
// Machine generated IDispatch wrapper
// class(es) created with ClassWizard

#include "stdafx.h"
#include "dispatch.h"

#ifdef _DEBUG
#define new DEBUG_NEW
#undef THIS_FILE
static char THIS_FILE[] = __FILE__;
#endif

/////////////////////////////////////////
// IDispatcher properties

long IDispatcher::GetBeepType()
   {
   long result;
   GetProperty(0x1, VT_I4, (void*)&result);
   return result;
   }

void IDispatcher::SetBeepType(long propVal)
   {
   SetProperty(0x1, VT_I4, propVal);
   }

/////////////////////////////////////////
// IDispatcher operations

void IDispatcher::Beep()
 {
 InvokeHelper(0x2, DISPATCH_METHOD, VT_EMPTY,
   NULL, NULL);
 }
```

Armed with this wrapper class, it is a simple matter to create and use this automation class. Listing 5.9 shows a simple program that displays a dialog. When you press OK, it creates an automation object and asks it to beep. Notice that MFC's AppWizard wrote most of the code. The only original lines are the include for the dispatch class and the code that handles the OK case in **InitInstance**.

Listing 5.9 An Automation controller.

```cpp
// User.cpp : Defines the class behaviors
// for the application.
//

#include "stdafx.h"
#include "User.h"
#include "UserDlg.h"
#include "dispatch.h"

#ifdef _DEBUG
#define new DEBUG_NEW
#undef THIS_FILE
static char THIS_FILE[] = __FILE__;
#endif

/////////////////////////////////////////
// CUserApp

BEGIN_MESSAGE_MAP(CUserApp, CWinApp)
    //{{AFX_MSG_MAP(CUserApp)
    //}}AFX_MSG
    ON_COMMAND(ID_HELP, CWinApp::OnHelp)
END_MESSAGE_MAP()

/////////////////////////////////////////
// CUserApp construction

CUserApp::CUserApp()
    {
    // TODO: add construction code here,
    // Place all significant initialization in InitInstance
    }

/////////////////////////////////////////
// The one and only CUserApp object

CUserApp theApp;

/////////////////////////////////////////
// CUserApp initialization

BOOL CUserApp::InitInstance()
    {
    // Initialize OLE libraries
    if (!AfxOleInit())
        {
        AfxMessageBox(IDP_OLE_INIT_FAILED);
        return FALSE;
        }

#ifdef _AFXDLL
```

```
    Enable3dControls();
#else
    Enable3dControlsStatic();
#endif

    // Parse the command line
    if (RunEmbedded() || RunAutomated())
        {
        COleTemplateServer::RegisterAll();
        return TRUE;
        }

    COleObjectFactory::UpdateRegistryAll();

    CUserDlg dlg;
    m_pMainWnd = &dlg;
    int nResponse = dlg.DoModal();
    if (nResponse == IDOK)
        {
        IDispatcher disp;
        disp.CreateDispatch("Beeper");   // ProgID
        disp.Beep();
        }
    else if (nResponse == IDCANCEL)
        {
// No action
        }

    return FALSE;
    }
```

Binding Time And Efficiency

If the **IDispatch** protocol seems like a lot of trouble, then you've been paying attention. The advantage is that you can perform late binding. That is, you can ask an object to do something without knowing anything at compile time about the object or what it does. You find out those things at run-time later, (hence, late binding). Early binding is what C++ normally does. Sure, you can manipulate objects, but only if you have detailed knowledge of the object at compile time. For that matter, ordinary ActiveX objects are about the same way. You can find interfaces at run time, but in general, you have to know what those interfaces do at compile time.

Of course, constructing a **DISPPARMS** structure, converting strings to **DISPID**s, and unpacking and coercing **VARIANT**s all takes time (even if you let MFC do it for you). If you need late binding, then this is as good an answer as any. However, what happens if you only need late binding on occasion, and at other times, clients know at compile time exactly what they want to do?

There are many possible solutions to this problem. You could provide an **IDispatch** interface and custom interfaces. Clients would select whichever they wanted to use. Another approach is to define a dual interface. A dual interface is an interface that is derived (in the C++ sense) from **IDispatch**. The dual interface's first functions are identical to **IDispatch**. The remaining functions implement whatever interface you like. Clients may elect to use **IDispatch::Invoke** to use your interface or call functions directly using your custom interface (which happens to be the same as your **IDispatch** interface).

Creating a dual interface is as simple as creating the appropriate functions and marking the interface with the **dual** keyword in the ODL file. Each member must return an **HRESULT** and all arguments must be scripting compatible (that is, something that fits in a **VARIANT**). Unfortunately, there is no simple way to create dual interfaces in MFC. (You can copy the ACDUAL sample inclued with MFC.)

IDataObject

In traditional Windows programming, the clipboard was the primary means by which applications used to share data. Although this model works pretty well for user-driven cut and paste of simple data items, it falls short when handling more complex types. Even where the model works, it isn't very efficient.

For example, consider a large bitmap in a file. When a program places it on the clipboard, it has to copy all of the data from the bitmap to memory for the clipboard. Then, when another application wants to read the bitmap, it has to copy all of the data back to another place, which might even be a file.

It would be much smarter if the programs could simply share the name of the bitmap file. Of course, other programs may not want the file, so you can't do that.

To solve all of these problems, ActiveX defines a protocol, often known as *Uniform Data Transfer*, that revolves around the **IDataObject** interface. This interface allows objects to signify that they have some data available and what formats they can provide. A program that wants data from an object simply asks for the object's **IDataObject** interface. Also, you can put an **IDataObject** on the clipboard. Although the **IDataObject** on the clipboard is small, it may reference gigantic objects that don't need to be on the clipboard.

Don't be fooled. Data objects, that is objects that support the **IDataObject** interface, are used throughout ActiveX for many purposes. They are not just for clipboard operations. In general, any time you want to pass formatted data between objects, you'll want to use **IDataObject**.

The **IDataObject** interface is not trivial to implement. However, ActiveX provides some helper functions that can make life simpler. There are two data structures central to **IDataObject**: **FORMATETC** and **STGMEDIUM**.

When a caller wants data in a certain format, it fills in a **FORMATETC** structure (see Table 5.30). This structure identifies the format of the data (as a clipboard format), what kind of device the data applies to, how to render the data, and where the caller wants the data. This allows a caller to ask, for example, for a bitmap for a 300DPI printer stored in a disk file. You can ask for a format to be the object's contents (**DVASPECT_CONTENT**) or an icon (**DVASPECT_ICON**).

The **tymed** field allows the caller to ask for data in a certain format (see Table 5.31). Of course, any given data object may not support every format, storage medium, or aspect, for its data. Callers need to check for successful return codes from data object function calls.

Having all of these possible return types leads to a problem: How can one function return all of these different types. Of course, you could have separate functions for each type, but that would be cumbersome. Instead, ActiveX defines a special union (the **STGMEDIUM**; see Table 5.32) to contain all types of data. This is actually a structure that contains a **tymed** field and a union for the data. Which union field you use depends on the value of **tymed**.

Table 5.30 The FORMATETC structure.

Field	Meaning
cfFormat	Clipboard-style format type
ptd	Device where data will appear, may be NULL if data is not device dependent
dwAspect	Type of rendering (usually DVASPECT_CONTENT, but may be DVASPECT_ICON, DVASPECT_THUMBNAIL, or DVASPECT_DOCPRINT); not all objects support all aspects
lindex	Optional portion of data (e.g., a specific page); usually -1 for all data
tymed	Type of medium (i.e., file, global memory, etc.) caller wants

Interface Bestiary

Table 5.31 Legal tymed values.

Value	Meaning
TYMED_HGLOBAL	Global memory handle
TYMED_FILE	Disk file
TYMED_ISTREAM	An IStream
TYMED_ISTORAGE	An IStorage
TYMED_GDI	Bitmap
TYMED_MFPICT	Metafile
TYMED_ENHMF	Enhanced metafile

The **STGMEDIUM** structure has one other field that is not part of the union. This is the **pUnkForRelease** field. If this field is **NULL**, the caller should use normal methods to free the incoming data. If the field is not **NULL**, then the caller should release the specified interface in order to free the data. This allows data objects to handle how it frees memory or to not worry about it. An example where this might be important is for a data object that passes the same data to many callers. The data object can't allow any caller to free the data. Instead, they notify the data object via **pUnkForRelease**. Normally, the caller will simply call **ReleaseStgMedium** that does the right thing for all data types and respects **pUnkForRelease**.

Table 5.32 The STGMEDIUM union.

Field	Type	Tymed	Meaning
tymed	DWORD	N/A	Type of data
pUnkForRelease	IUnknown *	N/A	Interface to release the data
hBitmap	HBITMAP	TYMED_GDI	Bitmap
hMetaFilePict	HMETAFILEPICT	TYMED_MFPICT	Metafile
hEnhMetaFile	HENHMETAFILE	TYMED_ENHMF	Enhanced metafile
hGlobal	HGLOBAL	TYMED_HGLOBAL	Global memory (use GlobalLock, etc.)
lpszFileName	LPWSTR	TYMED_FILE	Name of file on disk
pstm	IStream *	TYMED_ISTREAM	IStream interface pointer
pstg	IStorage *	TYMED_ISTORAGE	IStorage interface pointer

So now you know how to build a structure to ask for a particular piece of data and how the data appears. But how do you actually ask and receive data? That's the purpose of the **IDataObject** member functions (see Table 5.33).

That seems like a lot of functions, but it really isn't so bad. ActiveX provides a **CreateDataAdviseHolder** that does practically all the work for the last three advise functions. Also, if you have a list of formats in the registry, you can use the **OleRegEnumFormatEtc** function to handle the **EnumFormatEtc** call.

If you elect to implement **EnumFormatEtc** yourself, you should know a few things about it. The caller can request an enumerator of formats you can provide (via **GetData** and its related calls) or one for the formats you can accept via **SetData**. Naturally, if you don't accept data, you return error when callers ask for that enumerator.

Another quirk about **EnumFormatEtc** is that you don't have to actually support all formats at all times. Therefore, you can return formats that you might accept under some situations, even though you are not in a position

Table 5.33 IDataObject.

Function	Meaning
GetData	Takes a FORMATETC and returns data via a STGMEDIUM
GetDataHere	Takes a FORMATETC and fills in a caller-provided STGMEDIUM
QueryGetData	Takes a FORMATETC and indicates if the request would succeed
GetCanonicalFormat	Converts a FORMATETC into a FORMATETC that the data object prefers, but that contains the same data (the data object may not care, and return DATA_S_SAMEFORMATETC
SetData	Allows the caller to attempt to send data to the data object; some data objects do not support this and return E_NOTIMPL
EnumFormatEtc	Returns an enumerator that lists supported formats
DAdvise	Sets up a connection to an advise sink that receives data change notifications
DUnadvise	Terminates an advise connection
EnumDAdvise	Returns an enumerator that lists all advise connections

to accept them at the current time. **EnumFormatEtc** returns hints about what formats you might accept. It doesn't guarantee that you will accept them at all times.

The get and set data calls are straightforward if you understand **FORMATETC** and **STGMEDIUM**. The only other call that is odd is **GetCanonicalFormatEtc**. This call allows you to reduce a **FORMATETC** structure to its most basic form. This can prevent callers from asking for multiple data items that are really the same. For example, suppose you write a data object that renders a logo via metafiles. You don't care what device is in use. A smart caller might ask for the canonical format for a screen rendering and a printer rendering. Noting that the canonical formats for these are the same, it wouldn't request extra data to use during printing. You are free to ignore this call and just always return **DATA_S_SAMEFORMATETC**, if you don't care to implement this.

If you ever implement a data object, make sure you know what the caller expects. This can often save you some trouble. If the caller only expects **TYMED_MFPICT** data in an **HGLOBAL** for **DVASPECT_CONTENT**, then that is all you need to implement. You don't need other aspects or mediums. You also probably don't need **SetData**. Frequently, callers will make known what they expect, and you can significantly reduce your effort by writing to those expectations.

The End Of The Bestiary?

There are an endless number of interfaces, with new ones defined all the time. Of course, you can define your own interface specifications, too. However, the interfaces in this chapter are the ones you'll need to get started with ActiveX controls. There are many more interfaces that are specific to controls, but the ones in this chapter form a foundation on which many ActiveX technologies build.

When you encounter a new interface, try finding it in your compiler's online help. Be sure to notice if it is derived from another interface. Then try to understand what each function does. Also, see if the specification allows you to not implement certain portions of the interface. For many interfaces, you can simply return **E_NOTIMPL** from functions you elect not to provide.

Interfaces can be simple, like **IProvideClassInfo**, or complex, like **IMoniker**. The interaction between clients and servers via complicated interfaces is where ActiveX programming gets its bad reputation. If you try to understand each interface a little at a time, you'll have no problems.

ActiveX Controls

'Tis well said again;
And 'tis a kind of good deed to say as well;
And yet words are no deed.

—King Henry VIII

SO FAR, THIS BOOK HAS HAD quite a lot to say about ActiveX components and interfaces. Now it's time to put it all together to make ActiveX controls that you can put in Web pages as well as other ActiveX containers.

Now for some good news and bad news: The good news is that the objects you wrote in earlier chapters will work on Web pages already. The bad news is that they don't do anything useful. However, certain classes of controls are no more difficult to write. The more interaction you want with the Web browser, the more involved writing a control becomes.

If you are willing to use a tool kit such as MFC, writing an ActiveX control can be easy—in fact very easy, since MFC has specific support for ActiveX controls. Still, understanding what's happening at a detailed level will assist you in understanding your code—especially when debugging.

If MFC is so easy, you might ask, why not always use it to write controls (or some comparable tool kit)? The problem is efficiency. If you have simple controls you want to field over the Internet, you may not want the overhead of MFC controls. However, in many cases, the overhead is acceptable. For instance, local controls are usually unconcerned with MFC's overhead. Also, if you expect your users to already have MFC's DLLs, you won't have much of a problem. Another case is where you have many controls. Downloading the single MFC DLL once may not be as expensive when amortized over many controls.

In any case, we'll use this chapter to investigate the interfaces a proper ActiveX control must support. We'll also see how to code a control using MFC. You can decide which method is best for you.

Recently, Microsoft began an open beta of its ActiveX Template Library (ATL). This library uses C++ templates to let you create ActiveX objects. While this method is quite efficient, it requires you to know quite a bit of detail about your controls and their interfaces. And though it provides support for things like class factories and connection points, you still have to create much of your objects manually. As you'll see, this can be difficult if you are writing a traditional control.

Some History

When Microsoft first introduced the OLE Control Extensions (OCX), they were supposed to replace Visual Basic Controls (VBX). VBX controls were 16-bit creatures and not easy to port to 32 bits. Therefore, OCX was the heir, apparent for rich controls to drop into Visual Basic (and even C++) programs. No one had any idea that OCXs (which would become ActiveX controls) would turn into Internet controls.

The original specification called for OCXs to contain no fewer than 12 interfaces. Some of these interfaces are quite complex (including **IDispatch**, and several other elaborate interfaces). This led to large controls, especially if you used a general-purpose framework to help simplify constructing them.

Later, when Microsoft decided to pit ActiveX controls against Java in the Internet arena, a problem appeared. Large ActiveX controls are not particularly Internet-friendly, and most users don't want to wait 10 minutes or more for a control to travel across the Net to their computers. The same problem occurs when a control wants to load a large file (such as an MPEG video). Users don't want the machine to stop while the control loads the entire file, but using a standard **IPersist**-based interface to load the MPEG does just that.

To overcome this problem, Microsoft changed the ActiveX control specification. Now a control is any ActiveX object that exposes **IUnknown** and supports self-registration (in other words, practically all ActiveX objects). Of course, since a control container creates the object with **CoCreateInstance**, you'll also need to create a class factory for your control.

In addition to changing the specification, Microsoft added several things to help boost the efficiency of ActiveX over networks. For example, component categories now allow containers to create objects only if they are almost certain the object will do what the container wants. Asynchronous monikers (which we'll discuss in Chapter 7) are another example. These monikers allow you to start a file transfer or other operation before the transfer is completed.

The Simplest Web Control

Listing 6.1 is essentially the **AAWSound** object from Chapter 4. In this case, we don't care about the **IAAWSound** interface (since the Web browser doesn't know about that interface). Instead, I've added a few lines to the object constructor to create a new window of type **CSimpleWin** (as shown in Listing 6.2).

Listing 6.1   A Simple control.

```
// AAWSound.cpp : implementation file
//

#include "stdafx.h"
#include "mfcdll.h"
#include "simplewin.h"
#include "IAAWSound.h"
#include "AAWSound.h"
#include "mmsystem.h"


#ifdef _DEBUG
#define new DEBUG_NEW
#undef THIS_FILE
static char THIS_FILE[] = __FILE__;
#endif


/////////////////////////////////////////////////////////
// CAAWSound

IMPLEMENT_DYNCREATE(CAAWSound, CCmdTarget)
// Step 8a: Add IMPLEMENT_OLECREATE
IMPLEMENT_OLECREATE(CAAWSound,"AAW.Sound",
```

```
    0xf4512327, 0x9e89, 0x11cf,
    0xa7, 0xb2, 0x44, 0x45,
    0x53, 0x54, 0x0, 0x0);

CAAWSound::CAAWSound()
{
// Step 3: Delete this line: EnableAutomation();
    options=SND_NODEFAULT|SND_SYNC;
// Extra code added to create simple HTML active
// object
    win=new CSimpleWindow;
    win->CreateEx(WS_EX_TOPMOST,NULL,"Active!",
        WS_VISIBLE|WS_POPUP|WS_BORDER|WS_CAPTION,
        0,0,50,50,NULL,NULL);
}

CAAWSound::~CAAWSound()
{
    if (win&&IsWindow(win->m_hWnd)) win->DestroyWindow();
}


void CAAWSound::OnFinalRelease()
{
        CCmdTarget::OnFinalRelease();
        // Here we will close app but if this were a
        // MDI app, you'd need to make sure there were
        // no more open sessions—especially user
        // initiated windows
}


BEGIN_MESSAGE_MAP(CAAWSound, CCmdTarget)
        //{{AFX_MSG_MAP(CAAWSound)
        //}}AFX_MSG_MAP
END_MESSAGE_MAP()

// Step 4a: Remove dispatch map
//BEGIN_DISPATCH_MAP(CAAWSound, CCmdTarget)
//        //{{AFX_DISPATCH_MAP(CAAWSound)
//        //}}AFX_DISPATCH_MAP
//END_DISPATCH_MAP()

// Step 5: Change or remove this ID if you need to
//static const CLSID ID_AAWSound =
//{ 0xf4512327, 0x9e89, 0x11cf, { 0xa7, 0xb2, 0x44, 0x45,
// 0x53, 0x54, 0x0, 0x0 } };


// Step 6: fix up Interface map
BEGIN_INTERFACE_MAP(CAAWSound, CCmdTarget)
        INTERFACE_PART(CAAWSound, IID_IAAWSOUND, Aaw)
END_INTERFACE_MAP()
```

ActiveX Controls

```
///////////////////////////////////////////////////
// CAAWSound message handlers
// Step 9: Write methods
ULONG FAR EXPORT CAAWSound::XAaw::AddRef()
{
    METHOD_PROLOGUE(CAAWSound, Aaw)
    return pThis->ExternalAddRef();
}

ULONG FAR EXPORT CAAWSound::XAaw::Release()
{
    METHOD_PROLOGUE(CAAWSound, Aaw)
    return pThis->ExternalRelease();
}

HRESULT FAR EXPORT CAAWSound::XAaw::QueryInterface(
    REFIID iid, void FAR* FAR* ppvObj)
{
    METHOD_PROLOGUE(CAAWSound, Aaw)
    return
    (HRESULT)pThis->ExternalQueryInterface(&iid, ppvObj);
}

HRESULT FAR EXPORT
  CAAWSound::XAaw::Play(char const *file)
{
    METHOD_PROLOGUE(CAAWSound, Aaw)
    return sndPlaySound(file,pThis->options)?
            S_OK:E_FAIL;
}

HRESULT FAR EXPORT CAAWSound::XAaw::GetOptions(DWORD *w)
{
    METHOD_PROLOGUE(CAAWSound, Aaw)
        if (w) *w=pThis->options;
        return w?S_OK:E_FAIL;
}

HRESULT FAR EXPORT CAAWSound::XAaw::SetOptions(DWORD w)
{
    METHOD_PROLOGUE(CAAWSound, Aaw)
        pThis->options=w;
        return S_OK;
}
```

Listing 6.2 The Simple window.

```
// SimpleWin.cpp : implementation file
//

#include "stdafx.h"
#include "mfcdll.h"
#include "SimpleWin.h"
```

```
#ifdef _DEBUG
#define new DEBUG_NEW
#undef THIS_FILE
static char THIS_FILE[] = __FILE__;
#endif

// CSimpleWindow

CSimpleWindow::CSimpleWindow()
{
tick=10;
}

CSimpleWindow::~CSimpleWindow()
{
}


BEGIN_MESSAGE_MAP(CSimpleWindow, CWnd)
    //{{AFX_MSG_MAP(CSimpleWindow)
    ON_WM_CREATE()
    ON_WM_TIMER()
    ON_WM_PAINT()
    ON_WM_DESTROY()
    //}}AFX_MSG_MAP
END_MESSAGE_MAP()


/////////////////////////////////////////////////////////
// CSimpleWindow message handlers

int CSimpleWindow::OnCreate
   (LPCREATESTRUCT lpCreateStruct)
{
    if (CWnd::OnCreate(lpCreateStruct) == -1)
        return -1;

    SetTimer(1,1000,NULL);

    return 0;
}

void CSimpleWindow::OnTimer(UINT nIDEvent)
{
    CRect boundry;
    tick--;
    GetWindowRect(&boundry);
    boundry+=CPoint(20,20);
    MoveWindow(boundry,TRUE);
    InvalidateRect(NULL);
    if (!tick) DestroyWindow();
}
```

ActiveX Controls 183

```
void CSimpleWindow::OnPaint()
{
    CPaintDC dc(this); // device context for painting
    CRect r;
    CString s;
    s.Format("%d",tick);
    GetClientRect(&r);
    // Clear window
     dc.PatBlt(0,0,r.right,r.bottom,WHITENESS);
    // Draw number
    dc.DrawText(s,s.GetLength(),
     &r,DT_CENTER|DT_VCENTER|DT_SINGLELINE);
}

void CSimpleWindow::OnDestroy()
{
    CWnd::OnDestroy();
    KillTimer(1);
}

BOOL CSimpleWindow::PreCreateWindow(CREATESTRUCT& cs)
{
   cs.lpszClass=AfxRegisterWndClass(0);
   return CWnd::PreCreateWindow(cs);
}
```

This window has a life of its own. It is a topmost window so it floats over other ordinary windows. It is also a main window, so it isn't subordinate to any other window. It can only move from left to right while counting down from 10. At the end of the count, the window disappears.

You might be able to think of a use for this control. Even better, you might be able to think of something more interesting to draw in this window. The point is, this is a control you can use in a Web page.

Of course, to put this control in a Web page, you'll need some HTML construct to specify this object. HTML is the language you use to construct Web pages. You also need to install this control. Just run the REG file. If you have used the earlier examples, it might be a good idea to remove the old entries from the registry, just to be safe.

Once the component is on your system, you can write an HTML script like the one in Listing 6.3. The **<OBJECT>** tag tells the Web browser you want some kind of object. This object might be Java code, an ActiveX control, or any of several other things. The **CLASSID** and the related **clsid:** modifier confirms that we are using ActiveX. The actual CLSID appears in this tag, as well as a height and width parameter.

Listing 6.3 ActiveX HTML.

```
<HTML>
<TITLE> Hi Bunky! </TITLE>

start of meaningless text
<OBJECT CLASSID=clsid:F4512327-9E89-11CF-A7B2-
   444553540000>
Error! Object doesn't exist, bunky!
</OBJECT>
<P>
end of meaningless text
```

You can follow the object tag with parameters, but this control doesn't need them. You can also place ordinary HTML text or images that will load if the browser is not able to display the control (at least, in most cases). If you want to see the text, disable the ActiveX controls in your browser's Options window (an example option dialog appears in Figure 6.1).

The end of the object's HTML is the **</OBJECT>** tag. After this tag, everything is just normal HTML again. This document should work on your machine (just point the browser at the file instead of an Internet address). However, this brings up several questions: How does the ActiveX server wind up on any arbitrary user's machine? How does the user's registry get updated? What if someone writes an ActiveX virus? You'll have to wait until Chapter 7 for the answers to these questions. For now, take it on faith that the code resides—already installed—on the machine that displays the Web page.

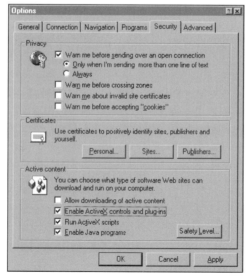

Figure 6.1 Disabling ActiveX content.

ActiveX Controls 185

Now that you've seen the page in action (or looked at Figure 6.2), go back and study the code more carefully. The server is completely ordinary. I used the MFC techniques discussed in Chapter 4 to build it, but it is so simple I could have easily used any method. I left the sound-playing capabilities of the object intact (though there is no good reason for doing so in this example). The browser creates this object as type **IUnknown**, then it tries to find other interfaces that it knows about. When it can't find one, it assumes it is just some anonymous object with its own tasks to perform and leaves it alone.

This process is exactly the one you want your browser to follow. Our object requires no interaction with the browser. It has its own independent window and uses a timer tick to decide when to advance. This might seem contrived, but you could use this technique anytime you want a separate windowed view.

Traditional Controls—A User's View

This simple example is only an ActiveX control by fiat since Microsoft now calls anything with an **IUnknown** an ActiveX control. However, traditional ActiveX controls are much more complex. They must expose many different interfaces, depending on the functions they want.

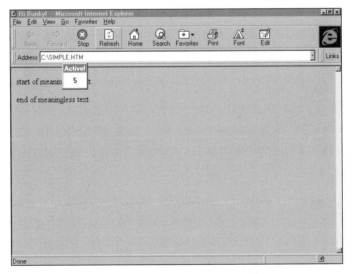

Figure 6.2 A Web page displaying a simple ActiveX control.

Before we see what interfaces these controls require, let's look at a full-blown ActiveX control from the user's point of view. *User*, in this context, means some programmer or HTML page designer who is using a control. An end user–someone reading the page–usually isn't aware that the control exists, per se.

Properties

ActiveX controls often expose most of their functionality via *properties*. To the user's perspective, a property is a variable inside the control. Some properties are read-only, others are write-only, but many allow full access to their contents.

From the control's perspective, a property may really be an internal variable. However, ActiveX can call a special function in the object when the user modifies the variable.

Instead of using a real variable, the control can elect to have a function actually set the property and read it. Consider a control that knows about some distance. It might expose a length property that users believe is in centimeters. However, the internal representation of distances is in .001-inch units. By reading and writing this property via functions, the control can always provide appropriate conversions. Then, if a user tries to put a negative value into the property, the control can report an error and prevent the variable from taking on an illegal value.

Another use of function-based properties is creating read-only or write-only properties. If you omit the read function, you have a write-only property. If you omit the write function, you create a read-only property. Omitting both functions really serves no useful purpose.

The important part to remember is that from the user's point of view, these properties all look the same: They look like variables. Suppose you rewrote the last example control to really store units in centimeters. Then you might change the property to be a true variable. The users would never know the difference, unless, of course, a user inadvertently stored a negative number in the variable.

Do properties sound familiar? They should. These are the same type of properties that dispatch interfaces provide (as we discussed in Chapter 5). You shouldn't find it too surprising to know that controls containing properties provide an **IDispatch** interface.

Another type of property is an *ambient property*. These are properties that containers (programs that hold controls) expose to controls. The Web browser, for example, might expose a background color ambient property, which allows controls to use the same background color as the rest of the document. This technique is a good idea since you don't want an orange-colored page to hold buttons with blue backgrounds.

Although the container exposes ambient properties, it can't enforce them. The control may use them or ignore them, however it sees fit. You'll find a list of standard ambient properties in Table 6.1.

In HTML, you can specify properties to an ActiveX control by using the **<PARAM>** tag. Simply specify a property name and its value. You can place as many **Param** tags as you like between the **<OBJECT>** and **</OBJECT>** tags. You'll see a control that uses properties and its HTML later in this chapter.

There is one other kind of special property you may encounter: the data bound (or bindable) property. Despite its name, a data bound property has nothing to do with data base access. At least, not directly. A data bound property can send an event to its container requesting permission to change values. Also, a data bound property can send a notification to its container after the value changes.

Table 6.1 Standard ambient properties.

Property	Meaning
BackColor	Background color
ForeColor	Foreground color
Font	Font to use for text
LocaleID	Locale (language ID)
UserMode	TRUE if not in user-mode
UIDead	Returns TRUE if control should not respond to user actions
SupportsMnemonics	True if container supports mnemonics
ShowGrabHandles	True if container wants grab handles on controls
ShowHatching	True if container wants control to show hatching when active (not in place active)
MessageReflect	True, if container will reflect messages
DisplayAsDefault	Cues a button-like control to display itself as the default button

That's all there is to bindable properties. The container can choose to disallow changes to the property and the container can learn when the property changes. This is useful for cases where the container has knowledge of the data within the control. Often, this is used to interface (or bind) a database record to a control, but that is not the only reason you might create a bindable property.

Methods

Another feature that dispatch interfaces have is *methods*. Controls may also have methods, which are simple function calls that perform some action.

Frequently, if you use properties correctly, you won't have many methods. For example, you don't need a method to set a sound file name. Instead, make that a property. You'll use methods for performing operations on the control, or in cases where you must coordinate several data items.

Events

Controls can send *events* back to the container, which supplies its own **IDispatch** interface. Buttons, for example, send the container a notification when the user clicks them. What the container does with an event depends on the container. The Web browser typically doesn't do anything with them unless it is running a script program that knows how to interpret them.

Extended Controls

Some containers may aggregate a control into a super control that has specific knowledge about the container. For example, an ordinary control doesn't know anything about the location it occupies in the container. Instead, an ordinary container has to store that information somewhere that it associates with the control.

A sophisticated container, on the other hand, might create a wrapper component that aggregates (and contains) the actual control. In this way, the control works as it always did, but the container can depend on properties and methods that it needs from the partial control. This type of control is an *extended control*.

When you write a control, you should realize that some containers may attempt to aggregate your control in this manner. However, there isn't much value to this for the control. It is strictly a convenience to the container.

Stock Properties, Methods, And Events

ActiveX defines many properties, methods, and events that have common meanings. These are the so-called stock properties, methods, and events. For example, **ForeColor** and **BackColor** are the conventional places to put your foreground and background colors. Mouse click events are typically called **Click**. You'll find a list of stock properties in Table 6.2. You'll also find a list of stock methods in Table 6.3 and stock events in Table 6.4.

Table 6.2 Standard properties.

Property	Description
Caption	Control's text
Text	Synonym for Caption
Enabled	True if control enabled
ForeColor	Foreground color
BackColor	Background color
FillColor	Color to fill areas
BorderColor	Color of border
BackStyle	Background style
FillStyle	Fill style
BorderStyle	Border style
BorderWidth	Width of border
BorderVisible	True if border should be visible
DrawStyle	Style of drawing
DrawWidth	Draw width
Font	Font to use for text
Window	Control's window handle
Name*	Name of control
Visible*	True if control is visible
Parent*	Parent of control
Default*	True if control is default
Cancel*	True if control handles cancel semantics

*Stock extended properties provided by container (see text)

Table 6.3 Stock methods.

Method	Description
Refresh	Redraw
DoClick	Fires a Click event
AboutBox	Show About box

Table 6.4 Stock events.

Event	Description
Click	Mouse activity
DblClick	Double-click mouse action
KeyDown	Virtual key down
KeyPress	Character key code
KeyUp	Virtual key up
MouseMove	Mouse moving
MouseUp	Mouse button up
Error	Error occurred

You are, of course, free to define your own properties and events for any purpose. However, you should avoid defining custom properties (or events) that mimic the stock ones. Using stock items makes your object easier to use and better able to cooperate with other controls and containers. Besides, MFC and similar tool kits often simplify handling stock items.

Persistence

Many controls support one or more of the **IPersist** interfaces. This allows a container to save their state and later reload it. For example, a button might store its current label and flags to indicate its check status and whether it is enabled.

Not all controls support persistence. This make sense because some controls might not have any persistent state. For instance, if you wrote an ActiveX control that shows a spinning company logo, there's no need to remember how far it turned last time it was accessed. When you re-create it, it just starts spinning. For cases like these, you can ignore persistence.

ActiveX Controls

Runtime State

Often, controls differentiate between a runtime state and a design-time state. When you are designing, for example, you might not do certain things. An ActiveX control that keeps a counter, for instance, shouldn't update during design of an HTML page. Of course, this assumes you are using some interactive design tool to build HTML. If you manually insert CLSIDs into an HTML page, the control will always operate in the runtime state.

Containers may wish to determine if an ActiveX object is running, to force an object to run, or to lock an object into the running state. This status is known as the runtime state. The system keeps a table of running objects and there is a special interface that controls provide to manipulate the runtime state.

Keyboard Handling

Controls often wish to use a custom accelerator table when they are active. In addition, many controls would like to have a keyboard mnemonic. That is, when the user presses a certain key, the control becomes active, even if it wasn't already.

Both of these capabilities may be present in a control. Some controls prefer to be always active, and therefore have little use for keyboard mnemonics. Others have no keyboard interface at all. These controls, of course, won't care about accelerators.

Frame Controls

Some controls can actually act as containers for other windows. A good example of this would be a box that groups several other controls. These controls are known as *frame controls* and require special techniques to make them work properly.

Traditional Control Interfaces

A full-blown, traditional ActiveX control has many interfaces. You can implement some or all of these interfaces depending on the functions your control requires. Table 6.5 shows the interfaces a traditional control may use and why a control would implement them.

Notice that some interfaces imply the presence of other related interfaces. You'll often find that once you start adding one interface, you'll start a chain reaction and have to implement more and more pieces.

Table 6.5 Control interfaces.

Interface	Description	Requires
IOleObject	Allows control to communicate with client	
IOleInPlaceObject	Enables in place activation	IOleObject, IOleInPlaceActiveObject
IOleInPlaceActiveObject	Supports in place activation	IOleObject, IOleInPlaceObject
IDataObject	Supplies control's graphics and/or property sets	
IViewObject or IViewObject2	Supplies non-in place active visuals	
IPersist...	Stores and loads the control's state	
IOleCache2	Cache for out-of-process display data	
IPerPropertyBrowsing	Describes each property and maps them to specific property pages	
IRunnableObject	Distinguishes between running and loaded states	
ISpecifyPropertyPages	Indicates which property Isheets to use for control	IOleObject
IConnectionPointContainer	Handles outgoing events	
IDispatch	Handles properties and methods	
IProvideClassInfo (or IProvideClassInfo2, or IProvideClassInfo3)	Dispenses type information	
IExternalInterface	Required for controls that can link to themselves	Moniker functions in IOleObject
IOleControl	Handles mnemonics, ambient properties, and event freezing (notification that the container is ignoring events)	For mnemonics: IOleObject andIOleIn PlaceObject; for ambient properties: IOleObject

We have already examined many of these interfaces in Chapter 5. In particular, you'll find details for **IDataObject**, **IDispatch**, **IProvideClassInfo**, and the **IPersist** family interfaces in the last chapter. These interfaces act as they usually do. The **IDispatch** interface manages the control's properties and methods. The **IDataObject** has a specific purpose: to provide a metafile representation of the control's visual state. Notice that the control doesn't usually draw itself. Instead, it provides a metafile via **IDataObject**.

The other interfaces are not overly complex. However, there are a lot of them. Some of them are not too important, while others are more substantial. However, if you approach them methodically, there is no reason you can't implement them. In the following sections, you'll find capsule sketches of these interfaces that will give you some insight into their construction and idiosyncrasies. You can find more specific details about these interfaces in your online help. Later, we will use MFC to write this code for us automatically.

IOleObject

One of the key interfaces that many ActiveX controls support is **IOleObject** (as shown in Table 6.6). This interface allows the control to communicate with its container in certain ways. One of the most important functions of the **IOleObject** interface is to receive a pointer to the container's **IOleClientSite** interface via the **SetClientSite** function (as shown later in Table 6.9). This interface provides a way for the control to request services from the container.

Not all of the members in this interface are necessary for most controls, so this interface isn't as intimidating as it might appear. For example, **SetMoniker** and **GetMoniker** are not useful for most controls. If you don't need to implement a particular function, just return **E_NOTIMPL** when the container calls that function.

Another way to simplify this interface is to use the built-in support for handling the **Advise**, **UnAdvise**, and **EnumAdvise** functions. These functions are used to store an **IAdviseSink** pointer (as shown in Table 6.7) that the control uses to signal the container when its data is being accessed. This is similar to a connection point, except it predates the introduction of the connection point interface.

To make your life a little easier, ActiveX provides a special object, **IOleAdviseHolder**, to manage these three functions for you (as shown in Table 6.8). You simply place an **IOleAdviseHolder** pointer in your object,

Table 6.6 The IOleObject interface.

Function	Description
SetClientSite	Informs object of its client site interface (as shown later in Table 6.9)
GetClientSite	Retrieves object's client site
SetHostNames	Communicates names of container application and container document
Close	Changes object from running to loaded state
SetMoniker	Informs object of its moniker
GetMoniker	Retrieves object's moniker
InitFromData	Initializes embedded object from specified data
GetClipboardData	Retrieves a data transfer object from the clipboard
DoVerb	Invokes one of the enumerated actions
EnumVerbs	Enumerates actions
Update	Updates the object
IsUpToDate	Checks if object is up to date
GetUserClassID	Returns object's class identifier
GetUserType	Retrieves object's user-type name
SetExtent	Sets extent of object's display area
GetExtent	Retrieves extent of object's display area
Advise	Establishes advisory connection with object
Unadvise	Destroys advisory connection with object
EnumAdvise	Enumerates object's advisory connections
GetMiscStatus	Retrieves status of object (see text)
SetColorScheme	Recommends color scheme to object

Table 6.7 IAdviseSink.

Function	Description
OnDataChange	Advises that data has changed
OnViewChange	Advises that view of object has changed
OnRename	Advises that name of object has changed
OnSave	Advises that object has been saved to disk
OnClose	Advises that object has been closed

ActiveX Controls

Table 6.8 IOleAdviseHolder.

Function	Description
Advise	Establishes advisory connection (surrogate for IOleObject::Advise)
Unadvise	Deletes advisory connection (surrogate for IOleObject::Unadvise)
EnumAdvise	Enumerates connections (surrogate for IOleObject::EnumAdvise)
SendOnRename	Advises that name of object has changed
SendOnSave	Advises that object has been saved
SendOnClose	Advises that object has been closed

create the object by calling **CreateOleAdviseHolder**, and delegate all the advisory calls to the new object. For example, your **Advise** function might look something like this:

```
HRESULT Advise(IAdviseSink *pAdvSink,
    DWORD *pdwConnection)
    {
    // holder is an IOleAdviseHolder class member
    if (Succeeded(CreateOleAdviseHolder(&holder))
        holder->Advise(pAdvSink,pdwConnection);
     else
        // yikes!
    }
```

When you need to inform the container that things have changed, you call the advise holder's **SendOnRename**, **SendOnClose**, or **SendOnSave** members. This in turn calls the corresponding **IAdviseSink** functions for each advise connection.

Another item worth mentioning is the **IOleObject::GetMiscStatus** function. This function informs the container about the object's behavior. You can return any number of bits from the list below to indicate various conditions. You can also store these status bits in the registry. If you do that, you can return **OLE_S_REG** to force ActiveX to read the values directly from the registry entries. Here are the status bits available:

- **OLEMISC_RECOMPOSEONRESIZE.** Indicates that when the container resizes the object, the object wants to recompose the presentation. This means that on resize, the object wants to do more than scale its picture. If this bit is set, the container should force the object to the running state and call **IOleObject::SetExtent** with the new size.

- **OLEMISC_ONLYICONIC.** Indicates that the object has no useful content view other than its icon. The object should still have a regular content; it will look the same as its icon view.
- **OLEMISC_INSERTNOTREPLACE.** Indicates that the object has initialized itself from the data in the container's current selection. Containers should examine this bit after calling **IOleObject::InitFromData** to initialize an object from the current selection. If set, the container should insert the object beside the current selection rather than replacing the current selection. If this bit is not set, the object being inserted replaces the current selection.
- **OLEMISC_STATIC.** Indicates that this object is a static object, which is an object that contains only a presentation (that is, only a drawing); it contains no native data.
- **OLEMISC_CANTLINKINSIDE.** Indicates that the object can't participate in internal linking.
- **OLEMISC_INSIDEOUT.** This object is capable of activating in place, without requiring installation of menus and toolbars to run. Several such objects can be active concurrently. Some containers, such as forms, may choose to activate such objects automatically, which makes this a useful bit for many controls.
- **OLEMISC_ACTIVATEWHENVISIBLE.** This bit is set only when **OLEMISC_INSIDEOUT** is set, and indicates that this object prefers to be activated whenever it is visible. Some containers may always ignore this hint. However, this is still a useful bit for controls.
- **OLEMISC_RENDERINGISDEVICEINDEPENDENT.** This object does not pay any attention to target devices. Its presentation data will be the same in all cases.

IOleClientSite

This interface (as shown in Table 6.9) is the one the container sends to your control via **IOleObject::SetClientSite**. The control uses this interface to communicate with the container. You might wonder why the control can't save itself. Don't forget, the container may have data pertaining to the control (for example, if it implements extended controls). The container must save this private data along with the control's ordinary data.

Before a control becomes visible, it will usually call **IOleClientSite::ShowObject**. This cues the container to scroll (if necessary) so that

ActiveX Controls

Table 6.9 The IOleClientSite interface.

Function	Description
SaveObject	Makes request for container to save the object
GetMoniker	Finds moniker for container
GetContainer	Returns IOleContainer pointer
ShowObject	Asks container to scroll so that object is visible
OnShowWindow	Function to call when control becomes visible
RequestNewObjectLayout	Informs container that control wants to change its size

the control is visible. Then when the control is actually visible, the control calls **IOleClientSite::OnShowWindow(TRUE)**. Later, the control can call **IOleClientSite::OnShowWindow(FALSE)** to indicate it is no longer visible.

IOleClientSite is the main interface the container exposes to the control. If your control needs another interface (such as **IOleControlSite**, which is described below), you can call **QueryInterface** on the **IOleClientSite** pointer.

IOleInPlaceObject

Controls that want to display something usually want to be in-place objects. An in-place object cooperates with its container so that it can share the container's display space. Contrast this to the simple control example at the beginning of this chapter. This control's presentation appears in its own independent window. An in-place control can appear directly in the container's document.

Table 6.10 IOleInPlaceObject.

Function	Description
GetWindow	Gets the control's window handle
ContextSensitiveHelp	Controls enabling of context sensitive help
InPlaceDeactivate	Deactivates active in-place object
UIDeactivate	Deactivates and removes UI of active object
SetObjectRects	Sets visible portion
ReactivateAndUndo	Reactivates previously deactivated object

In-place controls implement **IOleInPlaceObject** (as shown in Table 6.10). The container calls this interface to send commands to the control that allows the two to cooperate. In-place objects usually require **IOleInPlaceActiveObject** as well, which we'll discuss next.

IOleInPlaceActiveObject

The **IOleInPlaceActiveObject** interface allows the container to take charge of a control's activation, deactivation, and other state information (as shown in Table 6.11). Notice that in the documentation for this interface, the help files assume that you are writing a traditional OLE application. Therefore, there are many references to the container's frame and document windows. Although in-place activation requires a container to have a frame window (the main window) and a document window (the window holding the current document), it doesn't force the container to use separate windows for these functions. In other words, some containers may use one window for both the frame and the document windows.

IOleControl

The **IOleControl** interface (as shown in Table 6.12) allows controls to respond to keyboard events and supports ambient properties. Also, this interface informs the control when a container is not responding to events.

The **CONTROLINFO** structure that the control fills in for the **GetControlInfo** call is straightforward. This structure contains the accelerators for the control along with flags to indicate if the control wants to process the Enter and Escape keys.

Table 6.11 IOleInPlaceActiveObject.

Function	Description
GetWindow	Gets the control's window handle
ContextSensitiveHelp	Controls enabling of context sensitive help
TranslateAccelerator	Translates messages to interpret accelerator keys
OnFrameWindowActivate	Notifies the control when the state of the container's top-level frame changes
OnDocWindowActivate	Notifies the control when the state of the container's document window changes
ResizeBorder	Informs object that border requires resizing
EnableModeless	Enables or disables modeless dialog boxes

ActiveX Controls

If the control's **CONTROLINFO** structure changes, it should notify the container. The control can query for the **IOleControlSite** interface and send the notification that way (as shown in Table 6.13).

Table 6.12 The IOleControl interface.

Function	Description
GetControlInfo	Fills in a CONTROLINFO structure with information about a control's keyboard behavior
OnMnemonic	Informs control that the user has pressed a keystroke that the control specified through GetControlInfo and the control should perform the appropriate function
OnAmbientPropertyChange	Informs a control that one or more of the container's ambient properties has changed
FreezeEvents	Indicates whether the container ignores or accepts events from the control

Table 6.13 The IOleControlSite interface.

Function	Description
OnControlInfoChanged	Informs the container that the control's CONTROLINFO structure has changed and that the container should call the control's IOleControl::GetControlInfo for an update
LockInPlaceActivate	Indicates whether this control should remain active regardless of possible deactivation events
GetExtendedControl	Requests an IDispatch pointer to the extended control that the container uses to wrap the actual control
TransformCoords	Converts between a POINTL structure expressed in HIMETRIC units to a POINTF structure expressed in whatever units the container expects
TranslateAccelerator	Instructs the container to process a specified keystroke
OnFocus	Indicates whether the embedded control in this control site has gained or lost the focus
ShowPropertyFrame	Instructs the container to show a property page frame for the control object if the container so desires

IRunnableObject

Some controls differentiate between being *loaded* and *running*. This is especially important when you have a server that consists of a cooperating DLL and EXE file. The DLL might be present (loaded), but the EXE might not be running yet.

If you write a custom object handler, or for some other reason need to differentiate between being loaded and running, you'll want to implement **IRunnableObject** (as shown in Table 6.14). In fact, the default object handler (the DLL that stands in for an EXE server) provides this interface.

IViewObject And IViewObject2

Usually an ActiveX server that wants to have a visual representation on the screen provides a data object that sources a metafile. This metafile contains the object's visuals. However, some objects prefer to draw directly to a device context. In that case, you can implement **IViewObject** or **IViewObject2** (as shown in Table 6.15).

Since device contexts are only meaningful within a process, an object that implements this interface must reside in a DLL (or at least provide this interface in a DLL). This, of course, means that there is no marshaling support for **IViewObject**.

IOleCache And IOleCache2

Although objects usually provide data via **IDataObject**, it is often useful to cache some of the data or the presentation of the data. To this purpose, you can implement the **IOleCache** or **IOleCache2** interface (as shown in Table 6.16). This interface manages the cache and is especially useful when you have an object that resides in both a DLL and an EXE (that is, an object with a custom object handler).

Table 6.14 IRunnableObject.

Function	Description
GetRunningClass	Returns CLSID of a running object
Run	Forces an object to run
IsRunning	Determines if an object is running
LockRunning	Locks an object into a running state
SetContainedObject	Indicates that an object is embedded

Table 6.15 The IViewObject and IViewObject2 interfaces.

Function	Description
Draw	Draws a representation of the object onto a device context
GetColorSet	Returns the logical palette the object uses for drawing
Freeze	Freezes the drawn representation of an object so it will not change until a subsequent Unfreeze
Unfreeze	Unfreezes the drawn representation of an object
SetAdvise	Sets up a connection between the view object and an advise sink to forward change notifications
GetAdvise	Returns the information on the most recent SetAdvise
GetExtent*	Returns the size of the view object

*IViewObject2 only

Most controls don't need **IOleCache**, but you can implement it if you need its functions. The default object handler, by the way, provides an implementation of **IOleCache2**. You can reuse this implementation by calling **CreateDataCache** and aggregating the object it returns.

IPropertyPage And IPropertyPage2

Controls that want to show a property page must use objects with the **IPropertyPage** or **IPropertyPage2** interface (as shown in Table 6.17). This

Table 6.16 IOleCache and IOleCache2 interfaces.

Function	Description
Cache	Adds presentation to the data or view cache
Uncache	Removes a presentation previously added with IOleCache::Cache
EnumCache	Returns an object to enumerate the current cache
InitCache	Fills the cache with all the presentation data from the data object
SetData	Fills the cache with specified format of presentation data
UpdateCache*	Updates the specified cache
DiscardCache*	Discards cache

*IOleCache2 only

interface is straightforward and allows you to accept commands to show or hide your property pages. The **IPropertyPage2** interface has only one additional function: **EditProperty**. This function allows the container to select a specific field in the property page that will receive the focus when the page first appears.

The property page frame is responsible for calling each interface's **SetPageSite** function and passing a pointer to the corresponding **IPropertyPageSite** interface (as shown in Table 6.18). The property page can use this interface to communicate with the property page frame. Containers often use the **OleCreatePropertyFrame** or **OleCreatePropertyFrameIndirect** functions to create the **IPropertyPageSite** interface.

Table 6.17 IPropertyPage and IPropertyPage2.

Function	Description
SetPageSite	Initializes a property page and provides the page with a pointer to the IPropertyPageSite interface
Activate	Creates the dialog box window for the property page
Deactivate	Destroys the window created with Activate
GetPageInfo	Returns information about the property page
SetObjects	Provides the property page with an array of IUnknown pointers for objects associated with this property page
Show	Makes the property page dialog box visible or invisible
Move	Positions and resizes the property page dialog box within the frame
IsPageDirty	Indicates whether the property page has changed since activated or since the most recent call to Apply
Apply	Applies current property page values to underlying objects specified through SetObjects
Help	Invokes help in response to end user request
TranslateAccelerator	Provides a pointer to an MSG structure that specifies a keystroke to process
EditProperty*	Specifies which field is to receive the focus when the property page is activated

*IPropertyPage2 only

Table 6.18 IPropertyPageSite.

Function	Description
OnStatusChange	Indicates that values have changed
GetLocaleID	Returns the locale ID
GetPageContainer	Returns an IUnknown pointer for the object representing the entire property frame dialog box
TranslateAccelerator	Passes a keystroke to the property frame for processing

ISpecifyPropertyPages

An object that wants to use a property page must provide the container with the CLSIDs that correspond to the object that implements the pages (as shown above). To facilitate this, the container will call the **ISpecifyPropertyPages** interface. This interface has only one function: **GetPages**. To implement this function, the control fills in an array with the CLSIDs for each property page it wants to use.

When the container wishes to display property pages, it will call the control's **IOleObject::DoVerbs** with a special verb. These verbs are **OLEIVERB_PROPERTIES**, **OLEIVERB_PRIMARY**, **OLEIVERB_INPLACEACTIVE**, or **OLEIVERB_UIACTIVE.**

IPerPropertyBrowsing

This small interface allows the control to name its properties and inform the container of exactly which property page contains a particular property (as shown in Table 6.19).

Table 6.19 The IPerPropertyBrowsing interface.

Function	Description
GetDisplayString	Returns a text string describing a particular property
MapPropertyToPage	Returns the CLSID of the property page that allows manipulation of the specified property
GetPredefinedStrings	Returns an array of LPOLESTRs listing the descriptions of the values that the specified property can accept
GetPredefinedValue	Returns a VARIANT containing the value of a given property associated with a predefined string name as returned from IPerPropertyBrowsing::GetPredefinedStrings

IExternalConnection

The rare control that supports linking to itself requires the **IExternalConnection** interface (as shown in Table 6.20). If you need this capability, you'll have to be sure the moniker support in **IOleObject** is present as well. This interface manages an external reference count. You should not close the control as long as there are external locks outstanding. If you return the **OLEMISC_CANTLINKINSIDE** status bit during **IOleObject::GetMiscStatus**, then you don't need this interface.

Extra Registry Entries

In addition to these interfaces, a control usually has some additional registry entries. Of course, all the usual registry entries you use for any ActiveX component apply. In addition, most controls will want to register one or more category IDs (which we discussed in Chapter 3). Controls can signify that they are controls by registering the **CATID_Control CATID** (category ID) in their **Implemented** category key. For example:

```
HKEY_CLASSES_ROOT\CLSID\{your CLISD}\
    Implemented Categories\{CATID_Control}
```

Older programs don't recognize categories. To accommodate these older programs, you'll probably want to place the **Control** key in the registry. This cues older programs that your ActiveX server is a control and allows them to display it in lists of controls. This key appears under the control's main **CLSID** entry in the registry.

Other categories that a container might implement include **CATID_WindowlessObject** and **CATID_SimpleFrameControl**. Controls that only support one persistence model can indicate so by adding a **CATID** that specifies which model it supports. For example, a control that only allows stream persistence would use **CATID_PersistToStream**.

Some programs will display a toolbox with ActiveX controls on it. If you want a particular picture, you can specify it in the **ToolBoxBitmap32** registry key. This key appears under the control's ordinary CLSID key.

Table 6.20 The IExternalConnection interface.

Function	Description
AddConnection	Increments count of external locks
ReleaseConnection	Decrements count of external locks

Bad News/Good News

If all of these interfaces seem intimidating to you, join the club! Sure, a simple control only needs **IUnknown**, but if you add any of the optional interfaces, you wind up adding more and more because many of them are interdependent.

Still, the interfaces are no more difficult to work with than any other. However, you can use tool kits that take care of many of the details for you. MFC provides a Control Wizard that automatically generates almost all of the code you need to support a full-blown ActiveX control. The Class Wizard tool allows you to automatically generate properties, controls, and events. Using MFC makes writing ActiveX controls almost trivial.

If that's true, why did we spend so much time going into so much detail? There are a few reasons. First, MFC doesn't do everything. In the unlikely event that you need a control that MFC can't handle, you'll need to write your own code. Also, MFC controls have a fair amount of overhead inherent in the MFC DLLs. Of course, if your users already have those DLLs, the overhead disappears (a bare-bones control's file is only 20 to 30K long). Still, for some high-performance applications, you may not want to use MFC. Finally, consider this: You don't have to know how an engine works to drive a car. However, all the best professional drivers *do* know how engines work in great detail. Even if you always use MFC, knowing the ActiveX internal structure will help you build better controls, design smarter, and debug faster.

There are other tools that can help you build ActiveX controls. However, these operate at a much lower level than MFC. Instead of building around a framework, these tools help you define interfaces. You still have to assume most of the effort.

So, should you roll your own interfaces or use MFC? There isn't one right answer for everyone. However, once your users have the MFC DLLs, there is only a small penalty for using MFC—and enormous benefits. Besides, as network connection speeds increase, the time to download the MFC DLLs that first time is shrinking every day. Also, as more developers field MFC-based controls, the chances of a user already having the MFC DLLs on the target machine increases.

Getting Started With MFC

The basic steps for using MFC to create an ActiveX control are actually quite simple. First, you run a special wizard to create a basic control. The wizard automatically generates a UUID for your control and sets up all the necessary IDL and source files. If you build the project, you'll have a generic, useless (but functioning) control.

You'll want to add code to paint your control in a meaningful way. You'll also use a special tool—Class Wizard—to add properties, methods, and events. In some cases, Class Wizard will write all the code for you. In other cases, you'll have to write code to produce the desired effect. In either case, Class Wizard will at least start you in the right place and keep your IDL file and registry entries in line.

Of course, you'll also use the normal MFC mechanisms to handle messages, draw, and perform other mundane tasks. This is a plus, unless you don't know MFC. If you aren't familiar with it, don't worry. The amount of MFC you need to know to write most controls is minimal compared to the amount of MFC you need for a regular application. If you've struggled with document/view architecture and other MFC oddities, you'll be relieved to know you don't need all of that for a control.

Using Control Wizard

To start your control, select **New** from the **File** menu. Next, select **Project Workspace** to create a new project with its own makefile and sample source files. Once you select **Project Workspace**, you'll see an odd dialog box with a vertical strip of icons down the left side (as shown in Figure 6.3). Select the icon labeled **Control Wizard**. You can select a project name and directory using the right side of the dialog. Press the **Create** button to proceed.

You'll find that the Control Wizard uses two dialogs to collect information (as shown in Figures 6.4 and 6.5). The first dialog allows you to specify several things:

- How many controls you want in your project
- If you want a runtime license (that is, if you want to support a mechanism that requires developers to have a key to design with your control)
- If you want source file comments
- If you want skeletal help files

ActiveX Controls 207

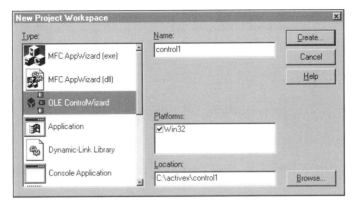

Figure 6.3 Starting a new ActiveX control.

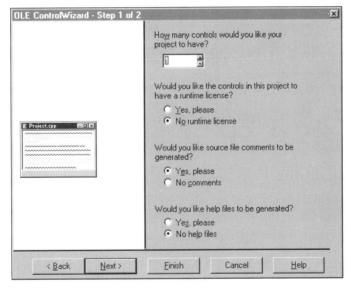

Figure 6.4 The first Wizard dialog.

Once you press the **Next** button, the final dialog box appears (see Figure 6.5). On this screen, you can edit the names of each class the wizard will create and change the file name it will use for each class (you'll usually accept the defaults). You can also select among several options. You can make:

- The control always activate when visible (containers may ignore this)
- The control invisible at runtime (may be ignored by some containers)
- The control appear in your ActiveX program's insert list (like any other OLE-style document)

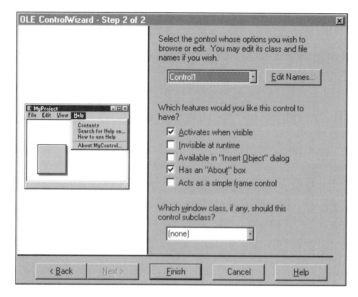

Figure 6.5 The second Wizard dialog.

- The wizard create an About box, if you request it
- The control act as a simple frame container that can contain other windows

You can also elect to subclass a standard Windows control (such as a button). This is very useful if you want a list box, for example, that happens to expose functions via properties, methods, and events. You don't have to write specific code to implement the drawing of such a class.

Code You Add

Often the only code you'll directly add to the files that the Control Wizard generates is the **OnDraw** function. This function paints the control on a device context. Instead of a normal Windows **DC**, this function receives an MFC **CDC**, which is just an object that encapsulates an ordinary device context. The **CDC** has member functions that correspond to ordinary device context functions. For example, in Windows, you might write:

```
TextOut(dc,0,0,"Help!",5);
```

in MFC, you'd write:

```
dc->TextOut(0,0,"Help!",5);
```

Since a **CDC** is a C++ object, it automatically frees itself when it goes out of scope. Therefore, you don't have to call **ReleaseDC** or worry about the device context's disposition.

MFC calls **OnDraw** in response to paint messages when the control is active. It also calls **OnDraw** when it needs to create a metafile to represent the inactive control. You can override **OnDrawMetafile** if you want the inactive representation to look different from the active window. Be aware that when the control is inactive, you can't assume anything about the **DC** passed to **OnDrawMetafile** or **OnDraw**. That means you'll have to setup any special brushes, pens, and fonts you need. It also means you don't know the current mapping mode.

The bounding rectangle and the invalid rectangle that the drawing functions receive use the current mapping mode, which presents an interesting dilemma. The solution is to convert the rectangles to device units (using **LPtoDP**). Then you can save the **DC** (using **SaveDC**), and change the mapping mode to suit you. Then you may convert the device units back to logical units (**DPtoLP**), if you like. For simple controls, you can often just use the current mapping mode, whatever it is. When you are done drawing, it is a good idea to restore the **DC** to its original state (if you called **SaveDC**, you can simply use **RestoreDC** to bring back the previous state).

Occasionally, you might want to add some custom code to the control's constructor or destructor. However, when it comes to adding properties, methods, and events, you'll use Class Wizard to either write the code or to place stub functions in the code that you will finish writing.

The other code you might add to a control is to handle ordinary window events. For example, a control that acts like a button might accept mouse events. You use Class Wizard to handle these events (instead of a traditional message function). This is exactly the same way that you use Class Wizard in the usual MFC program.

To handle a message in the control, start Class Wizard (you can press Control+W, or select it from the **View** menu or the toolbar). Make certain that the **Message Map** tab is active and that the control object is selected (as shown in Figure 6.6). In the left-hand list box, make sure the object is selected, and not a menu ID. Next, select the message of interest in the right-hand list box.

Once you have the correct items selected, click on the **Add Function** button (you can also double-click the message in the right-side list box).

210   Chapter 6

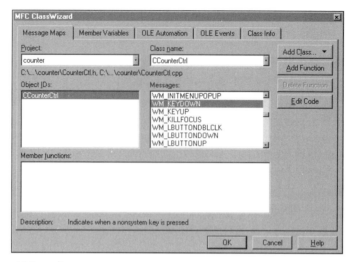

Figure 6.6 Class Wizard's message map screen.

This places a stub function in your code. If you want to edit the code immediately, just click on the **Edit Code** button. Make sure to press **OK** on the Class Wizard screen and not **Cancel** or the **Close** button. This makes sure the project retains your changes.

Class Wizard's stub functions often suggest what you should do, or have some simple example code in them. You can overwrite this code if you understand what you are doing. Often Class Wizard's code will include a call to the base class and a comment to indicate if you should do your work before or after this call. Again, if you are sure you want to ignore this advice, go ahead. Just be sure you understand the ramifications of doing so.

Adding Properties

Properties are the heart and soul of ActiveX controls, and adding them with Class Wizard couldn't be easier. Simply start Class Wizard, select the **OLE Automation** tab, then press **Add Property** (as shown in Figure 6.7). From here, you can select a stock property or name a new property. If you select a stock property, Class Wizard automatically arranges to store it and provides a notification function you can override to detect when the property changes. For example, when the stock **Text** property changes, the framework will call **OnTextChanged**. You can retrieve the text as a **BSTR** by using the **GetText** function, or as a **CString** by calling **InternalGetText**. You need only inform Class Wizard that you want the stock property.

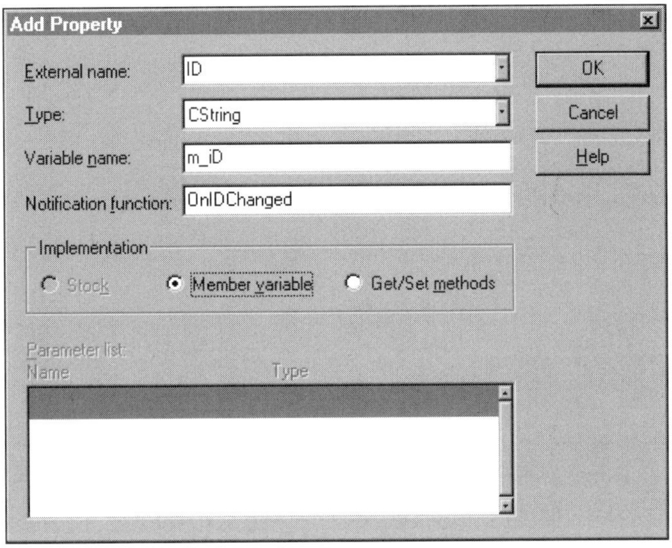

ActiveX Controls 211

Figure 6.7 Adding a property.

When you add a custom property, you can select between two types. The member variable type allows you to define a member variable that corresponds to the property. If you like, you can also define a function that the framework will call when the property changes. Class Wizard automatically provides the function's skeleton and an appropriate variable declaration.

Your other choice for properties is to use get and set member functions. In this case, you specify a member function that the framework calls when a container sets the property (the set function) and another function that supplies the value of the property (the get member function). You don't need to supply both functions if you want a read-only or write-only property.

When you create a member function property, Class Wizard automatically creates skeleton functions for you. The get function returns a value that has the same type as the property. The set function takes a value as an argument. You can also create pseudo-array properties by specifying additional arguments for these functions. What you do with these functions (and any extra arguments) is up to you. If you need a variable to store the property, you'll have to define it manually.

By default, stock properties are persistent. That is, the container saves them when it saves the control, and MFC arranges to load them back in when the container loads the control. If you want any custom properties to be persistent, you need to add a special **PX_** function to the **DoPropExchange** function. These macros (there is one for each common type) take the name of the property, the corresponding variable in your code, and a default value as arguments. Of course, some run-time properties may not require persistence. In those cases, you don't need to take any special action in the **DoPropExchange** function.

If you want to create a bindable property, click on Class Wizard's **Data Binding** button. This button brings up a simple dialog that allows you to specify that the property is bindable. It also allows you to select if you want to support edit requests, if you want the property to be visible to users, and if you want the property to be the default property.

Checking boxes in this dialog causes Class Wizard to make the necessary changes in your ODL file. However, it doesn't alter the code–you'll have to do that yourself. Usually, the changes are in the property set function (which implies you must use a Get/Set function property). If your property supports edit requests, call **BoundPropertyRequestEdit** to get permission to make a change. Assuming the call returns success, you can change the property and then call **BoundPropertyChanged**. Of course, if you don't check the **Sends OnRequestEdit** box in Class Wizard's **Data Binding** dialog, you don't need to ask for permission to change. Then, simply change the property and call **BoundPropertyChanged**.

Using Ambient Properties

While you use ambient properties (that is, properties supplied by the container) in your code, you don't define them. For common ambient properties, MFC provides simple functions to retrieve them (as shown in Table 6.21). You can also get any arbitrary ambient property by calling **GetAmbientProperty**. Of course, then you need to know the property's **DISPID**.

Adding Methods

When you want to add a method, simply select the **Add Method** button from Class Wizard's **OLE Automation** tab. This brings up a dialog you can use to create methods (as shown in Figure 6.8). Each method can have up to 16 parameters. Once Class Wizard creates a stub, you can fill in the appropriate code.

Frequently, you won't need many methods if you use properties correctly. For example, suppose you wanted to create a method called **Open** that

ActiveX Controls

Table 6.21 Standard ambient property functions.

Function

AmbientAppearance

AmbientBackColor

AmbientDisplayName

AmbientFont

AmbientForeColor

AmbientLocaleID

AmbientScaleUnits

AmbientTextAlign

AmbientUserMode

AmbientUIDead

AmbientShowGrabHandles

AmbientShowHatching

opens a file. Why not provide a **FileName** property instead? Then when the property changes, you can perform the open function.

The Web browser doesn't interact with control methods directly. However, scripting languages can call control methods. In this way, Web pages and Web servers can utilize scripting languages to orchestrate complex HTML content using ActiveX controls.

Adding Events

Class Wizard makes it easy to add events. To add one, simply select the **OLE Events** tab, then name the event (or select a stock event name). Events can have up to 15 arguments that you specify near the bottom of the dialog (as shown in Figure 6.9).

Class Wizard automatically writes a complete function that will trigger the event (the function will start with **Fire**, as in **FireClick**). That's it! You don't need to take any further action. When you want to fire the event, just call this firing function. Of course, you have to pass any arguments that you specified when you created the event.

The default MFC code will fire some stock events automatically. For example, when the control detects a character (a **WM_CHAR** message), it calls

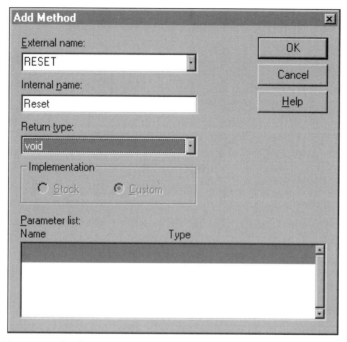

Figure 6.8 Adding a method.

FireKeyPress unless you override the **OnChar** message and don't call the base class. You'll find a list of window messages that MFC converts to events in Table 6.22.

The Web browser doesn't really care about control events. However, scripting languages that may be controlling the browser can handle events your controls generate.

Table 6.22 Automatic events.

Message	Event
WM_KEYUP	FireKeyUp
WM_KEYDOWN	FireKeyDown
WM_CHAR	FireKeyPress
WM_?BUTTONDOWN	FireMouseDown
WM_?BUTTONUP	FireMouseUp
WM_?BUTTONDOWN	FireClick
WM_MOUSEMOVE	FireMouseMove

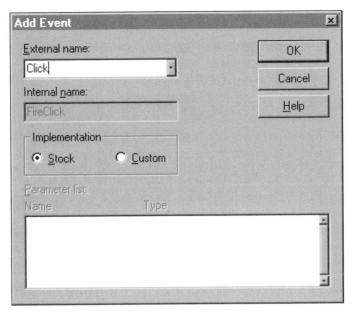

Figure 6.9 Adding an event.

Adding Property Sheets

Although it isn't mandatory, many ActiveX controls also support property pages. This allows a container to trigger the property page to set the properties by requesting the **OLEIVERB_PROPERTIES** action using **IOleObject::DoVerb**. As usual, MFC makes it quite simple to implement this feature.

The Control Wizard adds a blank property sheet in the dialog section of the resources. You can add controls (like edit controls) to the box in the usual way. To associate them with their corresponding ActiveX property, use Class Wizard's **Member Variables** tab. You can also associate a control with a variable and property, and Class Wizard takes care of the rest. Plus, you can even restrict entries by filling in the appropriate fields in the Class Wizard dialog. For example, you can limit integer properties to a certain range, or restrict a string property to a certain number of characters.

In addition to your normal property sheet, you can add more sheets by attaching them to the **BEGIN_PROPPAGEIDS** section of the source file. There are several standard property pages for things like fonts and colors that you can easily add. Use **CLSID_CColorPropPage** for colors, **CLSID_CPicturePropPage** for pictures, and **CLSID_CFontPropPage** for fonts. You'll see an example of adding a color property page later in this chapter.

More Sophisticated Additions

MFC uses the **COleControl** class to represent all ActiveX controls. You can find a wealth of functions in this base class that you can override to handle certain events. For example, if you want to know when ambient properties change, you can override **OnAmbientPropertyChange**. If you want to know when the container will ignore events, override **OnFreezeEvents**. You'll recognize many of these notifications from our earlier examination of the underlying interfaces that make them possible.

If you examine the source code for **COleControl**, you'll see that it uses the same **INTERFACE_PART** macros and other paraphernalia we used earlier to allow MFC's **CCmdTarget** class to create ActiveX servers. Since **COleControl** derives from **CWnd**, and **CWnd** derives from **CCmdTarget**, this isn't all that surprising. What it means is that you can use the techniques you learned in earlier chapters to add new interfaces to an ActiveX control–something you'll need to do when you get to Chapter 7.

Examining The Generated Files

When you use the Control Wizard to start a project, it generates three significant CPP files. The first file has the same name as your project. This file contains an object derived from **COleControlModule** and is the base class that represents the ActiveX control. If you need any customized code to execute when the control loads or unloads, you can add it here.

The same file that contains the **COleControlModule**-derived object also contains functions to support self-registration. You usually won't need to modify these functions.

The most important file that MFC generates has the same name as your project, along with the extension CTL (for example, PROJCTL.CPP). This file contains an object derived from **COleControl**. You'll make most of your changes—both automatic and manual—in this file. This is where the **OnDraw** function resides, along with all the events, properties, and methods in your control.

The final source file that MFC creates has the same name as your project with the extension PPG (for example, PROJPPG.CPP). In this file, you'll find an object that represents your main property page. This object derives from the base class **COlePropertyPage**. You won't need to change this file too often, except via Class Wizard.

ActiveX Controls 217

Testing And Using The Control

You can embed an MFC control in any appropriate container. However, you may find it especially useful to use the test container that comes with the Visual C++ tools. This container (as shown in Figure 6.10) allows you to embed any control in it. Then you can examine its properties, monitor its events, and set conditions like ambient properties.

To insert your control in the test container, you'll need to run TSTCON32.EXE (usually available on the **Tools** menu of the Visual C++ menu). Then, select **Insert Control** from the **Edit** menu. You can use items on the **Edit**, **View**, and **Options** menus to exercise and monitor the control. In particular, you can use the event log window (found on the **View** menu) to monitor events that the control fires. If you look at the notification log, you can work with data bound property requests and notifications.

If you want to test your control with other containers (for example, the Web browser), you'll need to insert the control using the method appropriate for that container. For the Web browser, you'll need to examine your source code to find the control's CLSID and write an HTML script that uses it. Alternately, you can use one of the HTML script generators to automatically insert your control from a list (much like the Test Container).

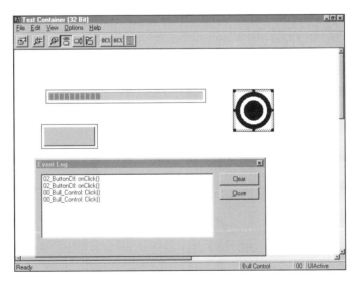

Figure 6.10 The Test Container.

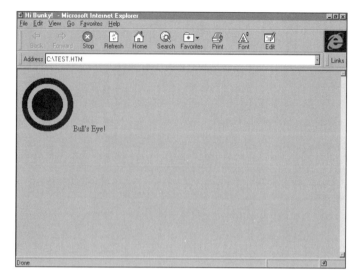

Figure 6.11 The Bull control.

A Simple Control

Figure 6.11 shows a very simple control, called the *Bull* control. This simplistic control looks somewhat like an archery target. You can control the colors and the size of the concentric circles via properties. You can also detect (by monitoring events) when the user clicks on the control.

As controls go, Bull is very simplistic. The control defines three properties and one event. It also uses the ambient background color to fill in behind the target. With MFC, this control is very easy to construct. The only part that requires any significant code is the **OnDraw** function (as shown in Listing 6.4).

Listing 6.4 The Bull control.

```
// BullCtl.cpp : Implementation of the CBullCtrl OLE
// control class.

#include "stdafx.h"
#include "bull.h"
#include "BullCtl.h"
#include "BullPpg.h"


#ifdef _DEBUG
#define new DEBUG_NEW
#undef THIS_FILE
```

```
static char THIS_FILE[] = __FILE__;
#endif


IMPLEMENT_DYNCREATE(CBullCtrl, COleControl)


/////////////////////////////////////////////////////////
// Message map

BEGIN_MESSAGE_MAP(CBullCtrl, COleControl)
    //{{AFX_MSG_MAP(CBullCtrl)
    ON_WM_LBUTTONDOWN()
    //}}AFX_MSG_MAP
    ON_OLEVERB(AFX_IDS_VERB_PROPERTIES, OnProperties)
END_MESSAGE_MAP()


/////////////////////////////////////////////////////////
// Dispatch map

BEGIN_DISPATCH_MAP(CBullCtrl, COleControl)
    //{{AFX_DISPATCH_MAP(CBullCtrl)
    DISP_PROPERTY_NOTIFY(CBullCtrl, "Step",
      m_step, OnStepChanged, VT_I2)
    DISP_STOCKPROP_FORECOLOR()
    DISP_STOCKPROP_BACKCOLOR()
    //}}AFX_DISPATCH_MAP
    DISP_FUNCTION_ID(CBullCtrl, "AboutBox",
      DISPID_ABOUTBOX, AboutBox, VT_EMPTY, VTS_NONE)
END_DISPATCH_MAP()


/////////////////////////////////////////////////////////
// Event map

BEGIN_EVENT_MAP(CBullCtrl, COleControl)
    //{{AFX_EVENT_MAP(CBullCtrl)
    EVENT_STOCK_CLICK()
    //}}AFX_EVENT_MAP
END_EVENT_MAP()


/////////////////////////////////////////////////////////
// Property pages

// TODO: Add more property pages as needed.
//   Remember to increase the count!
BEGIN_PROPPAGEIDS(CBullCtrl, 2)
    PROPPAGEID(CBullPropPage::guid)
    PROPPAGEID(CLSID_CColorPropPage)
END_PROPPAGEIDS(CBullCtrl)
```

```cpp
/////////////////////////////////////////////////////////
// Initialize class factory and guid

IMPLEMENT_OLECREATE_EX(CBullCtrl, "BULL.BullCtrl.1",
    0x59e8a903, 0xe0c6, 0x11cf, 0xa7, 0xb2, 0x44,
    0x45, 0x53, 0x54, 0, 0)


/////////////////////////////////////////////////////////
// Type library ID and version

IMPLEMENT_OLETYPELIB(CBullCtrl, _tlid, _
   wVerMajor, _wVerMinor)


/////////////////////////////////////////////////////////
// Interface IDs

const IID BASED_CODE IID_DBull =
        { 0x59e8a901, 0xe0c6, 0x11cf, { 0xa7, 0xb2,
          0x44, 0x45, 0x53, 0x54, 0, 0 } };
const IID BASED_CODE IID_DBullEvents =
        { 0x59e8a902, 0xe0c6, 0x11cf, { 0xa7, 0xb2,
          0x44, 0x45, 0x53, 0x54, 0, 0 } };


/////////////////////////////////////////////////////////
// Control type information

static const DWORD BASED_CODE _dwBullOleMisc =
    OLEMISC_ACTIVATEWHENVISIBLE |
    OLEMISC_SETCLIENTSITEFIRST |
    OLEMISC_INSIDEOUT |
    OLEMISC_CANTLINKINSIDE |
    OLEMISC_RECOMPOSEONRESIZE;

IMPLEMENT_OLECTLTYPE(CBullCtrl, IDS_BULL, _dwBullOleMisc)


/////////////////////////////////////////////////////////
// CBullCtrl::CBullCtrlFactory::UpdateRegistry -
// Adds or removes system registry entries for CBullCtrl

BOOL CBullCtrl::CBullCtrlFactory::UpdateRegistry(
  BOOL bRegister)
{
    if (bRegister)
        return AfxOleRegisterControlClass(
            AfxGetInstanceHandle(),
            m_clsid,
            m_lpszProgID,
            IDS_BULL,
            IDB_BULL,
            afxRegApartmentThreading,
```

```
                _dwBullOleMisc,
                _tlid,
                _wVerMajor,
                _wVerMinor);
    else
        return
        AfxOleUnregisterClass(m_clsid, m_lpszProgID);
}


/////////////////////////////////////////////////////////
// CBullCtrl::CBullCtrl - Constructor

CBullCtrl::CBullCtrl()
{
    InitializeIIDs(&IID_DBull, &IID_DBullEvents);

}


/////////////////////////////////////////////////////////
// CBullCtrl::~CBullCtrl - Destructor

CBullCtrl::~CBullCtrl()
{
    // TODO: Clean up your control's instance data
    // here.
}


/////////////////////////////////////////////////////////
// CBullCtrl::OnDraw - Drawing function

void CBullCtrl::OnDraw(
        CDC* pdc, const CRect& rcBounds,
        const CRect& rcInvalid)
{
    COLORREF fore=TranslateColor(GetForeColor());
    COLORREF back=TranslateColor(GetBackColor());
    COLORREF backgrnd=TranslateColor(AmbientBackColor());
    CBrush br1(fore);
    CBrush br2(back);
    CBrush *old;
    CRect r=rcBounds;
    int step=min(r.Width(),r.Height())/m_step;
    pdc->SetBkColor(backgrnd);
    pdc->ExtTextOut(0,0,ETO_OPAQUE,&r,"",NULL);
    old=pdc->SelectObject(&br1);
    pdc->Ellipse(&r);
    pdc->SelectObject(&br2);
    r.InflateRect(-step,-step);
    pdc->Ellipse(&r);
    pdc->SelectObject(&br1);
    r.InflateRect(-step,-step);
```

```cpp
        pdc->Ellipse(&r);
        pdc->SelectObject(old);
}


/////////////////////////////////////////////////////////
// CBullCtrl::DoPropExchange - Persistence support

void CBullCtrl::DoPropExchange(CPropExchange* pPX)
{
    ExchangeVersion(pPX,
    MAKELONG(_wVerMinor, _wVerMajor));
    COleControl::DoPropExchange(pPX);
    PX_Short(pPX,"Step",m_step,8);
}


/////////////////////////////////////////////////////////
// CBullCtrl::OnResetState - Reset control's state

void CBullCtrl::OnResetState()
{
// Resets defaults found in DoPropExchange
    COleControl::OnResetState();
// TODO: Reset any other control state here.
}


/////////////////////////////////////////////////////////
// CBullCtrl::AboutBox - Display an "About" box

void CBullCtrl::AboutBox()
{
    CDialog dlgAbout(IDD_ABOUTBOX_BULL);
    dlgAbout.DoModal();
}


/////////////////////////////////////////////////////////
// CBullCtrl message handlers

void CBullCtrl::OnStepChanged()
{
    InvalidateRect(NULL);
    SetModifiedFlag();
}

void CBullCtrl::OnLButtonDown(UINT nFlags, CPoint point)
{
    FireClick();
    // Actually, base class fires this event for
    // you...
    // COleControl::OnLButtonDown(nFlags, point);
}
```

ActiveX Controls 223

The **OnDraw** function must respect the color properties the control supports. Since the foreground and background colors are stock properties, the code simply calls **GetForeColor** and **GetBackColor** to learn what values to use. In response, these functions return an **OLE_COLOR**. This is similar to a regular **COLORREF**. Although a **COLORREF** is 32 bits wide, it only uses the lower 24 bits (eight bits each for red, green, and blue). An **OLE_COLOR**, on the other hand, uses the top eight bits to specify the type of color it contains. If the top byte is zero, the bottom 24 bits are a **COLORREF**. That means you can pass an RGB value as an **OLE_COLOR** with no conversion. However, if the top eight bits are, for instance, 0x80, then the bottom byte is a system color index (the same values you pass to **GetSysColor**). There are more rules, but you don't need to know them. You can just call **TranslateColor** to get the correct RGB value.

The control draws the area outside the target using the ambient background color. The **OnDraw** function retrieves this with the **AmbientBackColor** function. Again, this function returns an **OLE_COLOR** and requires **TranslateColor** to convert it into an RGB value.

The remaining drawing code is just ordinary MFC programming. The **step** variable corresponds to the custom property that defines the size of the concentric circles. Although stock properties take care of themselves, in many cases you do have to add a line of code to make a custom property like **step** work. If you don't want to save the property in the control's persistent state, you don't have to do anything outside of Class Wizard to define a property. However, if you do want the property to be persistent, you'll need to add a **PX_** function to the **DoPropExchange** function (as shown in Listing 6.4).

DoPropExchange maps properties to persistent storage. There is a **PX_** function for most common types (as shown in Table 6.23). You provide the context (an argument passed into **DoPropExchange**, the external property name, the internal property name, and (optionally) a default value for the property.

Why does **Step** need to be persistent? A programming tool might want to save the control and reload it later, and it should look the same when it reloads. Also, if you plan on using the Bull control with the Web browser, it uses persistence to load the values specified in the HTML. For example, consider the following HTML code:

Table 6.23 PX_ Exchange functions.

Macro

PX_Blob

PX_Bool

PX_Color

PX_Currency

PX_Double

PX_Float

PX_Font

PX_IUnknown

PX_Long

PX_Picture

PX_Short

PX_String

PX_ULong

PX_UShort

PX_VBXFontConvert

```
<OBJECT CLASSID=clsid:59e8a903-e0c6-11CF-A7B2-
    444553540000 WIDTH=100
    HEIGHT=100>
Error! Object doesn't exist!
<PARAM NAME="Step" VALUE=10>
</OBJECT>
end
```

Try taking out the **PX_** function and running this code. You'll see that the control will ignore the **Step** value unless you include the **PX_** function.

Another piece of code associated with the **Step** property is the change notification. If the container changes the step size, the control should redraw itself. This is the purpose of the **OnStepChanged** function. This simple function has two lines: **InvalidateRect** causes the control to redraw, and **SetModifiedFlag** marks the control as "dirty"—that is, the control needs to be saved.

One other refinement that is a good idea to implement is property pages. MFC makes these easy to implement, too. Near the top of Listing 6.4 is a

ActiveX Controls 225

BEGIN_PROPPAGEIDS macro. The last argument to this macro is the number of property pages defined for the control, initially set to 1. The MFC tools create a skeleton dialog box for that property page. You can customize the page (using the resource editor) to handle the step property by inserting an edit control (as shown in Figure 6.12). Then use Class Wizard to connect the edit control to the property (by using the **Member Variables** tab, as shown in Figure 6.13). Be sure to include the ActiveX name of the property when you're prompted for it.

The color properties are more problematic. How can you easily supply a nice interface for changing colors? The answer is, you don't have to since MFC provides one for you. Simply change the number of property pages in the **BEGIN_PROPPAGEIDS** line to 2, and add a **PROPPAGEID(CLSID-**

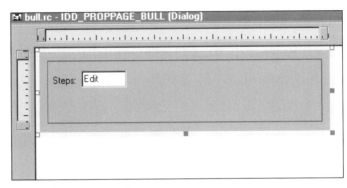

Figure 6.12 Creating the property sheet.

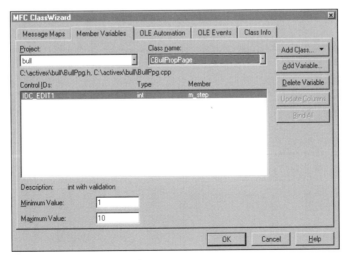

Figure 6.13 Connecting the property sheet.

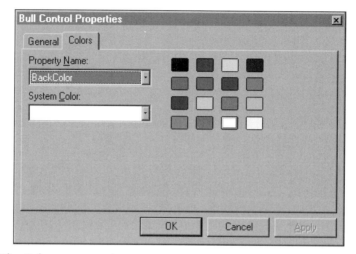

Figure 6.14 The Color property sheet.

_**CColorPropPage)** command to the list of property pages. This produces the color dialog you'll see in Figure 6.14.

MFC also produces a file to represent the default property page (BULLPPG.CPP; as shown in Listing 6.5). This is a relatively straightforward MFC property page with some ActiveX enhancements. Usually, you won't need to make any manual changes to this file. Class Wizard's **Member Variables** tab does all the work.

Listing 6.5 Bull's property page class.

```
// BullPpg.cpp : Implementation of the CBullPropPage
// property page class.

#include "stdafx.h"
#include "bull.h"
#include "BullPpg.h"

#ifdef _DEBUG
#define new DEBUG_NEW
#undef THIS_FILE
static char THIS_FILE[] = __FILE__;
#endif


IMPLEMENT_DYNCREATE(CBullPropPage, COlePropertyPage)


/////////////////////////////////////////////////////////
// Message map
```

```
BEGIN_MESSAGE_MAP(CBullPropPage, COlePropertyPage)
    //{{AFX_MSG_MAP(CBullPropPage)
    //}}AFX_MSG_MAP
END_MESSAGE_MAP()


/////////////////////////////////////////////////////////
// Initialize class factory and guid

IMPLEMENT_OLECREATE_EX(CBullPropPage, "BULL.BullPropPage.1",
    0x59e8a904, 0xe0c6, 0x11cf, 0xa7,
    0xb2, 0x44, 0x45, 0x53, 0x54, 0, 0)

/////////////////////////////////////////////////////////
// CBullPropPage::CBullPropPageFactory::UpdateRegistry -
// Adds or removes system registry entries

BOOL
    CBullPropPage::CBullPropPageFactory::
    UpdateRegistry(BOOL bRegister)
{
    if (bRegister)
        return AfxOleRegisterPropertyPageClass(
          AfxGetInstanceHandle(),
            m_clsid, IDS_BULL_PPG);
    else
        return AfxOleUnregisterClass(m_clsid, NULL);
}


/////////////////////////////////////////////////////////
// CBullPropPage::CBullPropPage - Constructor

CBullPropPage::CBullPropPage() :
    COlePropertyPage(IDD, IDS_BULL_PPG_CAPTION)
{
    //{{AFX_DATA_INIT(CBullPropPage)
    m_step = 0;
    //}}AFX_DATA_INIT
}


/////////////////////////////////////////////////////////
// CBullPropPage::DoDataExchange - Moves data between page and properties

void CBullPropPage::DoDataExchange(CDataExchange* pDX)
{
    //{{AFX_DATA_MAP(CBullPropPage)
    DDP_Text(pDX, IDC_EDIT1, m_step, _T("Step") );
    DDX_Text(pDX, IDC_EDIT1, m_step);
    DDV_MinMaxInt(pDX, m_step, 1, 10);
    //}}AFX_DATA_MAP
    DDP_PostProcessing(pDX);
}
```

```
//////////////////////////////////////////////////////////
// CBullPropPage message handlers
```

The other source file that MFC automatically creates represents the entire control (BULL.CPP in Listing 6.6). Again, this file is usually exactly what you need and requires no changes. You can spot the DLL registration calls and other items that you have to put in by hand if you are not using MFC.

Listing 6.6 BULL.CPP.

```cpp
// bull.cpp : Implementation of CBullApp

#include "stdafx.h"
#include "bull.h"

#ifdef _DEBUG
#define new DEBUG_NEW
#undef THIS_FILE
static char THIS_FILE[] = __FILE__;
#endif


CBullApp NEAR theApp;

const GUID CDECL BASED_CODE _tlid =
        { 0x59e8a900, 0xe0c6, 0x11cf,
         { 0xa7, 0xb2, 0x44, 0x45, 0x53,
           0x54, 0, 0 } };
const WORD _wVerMajor = 1;
const WORD _wVerMinor = 0;


//////////////////////////////////////////////////////////
// CBullApp::InitInstance - DLL initialization

BOOL CBullApp::InitInstance()
{
    BOOL bInit = COleControlModule::InitInstance();

    if (bInit)
    {
        // TODO: Add your own module initialization
        // code
    }

    return bInit;
}


//////////////////////////////////////////////////////////
// CBullApp::ExitInstance - DLL termination
```

```
int CBullApp::ExitInstance()
{
    // TODO: Add your own module termination code
    // here.

    return COleControlModule::ExitInstance();
}


/////////////////////////////////////////////////////////
// DllRegisterServer - Adds entries to the registry

STDAPI DllRegisterServer(void)
{
    AFX_MANAGE_STATE(_afxModuleAddrThis);

    if (!AfxOleRegisterTypeLib(
        AfxGetInstanceHandle(), _tlid))
            return ResultFromScode(SELFREG_E_TYPELIB);

    if (!COleObjectFactoryEx::UpdateRegistryAll(TRUE))
        return ResultFromScode(SELFREG_E_CLASS);

    return NOERROR;
}


/////////////////////////////////////////////////////////
// DllUnregisterServer - Removes entries from registry

STDAPI DllUnregisterServer(void)
{
    AFX_MANAGE_STATE(_afxModuleAddrThis);

    if (!AfxOleUnregisterTypeLib(_tlid))
        return ResultFromScode(SELFREG_E_TYPELIB);

    if (!COleObjectFactoryEx::UpdateRegistryAll(FALSE))
        return ResultFromScode(SELFREG_E_CLASS);

    return NOERROR;
}
```

A More Useful Control

No Internet programming book would be complete without an example of a counter. The usual CGI-based counter counts the number of users who view a particular page. However, with ActiveX, you can maintain a counter per user and track the number of times each user visits the page. Of course, the control stores the count on the user's machine, so it is only visible to the user, which alleviates any privacy concerns.

The basic idea is simple: Provide an ActiveX control that displays a counter. The counter finds its value in the system registry, then each time a container creates the control, it increments the counter. Of course, if the special registry entry doesn't exist, then the control uses an initial count of 1 and stores that in the registry. Each instance of the control can have a unique ID (specified by a property). The ID makes a special entry in the registry so that each control can have its own count. Without this feature you'd be unable to use the counter to maintain more than one count.

If you're like most Internet programmers, you'd probably like to have multiple counters available, so the control defines an **ID** property as a name to use when searching the registry. The count is in the registry under the AWC-Coriolis key.

To create the control, you can run the Control Wizard (as shown in Listing 6.7). Use Class Wizard to add the **ID** property and add the appropriate **PX_** function to make the property persistent.

Listing 6.7 The Counter control.

```
// CounterCtl.cpp :

#include "stdafx.h"
#include "counter.h"
#include "CounterCtl.h"
#include "CounterPpg.h"


#ifdef _DEBUG
#define new DEBUG_NEW
#undef THIS_FILE
static char THIS_FILE[] = __FILE__;
#endif


IMPLEMENT_DYNCREATE(CCounterCtrl, COleControl)


/////////////////////////////////////////////////////////
// Message map

BEGIN_MESSAGE_MAP(CCounterCtrl, COleControl)
    //{{AFX_MSG_MAP(CCounterCtrl)
    //}}AFX_MSG_MAP
    ON_OLEVERB(AFX_IDS_VERB_PROPERTIES, OnProperties)
END_MESSAGE_MAP()
```

```
//////////////////////////////////////////////////////
// Dispatch map

BEGIN_DISPATCH_MAP(CCounterCtrl, COleControl)
    //{{AFX_DISPATCH_MAP(CCounterCtrl)
    DISP_PROPERTY(CCounterCtrl, "ID", name, VT_BSTR)
    //}}AFX_DISPATCH_MAP
    DISP_FUNCTION_ID(CCounterCtrl, "AboutBox",
            DISPID_ABOUTBOX, AboutBox, VT_EMPTY, VTS_NONE)
END_DISPATCH_MAP()


//////////////////////////////////////////////////////
// Event map

BEGIN_EVENT_MAP(CCounterCtrl, COleControl)
    //{{AFX_EVENT_MAP(CCounterCtrl)
    //}}AFX_EVENT_MAP
END_EVENT_MAP()


//////////////////////////////////////////////////////
// Property pages

// TODO: Add more property pages as needed.
BEGIN_PROPPAGEIDS(CCounterCtrl, 1)
    PROPPAGEID(CCounterPropPage::guid)
END_PROPPAGEIDS(CCounterCtrl)


//////////////////////////////////////////////////////
// Initialize class factory and guid

IMPLEMENT_OLECREATE_EX(CCounterCtrl,
   "COUNTER.CounterCtrl.1",
     0xd41456c3, 0xe21f, 0x11cf, 0xa7, 0xb2, 0x44, 0x45,
   0x53, 0x54, 0, 0)


//////////////////////////////////////////////////////
// Type library ID and version

IMPLEMENT_OLETYPELIB(CCounterCtrl, _tlid, _wVerMajor,
   _wVerMinor)


//////////////////////////////////////////////////////
// Interface IDs

const IID BASED_CODE IID_DCounter =
        { 0xd41456c1, 0xe21f, 0x11cf, { 0xa7, 0xb2,
          0x44, 0x45, 0x53, 0x54, 0, 0 } };
const IID BASED_CODE IID_DCounterEvents =
        { 0xd41456c2, 0xe21f, 0x11cf, { 0xa7, 0xb2,
          0x44, 0x45, 0x53, 0x54, 0, 0 } };
```

```
//////////////////////////////////////////////////////////
// Control type information

static const DWORD BASED_CODE _dwCounterOleMisc =
    OLEMISC_ACTIVATEWHENVISIBLE |
    OLEMISC_SETCLIENTSITEFIRST |
    OLEMISC_INSIDEOUT |
    OLEMISC_CANTLINKINSIDE |
    OLEMISC_RECOMPOSEONRESIZE;

IMPLEMENT_OLECTLTYPE(CCounterCtrl, IDS_COUNTER, _dwCounterOleMisc)


//////////////////////////////////////////////////////////
// CCounterCtrl::CCounterCtrlFactory::UpdateRegistry -
// Adds or removes system registry entries

BOOL CCounterCtrl::CCounterCtrlFactory::UpdateRegistry(BOOL
  bRegister)
{
    if (bRegister)
        return AfxOleRegisterControlClass(
            AfxGetInstanceHandle(),
            m_clsid,
            m_lpszProgID,
            IDS_COUNTER,
            IDB_COUNTER,
            afxRegApartmentThreading,
            _dwCounterOleMisc,
            _tlid,
            _wVerMajor,
            _wVerMinor);
    else
        return AfxOleUnregisterClass(m_clsid,
          m_lpszProgID);
}


//////////////////////////////////////////////////////////
// CCounterCtrl::CCounterCtrl - Constructor

CCounterCtrl::CCounterCtrl()
{
    InitializeIIDs(&IID_DCounter, &IID_DCounterEvents);
    first=0;
    // Can't read count here because name isn't valid
}


//////////////////////////////////////////////////////////
// CCounterCtrl::~CCounterCtrl - Destructor

CCounterCtrl::~CCounterCtrl()
{
```

```
    // TODO: Clean up your control's instance data
    // here.
}


/////////////////////////////////////////////////////////
// CCounterCtrl::OnDraw - Drawing function

void CCounterCtrl::OnDraw(
            CDC* pdc, const CRect& rcBounds, const
                CRect& rcInvalid)
{
// cheapo hack to read count once after name is set up
if (first==0)
    {
    count=AfxGetApp()->GetProfileInt("Count",name,0);
    count++;
    AfxGetApp()->WriteProfileInt("Count",name,count);
    first=1;
    }

    COLORREF backcolor=TranslateColor(
    AmbientBackColor());
    CBrush br(backcolor);
    CString ctr;
    CRect r=rcBounds;
    ctr.Format("%d",count);
    pdc->SetBkColor(backcolor);
    pdc->FillRect(rcBounds,&br);
    pdc->DrawText(ctr,&r,
     DT_SINGLELINE|DT_VCENTER|DT_RIGHT);
}


/////////////////////////////////////////////////////////
// CCounterCtrl::DoPropExchange - Persistence support

void CCounterCtrl::DoPropExchange(CPropExchange* pPX)
{
    ExchangeVersion(pPX,
     MAKELONG(_wVerMinor, _wVerMajor));
    COleControl::DoPropExchange(pPX);
    PX_String(pPX,"ID",name,".DEFAULT");
}


/////////////////////////////////////////////////////////
// CCounterCtrl::OnResetState - Reset control

void CCounterCtrl::OnResetState()
{
// Resets defaults found in DoPropExchange    COleControl::OnResetState();
```

```
        // TODO: Reset any other control state here.
}


/////////////////////////////////////////////////////////
// CCounterCtrl::AboutBox - Display an "About" box

void CCounterCtrl::AboutBox()
{
    CDialog dlgAbout(IDD_ABOUTBOX_COUNTER);
    dlgAbout.DoModal();
}


/////////////////////////////////////////////////////////
// CCounterCtrl message handlers
```

With MFC, you can set a registry key to use for profile information by calling **SetRegistryKey** in the application object. However, this call is a private function. Therefore, you must modify the application object's **InitInstance** function to make this call (as shown in Listing 6.8). This is one of the few cases where you'll need to make changes in this file. Once you have this key set, you can use **ReadProfileInt** and **WriteProfileInt** to access the counter.

Listing 6.8 The Counter's main file.

```
// counter.cpp : Implementation of CCounterApp

#include "stdafx.h"
#include "counter.h"

#ifdef _DEBUG
#define new DEBUG_NEW
#undef THIS_FILE
static char THIS_FILE[] = __FILE__;
#endif


CCounterApp NEAR theApp;

const GUID CDECL BASED_CODE _tlid =
        { 0xd41456c0, 0xe21f, 0x11cf, { 0xa7, 0xb2,
            0x44, 0x45, 0x53, 0x54, 0, 0 } };
const WORD _wVerMajor = 1;
const WORD _wVerMinor = 0;


/////////////////////////////////////////////////////////
// CCounterApp::InitInstance - DLL initialization
```

```
BOOL CCounterApp::InitInstance()
{
    BOOL bInit = COleControlModule::InitInstance();
// Use our registry key for profile info!!!
    SetRegistryKey("AWC-Coriolis");

    if (bInit)
    {
    }

    return bInit;
}


/////////////////////////////////////////////////////////
// CCounterApp::ExitInstance - DLL termination

int CCounterApp::ExitInstance()
{
    // TODO: Add your own module termination code here.

    return COleControlModule::ExitInstance();
}


/////////////////////////////////////////////////////////
// DllRegisterServer - Adds entries to the registry

STDAPI DllRegisterServer(void)
{
    AFX_MANAGE_STATE(_afxModuleAddrThis);

    if (!AfxOleRegisterTypeLib(AfxGetInstanceHandle(),
            _tlid))
        return ResultFromScode(SELFREG_E_TYPELIB);

    if (!COleObjectFactoryEx::UpdateRegistryAll(TRUE))
        return ResultFromScode(SELFREG_E_CLASS);

    return NOERROR;
}


/////////////////////////////////////////////////////////
// DllUnregisterServer - Removes entries from registry

STDAPI DllUnregisterServer(void)
{
    AFX_MANAGE_STATE(_afxModuleAddrThis);

    if (!AfxOleUnregisterTypeLib(_tlid))
        return ResultFromScode(SELFREG_E_TYPELIB);
```

```
    if (!COleObjectFactoryEx::UpdateRegistryAll(FALSE))
        return ResultFromScode(SELFREG_E_CLASS);

    return NOERROR;
}
```

Each call that accesses the counter uses the **ID** property as an argument to the profile calls. This allows for separate counts for each counter. However, you must be careful not to access the count until the **ID** property is valid. That means you can't read and update the counter in the object's constructor (which, otherwise, would make sense).

There are several ways you can run this code. The counter control simply maintains a flag (**first**) that allows you to detect the first time the **OnDraw** function executes. On the very first invocation of **OnDraw**, the control reads the count, increments it, then stores it back into the registry.

The remaining portions of **OnDraw** are unremarkable. You simply format the count into a string and draw it into the rectangle defined by the control's window.

Once completed, the counter is ready to use. You can find an example HTML page that uses it in Listing 6.9. If you fail to supply an **ID** property, the control uses the value **.DEFAULT**.

Listing 6.9 Counter HTML.

```
<HTML>
<TITLE> Count Tester </TITLE>

You have accessed this page:
<OBJECT CLASSID=clsid:d41456c3-e21f-11CF-A7B2-444553540000 WIDTH=50 HEIGHT=10>
<PARAM NAME="ID" VALUE="Test001">
[Error! Counter object doesn't exist...]
</OBJECT> times

</HTML>
```

A Subclassed Control

Frequently, you'll want a control that works like an ordinary Windows control, but exposes functionality via ActiveX properties, events, and methods. Luckily, MFC makes this a simple task.

All MFC ActiveX controls derive from **COleControl,** which in turn derives from **CWnd**. **CWnd** is the class that represents all windows. Don't think of a **CWnd** object as an actual window, however. Instead, think of **CWnd** as a bottle that holds an ordinary Windows **HWND** (window handle).

When you create a **CWnd** (or a **CWnd**-derived class), it doesn't cause a window to spring into being on the screen. Instead, it just constructs an empty bottle. To actually fill the bottle up, you need to make an additional call (MFC pros call this two-phase construction).

The conventional way to create a window is to call **Create**. This call makes a new actual window and fills the **CWnd** bottle. As part of its work, **Create** calls the **CWnd**'s **PreCreateWindow** function. This function lets you change many parameters about the soon-to-be-created window. In particular, you can change the class name.

When you ask the Control Wizard to create a project based on an existing window class, it does five things:

1. As usual, it creates a derived **COleControl** object to represent your new control.
2. The wizard overrides the **PreCreateWindow** function and sets the class name of your control to correspond to the underlying window class you want to emulate. In this way, your C++ class has its own functions and variables, yet the actual Windows class is the control you want to subclass.
3. The wizard provides an **IsSubclassedControl** function that returns **TRUE**.
4. If the control sends you any notification messages, the wizard routes them to **OnOcmCommand** and writes a stub function for you.
5. In the **OnDraw** function, the wizard arranges to have the control paint itself by calling **DoSuperclassPaint**.

Then you can add properties, methods, and events as usual. You can see a simple example of this technique applied to the Windows progress bar in Listing 6.10 and Figure 6.15.

Listing 6.10 The ActiveX progress bar control.

```
// ProgressCtl.cpp

#include "stdafx.h"
#include "progress.h"
#include "ProgressCtl.h"
#include "ProgressPpg.h"
```

```cpp
#ifdef _DEBUG
#define new DEBUG_NEW
#undef THIS_FILE
static char THIS_FILE[] = __FILE__;
#endif


IMPLEMENT_DYNCREATE(CProgressCtrl, COleControl)


/////////////////////////////////////////////////////////
// Message map

BEGIN_MESSAGE_MAP(CProgressCtrl, COleControl)
    //{{AFX_MSG_MAP(CProgressCtrl)
    //}}AFX_MSG_MAP
    ON_MESSAGE(OCM_COMMAND, OnOcmCommand)
    ON_OLEVERB(AFX_IDS_VERB_PROPERTIES, OnProperties)
END_MESSAGE_MAP()


/////////////////////////////////////////////////////////
// Dispatch map

BEGIN_DISPATCH_MAP(CProgressCtrl, COleControl)
    //{{AFX_DISPATCH_MAP(CProgressCtrl)
    DISP_PROPERTY_NOTIFY(CProgressCtrl, "HI",
        m_hi, OnHILOChanged, VT_I2)
    DISP_PROPERTY_NOTIFY(CProgressCtrl, "LO",
        m_lo, OnHILOChanged, VT_I2)
     DISP_PROPERTY_NOTIFY(CProgressCtrl, "POS",
        m_pos, OnPOSChanged, VT_I2)
    DISP_FUNCTION(CProgressCtrl, "RESET", reset,
         VT_EMPTY, VTS_NONE)
    //}}AFX_DISPATCH_MAP
    DISP_FUNCTION_ID(CProgressCtrl, "AboutBox",
         DISPID_ABOUTBOX, AboutBox, VT_EMPTY, VTS_NONE)
END_DISPATCH_MAP()


/////////////////////////////////////////////////////////
// Event map

BEGIN_EVENT_MAP(CProgressCtrl, COleControl)
    //{{AFX_EVENT_MAP(CProgressCtrl)
    //}}AFX_EVENT_MAP
END_EVENT_MAP()


/////////////////////////////////////////////////////////
// Property pages

// TODO: Add more property pages as needed.
BEGIN_PROPPAGEIDS(CProgressCtrl, 1)
```

```cpp
        PROPPAGEID(CProgressPropPage::guid)
END_PROPPAGEIDS(CProgressCtrl)


///////////////////////////////////////////////////////
// Initialize class factory and guid

IMPLEMENT_OLECREATE_EX(CProgressCtrl,
 "PROGRESS.ProgressCtrl.1",
  0xd0fec723, 0xe866, 0x11cf, 0xa7, 0xb2, 0x44,
        0x45, 0x53, 0x54, 0, 0)


///////////////////////////////////////////////////////
// Type library ID and version

IMPLEMENT_OLETYPELIB(CProgressCtrl, _tlid, _
        wVerMajor, _wVerMinor)


///////////////////////////////////////////////////////
// Interface IDs

const IID BASED_CODE IID_DProgress =
        { 0xd0fec721, 0xe866, 0x11cf, { 0xa7, 0xb2,
        0x44, 0x45, 0x53, 0x54, 0, 0 } };
const IID BASED_CODE IID_DProgressEvents =
            { 0xd0fec722, 0xe866, 0x11cf, { 0xa7, 0xb2,
            0x44, 0x45, 0x53, 0x54, 0, 0 } };


///////////////////////////////////////////////////////
// Control type information

static const DWORD BASED_CODE _dwProgressOleMisc =
    OLEMISC_ACTIVATEWHENVISIBLE |
    OLEMISC_SETCLIENTSITEFIRST |
    OLEMISC_INSIDEOUT |
    OLEMISC_CANTLINKINSIDE |
    OLEMISC_RECOMPOSEONRESIZE;

IMPLEMENT_OLECTLTYPE(CProgressCtrl, IDS_PROGRESS, _dwProgressOleMisc)


///////////////////////////////////////////////////////
// CProgressCtrl::CProgressCtrlFactory::UpdateRegistry -

BOOL CProgressCtrl::CProgressCtrlFactory::UpdateRegistry(BOOL bRegister)
{
    if (bRegister)
        return AfxOleRegisterControlClass(
            AfxGetInstanceHandle(),
            m_clsid,
            m_lpszProgID,
```

```cpp
                IDS_PROGRESS,
                IDB_PROGRESS,
                afxRegApartmentThreading,
                _dwProgressOleMisc,
                _tlid,
                _wVerMajor,
                _wVerMinor);
    else
        return AfxOleUnregisterClass(m_clsid, m_lpszProgID);
}


/////////////////////////////////////////////////////////
CProgressCtrl::CProgressCtrl - Constructor

CProgressCtrl::CProgressCtrl()
{
    InitializeIIDs(&IID_DProgress, &IID_DProgressEvents);

    // TODO: Initialize your control's instance data
}


/////////////////////////////////////////////////////////
// CProgressCtrl::~CProgressCtrl - Destructor

CProgressCtrl::~CProgressCtrl()
{
    // TODO: Clean up your control's instance data here.
}


/////////////////////////////////////////////////////////
// CProgressCtrl::OnDraw - Drawing function

void CProgressCtrl::OnDraw(
            CDC* pdc, const CRect& rcBounds,
              const CRect& rcInvalid)
{
    DoSuperclassPaint(pdc, rcBounds);
}


/////////////////////////////////////////////////////////
// CProgressCtrl::DoPropExchange - Persistence support

void CProgressCtrl::DoPropExchange(CPropExchange* pPX)
{
    ExchangeVersion(pPX,
        MAKELONG(_wVerMinor, _wVerMajor));
    COleControl::DoPropExchange(pPX);

    // TODO: Call PX_ functions for each persistent
```

ActiveX Controls

```
    PX_Short(pPX,"HI",m_hi,100);
    PX_Short(pPX,"LO",m_lo,0);
    PX_Short(pPX,"POS",m_pos,0);
}


/////////////////////////////////////////////////////////
// CProgressCtrl::OnResetState - Reset control to
// default

void CProgressCtrl::OnResetState()
{
// Resets defaults found in DoPropExchange
// COleControl::OnResetState();

// TODO: Reset any other control state here.
}


/////////////////////////////////////////////////////////
// CProgressCtrl::AboutBox - Display an "About" box

void CProgressCtrl::AboutBox()
{
    CDialog dlgAbout(IDD_ABOUTBOX_PROGRESS);
    dlgAbout.DoModal();
}


/////////////////////////////////////////////////////////
// CProgressCtrl::PreCreateWindow - Modify class

BOOL CProgressCtrl::PreCreateWindow(CREATESTRUCT& cs)
{
// use progress bar class name
    cs.lpszClass = _T("msctls_progress32");
    return COleControl::PreCreateWindow(cs);
}


/////////////////////////////////////////////////////////
// CProgressCtrl::IsSubclassedControl - Yes!

BOOL CProgressCtrl::IsSubclassedControl()
{
    return TRUE;
}


/////////////////////////////////////////////////////////
// CProgressCtrl::OnOcmCommand - Handle command messages

LRESULT CProgressCtrl::OnOcmCommand(WPARAM wParam, LPARAM lParam)
{
```

```
#ifdef _WIN32
    WORD wNotifyCode = HIWORD(wParam);
#else
    WORD wNotifyCode = HIWORD(lParam);
#endif

    // TODO: Switch on wNotifyCode here.

    return 0;
}


/////////////////////////////////////////////////////////
// CProgressCtrl message handlers

void CProgressCtrl::OnHILOChanged()
{
// This control is derived from CWnd, but it really
// should be a CProgressCtrl, and we know this.
// On the other hand
// we can't permanently attach it since it is
// already attached
// Also, we can't treat it as a CProgressCtrl since
// this class might not have the same layout, so we
// have to treat the thing as an ordinary progress
// control, not an MFC one
SendMessage(PBM_SETRANGE,0,MAKELPARAM(m_lo,m_hi));
SetModifiedFlag();
}


void CProgressCtrl::OnPOSChanged()
{
    SendMessage(PBM_SETPOS,m_pos);

    SetModifiedFlag();
}
void CProgressCtrl::reset()
{
    SendMessage(PBM_SETPOS,0);
}
```

The progress bar exposes three properties (**HI**, **LO**, and **POS**). In addition, it exposes a single method (**RESET**) so that you can clear the control. Since the progress bar already supports these functions, you simply translate the ActiveX property change notifications (and method) into corresponding messages to the control.

There is only one problem. We *know* that the window is a certain type of control (a progress bar), and therefore it is tempting to try to represent it as

ActiveX Controls 243

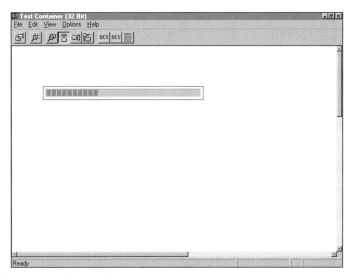

Figure 6.15 The progress bar in the Test Container.

a **CProgressCtrl** (the MFC class that allows you to work with progress bars). However, only the underlying window handle is a progress control. The C++ class is not. Since a **CWnd**-derived class already owns the window, you can't use **Attach**, **SubclassWindow**, or **FromHandle** to set it into a **CProgressCtrl**. Instead, the program directly sends window messages to the control as if it were an ordinary control and not an MFC window.

Subclassing A Custom Control

Although the Control Wizard will help you subclass built-in Windows controls, it doesn't help you with any custom controls you may have. You can only select the built-in controls from the list.

In fact, any ordinary Windows control can become an ActiveX control via subclassing. The only requirement is that the control must be able to paint itself to an arbitrary device context—and there was even an undocumented feature in many Windows controls that allowed for this. If you send an ordinary control a **WM_PAINT** message, but set the **wParam** parameter to an **HDC**, the control would paint to that device context instead of using the usual **BeginPaint** call to obtain an **HDC**.

This feature wasn't officially documented anywhere (although several MFC samples relied on this fact). With Windows 95, however, there is an official way to ask a control to paint to a specific device context. This is the **WM_PRINT** message. **WM_PRINT** takes the **HDC** in its **wParam** argument and a function code in the **lParam** argument. In either case, MFC needs a way to force the control to paint to a metafile. This metafile becomes the presentation for the subclassed control when it is in the inactive state.

If you need to work with a custom control, you'll have to make sure it supports these painting features. If not, you may have to do a lot of work to draw the control. If you have the source code for the control, it may be a very simple modification to make the control aware of this protocol. For example, suppose your control's source code had a section of code that looked like this:

```
case WM_PAINT:
    dc=BeginPaint(hWnd,&ps);
         .
         .
         .
    EndPaint(hWnd,&ps);
```

It would be simple to change it to look like this:

```
case WM_PAINT:
case WM_PRINT:
    if (!wParam)
        dc=BeginPaint(hWnd,&ps);
    else
        dc=(HDC)wParam;
         .
         .
         .
    if (!wParam)
        EndPaint(hWnd,&ps);
```

Note that although this example doesn't provide a full implementation of the **WM_PRINT** message, it is adequate, at least for creating an ActiveX control. Also, this code assumes you don't use any of the information out of the **PAINTSTRUCT** (like the rectangle to redraw), which is often the case. If it isn't, you'll have to come up with suitable fake values for the **PAINTSTRUCT** when **wParam** is not **NULL**. Usually, this means using the client rectangle for the bounding box and appropriate defaults for the flags.

A Custom Control

Listing 6.11 shows a simple control that is written in C. This control creates a countdown timer not unlike the one you see on movie reels (you know,

ActiveX Controls 245

that stuff we used back before video tape). The DLL registers a custom window class, and that class implements the countdown timer. Notice that the timer may not be accurate in certain situations. If the system is slow, the timer will countdown every time it receives a **WM_TIMER** message. This may cause the timer to count more slowly than is accurate, but it does allow the user to see the entire time elapse.

Listing 6.11 The Custom control.

```
#include <windows.h>
#include <stdlib.h>
#include "tcontrol.h"

HANDLE hInst;

// Dummy function allows callers to link with DLL
__declspec(dllexport) void FAR PASCAL TControl_Init(void)
  {
  }

LONG FAR PASCAL ControlProc(HWND w,UINT cmd,
  WPARAM wParam,LPARAM lParam)
  {
  switch (cmd)
    {
    case WM_PAINT:
     case WM_PRINT:
       {
       RECT r,rct;
        int x,y;
       int tick,amt;
       char tmp[5];
       HDC dc;
       HBRUSH br,old,back;
       PAINTSTRUCT ps;
       if (!wParam)
            dc=BeginPaint(w,&ps);
        else
            {
            dc=(HDC)wParam;
            SaveDC(dc);
            }
       br=CreateSolidBrush(RGB(0xFF,0,0));
        back=CreateSolidBrush(GetWindowLong(w,BACK));
       SetMapMode(dc,MM_ISOTROPIC);
       GetClientRect(w,&r);
       SetWindowExtEx(dc,20,20,NULL);
       SetViewportExtEx(dc,r.right,r.bottom,NULL);
       tick=GetWindowLong(w,TICK);
       amt=GetWindowLong(w,TIMELEFT);
        old=SelectObject(dc,back);
        PatBlt(dc,0,0,20,20,PATCOPY);
```

```
       if (tick!=8) Ellipse(dc,0,0,20,20);
       /* Select new brush */
       SelectObject(dc,br);
       switch (tick)
           {
           case 0:
              x=10;
              y=0;
              break;
           case 1:
              x=15;
              y=2;
              break;
           case 2:
              x=20;
              y=10;
              break;
           case 3:
              x=15;
              y=18;
              break;
           case 4:
              x=10;
              y=20;
              break;
           case 5:
              x=5;
              y=18;
              break;
           case 6:
              x=0;
              y=10;
              break;
           case 7:
              x=5;
              y=2;
              break;
           }

      if (tick==8)
          Ellipse(dc,0,0,20,20);
      else
         if (!Pie(dc,0,0,20,20,x,y,10,0))
             MessageBeep((UINT)-1);
       SelectObject(dc,old);
      DeleteObject(br);
       DeleteObject(back);

/* Write text */
      rct.top=rct.left=0;
      rct.right=rct.bottom=20;
      itoa(amt,tmp,10);
      SetBkMode(dc,TRANSPARENT);
      DrawText(dc,
```

```
              tmp,-1,&rct,
              DT_CENTER|DT_VCENTER|DT_SINGLELINE);
          if (!wParam)
              EndPaint(w,&ps);
           else
              RestoreDC(dc,-1);
          return 0;
          }

      case WM_TIMER:
        {
        int tick,amt;
        HWND parent=GetParent(w);
        tick=GetWindowLong(w,TICK);
        if (++tick==9)
          {
          tick=0;
          amt=GetWindowLong(w,TIMELEFT);
          SetWindowLong(w,TIMELEFT,-amt);
          PostMessage(parent,WM_COMMAND,
              MAKELONG(0,TC_TICK),amt);
          if (!amt)
            {
            KillTimer(w,1);
            }
          }
        SetWindowLong(w,TICK,tick);
        InvalidateRect(w,NULL,FALSE);
        return 0;
        }

      case TC_SET:
        SetWindowLong(w,TIMELEFT,wParam);
        SetWindowLong(w,TICK,0);
        InvalidateRect(w,NULL,FALSE);
        return 0;

      case TC_GETTIME:
        return GetWindowLong(w,TIMELEFT);

      case TC_GO:
        if (wParam)
          SetTimer(w,1,125,NULL); /* 1/8th second */
        else
          KillTimer(w,1);
        return 0;
      }
    return DefWindowProc(w,cmd,wParam,lParam);
    }

BOOL WINAPI DllMain(HANDLE _hInst,ULONG reason,LPVOID na)
    {
    WNDCLASS wc;
    if (reason==DLL_PROCESS_ATTACH)
```

```
    {
    hInst=_hInst;
    wc.lpszClassName=TIMECTRL;
    wc.hInstance=hInst;
    wc.style=CS_GLOBALCLASS;
    wc.lpfnWndProc=ControlProc;
    wc.hbrBackground=(HBRUSH)(COLOR_WINDOW+1);
    wc.hCursor=LoadCursor(NULL,IDC_ARROW);
    wc.hIcon=NULL;
    wc.lpszMenuName=NULL;
    wc.cbClsExtra=0;
    wc.cbWndExtra=12;
    if (!RegisterClass(&wc)) return FALSE;
    }
  if (reason==DLL_PROCESS_DETACH)
    UnregisterClass(TIMECTRL,hInst);
  return TRUE;
  }
```

The protocol for using the timer is a combination of Windows messages and window extra words. When you register a window class, you can reserve a number of extra words that act like per-window variables. Other programs can access these words by specifying an offset. What these words are for is strictly up to the window. Programs that want to manipulate the timer, have to place values in these extra words and send messages.

You'll find several messages and constant extra word offsets in Listing 6.12. In addition to the messages, you can set the control's background color by manipulating its extra window words starting at offset 8. The **DWORD** at this address sets the color in the usual RGB format. You can use **SetWindowLong** and **GetWindowLong** to read or change the value.

Listing 6.12   The TCONTROL header file.

```
#define TIMECTRL  "TimeCtrl"
#define TC_SET (WM_USER)
#define TC_GO (WM_USER+1)
#define TC_TICK (WM_USER+2)
#define TC_GETTIME (WM_USER+3)

#define TIMELEFT 0
#define TICK  4
#define BACK  8

__declspec(dllimport) void FAR PASCAL TControl_Init(void);
```

When you want to set the timer to a specific number of seconds, use the **TC_SET** message (place the number of seconds in **wParam**). The

TC_GETTIME message returns the current number of seconds. To start or stop the timer, send a **TC_GO** message. If the **wParam** parameter is 1, the timer starts. If it is 0, the timer stops.

When each second elapses (which may not be a true second), the timer sends a **WM_CONTROL** message with the **TC_TICK** notification code in the high part of **wParam**. The current time count is in **lParam**. When the count reaches zero, the period is complete and the timer automatically stops.

To use the control in an ordinary C or C++ program, you can load its DLL using the **LoadLibrary** call. Alternately, you can link with the corresponding **IMPLIB**. The dummy function **TControl_Init** provides you with a function to call so the linker will include the DLLfi you elect to use the latter method.

You'll notice in the source code that this control properly handles **WM_PAINT** and **WM_PRINT**. However, if it didn't (and, in fact, it originally did not), it would be simple to change the code.

So that's how you can use this control from an ordinary program. How can you use it with the Web browser (or Visual Basic for that matter)? Just as we subclassed the progress bar control, we might just as well subclass this control and convert it into an ActiveX component.

Subclassing The Control

Although Control Wizard won't allow us to subclass a custom control directly, we can ask it to subclass a standard control and make changes. I usually choose to subclass from a **STATIC** on the theory that this should be innocuous, but it doesn't seem to make any real difference. There are 9 Steps you'll need to take after you generate a standard subclassed control:

1. Add the TCONTROL.H file to the control's CPP file
2. Find the name of the subclass in the **PreCreateWindow** method and change it to reflect the custom control's name
3. Load the library (or make the dummy call to load the library) in the application's **InitInstance** member
4. Add properties (use Class Wizard)
5. Add **PX_** functions to implement persistent properties
6. Add methods (use Class Wizard)

7. Add events (use Class Wizard)
8. Add message map entries and message functions to fire events
9. Modify the property page

For this control, I decided to implement a **Count** property that corresponds to the current count, **Go** and **Stop** methods, and a **Tick** event that fires with the **TC_TICK** message. The results are shown in Listing 6.13.

Listing 6.13 The Subclassed control.

```cpp
// CountdnCtl.cpp

#include "stdafx.h"
#include "countdn.h"
#include "CountdnCtl.h"
#include "CountdnPpg.h"
#include "tcontrol.h"

#ifdef _DEBUG
#define new DEBUG_NEW
#undef THIS_FILE
static char THIS_FILE[] = __FILE__;
#endif


IMPLEMENT_DYNCREATE(CCountdnCtrl, COleControl)


/////////////////////////////////////////////////////////
// Message map

BEGIN_MESSAGE_MAP(CCountdnCtrl, COleControl)
    //{{AFX_MSG_MAP(CCountdnCtrl)
    ON_WM_CREATE()
    //}}AFX_MSG_MAP
// Handle reflected command message
    ON_MESSAGE(OCM_COMMAND, OnOcmCommand)
    ON_OLEVERB(AFX_IDS_VERB_PROPERTIES, OnProperties)
END_MESSAGE_MAP()


/////////////////////////////////////////////////////////
// Dispatch map

BEGIN_DISPATCH_MAP(CCountdnCtrl, COleControl)
    //{{AFX_DISPATCH_MAP(CCountdnCtrl)
    DISP_PROPERTY_NOTIFY(CCountdnCtrl, "Count",
        m_count, OnCountChanged, VT_I4)
    DISP_FUNCTION(CCountdnCtrl, "Go", Go,
        VT_EMPTY, VTS_NONE)
    DISP_FUNCTION(CCountdnCtrl, "Stop", Stop,
        VT_EMPTY, VTS_NONE)
```

ActiveX Controls

```
        //}}AFX_DISPATCH_MAP
        DISP_FUNCTION_ID(CCountdnCtrl, "AboutBox", DISPID_ABOUTBOX, AboutBox,
        VT_EMPTY, VTS_NONE)
END_DISPATCH_MAP()


/////////////////////////////////////////////////////////
// Event map

BEGIN_EVENT_MAP(CCountdnCtrl, COleControl)
        //{{AFX_EVENT_MAP(CCountdnCtrl)
        EVENT_CUSTOM("Tick", FireTick, VTS_I4)
        //}}AFX_EVENT_MAP
END_EVENT_MAP()


/////////////////////////////////////////////////////////
// Property pages

BEGIN_PROPPAGEIDS(CCountdnCtrl, 1)
        PROPPAGEID(CCountdnPropPage::guid)
END_PROPPAGEIDS(CCountdnCtrl)


/////////////////////////////////////////////////////////
// Initialize class factory and guid

IMPLEMENT_OLECREATE_EX(CCountdnCtrl, "COUNTDN.CountdnCtrl.1",
        0xa7e2a563, 0xe914, 0x11cf, 0xa7, 0xb2, 0x44, 0x45, 0x53, 0x54, 0, 0)


/////////////////////////////////////////////////////////
// Type library ID and version

IMPLEMENT_OLETYPELIB(CCountdnCtrl, _tlid, _
        _wVerMajor, _wVerMinor)


/////////////////////////////////////////////////////////
// Interface IDs

const IID BASED_CODE IID_DCountdn =
        { 0xa7e2a561, 0xe914, 0x11cf, { 0xa7, 0xb2,
        0x44, 0x45, 0x53, 0x54, 0, 0 } };
const IID BASED_CODE IID_DCountdnEvents =
        { 0xa7e2a562, 0xe914, 0x11cf, { 0xa7, 0xb2,
        0x44, 0x45, 0x53, 0x54, 0, 0 } };


/////////////////////////////////////////////////////////
// Control type information

static const DWORD BASED_CODE _dwCountdnOleMisc =
        OLEMISC_ACTIVATEWHENVISIBLE |
```

```
            OLEMISC_SETCLIENTSITEFIRST |
            OLEMISC_INSIDEOUT |
            OLEMISC_CANTLINKINSIDE |
            OLEMISC_RECOMPOSEONRESIZE;

IMPLEMENT_OLECTLTYPE(CCountdnCtrl, IDS_COUNTDN, _dwCountdnOleMisc)


/////////////////////////////////////////////////////////
// CCountdnCtrl::CCountdnCtrlFactory::UpdateRegistry -
// Adds or removes system registry entries

BOOL CCountdnCtrl::CCountdnCtrlFactory::UpdateRegistry(
        BOOL bRegister)
{
    if (bRegister)
        return AfxOleRegisterControlClass(
            AfxGetInstanceHandle(),
            m_clsid,
            m_lpszProgID,
            IDS_COUNTDN,
            IDB_COUNTDN,
            afxRegApartmentThreading,
            _dwCountdnOleMisc,
            _tlid,
            _wVerMajor,
            _wVerMinor);
    else
        return AfxOleUnregisterClass(
                m_clsid, m_lpszProgID);
}


/////////////////////////////////////////////////////////
// CCountdnCtrl::CCountdnCtrl - Constructor

CCountdnCtrl::CCountdnCtrl()
{
    InitializeIIDs(&IID_DCountdn, &IID_DCountdnEvents);

}


/////////////////////////////////////////////////////////
// CCountdnCtrl::~CCountdnCtrl - Destructor

CCountdnCtrl::~CCountdnCtrl()
{
    // TODO: Clean up your control's instance data
    // here.
}


/////////////////////////////////////////////////////////
```

```
// CCountdnCtrl::OnDraw - Drawing function

void CCountdnCtrl::OnDraw(
            CDC* pdc, const CRect& rcBounds,
                const CRect& rcInvalid)
{
    DoSuperclassPaint(pdc, rcBounds);
}


/////////////////////////////////////////////////////////
// CCountdnCtrl::DoPropExchange - Persistence support

void CCountdnCtrl::DoPropExchange(CPropExchange* pPX)
{
    ExchangeVersion(pPX,
        MAKELONG(_wVerMinor, _wVerMajor));
    COleControl::DoPropExchange(pPX);
    PX_Long(pPX,"Count",m_count,60);
}


/////////////////////////////////////////////////////////
// CCountdnCtrl::OnResetState - Reset control

void CCountdnCtrl::OnResetState()
{
// Resets defaults found in DoPropExchange
COleControl::OnResetState();
}


/////////////////////////////////////////////////////////
// CCountdnCtrl::AboutBox - Display an "About" box

void CCountdnCtrl::AboutBox()
{
    CDialog dlgAbout(IDD_ABOUTBOX_COUNTDN);
    dlgAbout.DoModal();
}


/////////////////////////////////////////////////////////
// CCountdnCtrl::PreCreateWindow - Modify parameters

BOOL CCountdnCtrl::PreCreateWindow(CREATESTRUCT& cs)
{
    cs.lpszClass = _T(TIMECTRL);
    return COleControl::PreCreateWindow(cs);
}


/////////////////////////////////////////////////////////
// CCountdnCtrl::IsSubclassedControl - Yes!
```

```
BOOL CCountdnCtrl::IsSubclassedControl()
{
    return TRUE;
}


/////////////////////////////////////////////////////////
// CCountdnCtrl::OnOcmCommand - Handle command messages

LRESULT CCountdnCtrl::OnOcmCommand(WPARAM wParam,
      LPARAM lParam)
{
#ifdef _WIN32
    WORD wNotifyCode = HIWORD(wParam);
#else
    WORD wNotifyCode = HIWORD(lParam);
#endif

    if (wNotifyCode==TC_TICK) OnTick(lParam);

    return 0;
}


/////////////////////////////////////////////////////////
// CCountdnCtrl message handlers


void CCountdnCtrl::Go()
{
    SendMessage(TC_GO,1);
}

void CCountdnCtrl::OnTick(long ct)
{
   m_count=ct;
   FireTick(ct);
}

void CCountdnCtrl::Stop()
{
    SendMessage(TC_GO); // wParam==0 so stop

}

void CCountdnCtrl::OnCountChanged()
{
    SendMessage(TC_SET,m_count);
    InvalidateControl();
}

int CCountdnCtrl::OnCreate(LPCREATESTRUCT lpCreateStruct)
{
```

```
        if (COleControl::OnCreate(lpCreateStruct) == -1)
            return -1;
    ::SetWindowLong(m_hWnd,BACK,
            TranslateColor(AmbientBackColor()));
    SendMessage(TC_SET,m_count);

    return 0;
}

void CCountdnCtrl::OnAmbientPropertyChange(DISPID)
{
// background may have changed, so
  ::SetWindowLong(m_hWnd,BACK,
      TranslateColor(AmbientBackColor()));
  InvalidateControl();
}
```

There are two major twists to subclassing a control like this. First, the window is not created until the first **OnDraw**. That means you can't do anything that requires a window handle (for example, send messages) until after that point.

The other issue is that the **TC_TICK** notification goes to the control's parent window, not the control itself. This poses a problem since you need to handle the **TC_TICK** notification in the **COleControl**-derived class that represents the control, not in some class that represents the parent window.

Luckily, the solutions to these problems are straightforward. You must refrain from sending messages or otherwise manipulating the window during **DoPropExchange**, **OnResetState**, or any other place where the window may not be valid. Instead, remember the state of the control, and initialize it during **WM_CREATE** processing. You can use Class Wizard to handle **WM_CREATE**. Naturally, when **WM_CREATE** occurs, the window will be valid.

The notification problem is even simpler. MFC arranges to reflect certain messages (including **WM_COMMAND**) from the parent window to the control window. When the parent window receives a **WM_COMMAND**, it reflects an **OCM_COMMAND** message to the control. You can handle this with an **ON_MESSAGE** message map entry (although Class Wizard will not make it for you). The Control Wizard automatically sets this up for you in the case of **WM_COMMAND**.

There are several other messages that MFC reflects (as shown in Table 6.24). You can handle these using **ON_MESSAGE** the same way the example handles **OCM_COMMAND**.

Table 6.24 Window message reflection.

Message to Parent	Reflected Control Message	Notes
WM_COMMAND	OCM_COMMAND	
WM_CTLCOLOR	OCM_CTLCOLOR	MFC reflects this for all Win32 CTL COLOR messages
WM_DRAWITEM	OCM_DRAWITEM	
WM_MEASUREITEM	OCM_MEASUREITEM	
WM_DELETEITEM	OCM_DELETEITEM	
WM_VKEYTOITEM	OCM_VKEYTOITEM	
WM_CHARTOITEM	OCM_CHARTOITEM	
WM_COMPAREITEM	OCM_COMPAREITEM	
WM_HSCROLL	OCM_HSCROLL	
WM_VSCROLL	OCM_VSCROLL	
WM_NOTIFY	OCM_NOTIFY	
WM_PARENTNOTIFY	OCM_PARENTNOTIFY	

The **Count** property requires special handling since the window is not valid until the first paint operation occurs. The special variable **m_count** holds a local counter that the control object maintains in the usual way. Then, during **WM_CREATE** processing, the code sends the **TC_SET** message to the control to synchronize the control object's property with the real value in the custom control.

Using The Control

Once the control is working, it operates like any other ActiveX control (as shown in Figure 6.16). If you plan on shipping a subclassed control, however, be aware that you have to ship both the control and the DLL that contains the original control. This assumes you have the right to distribute that DLL, of course.

When you install your files on a different machine, you must be sure that the custom control's DLL resides where the ActiveX control can find it. The standard SYSTEM directory is often a good choice. Without access to the base control's DLL, any attempts to use the ActiveX control will fail.

ActiveX Controls 257

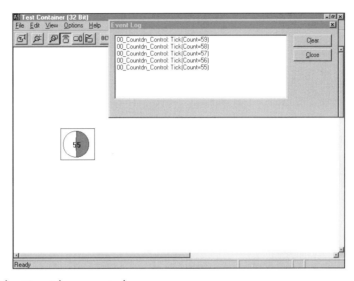

Figure 6.16 The Countdown control.

Summary

From an efficiency standpoint, it is desirable to use as few interfaces as possible when constructing ActiveX Internet controls. However, if you add many interfaces, you may find it easier to go ahead and use a class library like MFC. Of course, if you want to use MFC in your control, you'll be taking the overhead penalty anyway, so you might just as well use MFC in the first place.

A classic ActiveX control is no different from the ActiveX components you wrote in earlier chapters, they just have more interfaces with a complex protocol. While it is a lot of work to write these by hand, it is possible.

Either way you go, understanding the complex protocol that ActiveX containers expect of controls will pay off. Knowing these details will help you design better and more efficient controls, and debugging will usually be easier, as well.

Like many programming tasks, ActiveX controls can be as simple or as complex as you like depending on how much control you are willing to turn over to a tool kit. If you use MFC, programming an ActiveX control is almost trivial. If you don't use MFC, it isn't difficult, but the sheer number of interfaces can make it tedious.

There are still a few other issues surrounding Internet awareness and efficiency, which will be the topic of Chapter 7. However, even without these enhancements, you can put controls on the Net.

PART 3

ActiveXing The Internet

ActiveX And The Internet 261

Other Interface Building
    Techniques 315

The End? 343

7
ActiveX And The Internet

O Brave new world that has such people in't!
—The Tempest

IF YOU HAVE ANY FAMILIARITY with OCX controls, you might wonder what all the fuss is about when it comes to ActiveX. Well, as radio personality Paul Harvey says, here's the *rest* of the story.

It is true that ActiveX controls and OCX controls have a lot in common. However, there are several new additions to the standard for controls that allow them to work better—or at least faster—on the Internet.

You've already seen that an official ActiveX control only needs to expose **IUnknown** and support self-registration. That's a big difference from traditional controls, which had to support all of the control interfaces, even if they didn't specifically use them. That means, however, that containers have to query for each interface they want to use and do something appropriate if that interface does not exist.

ActiveX also has protocols to allow asynchronous data transfer, the referencing of URLs via monikers, and digital signatures to authenticated code. Controls destined for the Internet will probably want to avail themselves of these new technologies.

The final way that ActiveX accommodates the Internet is with the Internet Control Pack (ICP). ICP is a set of ActiveX controls that you can use to simplify many Internet programming chores. Need to do an FTP file transfer? You can use an ActiveX control from the ICP. Want to read a Web page (or display it)? You can use another control from the ICP. Since these are ActiveX controls, you can put them anywhere, including in Visual Basic, C++, or Delphi programs. You'll find a list of the ICP components in Table 7.1. You can also download the ICP from Microsoft's Web site at **www.microsoft.com**.

Another important ActiveX control is the **MSHTML** control. This single control encapsulates all of the features of Microsoft's Internet Explorer. In fact, Internet Explorer is really nothing more than a simple container for the **MSHTML** control. Imagine what that means: If you want a full-featured Web browser in your program, you can just drop the **MSHTML** control into your program. This is the kind of power that ActiveX brings to programs—the power to reuse complete functional blocks, even if they happen to be the entire Internet Explorer!

Currently the ICP contains an HTML control that isn't as powerful as the **IExplorer** control, however it is simple to use. Listing 7.1 contains an ActiveX program that uses the HTML control (as shown in Figure 7.1). This

Table 7.1 ICP components.

Component	Function
FTP	Transfer files using FTP
HTML	Display HTML documents (including Web pages)
HTTP	Retrieve documents from the network using the HTTP protocol
NNTP	Retrieve and post news articles
POP3	Receive mail using a POP server
SMTP	Send mail using SMTP
TCP	Create or connect to a reliable socket to exchange data
UDP	Create or connect to an unreliable (datagram) socket to exchange data

ActiveX And The Internet 263

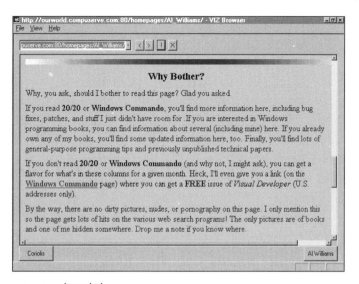

Figure 7.1 A customized Web browser.

program is a good introduction to writing a large-scale ActiveX container using MFC. You can find out more about the HTML control in Table 7.2.

Listing 7.1 A specialized Web browser.

```
// vizbrowzView.cpp : Implementation
//

#include "stdafx.h"
#include "vizbrowz.h"

#include "vizbrowzDoc.h"
#include "vizbrowzView.h"
#include "mainfrm.h"
#ifdef _DEBUG
#define new DEBUG_NEW
#undef THIS_FILE
static char THIS_FILE[] = __FILE__;
#endif

/////////////////////////////////////////////////////
// CVizbrowzView

IMPLEMENT_DYNCREATE(CVizbrowzView, CFormView)

BEGIN_MESSAGE_MAP(CVizbrowzView, CFormView)
        //{{AFX_MSG_MAP(CVizbrowzView)
        ON_BN_CLICKED(IDC_LOAD, OnLoad)
        ON_BN_CLICKED(IDC_FORWARD, OnForward)
        ON_BN_CLICKED(IDC_BACK, OnBack)
```

```
                        ON_CBN_SELCHANGE(IDC_HISTORY,
                        OnSelchangeHistory)
            ON_BN_CLICKED(IDC_STOP, OnStop)
            ON_WM_SIZE()
            ON_COMMAND(ID_LOAD, OnLoad)
            ON_COMMAND(ID_BACK, OnBack)
            ON_COMMAND(ID_FORWARD, OnForward)
            ON_BN_CLICKED(IDC_AAW, OnAaw)
            ON_BN_CLICKED(IDC_CORIOLIS, OnCoriolis)
            //}}AFX_MSG_MAP
END_MESSAGE_MAP()

/////////////////////////////////////////////////////
// CVizbrowzView construction/destruction

CVizbrowzView::CVizbrowzView()
            : CFormView(CVizbrowzView::IDD)
{
            //{{AFX_DATA_INIT(CVizbrowzView)
            url = _T("");
            //}}AFX_DATA_INIT
            // TODO: Add construction code here

}

CVizbrowzView::~CVizbrowzView()
{
}

void CVizbrowzView::DoDataExchange(CDataExchange* pDX)
{
            CFormView::DoDataExchange(pDX);
            //{{AFX_DATA_MAP(CVizbrowzView)
            DDX_Control(pDX, IDC_HISTORY, history);
            DDX_CBString(pDX, IDC_HISTORY, url);
            DDX_Control(pDX, IDC_HTML, html);
            //}}AFX_DATA_MAP
}

BOOL CVizbrowzView::PreCreateWindow(CREATESTRUCT& cs)
{
            return CFormView::PreCreateWindow(cs);
}

/////////////////////////////////////////////////////
// CVizbrowzView diagnostics

#ifdef _DEBUG
void CVizbrowzView::AssertValid() const
{
            CFormView::AssertValid();
}

void CVizbrowzView::Dump(CDumpContext& dc) const
```

```
{
          CFormView::Dump(dc);
}

// Non-debug version is inline CVizbrowzDoc* CVizbrowzView::GetDocument()
{
          ASSERT(m_pDocument->
          IsKindOf(RUNTIME_CLASS(CVizbrowzDoc)));
          return (CVizbrowzDoc*)m_pDocument;
}
#endif //_DEBUG

/////////////////////////////////////////////////////
// CVizbrowzView message handlers



void CVizbrowzView::OnLoad()
{
  int n;
  UpdateData(TRUE);
  n=history.GetCurSel();
  if (n==-1)
     {
     n=history.InsertString(-1,url);
     history.SetCurSel(n);
     }
  html.RequestDoc(url);
}

void CVizbrowzView::OnForward()
{
   int n=history.GetCurSel();
   if (n!=CB_ERR&&n!=history.GetCount()-1)
      {
      history.SetCurSel(++n);
      UpdateData(TRUE);
      html.RequestDoc(url);
      }
   ResetDefButton(IDC_FORWARD);
   }

void CVizbrowzView::OnBack()
{

   int n=history.GetCurSel();
   if (n!=CB_ERR&&n!=0)
      {
      history.SetCurSel(-n);
      UpdateData(TRUE);
      html.RequestDoc(url);
      }
   ResetDefButton(IDC_BACK);
```

```
    }
void CVizbrowzView::OnSelchangeHistory()
{
   UpdateData(TRUE);
   html.RequestDoc(url);
}

BEGIN_EVENTSINK_MAP(CVizbrowzView, CFormView)
    //{{AFX_EVENTSINK_MAP(CVizbrowzView)
        ON_EVENT(CVizbrowzView, IDC_HTML,
      4 /* BeginRetrieval */, OnBeginRetrieval, VTS_NONE)
        ON_EVENT(CVizbrowzView, IDC_HTML,
      -608 /* Error */, OnError, VTS_I2 VTS_PBSTR VTS_I4
      VTS_BSTR VTS_BSTR VTS_I4 VTS_PBOOL)
        ON_EVENT(CVizbrowzView, IDC_HTML,
      6 /* EndRetrieval */, OnEndRetrieval, VTS_NONE)
        //}}AFX_EVENTSINK_MAP
END_EVENTSINK_MAP()

void CVizbrowzView::OnBeginRetrieval()
{
        CString s=html.GetUrl(),msg;
   CMainFrame *frm=(CMainFrame *)AfxGetMainWnd();
   UpdateData(TRUE);
   msg="Loading ";
   msg+=s;
   msg+="...";
   frm->SetStatusMsg(msg);
   GetDocument()->SetTitle(s);   // Change frame title
   if (s!=url)
      {
      int n=history.InsertString(-1,s);
      history.SetCurSel(n);
      }
}

void CVizbrowzView::OnError(short Number,
   BSTR FAR* Description, long Scode, LPCTSTR Source,
   LPCTSTR HelpFile, long HelpContext,
   BOOL FAR* CancelDisplay)
{
   CString errmsg;
   errmsg=*Description;
   MessageBox(errmsg,"Error!");
}

void CVizbrowzView::OnEndRetrieval()
{
   CString empty;
   CMainFrame *frm=(CMainFrame *)AfxGetMainWnd();
   frm->SetStatusMsg(empty);
}

void CVizbrowzView::OnStop()
```

```
{
   VARIANT msg;
   msg.vt=VT_NULL;
   html.Cancel(msg);
}

void CVizbrowzView::OnSize(UINT nType, int cx, int cy)
{
         CFormView::OnSize(nType, cx, cy);
         // Relocate and resize control
   CRect offset;
   if (IsWindow(history.m_hWnd))
      {
      history.GetWindowRect(&offset);
      // Convert to client coords
      ScreenToClient(&offset.TopLeft());
      ScreenToClient(&offset.BottomRight());
      CWnd *b1=GetDlgItem(IDC_CORIOLIS);
      CWnd *b2=GetDlgItem(IDC_AAW);
      CRect brect;
      b1->GetWindowRect(&brect);
      b1->MoveWindow(offset.left,
        cy-brect.Height(),brect.Width(),brect.Height());
      b2->MoveWindow((cx-offset.left)-brect.Width(),
        cy-brect.Height(),brect.Width(),brect.Height());
      html.MoveWindow(offset.left,offset.bottom+5,
        cx-2*offset.left,
        cy-offset.Height()-brect.Height()-15);
      html.UpdateWindow();
      }
}

void CVizbrowzView::OnInitialUpdate()
{
         CFormView::OnInitialUpdate();
         CRect r;
   GetWindowRect(&r);
   // Force an inital resize now that
   // controls are ready
   MoveWindow(r.left,r.top,r.right,r.bottom);
   // Set init URL
   CString initurl;
   initurl.LoadString(IDS_URL);
   html.RequestDoc(initurl);
}

void CVizbrowzView::OnAaw()
{
html.RequestDoc(
 "http:// ourworld.compuserve.com/homepages/Al_Williams");
ResetDefButton(IDC_AAW);
}

void CVizbrowzView::OnCoriolis()
```

```
{
html.RequestDoc("http://www.coriolis.com");
ResetDefButton(IDC_CORIOLIS);
}

void CVizbrowzView::ResetDefButton(UINT id)
{
// Reset default button so enter always loads
    SendMessage(DM_SETDEFID,IDC_LOAD);
        GetDlgItem(IDC_LOAD)->SetFocus();
    ((CButton *)GetDlgItem(id))->
        SetButtonStyle(BS_PUSHBUTTON);
}
```

Building The Browser

To start the browser, run App Wizard and select the icon for a normal MFC program. Make sure to select the OLE Controls check box during Step 3 (as shown in Figure 7.2). For this particular program, you'll also want to make sure that the view class derives from **CFormView** (as shown in Figure 7.3). You can find out more about **CFormView**-based programs in the section later in the chapter, titled *About CFormView*.

Using an ActiveX control on a dialog is very simple, and therefore it is also simple in a form view-based program. The first step is to add the ActiveX control to your project, which you can accomplish using Component Gallery (as shown in Figure 7.4). Select the *OCX Control* tab, click on the HTML control, then click the *Insert* button. Of course, you have to have the Internet Control Pack from Microsoft installed first.

The Component Gallery does an amazing amount of work at this point: It adds a class wrapper for the HTML control (the **CHTML** class, as shown in Listings 7.2 and 7.3) to your project. This class provides C++ functions for all the properties and methods that the ActiveX control provides. It also arranges for Class Wizard to understand the control's events.

ActiveX And The Internet 269

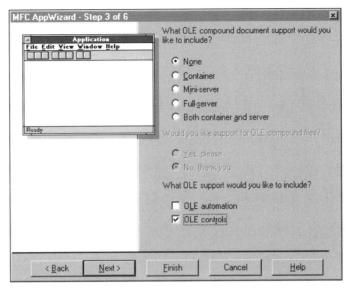

Figure 7.2 Selecting OLE control support.

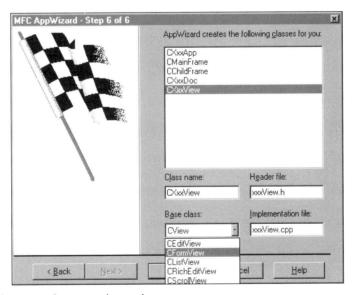

Figure 7.3 Changing the view's base class.

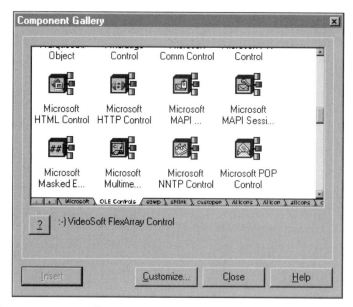

Figure 7.4 The Component gallery.

Table 7.2 Selected members of the ICP HTML control.

Name	Type	Description
DocInput loading	Property	Returns a DocInput object that controls http
DocOutput writes	Property	Returns a DocOutput object that controls http
ElemNotification	Property	Flag indicates if control should trigger a DoNewElement event for each HTML element (useful for parsing HTML)
LayoutDone	Property	TRUE when layout is complete
ParseDone	Property	TRUE when parsing is complete
Cancel	Method	Cancels pending request
RequestDoc	Method	Requests a URL
RequestSubmit	Method	Submits a form
BeginRetrieval	Event	Triggers when retrieval begins
DocInput	Event	Triggers when input data is pending
DocOuput	Event	Triggers when output data is pending

(continued)

Table 7.2 Selected Members of the ICP HTML control (Continued).

Name	Type	Description
DoNewElement	Event	Occurs when control parses a new HTML element (see ElemNotification, above)
EndRetrieval	Event	Triggers when transfer is complete
Error	Event	Fires when an error occurs
TimeOut	Event	Occurs when a transfer times out

Listing 7.2 The CHTML class declaration.

```
#ifndef __HTML_H__
#define __HTML_H__

// Machine generated IDispatch wrapper class(es) created
// by Microsoft Visual C++

// NOTE: Do not modify the contents of this file.  If
// this class is regenerated by
//  Microsoft Visual C++, your modifications will be
// overwritten.


// Dispatch interfaces referenced by this interface
class CDocInput;
class CDocOutput;
class CHTMLForms;
class COleFont;

/////////////////////////////////////////////////////
// CHTML wrapper class

class CHTML : public CWnd
{
protected:
        DECLARE_DYNCREATE(CHTML)
public:
        CLSID const& GetClsid()
        {
                static CLSID const clsid
                        = { 0xb7fc355e, 0x8ce7, 0x11cf, { 0x97,
                    0x54, 0x0, 0xaa, 0x0, 0xc0,
                    0x9, 0x8 } };
                return clsid;
        }
        virtual BOOL Create(LPCTSTR lpszClassName,
                LPCTSTR lpszWindowName, DWORD dwStyle,
        const RECT& rect,
        CWnd* pParentWnd, UINT nID,
        CCreateContext* pContext = NULL)
```

Chapter 7

```
    {
      return CreateControl(GetClsid(),
         lpszWindowName, dwStyle, rect, pParentWnd, nID); }
    BOOL Create(LPCTSTR lpszWindowName, DWORD dwStyle,
         const RECT& rect, CWnd* pParentWnd, UINT nID,
         CFile* pPersist = NULL, BOOL bStorage = FALSE,
         BSTR bstrLicKey = NULL)
    {
      return CreateControl(GetClsid(),
         lpszWindowName, dwStyle, rect, pParentWnd, nID,
         pPersist, bStorage, bstrLicKey); }

// Attributes
public:

// Operations
public:
    // Method 'QueryInterface' not emitted because of
    // invalid return type or parameter type
    unsigned long AddRef();
    unsigned long Release();
    // Method 'GetTypeInfoCount' not emitted because of
    // invalid return type or parameter type
    // Method 'GetTypeInfo' not emitted because of
    // invalid return type or parameter type
    // Method 'GetIDsOfNames' not emitted because of
    // invalid return type or parameter type
    // Method 'Invoke' not emitted because of invalid
    // return type or parameter type
    void AboutBox();
    CDocInput GetDocInput();
    CDocOutput GetDocOutput();
    CString GetUrl();
    CString GetRequestURL();
    CString GetBaseURL();
    CHTMLForms GetForms();
    long GetTotalWidth();
    long GetTotalHeight();
    long GetRetrieveBytesTotal();
    long GetRetrieveBytesDone();
    BOOL GetParseDone();
    BOOL GetLayoutDone();
    BOOL GetDeferRetrieval();
    void SetDeferRetrieval(BOOL bNewValue);
    BOOL GetViewSource();
    void SetViewSource(BOOL bNewValue);
    BOOL GetRetainSource();
    void SetRetainSource(BOOL bNewValue);
    CString GetSourceText();
    BOOL GetElemNotification();
    void SetElemNotification(BOOL bNewValue);
    long GetTimeout();
```

```cpp
    void SetTimeout(long nNewValue);
    BOOL GetRedraw();
    void SetRedraw(BOOL bNewValue);
    BOOL GetUnderlineLinks();
    void SetUnderlineLinks(BOOL bNewValue);
    BOOL GetUseDocColors();
    void SetUseDocColors(BOOL bNewValue);
    CString GetBackImage();
    void SetBackImage(LPCTSTR lpszNewValue);
    unsigned long GetBackColor();
    void SetBackColor(unsigned long newValue);
    unsigned long GetForeColor();
    void SetForeColor(unsigned long newValue);
    unsigned long GetLinkColor();
    void SetLinkColor(unsigned long newValue);
    unsigned long GetVisitedColor();
    void SetVisitedColor(unsigned long newValue);
    unsigned long GetDocBackColor();
    unsigned long GetDocForeColor();
    unsigned long GetDocLinkColor();
    unsigned long GetDocVisitedColor();
    COleFont GetFont();
    void SetFont(LPDISPATCH newValue);
    COleFont GetFixedFont();
    void SetFixedFont(LPDISPATCH newValue);
    COleFont GetHeading1Font();
    void SetHeading1Font(LPDISPATCH newValue);
    COleFont GetHeading2Font();
    void SetHeading2Font(LPDISPATCH newValue);
    COleFont GetHeading3Font();
    void SetHeading3Font(LPDISPATCH newValue);
    COleFont GetHeading4Font();
    void SetHeading4Font(LPDISPATCH newValue);
    COleFont GetHeading5Font();
    void SetHeading5Font(LPDISPATCH newValue);
    COleFont GetHeading6Font();
    void SetHeading6Font(LPDISPATCH newValue);
    void RequestDoc(LPCTSTR URL);
    void RequestAllEmbedded();
    void Cancel(const VARIANT& Message);
};

#endif // __HTML_H__
```

Listing 7.3 The implementation of CHTML.

```cpp
// Machine generated IDispatch wrapper class(es)
// created by Microsoft Visual C++

// NOTE: Do not modify the contents of this file.
// If this class is regenerated by
//  Microsoft Visual C++, your modifications
// will be overwritten.
```

```
#include "stdafx.h"
#include "html.h"

// Dispatch interfaces referenced by this interface
#include "docinput.h"
#include "docoutput.h"
#include "htmlforms.h"
#include "font.h"


/////////////////////////////////////////
// CHTML

IMPLEMENT_DYNCREATE(CHTML, CWnd)

/////////////////////////////////////////
// CHTML properties

/////////////////////////////////////////
// CHTML operations

unsigned long CHTML::AddRef()
   {
   unsigned long result;
   InvokeHelper(0x60000001, DISPATCH_METHOD,
      VT_I4, (void*)&result, NULL);
   return result;
   }

unsigned long CHTML::Release()
   {
   unsigned long result;
   InvokeHelper(0x60000002, DISPATCH_METHOD,
      VT_I4, (void*)&result, NULL);
   return result;
   }

void CHTML::AboutBox()
   {
   InvokeHelper(0xfffffdd8, DISPATCH_METHOD,
      VT_EMPTY, NULL, NULL);
   }

CDocInput CHTML::GetDocInput()
   {
   LPDISPATCH pDispatch;
   InvokeHelper(0x3ea, DISPATCH_PROPERTYGET,
      VT_DISPATCH, (void*)&pDispatch, NULL);
   return CDocInput(pDispatch);
   }

CDocOutput CHTML::GetDocOutput()
   {
   LPDISPATCH pDispatch;
```

```
    InvokeHelper(0x3eb, DISPATCH_PROPERTYGET,
      VT_DISPATCH, (void*)&pDispatch, NULL);
    return CDocOutput(pDispatch);
    }

CString CHTML::GetUrl()
    {
    CString result;
    InvokeHelper(0x3e9, DISPATCH_PROPERTYGET,
      VT_BSTR, (void*)&result, NULL);
    return result;
    }

CString CHTML::GetRequestURL()
    {
    CString result;
    InvokeHelper(0x2, DISPATCH_PROPERTYGET,
      VT_BSTR, (void*)&result, NULL);
    return result;
    }

CString CHTML::GetBaseURL()
    {
    CString result;
    InvokeHelper(0x3, DISPATCH_PROPERTYGET,
      VT_BSTR, (void*)&result, NULL);
    return result;
    }

CHTMLForms CHTML::GetForms()
    {
    LPDISPATCH pDispatch;
    InvokeHelper(0x4, DISPATCH_PROPERTYGET,
      VT_DISPATCH, (void*)&pDispatch, NULL);
    return CHTMLForms(pDispatch);
    }

long CHTML::GetTotalWidth()
    {
    long result;
    InvokeHelper(0x5, DISPATCH_PROPERTYGET,
      VT_I4, (void*)&result, NULL);
    return result;
    }

long CHTML::GetTotalHeight()
    {
    long result;
    InvokeHelper(0x6, DISPATCH_PROPERTYGET,
      VT_I4, (void*)&result, NULL);
    return result;
    }
```

```cpp
long CHTML::GetRetrieveBytesTotal()
   {
   long result;
   InvokeHelper(0x7, DISPATCH_PROPERTYGET,
      VT_I4, (void*)&result, NULL);
   return result;
   }

long CHTML::GetRetrieveBytesDone()
   {
   long result;
   InvokeHelper(0x8, DISPATCH_PROPERTYGET,
      VT_I4, (void*)&result, NULL);
   return result;
   }

BOOL CHTML::GetParseDone()
   {
   BOOL result;
   InvokeHelper(0x9, DISPATCH_PROPERTYGET,
      VT_BOOL, (void*)&result, NULL);
   return result;
   }

BOOL CHTML::GetLayoutDone()
   {
   BOOL result;
   InvokeHelper(0xa, DISPATCH_PROPERTYGET,
      VT_BOOL, (void*)&result, NULL);
   return result;
   }

BOOL CHTML::GetDeferRetrieval()
   {
   BOOL result;
   InvokeHelper(0xb, DISPATCH_PROPERTYGET,
      VT_BOOL, (void*)&result, NULL);
   return result;
   }

void CHTML::SetDeferRetrieval(BOOL bNewValue)
   {
   static BYTE parms[] =
      VTS_BOOL;
   InvokeHelper(0xb, DISPATCH_PROPERTYPUT,
      VT_EMPTY, NULL, parms, bNewValue);
   }

BOOL CHTML::GetViewSource()
   {
   BOOL result;
   InvokeHelper(0xc, DISPATCH_PROPERTYGET,
      VT_BOOL, (void*)&result, NULL);
```

ActiveX And The Internet 277

```
    return result;
    }

void CHTML::SetViewSource(BOOL bNewValue)
    {
    static BYTE parms[] =
        VTS_BOOL;
    InvokeHelper(0xc, DISPATCH_PROPERTYPUT,
      VT_EMPTY, NULL, parms, bNewValue);
    }

BOOL CHTML::GetRetainSource()
    {
    BOOL result;
    InvokeHelper(0xd, DISPATCH_PROPERTYGET,
      VT_BOOL, (void*)&result, NULL);
    return result;
    }

void CHTML::SetRetainSource(BOOL bNewValue)
    {
    static BYTE parms[] =
        VTS_BOOL;
    InvokeHelper(0xd, DISPATCH_PROPERTYPUT,
      VT_EMPTY, NULL, parms, bNewValue);
    }

CString CHTML::GetSourceText()
    {
    CString result;
    InvokeHelper(0xe, DISPATCH_PROPERTYGET,
      VT_BSTR, (void*)&result, NULL);
    return result;
    }

BOOL CHTML::GetElemNotification()
    {
    BOOL result;
    InvokeHelper(0xf, DISPATCH_PROPERTYGET,
      VT_BOOL, (void*)&result, NULL);
    return result;
    }

void CHTML::SetElemNotification(BOOL bNewValue)
    {
    static BYTE parms[] =
        VTS_BOOL;
    InvokeHelper(0xf, DISPATCH_PROPERTYPUT,
      VT_EMPTY, NULL, parms,
        bNewValue);
    }

long CHTML::GetTimeout()
    {
```

```
    long result;
    InvokeHelper(0x1fb, DISPATCH_PROPERTYGET,
        VT_I4, (void*)&result, NULL);
    return result;
    }

void CHTML::SetTimeout(long nNewValue)
    {
    static BYTE parms[] =
        VTS_I4;
    InvokeHelper(0x1fb, DISPATCH_PROPERTYPUT,
        VT_EMPTY, NULL, parms, nNewValue);
    }

BOOL CHTML::GetRedraw()
    {
    BOOL result;
    InvokeHelper(0x11, DISPATCH_PROPERTYGET,
        VT_BOOL, (void*)&result, NULL);
    return result;
    }

void CHTML::SetRedraw(BOOL bNewValue)
    {
    static BYTE parms[] =
        VTS_BOOL;
    InvokeHelper(0x11, DISPATCH_PROPERTYPUT,
        VT_EMPTY, NULL, parms, bNewValue);
    }

BOOL CHTML::GetUnderlineLinks()
    {
    BOOL result;
    InvokeHelper(0x12, DISPATCH_PROPERTYGET,
        VT_BOOL, (void*)&result, NULL);
    return result;
    }

void CHTML::SetUnderlineLinks(BOOL bNewValue)
    {
    static BYTE parms[] =
        VTS_BOOL;
    InvokeHelper(0x12, DISPATCH_PROPERTYPUT,
        VT_EMPTY, NULL, parms, bNewValue);
    }

BOOL CHTML::GetUseDocColors()
    {
    BOOL result;
    InvokeHelper(0x13, DISPATCH_PROPERTYGET,
        VT_BOOL, (void*)&result, NULL);
    return result;
    }
```

ActiveX And The Internet 279

```
void CHTML::SetUseDocColors(BOOL bNewValue)
   {
   static BYTE parms[] =
      VTS_BOOL;
   InvokeHelper(0x13, DISPATCH_PROPERTYPUT,
     VT_EMPTY, NULL, parms, bNewValue);
   }

CString CHTML::GetBackImage()
   {
   CString result;
   InvokeHelper(0x14, DISPATCH_PROPERTYGET,
     VT_BSTR, (void*)&result, NULL);
   return result;
   }

void CHTML::SetBackImage(LPCTSTR lpszNewValue)
   {
   static BYTE parms[] =
      VTS_BSTR;
   InvokeHelper(0x14, DISPATCH_PROPERTYPUT,
     VT_EMPTY, NULL, parms, lpszNewValue);
   }

unsigned long CHTML::GetBackColor()
   {
   unsigned long result;
   InvokeHelper(DISPID_BACKCOLOR, DISPATCH_PROPERTYGET,
     VT_I4, (void*)&result, NULL);
   return result;
   }

void CHTML::SetBackColor(unsigned long newValue)
   {
   static BYTE parms[] =
      VTS_I4;
   InvokeHelper(DISPID_BACKCOLOR, DISPATCH_PROPERTYPUT,
     VT_EMPTY, NULL, parms, newValue);
   }

unsigned long CHTML::GetForeColor()
   {
   unsigned long result;
   InvokeHelper(DISPID_FORECOLOR, DISPATCH_PROPERTYGET,
     VT_I4, (void*)&result, NULL);
   return result;
   }

void CHTML::SetForeColor(unsigned long newValue)
   {
   static BYTE parms[] =
      VTS_I4;
   InvokeHelper(DISPID_FORECOLOR, DISPATCH_PROPERTYPUT,
```

```
      VT_EMPTY, NULL, parms, newValue);
   }

unsigned long CHTML::GetLinkColor()
   {
   unsigned long result;
   InvokeHelper(0x15, DISPATCH_PROPERTYGET,
      VT_I4, (void*)&result, NULL);
   return result;
   }

void CHTML::SetLinkColor(unsigned long newValue)
   {
   static BYTE parms[] =
      VTS_I4;
   InvokeHelper(0x15, DISPATCH_PROPERTYPUT,
      VT_EMPTY, NULL, parms, newValue);
   }

unsigned long CHTML::GetVisitedColor()
   {
   unsigned long result;
   InvokeHelper(0x16, DISPATCH_PROPERTYGET,
      VT_I4, (void*)&result, NULL);
   return result;
   }

void CHTML::SetVisitedColor(unsigned long newValue)
   {
   static BYTE parms[] =
      VTS_I4;
   InvokeHelper(0x16, DISPATCH_PROPERTYPUT,
      VT_EMPTY, NULL, parms, newValue);
   }

unsigned long CHTML::GetDocBackColor()
   {
   unsigned long result;
   InvokeHelper(0x17, DISPATCH_PROPERTYGET,
      VT_I4, (void*)&result, NULL);
   return result;
   }

unsigned long CHTML::GetDocForeColor()
   {
   unsigned long result;
   InvokeHelper(0x18, DISPATCH_PROPERTYGET,
      VT_I4, (void*)&result, NULL);
   return result;
   }

unsigned long CHTML::GetDocLinkColor()
   {
```

```
   unsigned long result;
   InvokeHelper(0x19, DISPATCH_PROPERTYGET,
     VT_I4, (void*)&result, NULL);
   return result;
   }

unsigned long CHTML::GetDocVisitedColor()
   {
   unsigned long result;
   InvokeHelper(0x1a, DISPATCH_PROPERTYGET,
     VT_I4, (void*)&result, NULL);
   return result;
   }

COleFont CHTML::GetFont()
   {
   LPDISPATCH pDispatch;
   InvokeHelper(DISPID_FONT, DISPATCH_PROPERTYGET,
     VT_DISPATCH, (void*)&pDispatch, NULL);
   return COleFont(pDispatch);
   }

void CHTML::SetFont(LPDISPATCH newValue)
   {
   static BYTE parms[] =
      VTS_DISPATCH;
   InvokeHelper(DISPID_FONT, DISPATCH_PROPERTYPUT,
     VT_EMPTY, NULL, parms, newValue);
   }

COleFont CHTML::GetFixedFont()
   {
   LPDISPATCH pDispatch;
   InvokeHelper(0x1b, DISPATCH_PROPERTYGET,
     VT_DISPATCH, (void*)&pDispatch, NULL);
   return COleFont(pDispatch);
   }

void CHTML::SetFixedFont(LPDISPATCH newValue)
   {
   static BYTE parms[] =
      VTS_DISPATCH;
   InvokeHelper(0x1b, DISPATCH_PROPERTYPUT, VT_EMPTY,
     NULL, parms, newValue);
   }

COleFont CHTML::GetHeading1Font()
   {
   LPDISPATCH pDispatch;
   InvokeHelper(0x1c, DISPATCH_PROPERTYGET,
     VT_DISPATCH, (void*)&pDispatch, NULL);
   return COleFont(pDispatch);
   }
```

```cpp
void CHTML::SetHeading1Font(LPDISPATCH newValue)
    {
    static BYTE parms[] =
        VTS_DISPATCH;
    InvokeHelper(0x1c, DISPATCH_PROPERTYPUT,
        VT_EMPTY, NULL, parms, newValue);
    }

COleFont CHTML::GetHeading2Font()
    {
    LPDISPATCH pDispatch;
    InvokeHelper(0x1d, DISPATCH_PROPERTYGET,
        VT_DISPATCH, (void*)&pDispatch, NULL);
    return COleFont(pDispatch);
    }

void CHTML::SetHeading2Font(LPDISPATCH newValue)
    {
    static BYTE parms[] =
        VTS_DISPATCH;
    InvokeHelper(0x1d, DISPATCH_PROPERTYPUT,
        VT_EMPTY, NULL, parms, newValue);
    }

COleFont CHTML::GetHeading3Font()
    {
    LPDISPATCH pDispatch;
    InvokeHelper(0x1e, DISPATCH_PROPERTYGET,
        VT_DISPATCH, (void*)&pDispatch, NULL);
    return COleFont(pDispatch);
    }

void CHTML::SetHeading3Font(LPDISPATCH newValue)
    {
    static BYTE parms[] =
        VTS_DISPATCH;
    InvokeHelper(0x1e, DISPATCH_PROPERTYPUT,
        VT_EMPTY, NULL, parms, newValue);
    }

COleFont CHTML::GetHeading4Font()
    {
    LPDISPATCH pDispatch;
    InvokeHelper(0x1f, DISPATCH_PROPERTYGET,
        VT_DISPATCH, (void*)&pDispatch, NULL);
    return COleFont(pDispatch);
    }

void CHTML::SetHeading4Font(LPDISPATCH newValue)
    {
    static BYTE parms[] =
        VTS_DISPATCH;
    InvokeHelper(0x1f, DISPATCH_PROPERTYPUT,
```

```cpp
      VT_EMPTY, NULL, parms, newValue);
   }

COleFont CHTML::GetHeading5Font()
   {
   LPDISPATCH pDispatch;
   InvokeHelper(0x20, DISPATCH_PROPERTYGET,
      VT_DISPATCH, (void*)&pDispatch, NULL);
   return COleFont(pDispatch);
   }

void CHTML::SetHeading5Font(LPDISPATCH newValue)
   {
   static BYTE parms[] =
      VTS_DISPATCH;
   InvokeHelper(0x20, DISPATCH_PROPERTYPUT,
      VT_EMPTY, NULL, parms, newValue);
   }

COleFont CHTML::GetHeading6Font()
   {
   LPDISPATCH pDispatch;
   InvokeHelper(0x21, DISPATCH_PROPERTYGET,
      VT_DISPATCH, (void*)&pDispatch, NULL);
   return COleFont(pDispatch);
   }

void CHTML::SetHeading6Font(LPDISPATCH newValue)
   {
   static BYTE parms[] =
      VTS_DISPATCH;
   InvokeHelper(0x21, DISPATCH_PROPERTYPUT,
      VT_EMPTY, NULL, parms, newValue);
   }

void CHTML::RequestDoc(LPCTSTR URL)
   {
   static BYTE parms[] =
      VTS_BSTR;
   InvokeHelper(0x22, DISPATCH_METHOD,
      VT_EMPTY, NULL, parms, URL);
   }

void CHTML::RequestAllEmbedded()
   {
   InvokeHelper(0x23, DISPATCH_METHOD,
      VT_EMPTY, NULL, NULL);
   }

void CHTML::Cancel(const VARIANT& Message)
   {
   static BYTE parms[] =
      VTS_VARIANT;
```

```
  InvokeHelper(0x208, DISPATCH_METHOD,
    VT_EMPTY, NULL, parms, &Message);
}
```

Component Gallery doesn't stop there. It also creates classes for other ActiveX objects that the HTML control depends on. This includes the following classes: **CDocOutput**, **CDocHeader**, **CDocHeaders**, **CHTMLForm**, **CHTMLForms**, **COleFont**, **CDocInput**, and **CDocOutput**. These classes represent objects that the HTML control uses in some way. For example, you can use the **CDocHeaders** object to set or examine the HTTP protocol headers. The **CHTML** class, as well as these ancillary classes are little more than wrappers around the appropriate dispatch interface. Each function that sets values accepts a C++ argument, converts it to a **VARIANT** structure, and calls the dispatch interface with the correct **DISPID**. Functions that return values convert **VARIANT**s to C++ data types. Each object has a constructor that allows it to accept a dispatch interface pointer (an **LPDISPATCH**) and wrap it.

The final thing that Component Gallery does is to add an icon to the resource editor's control palette that represents the control. This allows you to easily drop the control on a dialog box template.

The browser's main form contains an HTML control, a combo box, and several buttons. You can see the form in Figure 7.1 earlier in this chapter, and you'll find the code in Listing 7.1, also shown earlier. The browser calls the HTML control's **RequestDoc** function to do all the work of loading a document. It also maintains a list of URLs in the combo box. In addition, the browser handles several events to better integrate with the HTML control:

- **Error.** This event occurs when the HTML control raises an error.
- **OnBeginRetrieval.** When the HTML control starts loading a page, it calls **OnBeginRetrieval.** The browser uses this event for two purposes. First, it checks to see if the URL is already at the top of the list in the combo box. If it isn't, the browser inserts it into the list. This usually means the user loaded a new page by selecting a link on the current page. The other action the browser takes when it processes this event is to update the status bar with text to show what the browser is doing.
- **OnEndRetrieval.** The browser also processes the ending notification so it can clear the status bar.

Form views scroll when the window containing them is not large enough to hold the dialog template. For the browser, this is not good behavior. Instead, the program catches the **WM_SIZE** message (in the **OnSize** function) and recalculates the layout of the dialog so that everything fits in the current window. If the HTML page doesn't fit in the control, the control will display scroll bars that allow the user to view the entire page.

The rest of the code is just straightforward MFC programming that handles various user interface events. When the user changes the URL in the combo box or presses one of the buttons, the program manipulates the HTML control to produce the desired result.

The browser should detect when you press the **Enter** key and load the URL that appears in the combo box. To accomplish this, the browser makes the load button the default button. When you click a button, special code executes to reset the default button so that the **Enter** key works correctly.

Considering that it is a functional Web browser, this is an amazingly small program. The trick is that it uses an ActiveX control to do all of the difficult work. Thanks to ActiveX, you don't need to know how to open a network connection, perform HTTP transfers, or perform HTML decoding.

Of course, the ICP HTML control is not capable of handling many newer HTML tags. It also won't handle embedded ActiveX objects (you'll need the **MSHTML** control for that). In the beta release, at least, the ICP HTML control has several quirks. For example, if a page contains an embedded image that the control can't load, the control generates an error. You can't restart the transfer after the error, so any portion of the page after the error occurs never appears.

About CFormView

MFC provides a framework that allows you to create many different types of programs. Most of these programs revolve around the document/view architecture. Although it is easy to get bogged down in the details of the approach, the essential elements are quite simple.

Suppose, for example, that you wrote a spreadsheet program for Windows. When you designed your code, you may not have thought about future requirements, so your code only takes into account the normal grid view of a spreadsheet. In the code there is no clear distinction between data storage, formula calculation, user input, and display.

For a while, things work fine. However, some time later, you decide that you need a pie chart representation of the data. Since the code is all together, you'll have to dig through it all to make the changes. If you introduce any bugs, they may affect unrelated areas (like formulas). Also, your pie chart code is now very specific to the spreadsheet. It would be difficult to reuse it in other programs.

Later, when you decide to add a scattergram or a bar chart, you have to repeat the whole process. Eventually, the program will become unmaintainable. This problem is especially troublesome when you model your C++ program in terms of the actions instead of the user interface. For example, you might select certain objects to represent a spreadsheet and other objects to represent a cell.

MFC takes a different approach. In many cases, MFC requires you to model the user interface separately from the program's actions. In particular, in MFC, you derive a document object (from **CDocument** or a class that itself derives from **CDocument**) and a view object (from **CView** or a related class). The document represents a model of what your program should display. It usually (but not always) corresponds to a file on disk. In the spreadsheet example, the document might know how to read and write files, evaluate formulas, and recalculate the spreadsheet contents. However, it won't know how to display the spreadsheet on the screen (or on a printer, for that matter). It also won't know how to accept keyboard or mouse input from the user.

These jobs (display, printing, and user input) are in part the responsibility of the view class. When view receives a request to draw part of the spreadsheet, it acquires data from the document, then draws the appropriate representation. When view receives input, it decides what action to take and either satisfies the request or passes the request on to the document object. This architecture has several advantages:

- The code that handles the user interface is separate from the code that does processing
- You can easily add different types of views without regard to the document's code
- A single document may have multiple views of any type
- If you design correctly, you may reuse views easily

Another advantage of this architecture is that MFC can supply an amazing amount of functionality in the base class for the view (**CView**). For example, if your view class knows how to draw itself, MFC can automatically supply print and print-preview code. It can also handle sophisticated operations like scrolling and managing split-screen windows (splitters) without any knowledge of your code.

In the spreadsheet example, you'd create a document object to represent the spreadsheet. That object is free to handle everything, or it can create other C++ objects to do the work (for example, your original spreadsheet and cell objects). Then, the code to draw the grid, accept input, and perform other user interface operations goes in the view object. Later, if you decide to add a different type of view, you'll have no trouble. Code you place in a new view object shouldn't affect code in the document or other views.

Because your view is in a separate object, MFC can supply two grids on a single spreadsheet (perhaps scrolled to different locations). Also, you can have a grid and a bar chart view with little difficulty, and changes you make in the grid appear in the bar chart right away.

An ordinary program that draws into a normal, non-scrolling window usually creates its view object by deriving from **CView**. If you want the window to scroll, you can use **CScrollView**. MFC provides another type of view (that derives from **CScrollView**) to support form-based programming. This is **CFormView**, which is used by the browser in this chapter.

CFormView knows how to read a dialog template and incorporate it in its display. This combines the ease of use of a dialog box with the advanced features of a view. But why not just use a dialog box? There are several reasons. First, a dialog box can't take advantage of MFC's support for printing, print preview, splitter windows, and so on. Also, a dialog box can't act as a proper MDI child window. Finally, a dialog window can't scroll to show a larger dialog than would fit in the window. A form view can do all of these things.

When you use App Wizard to create an application, you can change the base class used for the view on the final App Wizard dialog. Simply change this base class from **CView** to **CFormView,** and App Wizard generates your code, complete with a dummy dialog template for you to customize.

To further complete your code, you can more or less treat the view as a dialog box. That means you can use Class Wizard to link variables in your view object to items (like edit controls and buttons) on your form. You can also manipulate them in the more traditional way using **GetDlgItem** and similar calls.

Because a form's data is resident in the controls, it doesn't follow the document/view architecture in a strict way. A form-based application will either not use its document object, or it has to do special work to keep the document's variables in synch with the data in the controls. If the program doesn't use the document to hold data, then all document functions must either delegate to the view or query the view to learn the correct data. For example, a form program that wants to load and save data to disk must keep the document up to date, delegate the call that performs disk I/O to the view, or query the view during disk I/O (the **Serialize** function).

ActiveX And Non-Dialog Views

Adding an ActiveX control to a dialog is a snap. You add the control to your project with Component Gallery. You can then drop the control on any dialog template from the component toolbar. However, what happens if you want to add an ActiveX control to a non-dialog view? You can do that too, but it isn't quite as easy.

Microsoft recommends that you temporarily create a dialog and attach it to your view class. Class Wizard will complain, of course, but you can ignore that. Then you can add event handlers and otherwise work with the control. Later, you delete the dialog template. This works after a fashion, but it does require a great deal of manual changes. Here are the steps:

1. Create a dialog resource and add the ActiveX control.
2. Run Class Wizard from the dialog editor. Class Wizard will offer to create a new class to go with the dialog template.
3. Pick the *Select an Existing Class* option, and click the *OK* button. Class Wizard displays a list of classes.
4. Select your view class.
5. Class Wizard displays a dialog box explaining that your class doesn't use a dialog template. Ignore this error message by clicking on the *Yes* button.
6. Use Class Wizard to hook up event handlers in your code (you'll still need to create the control manually).
7. Once you've completed all the event handlers, delete the dialog template.

This is, at best, a hack. You might just as well add the necessary items manually, which isn't much more work, and you'll know exactly what you are doing and why, instead of relying on temporary dialog templates and other cheap tricks.

There are 9 steps required to add an ActiveX control to an ordinary view. You can follow along with these steps by looking at the code in Listings 7.4, 7.5, and 7.6. This code is a simple program that displays an AVI file and monitors its progress (as shown in Figure 7.5). Each important section of code has a comment near it that refers you to the appropriate step. Here are the steps:

1. Use Component Gallery to add the control to your application as usual.

2. Include the ActiveX control's header to the view's CPP file. Be sure to place it in front of **#include** for the view's header file. If any other CPP files include the view header, you'll need to modify them, too.

3. Add a member variable in the view class' definition to represent the ActiveX control.

4. Use Class Wizard to add a **Create** (or **OnCreate**) function, if one is not already present.

5. In the **Create** handler, after calling the base class **Create**, call the ActiveX control's **Create** function (using the variable declared in Step 2). You'll usually pass a **WS_VISIBLE** flag and the control's size, ID, and parent (the view).

6. Call the appropriate functions for the ActiveX control to set any properties you want initialized right after calling **Create**.

7. Add the **DECLARE_EVENTSINK_MAP** macro to the class declaration in the H file, which allows you to map events to functions.

8. Add the **BEGIN_EVENTSINK_MAP** and **END_EVENTSINK_MAP** macros to the CPP file. In between these macros, add macros to handle specific events (as shown in Table 7.3).

9. If you want to provide ambient properties, override the view's **OnAmbientProperty** function. In the function, examine the **DISPID** passed in and either return a **VARIANT** or call the base class.

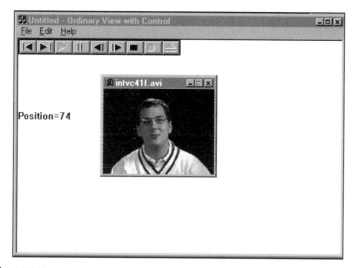

Figure 7.5 The VIEW program in action.

Listing 7.4 The VIEW.CPP file.

```
// view.cpp : Defines the class behaviors for the application.
//

#include "stdafx.h"
#include "view.h"

#include "MainFrm.h"
#include "viewDoc.h"
#include "mcictrl.h" /* !!2 */
#include "viewView.h"

#ifdef _DEBUG
#define new DEBUG_NEW
#undef THIS_FILE
static char THIS_FILE[] = __FILE__;
#endif

/////////////////////////////////////
// CViewApp

BEGIN_MESSAGE_MAP(CViewApp, CWinApp)
   //{{AFX_MSG_MAP(CViewApp)
   ON_COMMAND(ID_APP_ABOUT, OnAppAbout)
   //}}AFX_MSG_MAP
// Standard file based document commands
ON_COMMAND(ID_FILE_NEW, CWinApp::OnFileNew)
ON_COMMAND(ID_FILE_OPEN, CWinApp::OnFileOpen)
END_MESSAGE_MAP()
```

```
/////////////////////////////////////
// CViewApp construction

CViewApp::CViewApp()
    {
    // TODO: Add construction code here
    // Place all significant initialization in InitInstance
    }

/////////////////////////////////////
// The one and only CViewApp object

CViewApp theApp;

/////////////////////////////////////
// CViewApp initialization

BOOL CViewApp::InitInstance()
    {
    AfxEnableControlContainer();

#ifdef _AFXDLL
    Enable3dControls();
#else
    Enable3dControlsStatic();
#endif

    LoadStdProfileSettings(0);
    CSingleDocTemplate* pDocTemplate;
    pDocTemplate = new CSingleDocTemplate(
        IDR_MAINFRAME,
        RUNTIME_CLASS(CViewDoc),
        RUNTIME_CLASS(CMainFrame),    // Main SDI frame
            RUNTIME_CLASS(CViewView));
        AddDocTemplate(pDocTemplate);

    // Parse command line
    CCommandLineInfo cmdInfo;
    ParseCommandLine(cmdInfo);

    // Dispatch commands specified on the command line
    if (!ProcessShellCommand(cmdInfo))
        return FALSE;

    return TRUE;
    }

/////////////////////////////////////
// CAboutDlg dialog used for App About

class CAboutDlg : public CDialog
    {
```

Chapter 7

```
   public:
      CAboutDlg();

   // Dialog Data
      //{{AFX_DATA(CAboutDlg)
      enum { IDD = IDD_ABOUTBOX };
      //}}AFX_DATA

   // ClassWizard generated virtual function overrides
      //{{AFX_VIRTUAL(CAboutDlg)
      protected:
         virtual void DoDataExchange(CDataExchange* pDX);
      //}}AFX_VIRTUAL

   // Implementation
   protected:
         //{{AFX_MSG(CAboutDlg)
         // No message handlers
         //}}AFX_MSG
      DECLARE_MESSAGE_MAP()
   };

CAboutDlg::CAboutDlg() : CDialog(CAboutDlg::IDD)
   {
      //{{AFX_DATA_INIT(CAboutDlg)
      //}}AFX_DATA_INIT
   }

void CAboutDlg::DoDataExchange(CDataExchange* pDX)
   {
   CDialog::DoDataExchange(pDX);
      //{{AFX_DATA_MAP(CAboutDlg)
      //}}AFX_DATA_MAP
   }

BEGIN_MESSAGE_MAP(CAboutDlg, CDialog)
   //{{AFX_MSG_MAP(CAboutDlg)
   // No message handlers
   //}}AFX_MSG_MAP
END_MESSAGE_MAP()

// App command to run the dialog
void CViewApp::OnAppAbout()
   {
   CAboutDlg aboutDlg;
   aboutDlg.DoModal();
   }

/////////////////////////////////////////
// CViewApp commands
```

Listing 7.5   The View implementation.

```
// viewView.cpp : Implementation of the CViewView class
//
```

```cpp
#include "stdafx.h"
#include "view.h"

#include "viewDoc.h"
#include "mcictrl.h"   /* !!2 */
#include "viewView.h"

#ifdef _DEBUG
#define new DEBUG_NEW
#undef THIS_FILE
static char THIS_FILE[] = __FILE__;
#endif

/////////////////////////////////////
// CViewView

IMPLEMENT_DYNCREATE(CViewView, CView)

BEGIN_MESSAGE_MAP(CViewView, CView)
    //{{AFX_MSG_MAP(CViewView)
    //}}AFX_MSG_MAP
END_MESSAGE_MAP()


/* !!8 */
    BEGIN_EVENTSINK_MAP(CViewView,CView)
ON_EVENT(CViewView,1,0x1c,OnStatusUpdate,VTS_NONE)
END_EVENTSINK_MAP()

/////////////////////////////////////
// CViewView construction/destruction

CViewView::CViewView()
    {
    // TODO: Add construction code here

    }

CViewView::~CViewView()
    {
    }

BOOL CViewView::PreCreateWindow(CREATESTRUCT& cs)
    {
// Clip children so control will draw properly
    cs.style|=WS_CLIPCHILDREN;
    return CView::PreCreateWindow(cs);
    }

/////////////////////////////////////
// CViewView drawing

void CViewView::OnDraw(CDC* pDC)
```

```
    {
    CViewDoc* pDoc = GetDocument();
    ASSERT_VALID(pDoc);
// To draw, simply get current MCI position
// and print it
    long l=
        mci_control.GetPosition();
    CString s;
    s.Format("Position=%ld",l);
    pDC->TextOut(0,100,s);
    }


/////////////////////////////////////
// CViewView diagnostics

#ifdef _DEBUG
void CViewView::AssertValid() const
    {
    CView::AssertValid();
    }

void CViewView::Dump(CDumpContext& dc) const
    {
    CView::Dump(dc);
    }

CViewDoc* CViewView::GetDocument()
    {
    ASSERT(m_pDocument->
     IsKindOf(RUNTIME_CLASS(CViewDoc)));
    return (CViewDoc*)m_pDocument;
    }
#endif //_DEBUG


/////////////////////////////////////
// CViewView message handlers

/* !!4 */
    BOOL CViewView::Create(LPCTSTR lpszClassName,
      LPCTSTR lpszWindowName, DWORD dwStyle,
      const RECT& rect, CWnd* pParentWnd,
      UINT nID, CCreateContext* pContext)
        {
        BOOL rv= CWnd::Create(lpszClassName,
          lpszWindowName, dwStyle, rect,
          pParentWnd, nID, pContext);
        if (rv)
           {
           /* !!5 */
              CRect pos;
           GetClientRect(&pos);
           mci_control.Create(NULL,
             WS_VISIBLE|WS_CHILD|WS_CLIPSIBLINGS,pos,this,1);
```

```
           /* !!6 */
// NOTE: You'll need to set this to a valid AVI file name
        mci_control.SetFileName("d:\\vcmovie\\intvc41f.avi");
        mci_control.SetAutoEnable(TRUE);
        mci_control.SetEnabled(TRUE);
        mci_control.SetCommand("Open");
        }
     return rv;
     }

void CViewView::OnStatusUpdate()
   {
// When control updates, invalidate to redraw
   InvalidateRect(NULL);   /* !!9 */
   }

BOOL CViewView::DestroyWindow()
   {
   mci_control.SetCommand("Close");
   return CView::DestroyWindow();
   }

void CViewView::OnInitialUpdate()
   {
   CView::OnInitialUpdate();

// Oddly enough, this is how an SDI view knows
// it is initializing
   mci_control.SetCommand("CLOSE");
   mci_control.SetFileName("d:\\vcmovie\\intvc41f.avi");
   mci_control.SetCommand("Open");
   }

// Although our control ignores ambient props
// we do one anyway
// Kind of silly to do a switch here, but in general
// you will test for more than one, in which case
// the switch is a good idea...
BOOL CViewView::OnAmbientProperty( COleControlSite* pSite,
  DISPID dispid, VARIANT* pvar )
   {
   switch (dispid)
      {
      case DISPID_AMBIENT_BACKCOLOR:
         pvar->vt=VT_COLOR;
      pvar->lVal=RGB(0,0,0); // Black
      return TRUE;
      default:
         return CView::OnAmbientProperty(pSite,dispid,pvar);
      }
   }
```

Listing 7.6 The View header file.

```cpp
// viewView.h : Interface of the CViewView class
//
/////////////////////////////////////////

class CViewView : public CView
   {
   protected: // Create from serialization only
      CViewView();
   DECLARE_DYNCREATE(CViewView)
   // Attributes
   public:
      BOOL OnAmbientProperty( COleControlSite* pSite,
         DISPID dispid, VARIANT* pvar );
      void OnStatusUpdate();
      CMciCtrl mci_control;    /* !!3 */
         CViewDoc* GetDocument();

   // Operations
   public:

      // Overrides
      // ClassWizard generated virtual function overrides
         //{{AFX_VIRTUAL(CViewView)
         public:
            virtual void OnDraw(CDC* pDC);
         virtual BOOL PreCreateWindow(CREATESTRUCT& cs);
      virtual BOOL Create(LPCTSTR lpszClassName,
         LPCTSTR lpszWindowName, DWORD dwStyle,
         const RECT& rect, CWnd* pParentWnd,
         UINT nID, CCreateContext* pContext = NULL);
      virtual BOOL DestroyWindow();
      virtual void OnInitialUpdate();
      //}}AFX_VIRTUAL

   // Implementation
   public:
      virtual ~CViewView();
#ifdef _DEBUG
   virtual void AssertValid() const;
   virtual void Dump(CDumpContext& dc) const;
#endif

   protected:

      // Generated message map functions
      protected:
         //{{AFX_MSG(CViewView)
         //}}AFX_MSG
        DECLARE_MESSAGE_MAP()
      DECLARE_EVENTSINK_MAP() /* !!7 */
         };
```

```
#ifndef _DEBUG  // Debug version in viewView.cpp
inline CViewDoc* CViewView::GetDocument()
   { return (CViewDoc*)m_pDocument; }
#endif
```

If your control is a visible one, you'll usually want to force the view to clip its child windows, which you can easily do by overriding **PreCreateWindow**. This function receives a **CREATESTRUCT** that MFC will use when creating the view. Simply use a bit-wise **or** operation to add the **WS_CLIPCHILDREN** flag to the styles (you can see this back in Listing 7.5).

The only tricky part is handling events. Each event or property notification you want to handle requires a macro after the **BEGIN_EVENTSINK_MAP** map in the CPP file (shown in Step 8). The final argument to this macro is a list of argument types that the event passes. If the event takes multiple arguments, you separate them with a space (not a comma or a vertical bar as you might expect). For example, here is an event that takes a short and a Boolean as arguments:

```
ON_EVENT(CXXXView,IDC_CTL,33,OnSomeEvent,
   VTS_SHORT VTS_BOOL);
```

The other problem with **ON_EVENT** is that you need to know the **DISPID** for the event. This is in the control's type library, which you can easily view using the OLE Object Viewer available on the **Tools** menu in Visual C++. You can use the screen in Figure 7.6 to select the control. Then you can find the correct entry using the screen in Figure 7.7. The viewer refers to the **DISPID** as a **memid** (member ID).

The example program is simplistic. It creates a multimedia ActiveX control (this control comes with Visual C++, although it is technically a Visual Basic control). During execution of the **OnCreate** function, the program creates the control and loads an AVI file. The only event the program

Table 7.3 Event-handling macros.

Macro	Description
ON_EVENT	Handles an ordinary event
ON_PROPNOTIFY	Handles a property change notification
ON_EVENT_RANGE	Handles a range of events
ON_PROPNOTIFY_RANGE	Handles a range of property notifications

handles is the **StatusUpdate** event. This event takes no parameters and the OLE Object Viewer reveals that the **DISPID** for this event is 0x1C. For events that don't require any arguments, the **ON_EVENT** macro uses **VTS_NONE** as the final argument.

The control doesn't use any ambient properties. However, the example program provides an ambient background color just for the exercise.

By following these nine simple steps shown above, you can add ActiveX controls to any MFC view or window. You might find it interesting to return to the Web browser presented earlier in this chapter. Try to identify all the portions of the code that Class Wizard generated to support the HTML control. You'll find it looks very similar to the code you must add manually when using a non-dialog view.

Asynchronous Monikers

Remember monikers? Monikers are the ActiveX objects that refer to other things (like files or specific items within files). Instead of opening a file, you ask a moniker to bind. The moniker then returns a pointer to the correct kind of object.

The problem with monikers is that the binding process is usually synchronous. That is, you ask a moniker to bind, and then your program waits until the binding process is complete.

For controls destined to run on your local machine, that isn't a big problem. After all, how long could binding take? For potential Internet controls, however, synchronous binding could spell disaster. Suppose you have an ActiveX control that loads an AVI video clip from a remote Web server and plays it. The AVI file might be as large as several megabytes. Over a slow link, this could take many minutes—minutes that will frustrate the user waiting for a moniker to bind.

To prevent this problem, ActiveX defines a new kind of moniker: the asynchronous moniker. You should avoid placing large objects (like AVI data) in your control's direct properties. Instead, use a data path property, which is just a string that contains a URL for a data file (the URL may be absolute or relative). A data path property has the type **OLE_DATAPATH** (the same as **BSTR**). To load these properties, the browser creates a special type of asynchronous moniker. You can also use the monikers internally within your control to load anything you like (perhaps based on ordinary string properties).

ActiveX And The Internet 299

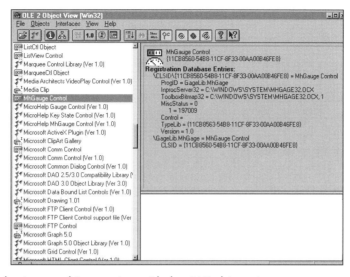

Figure 7.6 Selecting an object to view with the OLE object viewer.

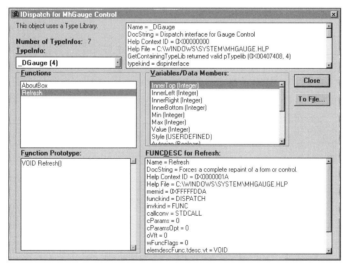

Figure 7.7 Viewing an interface with the OLE object viewer.

Often, the browser wants to show some status for a download operation. Therefore, you shouldn't create monikers directly. Instead, find the container's **IBindHost** interface. This interface has two functions: **ParseDisplayName** and **GetBindCtx**. The **ParseDisplayName** function takes the name of an item and returns a pointer to a moniker. Some containers may not supply **IBindHost**. In that case, you'll have to create the moniker in the usual way.

However, when you create your own moniker, the container isn't aware of the progress of the download.

To obtain an **IBindHost** interface, you need to query the **IClientSite** interface. That implies that you have to implement **IOleObject**—this interface is the traditional way for controls to learn their client site. However, this interface has 21 member functions, and you may not need that kind of overhead. Since ActiveX wants Internet controls to be lean, it provides the **IObjectWithSite** interface that you can use to learn your client site. This interface has only two members (other than **IUnknown**, of course): **SetSite** and **GetSite**.

Another important interface is **IPersistMoniker**, which is simply a moniker that can save itself (it derives from **IPersistStream**). **IPersistMoniker** is essentially **IPersistFile** reworked to use monikers instead of files, which is important when you are working with non-file types (such as URLs). You can find a description of **IPersistMoniker** in Table 7.4.

Controls that participate in asynchronous transfers usually implement **IBindStatusCallback** (as shown in Table 7.5). This interface allows the moniker to call the control when data is available and as the download progresses. You register your callback by calling **RegisterBindStatusCallback**. This call requires a pointer to the bind context, a pointer to the **IBindStatusCallback** interface, and some flags that indicate what events warrant a callback.

If you create a moniker via **IBindHost**, you can learn the bind context by calling **GetBindCtx**. If you create your monikers directly, you pass the bind context using **CreateBindCtx** and pass it to **IMoniker::BindToObject**.

Usually, you'll install your own **IBindStatusCallback** interface and respond to the calls it receives. However, you can elect to remove all other callbacks, install your own, and then selectively call the other callbacks as you see fit. This allows the control to modify what other programs see about the state of the transfer.

Controls that support asynchronous transfer should expose the **ReadyState** property and the **OnReadyStateChange** event (if they expose any properties and events). This allows the container to wait for the control to have the appropriate data before acting on it. Table 7.6 includes a list of ready state values. You don't need to supply all of these values since several of them won't make sense for every control, but each time you update the **ReadyState** property, you must fire the **OnReadyStateChange** event.

ActiveX And The Internet

Table 7.4 The IPersistMoniker interface.

Function	Description
GetClassID	Returns object's CLSID
IsDirty	Checks object for changes since last save
Load	Loads object using specified moniker
Save	Saves object to a destination moniker
SaveCompleted	Notifies object that save is complete
GetCurMoniker	Gets the current moniker for object

Table 7.5 The IBindStatusCallback interface.

Function	Description
GetBindInfo	Called by an asynchronous moniker to get bind info
OnStartBinding	Notifies the client which callback methods it is registered to receive
GetPriority	Gets data during asynchronous bind operations
OnProgress	Indicates the current progress of this bind operation
OnDataAvailable	Retrieves the current priority of this bind operation
OnObjectAvailable	Called by asynchronous monikers to pass the requested object interface pointer to the client
OnLowResource	An asynchronous moniker calls this method when it detects low resources
OnStopBinding	An asynchronous moniker calls this method to indicate the end of the bind operation

Since asynchronous monikers use **IMoniker** as their primary interface, you can't determine if a moniker is synchronous or asynchronous just by looking at that interface. However, all asynchronous monikers support a dummy interface named **IMonikerAsync** that is just any **IUnknown** interface (that is, it contains no functions itself). If you can successfully call **QueryInterface** on an **IMoniker** for an **IMonikerAsync** interface, then the moniker is asynchronous.

Table 7.6 Readystate values.

Value	State	Description
READYSTATE_LOADING	Loading	Control has initiated asynchronous loading
READYSTATE_LOADED	Loaded	Control has small properties loaded but is still transferring large properties
READYSTATE_INTERACTIVE	Interactive	Control has enough data to begin limited user interaction
READYSTATE_COMPLETED	Complete	Control is completely ready

URL Monikers

It's important to realize that the idea of an "asynchronous moniker" *per se* is an abstraction. Specific monikers, however, may be asynchronous. Currently the best example of an asynchronous moniker is a URL moniker (which is, obviously, a moniker that refers to a URL). You can create such a moniker with **CreateURLMoniker**.

CreateURLMoniker takes two input arguments: a URL (the display name), and a URL moniker that is the base URL for the display name. Of course, if the URL is an absolute URL, the base moniker can be **NULL**. Also, if the moniker can draw the base context from the binding context or from the left-hand portion of a composite moniker, you can use **NULL** for the base moniker.

If you do use a partial URL with a **NULL** base moniker, the URL moniker will call its binding context's **GetObjectParam** function with the **SZ_URLCONTEXT** argument. If the context returns a base URL, the moniker uses it. Presumably, this comes from the container that knows which URL refers to the current page.

Armed with a URL moniker, you can call **BindToObject** or **BindToStorage** to retrieve an object or a storage, respectively. The transfer takes place asynchronously and the container (or the object) can monitor the progress by registering with the bind context as discussed above (using **RegisterBindStatusCallback**).

Code Downloading

In Chapter 6, you saw how to place an ActiveX control in a Web page. However, all the examples assumed that the local machine already knew about the control. While this might be the case sometimes, what about when the local machine doesn't know about the control?

ActiveX defines a mechanism for a browser to load and install an ActiveX control when it first encounters it. To do this, it requires the control designer to specify where the control resides, the current version, and other information. A system administrator (or user) can specify where the browser should look for a control. In this way, you can search local libraries of controls (perhaps on a LAN) first. You can also prevent downloading any code, if you like.

Remember the **<OBJECT>** HTML tag? This is the tag you use to create an ActiveX object on a Web page. One of the attributes of this tag is the **CODEBASE** parameter, which is how the designer of a Web page specifies where an ActiveX control resides.

When a Web browser encounters an **<OBJECT>** tag, it searches for the object's CLSID in the system registry. If the object is already there (and at least the same version as the object specified in the **CODEBASE** parameter), the browser simply uses the existing object. If the object isn't already in the system registry, the browser searches for the control in a special search path. In this search path, the administrator can specify any number of URLs. The administrator can also indicate that the system should download the control from the URL specified in the **CODEBASE** parameter. Then the system downloads the control, checks its digital signature (see *Trust Verification* later in this chapter), and installs the control.

Naturally, this process uses URL monikers, so the process is asynchronous. In other words, you don't have to wait for the objects on a page to download before you can proceed. This is a good idea, since users may not want to watch the browser lock up while a few dozen ActiveX controls are downloaded.

The file argument can specify a normal ActiveX control file (usually with the extension OCX), an INF file, or a CAB file. Which one you should use depends on what your control requires in the way of support.

The easiest—and least useful—option is to specify an OCX file directly. This is usually not satisfactory, because there is no file compression, and if you need any supporting files (perhaps the MFC DLL), the system won't check for them.

A cabinet, or CAB file, is a special archive that can contain multiple files in a compressed format. CAB files are good if you need several files, or if you want to compress the files (almost always a good idea). The disadvantage to CAB files is that you have to download everything in the CAB file. Imagine, for instance, that you have an ActiveX control that uses one of the MFC DLLs. If you place the control and the DLL in the same CAB file, the system must load everything, even if the target computer already has the MFC DLLs. Also, if you want to support multiple platforms, you won't want to download versions for all platforms on each machine.

Within the CAB file, you place an INF file that tells the system how to install the files in the cabinet. You can also specify an INF file directly. Using an INF file by itself is the most general method since it can point to other files (including CAB files). The INF file won't benefit from compression, but INF files are usually small, so this isn't a problem. Of course, you may compress the files that the INF file calls for by using a cabinet.

Writing An INF File

The INF file format is quite simple and resembles ordinary Windows INI files. The first section is the **[Add.Code]** section. In that section, you place a line that specifies a tag and a section name for each file you need to install. Then you create the sections that contain commands for each file. For example:

```
[Add.Code]
FILE1.OCX=FILE1.OCX
FILE2.DLL=FILE2.DLL
[FILE1.OCX]
...
```

You don't have to use the file name for the section name, but it is common practice. Besides, it helps keep things straight.

In each file section, you can place the following lines:

- **FILE=url.** Specifies where the system can download the control.
- **FILE=thiscab.** Informs the system that the file is in this cabinet (only applies to INF files in a cabinet).
- **FILEVERSION=a,b,c,d.** Version numbers for the control.

ActiveX And The Internet

- **FILE-WIN32-X86=url.** Indicates URL to use for downloading a version of code for Win32 platforms using an x86 processor. You can also use MAC in place of WIN32 for the Macintosh. In place of X86, you can also specify PPC, MIPS, or ALPHA.
- **FILE-WIN32-X86=ignore.** Informs the system that the file is not required (or not available) for the target platform specified. Again, you may specify MAC, PPC, ALPHA, or MIPS.
- **CLSID={...}.** The CLSID for the control in the usual registry format.
- **DESTDIR=10.** Places the file in the \WINDOWS directory (or whatever is the equivalent location for this machine). If there is no DESTDIR command, the system places the file in a special object cache directory.
- **DESTDIR=11.** Places the file in the \WINDOWS\SYSTEM directory (or its equivalent).

You can find a simple example INF file in Listing 7.7. In addition, Listing 7.8 shows a similar INF file that handles multiple platforms.

Listing 7.7 An example INF file.

```
; Sample INF File
[Add.Code]
Sample.OCX=Sample.OCX
MFC40.DLL=MFC40.DLL

[Sample.OCX]
File=http://www.coriolis.com/not_real/sample.ocx
CLSID={12345678-1234-1234-123456789abc}
FileVersion=1,0,0,1

[MFC40.DLL]
File=http://www.coriolis.com/not_real/mfc40.dll
FileVersion=4,0,0,5
```

Note that you can handle multiple platforms without using INF files. The system adds an HTTP Accept header when it queries the server for a control file. By interpreting this header, it is possible to send the correct executable or CAB file for the given platform. However, using the INF file is a much easier solution and easier to keep straight.

Listing 7.8 An example multiplatform INF file.

```
; Sample INF File
[Add.Code]
Sample.OCX=Sample.OCX

[Sample.OCX]
```

```
file-win32-x86=http://www.coriolis.com/not_real/x86/sample.ocx
file-win32-alpha=http://www.coriolis.com/not_real/a/sample.ocx
file-mac-ppc=ignore ; no mac!
CLSID={12345678-1234-1234-123456789abc}
FileVersion=1,0,0,1
```

One important advantage to using INF files is that the system can selectively download only the files that are not on the system already. For example, if the INF file contains a reference to a control and a reference to the MFC DLL that it requires, the system need only load the files that are not already present.

Building A CAB File

For reasons known only to Microsoft, CAB files are often known as Diamond files. Therefore, to build one, you must construct a Diamond directive file (DDF). This file has a very simple format:

```
.Option Explicit
.Set CabinetNameTemplate=anyname.CAB
.Set Cabinet=on
.Set Compress=on
file1
.
.
.
fileN
```

In the above example, you create a cabinet named ANYNAME.CAB (of course, you could name it anything you like). The cabinet will contain file1, fileN, and whatever other files you name in between.

When you want to create the cabinet file, run the DIANTZ utility:

```
DIANTZ /f xxx.DDF
```

Of course, be sure to substitute the name of your DDF file in the above command line.

Seeking Components

Just because a Web page designer specifies a certain **CODEBASE** parameter, doesn't mean that the browser will automatically download from that location. Instead, the browser refers to a special registry key to decide where to search for the component.

For Microsoft's browser, the key in question is under HKEY_CURRENT_USER\Software\Microsoft\InternetExplorer\CodeBaseSearchPath. This key's

ActiveX And The Internet

value is a list of URLs separated by semicolons. If a URL has a special value (**CODEBASE**), then the browser will search the location specified by the **CODEBASE** parameter in the Web page. Consider the examples shown in Table 7.7.

This approach gives the system administrator a great deal of control over the search for components. The first case tries to optimize performance by searching local object stores, while the third case forbids downloading except from certain known servers.

You might think that the third search path would allow a certain amount of security. That's true, although it is a bit draconian. If this were the sole method of controlling access, only controls that were on the trusted servers would be usable. If you are especially paranoid, that might be a good idea. However, most people would prefer a better solution. That's why the trust verification services exist.

Trust Verification

Every time you download a piece of code from the Internet, you risk infecting your system with a virus. That's a problem when you consciously transfer a file. Now that ActiveX can automatically download, install, and run an ActiveX component, the problem increases many times over. How can you be sure that the code that runs won't wipe out your hard disk or play other malicious tricks on you?

ActiveX provides trust verification services that allow you to control what code gets to execute on your machine. Here's the basic idea:

1. A software developer gets a certificate file from a trusted certificate authority. The authority verifies that the developer is legitimate.

Table 7.7 Codebase values and their meanings.

Codebase Value	Meaning
CodeBaseSearchPath=http://m1;http://m2;CODEBASE	Search local object stores first, then specified URL
CodeBaseSearchPath=CODEBASE	Always look where specified
CodeBaseSearchPath=http://m1;http://m2	Never download code from the specified location

2. The developer encrypts a digest of a file (similar to a checksum, but much longer) and combines it with the certificate to form a signature block.

3. The developer finally stores the signature block in the file.

When ActiveX downloads your file, it checks the signature block. It scans the certificate to see if it comes from a certificate authority that the system administrator trusts. It also checks the digest to verify that the file is unmodified. If there is no signature, the certificate is not trustworthy, and if the file appears modified, the system considers the file unsafe. If everything checks out, installation of the file proceeds.

Each certificate knows about the authority that issued it and the authority that certified the originating authority. That means your machine can trust authorities that it doesn't know about directly. Suppose, for example, that authority "A" trusts authority "B" and authority "B" issues the Coriolis Group a code certificate.

When you download a Coriolis control, your machine notes that the certificate originates from authority "B." Your machine doesn't know about authority "B," but by tracing the certificate chain, the system discovers that authority "B" has a certificate from authority "A." Therefore, the trust verification service concludes that the code is trustworthy.

If the system doesn't trust code, one of several things may happen, depending on the settings you use in the browser (as shown in Figure 7.8). For most users, the machine will refuse to load the offending component. However, you can elect to have the browser warn you that the code is not trustworthy, and then decide whether to load it. Finally, you can tell the browser to always load code, regardless of its trust status (a dangerous proposition).

This raises some interesting questions: Who trusts the authorities? Microsoft? A third-party group? If your machine becomes infected, who is liable? Will small-time developers be able to get certificates? How much will they cost? The answers to these questions are far from clear today. Only time will tell how safe—or how sinister—trust verification is.

Using Trust Verification

You can use the **MAKECERT** program to generate your keys and certificate file. Here's a typical command line:

Figure 7.8 Browser security settings.

```
MAKECERT -C -u:keyset -k:keyfile.pvk -n:"CN=CertName" mycert.cer
```

The arguments, in no particular order, are shown in Table 7.8.

Once you have a certificate file, you have to generate a signature block (sometimes known as credentials) by combining it with your trusted certificate. To test, you may use the ROOT.CER file that Microsoft provides. Run CERT2SPC to make your signature block:

```
CERT2SPC \inetsdk\bin\root.cer my.cer my.spc
```

The output of this command is the my.spc file. This file contains all of the certificates listed in the input (you can specify as many as you like).

Finally, you'll need to run the SIGNCODE wizard to add the Spc file to your code. Although this program has a wizard-style interface, you may prefer to provide command line options if you are running it as part of a lengthy build. The command line options are shown in Table 7.9.

You can see the results by running the CHKTRUST utility. This program checks your trust in the same way a user's browser will. Don't forget: Every time you change your code, you must resign your code.

Table 7.8 Arguments for the MakeCert program.

Argument	Meaning
-u	The keyset file used for the developer's public/private key pair. If this keyset does not exist, it is created.
-U	Use existing certificate and keys.
-k	The PVK file that contains the key pair. If this file doesn't exist, it is created.
-n	The name of the developer's certificate (the name must begin with CN= as in "CN=Al Williams Consulting").
-s	The issuer's key file (default to the test root key).
-i	The issuer's certificate.
-l	A URL to the policy information about this certification.
-I	Marks certificate as an individual certificate.
-C	Marks certificate as a commercial developer certificate (use :f to set financial criteria).
-S	Sets session.
-P	Sets purpose for certificate (default is code signing).
-x	Sets crypto provider.
-y	Sets crypto provider type.
-K	Type of key (S=signature, E=exchange).
-B	Start of valid period (defaults to now).
-D	Sets number of months certificate is valid.
-E	Sets end date of valid period (default is 2039).
-h	Sets maximum number of child certificates this certificate may have.
-t	Certificate type (E=end of hierarchy; C=potential root; may use both).
-g	Creates a glue certificate for encapsulating multiple certificates.
-r	Create a self-signed (no root) certificate.
-m	Uses MD5 hashing (default).
-a	Uses SHA1 hashing.
-N	Includes Netscape client authorization extension.
-#	Overrides default serial number (not recommended).

Table 7.9 Command-line options for SignCode.

Option	Meaning
-prog	Program name
-spc	Credential file
-pvk	Public/private key file or keyset name
-name	Program name
-info	URL or file for more information
-nocerts	No certification
-provider	Specifies which crypto provider to use
-providerType	Specifies what type of crypto provider to use
-individual	Marks as an individual developer (default)
-commercial	Marks as a commercial developer
-md5	Encrypts using MD5 hashing (default)
-sha	Encrypts using SHA1 hashing
-gui	Uses GUI to gather any additional arguments (without this option, incomplete command line options cause the operation to fail)

To summarize, here are the steps you must take along with example command lines:

1. Run MAKECERT to create a pair of keys (public and private keys) and associate the keys with a readable name, as in the example:

   ```
   MAKECERT -u:mykeys -n:CN=Coriolis newcert.cer
   ```

2. Run CERT2SPC to place the root certificate (presumably from a third-party) and the user certificate (from Step 1) into a signature block, as in the example:

   ```
   CERT2SPC root.cer newcert.cer coriolis.spc
   ```

3. Execute SIGNCODE to add the signature block to your executable file. If you just run the SIGNCODE program, you can fill in a wizard-like form to specify arguments. You may also use command line arguments, as in the example:

   ```
   SIGNCODE -prog myprogram.exe -spc coriolis.spc -pvk mykeys
   ```

Once these steps are complete, you can verify that the certificate is present by running PESIGMGR (Portable Executable SIGnature ManaGeR):

```
PESIGMGR -l myprogram.exe
```

You can also specify a variety of arguments to PESIGMGR to manually add and delete certificates (use PESIGMGR /? to find out more). Usually, you'll let SIGNCODE do all the work for you.

You can also manually check the file for trustworthiness by running CHKTRUST. Just specify your executable file name as an argument to this program. For practice, try making a copy of Solitaire (or any other small program), run CHKTRUST on it, and then sign it with your own signature. If you do this, try changing the file with a binary editor and note the results. The signature is only valid if the file is intact. While there is a small possibility that you could alter a file in such a way that the digest (basically a very long checksum) would not detect it, the chances of that are astronomically slim.

If you ever want to write a program to manually check a signature, you can call **WinVerifyTrust**. This API call finds the signature, validates it, and tells you whether the code is trustworthy.

The browser has a special setup dialog that allows you to confer trustworthy status to particular agencies or types of developers (as shown earlier in Figure 7.8). Also, if the browser prompts you for an unsafe component, you can ask it to consider other components from the same source as trustworthy (as shown in Figure 7.9).

Summary

Using ActiveX Internet controls can make writing Net-aware programs almost trivial. In the past, you needed to understand network software, communications layers, and complex protocols. Now, you just drop a control into your program and it handles all the details. The Web browser shown at the beginning of this chapter is a perfect example of this. By using a control, you don't need to know about networking protocols, HTML syntax, or address resolution. You simply provide URLs and the control does the rest.

If you want to write your own Internet controls, you don't necessarily need any special code to be Internet-aware. However, by using asynchronous

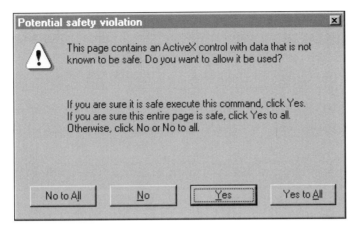

Figure 7.9 A security warning dialog.

URL monikers, you can improve the subjective performance of your code considerably. However, many practical controls don't download much data. In that case, you are free to ignore this special moniker interface.

On the other hand, you probably can't ignore the download and trust verification system. If you expect any one to be able to view your pages, you need to allow automatic downloading of your code. Of course, if you are creating a private service (perhaps on an Intranet or a subscription service), you might be able to assume the user already has the ActiveX code required. You might even depend on that as a rudimentary security measure. If users have not installed your software, your Web pages won't work properly.

However, generally, you'll need to automatically download code to each user's machine. The catch is trust verification. How easy will it be for small software developers to get adequate trust certificates? No one knows, and this has the potential of being a major barrier to small vendors and independent developers.

Because ActiveX is extensible, there is always something new. ActiveX is not a static entity. The pieces in this chapter are relatively new. In many cases, the interfaces and controls are still in beta release form and subject to change.

Still, this is what makes ActiveX so powerful. It has the ability to change and mutate to fit needs never dreamed of by the original designers. With proper forethought, new features can coexist with older controls and containers.

If you are old enough, you might remember a time when computer software always read data directly from disk. In those days, you always read a sector of data. If your data records didn't exactly fill a sector, it was your job to extract the record (or build the record from multiple sectors). Since everyone wrote code to do this, operating system designers eventually moved that functionality into the system code. Look for even more Internet-specific extensions to ActiveX in the future. As the Internet grows in importance, more and more Net features will become part of the operating system and less trouble to use in ordinary programs.

OTHER INTERFACE BUILDING TECHNIQUES

Unthread the rude eye of rebellion,
And welcome home again discarded faith.

— King John

PROGRAMMERS ARE A FAITHFUL BUNCH. Not necessarily in the traditional sense, mind you. I mean they get some tool, operating system, or hardware platform, and they stick with it no matter what. I'm often amused by the jihad that ensues if you ask a room full of Unix programmers if they use VI or Emacs. Of course, the C++ versus Pascal versus Basic versus (your favorite language here) wars never end. Even the various flavors of C or C++ have adherents who would rather fight than switch.

You don't find this mentality in most other creative or technical endeavors. I can't imagine a carpenter's convention shunning the guys who use saws (everyone knows hammers are wonderful). How many doctors still prescribe sulfa drugs for upper respiratory infections? How many banks still have hundreds of clerks with Underwood adding machines keeping the books?

Chapter 8

As a long-time consultant, I've been forced to work on many languages, operating systems, platforms, design methodologies—you name it. While I have my clear preferences (most of which I'll keep to myself so as not to offend anyone), I also know that some jobs are best done with certain tools. I rarely drive nails with a screwdriver (okay, sometimes I do, but rarely). I never cut wood with one. There just isn't a single best tool that fits every situation.

This book shows you several techniques you can use to construct ActiveX objects. You can use straight C++, or use MFC techniques to create your interfaces one at a time. If you are creating a classic ActiveX control, you can also use the Control Wizard to build a complete project. I'll admit that I have a strong C++ bias. But some would tell you that you should write ActiveX programs in Visual Basic (which might be a good thing in certain cases).

However, there is some middle ground. Often, you'll want to build some interfaces and you'd like some support to help you do that. However, you don't want all the interfaces a classic ActiveX control requires. To help in this situation, Microsoft recently introduced the ActiveX Template Library (ATL). This library uses C++ templates to give you the basic frame you need to build a generic ActiveX control. In addition, it provides support for common things like **IUnknown**, class factories, aggregation, connection points, **IEnum** interfaces, tear-off interfaces, and dual interfaces.

Should you use ATL? That depends. If you don't want to use MFC, ATL will allow you to create very small ActiveX controls. If you are using MFC anyway, ATL isn't much different from using the other techniques in this book. For completeness, this chapter shows you how to build a simple ActiveX control with ATL and discusses some of the issues you'll encounter if you try using ATL yourself. Be aware that this material is based on a beta release of ATL, and there may be slight differences in the version you are using.

As the name implies, ATL makes extensive use of C++ templates. If you aren't familiar with C++ templates, this would be a good time to read the next section, *About Templates*.

About Templates

Already know about templates?
If you're already familiar with templates, you might want to skip this section and go directly to the following section on "Key Features in the ActiveX Template Library."

Templates are a relatively new addition to the C++ language. Templates allow you to write functions and classes that are easy to reuse. They do this by transforming code at compile time so that you can ignore data types. Think about a function that is supposed to return the maximum of two values. Here's a version for integers:

```
int Max(int v1,int v2)
  {
  return v1>v2?v1:v2;
  }
```

The logic for this code only depends on the greater-than operator. There is no reason this code shouldn't work for any type that has such an operator. Of course, it won't work because the type **int** is hard-coded in the function. The integers are the function's data, but the greater-than operation is the function's logic or algorithm. Templates solve this type of problem by allowing you to specify the function's algorithm independently of the data involved. Consider this code:

```
template <class TYPE> TYPE Max(TYPE v1, TYPE v2)
  {
  return v1>v2?v1:v2;
  }
```

Now, when you call function **Max** with two integer arguments, the compiler will automatically create a function just like the first example. However, if you later call **Max** with two floating point arguments, the compiler will generate another function for floating point. Remember, C++ allows you to have multiple functions with the same name provided the arguments are different (function overloading). Notice that even though the syntax uses the **class** keyword, that doesn't imply a user-defined class. You can use user-defined classes or built-in types (like **int**, **char ***, or **float**, to name a few).

Templates are especially useful for encapsulating algorithms in classes. Suppose you wanted a class that accepted two values and always returned the larger one. Here's some template code that accomplishes that for any data type:

```
template <class TYPE> class Selector
  {
  private:
  TYPE v1;
  TYPE v2;
   public:
   Selector(TYPE xv1, TYPE xv2)  { v1=xv1; v2=xv2; };
   void Set1(TYPE v) { v1=v;};
   void Set2(TYPE v) { v2=v;};
    TYPE GetMax(void) { return v1>v2?v1:v2; };
    };
  };
```

Again, the class algorithm is separate from the data types. To create a **Selector** class for integers, you can write:

```
Selector<int> sel;
Selector<int> *selptr;
```

This can lead to some unwieldy type casts. You might prefer to simplify things with a **typedef**:

```
typedef Selector<int> IntSelector;
IntSelector sel, *selptr;
```

Notice that everywhere the parameter **TYPE** appears in the template, **int** appears in the final code. Of course, you can create as many kinds of **Selector** classes as you need (one for **float**; another for **CString**, for example). The compiler only generates functions for those you use. You don't have to write the functions inline, by the way. If you wanted to write the **GetMax** function in the conventional way, it would look like this:

```
template <class TYPE>
 TYPE Selector<TYPE>::GetMax(TYPE v1,TYPE v2)
    {
    return v1>v2?v1:v2;
    }
```

Although the function does not need to be inline, source files that use the template must have the entire function visible. Therefore, you'll almost always put the functions (inline or not) in a header file. The only exception would be where you place a template in the same CPP file that uses it and no other source file needs the same template.

The above examples were straightforward because none of the code changed for specific types. However, frequently, you'll want to have some specialized code depending on the type. Then you can create a generic base class with virtual functions. For example, suppose you wanted to extend the above class so that it could print the type formatted in a way specific to each type. Further suppose that the default stream I/O formatting was not adequate. You can still use templates:

```
template <class TYPE> class SelectorBase
   {
   private:
   TYPE v1;
   TYPE v2;
    public:
    SelectorBase(TYPE xv1, TYPE xv2)  { v1=xv1; v2=xv2; };
    void Set1(TYPE v) { v1=v;};
    void Set2(TYPE v) { v2=v;};
     TYPE GetMax(void) { return v1>v2?v1:v2; };
// pure virtual function - sub class must override
     virtual void PrintMax(void) =0;
     };
class IntSelector : public SelectorBase<int>
    {
    void PrintMax(void) { printf("Largest integer=%d (0x%x)\n",GetMax()); };
    };
```

Although type parameters are useful, you can also specify other constant arguments to a template. Suppose you wanted a selector class that could handle more than two entries. Here's some code to consider:

```
template <class T, int ct> class ArySelect
   {
   T * ary;
   public:
   ArySelect() { ary=new T[ct]; };
   ~ArySelect() { delete [] ary; };
   void Set(int n,T v) { ary[n]=v; };
   T GetMax(void);
    };
template <class T,int ct>
   T ArySelect<T,ct>::GetMax(void)
      {
      T maxv=ary[0];
      for (int n=1;n<ct;n++)
         if (maxv<ary[n]) maxv=ary[n];
      return maxv;
      }
```

This code passes an integer counter to define the size of the array. It is easy to imagine a simple template that didn't do any type manipulation at all. For example:

```
template <int sz> struct dataholder
    {
    char *name[sz];
    int score[sz];
    struct dataholder<sz> *links[2*sz];
    };
```

There is one other special case you'll find for template arguments. Suppose you have a class that you want to work one way for nearly every type. However, you want some special processing for character pointers and **CString** types. You could write something like this:

```
template <class T>
    class Special
    {
    // general code
    };
template <char *>
    class Special
    {
    // char * only code
    };
template <CString>
    class Special
    {
    // CString only code
    };
```

Templates are a powerful way to write generic code. ATL provides many templates that, combined with multiple inheritance, help you create COM interfaces of different kinds. Although the ATL templates are often quite complex, they all follow the same rules as these simple examples.

Key Features Of The ActiveX Template Library

ATL is a template library. That means it generates code based on your requirements each time you use it. Therefore, there are no libraries or DLLs that you have to include in your project. You only need a few H and CPP files. The code compiles right in with your choice of compiler options. Of course, if you want to use MFC (or some other library), you'll still need the DLLs and libraries for those.

When you use ATL, you'll typically derive a class from multiple base classes that exist as templates (or, more frequently, you'll let the ATL's wizard create the class for you). The class that represents your interfaces will almost always be derived from **CComObjectBase** (a template class). This provides all the common housekeeping required of an ActiveX object. If you are creating ordinary ActiveX interfaces, your class will also derive (via multiple inheritance) from the class that directly represents your interface functions (in other words, a C++ class that only contains your interface's member functions as pure virtual functions). That class typically is in a file that the **MKTYPLIB** utility creates. If you support multiple interfaces, your main class will derive from each of them.

Objects that implement a dual **IDispatch** interface derive from **CComObjectBase**. They also derive from **CComDualImpl** which supports the combination of **IDispatch** and a custom interface.

You can also use the **CComTearOffObject** class. This class allows you to have interfaces that are individually reference counted. When a client queries for a complex interface, you can create it at that time. When there are no more references on that interface, you can destroy it (leaving the object intact). Later, if there is another reference to the interface, the object can reconstruct it at that time. Of course, from the client's point of view, tear off interfaces are no big deal. However, if you have a complex interface that consumes resources, you can greatly improve efficiency by using a tear off interface.

ATL provides templates that allow you to easily create **IEnum** interfaces. Remember, there is no such thing as an **IEnum** interface. It is simply the algorithm that enumerators use. You have to have a specific enumerator for each data type you want to enumerate. What a perfect place to use templates. A template allows ATL to encapsulate the algorithm independent of the data type.

ATL also provides basic support for the server in the **CComModule** class. Usually, you'll just use this class as-is. However, you can derive your own class from it if you need to customize its behavior.

Like MFC, ATL also uses maps to organize certain parts of your code. The object map is a list of objects in your project. In the main CPP file, you'll find an object map. This map defines the objects you support and informs ATL how it should create those objects. Another map, the COM map, appears in each object's CPP file. It maps the interface **IID**s to the individual C++ classes that constitute the object.

Drawbacks Of ATL

Like everything else, ATL has its problems. First, you have to create each interface you want to use. This is not as simple as using the MFC Control Wizard to automatically generate a complete control. Of course, it is no worse than other methods you use when you want to create your own interfaces.

ATL also has no support for using Class Wizard to automatically manipulate your code or keep your ODL and IDL files in synch. Again, this isn't much different from other interface-by-interface methods, but it is a big drawback compared to the MFC Control Wizard-method.

When you generate an ATL project, you'll find that there are many subordinate classes that appear in the project's Class View. These classes work behind the scenes, and they clutter up the interface and can cause confusion.

One other problem with ATL is that the wizard you use to start an ATL project leaves a bit to be desired. There are many things you can't do directly from the wizard. Also, it has several quirks in the generated code. For example, you can create multiple objects at once, but they all start with the same number of interfaces. Sure, you can fix up the code manually, but it defeats the purpose of a wizard.

For its faults, ATL is a robust way to create ActiveX objects interface by interface. If you are comfortable working with templates, give it a try. Of course, if you are creating a full-blown control and want to use MFC anyway, the MFC Control Wizard does a good job and is much easier to use. ATL is best for cases when you want to squeeze every last byte out of your control.

Getting Started With ATL

The best way to start an ATL control is to use the custom wizard. Select New from the File menu. Then pick **Project Workspace**. From the dialog that appears, select the **OLE COM AppWizard** icon and fill in the other information, as shown in Figure 8.1.

This leads to a screen where you will enter information about your project, as shown in Figure 8.2. Although the wizard allows you to create multiple objects per project, it always creates the objects with the same number of interfaces. If you want a completely custom interface, select the **Custom Interface** checkbox. If you are creating a dispatch interface, select **Dual Interface**, instead.

Other Interface Building Techniques 323

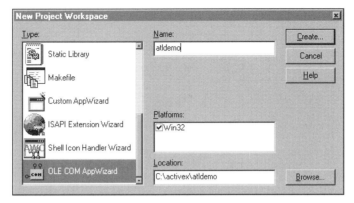

Figure 8.1 Starting an ATL Project.

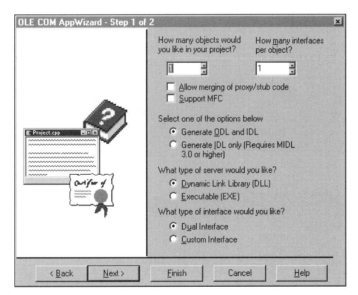

Figure 8.2 The first ATL wizard screen.

When you click on **Next**, you'll see a screen that contains a list of objects you asked to create. You can pick any one of them and modify their information from this screen, shown in Figure 8.3. When you are satisfied, click on **Finish** to generate the project.

After the wizard builds the project, you'll need to add a few build steps to process the IDL file and register the server. The instructions for adding these steps are in the comments for the main source file. You'll also see how to do this in the example later in this chapter.

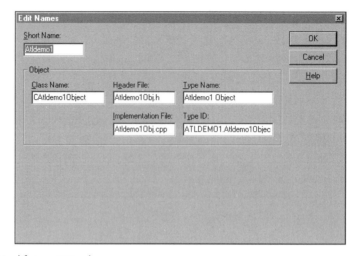

Figure 8.3 Modifying ATL's class names.

The wizard generates several files. Suppose your project name is CTL. The main code for your module is then in CTL.CPP. Your object will be in CTLOBJ.CPP and CTLOBJ.H (assuming you didn't change the names). Of course, the wizard also creates your RC, ODL, IDL, and MAK files. It also generates a file, PS.MAK, that you may use to generate the proxy DLL, if you need it (this is mainly for local servers or remote DLL servers).

Working With Maps

ATL uses an object map in your main CPP file to organize the objects a project contains. These maps are simply an array of data that you construct with special macros. The array contains several things for each object:

- The CLSID of the object
- A method ATL can use to create the object
- The object's PROGID
- The object's version-specific PROGID
- A string table entry for the object's description
- Flags that specify options (such as the chosen threading model)

There are three macros you can use to construct an object map:

- **RAWOBJECT_ENTRY.** Used to specify an object when you supply an object that returns a class factory capable of creating the object.

- **OBJECT_ENTRY.** Used to specify an object that uses the default class factory.
- **FACTORYOBJECT_ENTRY.** Used to specify an object that has an explicit class factory.

These macros appear between the **BEGIN_OBJECT_MAP** and **END_OBJECT_MAP** macros. The wizard automatically places these in the correct place in your main CPP file.

This map tells ATL about each object in your project. Another map, the COM map, tells ATL about each interface in a particular object (each object has its own COM map). This information is especially important for the default **QueryInterface** implementation.

The COM table begins with a **BEGIN_COM_MAP** macro and ends with an **END_COM_MAP** entry. In between those entries (which the wizard automatically generates in your object's header file) you can use any of the following macros:

- **COM_INTERFACE_ENTRY.** Used when you specify the class name only; ATL prepends IID_ to the name to generate the IID. Example: COM_INTERFACE_ENTRY(ICustomInterface).
- **COM_INTERFACE_ENTRY_IID.** Used when you want to specify the class name and the IID independently. This is useful when you have an object that implements a class but you want it to respond as a base class. For example: COM_INTERFACE_ENTRY_IID(IID_IProvideClassInfo, IProvideClassInfo2).
- **COM_INTERFACE_ENTRY2.** Used when you have several objects that implement the same interface. For example, when you have multiple dual interfaces, you can't refer to **IDispatch** since all the dual interfaces use **IDispatch** as a base class. This entry lets you specify a specific class. Example: COM_INTERFACE_ENTRY2(IDispatch, IDual2).
- **COM_INTERFACE_ENTRY2_IID.** Same as COM_INTERFACE_ENTRY2 except this macro takes an explicit IID.
- **COM_INTERFACE_ENTRY_TEAR_OFF.** Specifies a tear off interface.
- **COM_INTERFACE_ENTRY_AGGREGATE.** Specifies that this interface is aggregated from another object.

Don't forget, the wizard provides an object map and a COM map for you to start with. Often, you won't need to change these at all. Sometimes, you'll want to manually add more interfaces or objects (for example, if you have objects with a different number of interfaces). Also, the wizard doesn't generate code for tear off interfaces or aggregation. You'll have to modify the maps in those cases, too.

Customizing Interfaces

The wizard automatically sets up your maps so that each interface has its own empty object. If you are writing a custom interface, the object derives from your interface and **CComObjectBase**. If the interface is a dual interface (that is, it implements **IDispatch** and a custom interface), it will derive from **CComObjectBase** and **CComDualImpl**.

To flesh out your interface, you'll need to modify the ODL and IDL files. You'll also have to add your interface function to the header and CPP files. You can easily do both files in one step if you use Visual C++'s Class View, shown in Figure 8.4. Just right-click on the class you want to augment. Select **Add Function** from the pop-up menu. Then, fill in the dialog that appears, as shown in Figure 8.5. This conveniently adds the function prototype to the header and places the function stub in the CPP file. Of course, this still leaves the ODL and IDL files for you to handle yourself.

For a simple ATL object, that's all you need. The ATL code automatically handles **AddRef**, **Release**, and **QueryInterface** (via the COM maps). The object map takes care of class factory problems, so you won't need to write a class factory either.

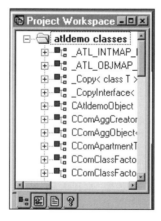

Figure 8.4 Class View.

Other Interface Building Techniques 327

Figure 8.5 Adding a function.

Decreasing Code Size

Because one of the main reasons you might use ATL is to write a very small control, you might wonder if there is any way to further shrink the code. If you don't need support from the C runtime library, there is a way. You can shed about 20K of space by forcing the compiler to omit the C runtime startup code. If you rely on global classes that require construction, you can't use this technique. The C runtime startup constructs global objects. But if you don't need that, here's what to do:

1. Turn off exception handling. You can do this in the **Build Settings** menu item. Look for the **C++** tab and select the **C++ Language** category. You'll find a checkbox from exception handling that you can clear. Of course, that implies that you don't use exception handling. If you do, you can't use this technique.

2. Define **_ATL_MINCRT** so that ATL will supply **new** and **delete** functions (these usually come from the C runtime library).

3. Specify **DllMain** as the entry point for the code. You can do this in the **Build Settings** menu item. Find the **Link** tab and select the **Output** category. You'll see a field where you can specify the entry point.

Aggregation And ATL

ATL does simplify aggregation support considerably. Each object has a macro in its header file that—behind the scenes—arranges for a class factory. You can select one of two macros, depending on your wishes for aggregation.

—If you want to disallow aggregation, use the **DECLARE_NOT_AGGREGATABLE** macro. If you want to allow aggregation, use **DECLARE_AGGREGATABLE** instead. However, if a client creates your object without aggregation, there is no penalty for using **DECLARE_AGGREGATABLE**. The code is exactly the same except for the case where a client actually aggregates your object.

You can also aggregate other objects with ATL. Simply override **FinalConstruct** and create your subordinate objects there. This is also a good place to create objects you want to contain, or do any other initialization that requires a completely constructed object. The base class constructor calls **FinalConstruct** after the object is built. Of course, if you are creating an object for aggregation, don't forget to pass your **IUnknown** pointer as the controlling unknown. You can easily get your **IUnknown** pointer by calling **InternalQueryInterface**.

Creating Enumeration Classes

To create an enumeration class, you'll derive from **CComEnumImpl**. This is a template that takes four template arguments. The first is the base class. That is, the enumeration class you are implementing. For example, you might use **IEnumVariant**. The second argument is the enumeration's **IID**. Next comes the type of the data the enumeration returns. The final argument is a class that knows how to copy, construct, and delete the data types.

You might wonder why this is easier than creating an enumeration from scratch. Well, ATL provides a default **_Copy** template object that works for items that you can manage simply by copying bits. It also provides special versions of **_Copy** that work with **VARIANT**s and **CONNECTDATA** structures. There is also a **_CopyInterface** template that correctly manages interfaces for an enumeration that returns interface pointers.

You can use these classes, or you can use them as a model to help you create your own copy objects. Here's the code for copying **VARIANT**s:

```
class _Copy<VARIANT>
{
public:
        static void copy(VARIANT* p1, VARIANT* p2) {VariantCopy(p1, p2);}
        static void init(VARIANT* p) {VariantInit(p);}
        static void destroy(VARIANT* p) {VariantClear(p);}
};
```

Then, if you want to enumerate **VARIANT**s, you can generate a class like this:

```
typedef CComEnumImpl<IEnumVariant,&IID_IEnumVariant,VARIANT
    ,_Copy<VARIANT>> VarEnum;
VarEnum a_varient_enumerator; // create class
```

The object assumes that your data is in an array. You'll call the **Init** member to set up the data in the enumerator. This call takes five arguments:

- **begin.** A pointer to the beginning of the enumeration data.
- **end.** A pointer to the end of the enumeration data.
- **pUnk.** An optional pointer to an object whose lifetime controls the enumerated data.
- **bCopy.** If **TRUE**, the enumeration makes a private copy of the data during the **Init** call.
- **bNoInitialUnkAddRef**. If **TRUE**, the enumeration ignores the **pUnk** argument to **Init**.

One special case you'll see in the ATL source code is when some code creates a list for enumeration, and then wants the enumerator to destroy it. In that case, the caller will pass **FALSE** for **Init**'s **bCopy** flag, but later set it directly using the **m_dwFlags** member. That way, when the enumerator's destructor executes, it will clean up the array.

If you want to create a complete object that only contains an enumeration interface, you can use this syntax:

```
CSomeEnumObj *obj=new CComObject<CSomeEnumInterface>;
```

You can find several examples of using the enumeration classes in the ATL source code. ATL uses enumerators to support connection points.

Connection Point Containers

To create a connection point container, you need to create a **CComConnectionPointContainerImpl** object. This is a template and takes a single argument. That argument tells the container what type of array to use to hold the connections.

The most general type of array is the **CComDynamicArrayCONNECTDATA** array. This array can handle any number of connections. If you know how many connections the container must handle, you can elect to use

CComStaticArrayCONNECTDATA. This array is more efficient, since you pass it an upper boundary as a template argument. To further boost efficiency, there is a special case in which you specify that there is only one connection possible. This produces the most efficient code. Why manage an array when there is only one connection?

The **CComConnectionPointContainerImpl** object contains **CComConnectionPoint** objects. This class is the one that actually uses the array specified for the connection container.

Tear-off Interfaces

If you want, you can group one or more interfaces into another object. This allows ATL to create that object only when a client requests one of its interfaces.

This would be a complex task without ATL. With ATL, it is simple, albeit not trivial. First, derive a class from the interface classes you want in the tear off and derive it from **CComTearOffObjectBase**. This template class takes parameters to indicate the main class (that is the class with the non-tear-off interfaces) and the CLSID for the object. In this object, you create a normal COM map to assign interface IDs. However in the main class, you use the **COM_INTERFACE_ENTRY_TEAR_OFF** macro to specify the **IID** and the object that provides that tear-off interface.

You won't have a frequent need to create tear-off interfaces. However, if you need them, ATL makes them significantly easier to create.

Error Handling

All objects you create with ATL's wizard also derive from **ISupportErrorInfo**. This class allows extended error reporting to programs that support it. The interface has a single member function (**InterfaceSupportsErrorInfo**) that returns an indication that the object supports extended error information via the **IErrorInfo** interface, shown in Table 8.1.

All objects derived from **CComObject** can call one of the **Error** functions to automatically create an object that has the **IErrorInfo** interface. Then, the primary **Error** function calls the global function **SetErrorInfo** with the object.

There are several variations of the **Error** function, depending on what you want to pass. The primary function requires your **CLSID**, a string describing

Other Interface Building Techniques 331

Table 8.1 The IErrorInfo interface.

Function	Description
GetDescription	Returns an error message
GetGUID	Returns the CLSID corresponding to the program raising the error
GetHelpContext	Retrieve the help ID for the error
GetHelpFile	Returns the help file for the error
GetSource	Returns the PROGID of the program raising the error (language-dependent)

the error, an **IID**, and the **HRESULT**. The other versions take different types of strings or a string ID so you can load the description string from the program's resources.

An ATL Project

To see how ATL creates a real control, look at Listings 8.1 and 8.2. This very simple control illustrates a dual interface **IDispatch** control. It only has one function, **Beep**. To start this control, run the ATL Wizard and select one object with one interface. In addition, tell ATL that you want a dual interface (as opposed to a custom interface).

Listing 8.1 An ATL control (H file).

```
// AtldemoObj.h : Declaration of the CAtldemoObject
#include "resource.h"       // main symbols
/////////////
// atldemo
class CAtldemoObject :
   public CComDualImpl<IAtldemo, &IID_IAtldemo, &LIBID_ATLDEMOLib>,
   public ISupportErrorInfo,
   public CComObjectBase<&CLSID_Atldemo>
{
public:
   CAtldemoObject() {}
BEGIN_COM_MAP(CAtldemoObject)
   COM_INTERFACE_ENTRY(IDispatch)
   COM_INTERFACE_ENTRY(IAtldemo)
   COM_INTERFACE_ENTRY(ISupportErrorInfo)
END_COM_MAP()
// Use DECLARE_NOT_AGGREGATABLE(CAtldemoObject)
// if you don't want your object  to support aggregation
DECLARE_AGGREGATABLE(CAtldemoObject)
```

```
// ISupportsErrorInfo
   STDMETHOD(InterfaceSupportsErrorInfo)(REFIID riid);
// IAtldemo
// Our custom function(s)
   STDMETHOD(Beep)(void);
public:
};
```

Listing 8.2   The ATL object's CPP file.

```
// AtldemoObj.cpp : Implementation of CatldemoApp and DLL registration.

#include "stdafx.h"
#include "atldemo.h"
#include "AtldemoObj.h"

/////////////////////////
//
// The wizard wrote this to indicate that we support
// extended error info
STDMETHODIMP CAtldemoObject::InterfaceSupportsErrorInfo(REFIID riid)
{
   if (riid == IID_IAtldemo)
      return S_OK;
   return S_FALSE;
}

// Custom function ID=1
STDMETHODIMP CAtldemoObject::Beep(void)
   {
   MessageBeep((unsigned)-1);
   return S_OK;
   }
```

Before you begin modifying the object, you'll need to add a few build steps that the wizard fails to incorporate into your project. You'll find the instructions embedded in your main CPP file as comments. If you need proxies and stubs, you'll need to run the MIDL compiler to generate them. Open up the Build Settings dialog and select the Custom Build Steps tab. On the left side, expand both the debug and release projects so that you can see the files inside. Click on the IDL file in one branch, then hold down the control key and click on the same IDL file in the other branch. Then fill in the compile steps, as shown in Figure 8.6.

You also need to add a step to register the server. You do that in the same way, except that this time, you select both projects: you'll have to collapse them first. The proper entry is: REGSVR32 /s /c "$(TargetPath)"?.

Once you add the extra build steps, you are ready to add your own functions. The first step is to alter the ODL and IDL files (see Listings 8.3 and

Other Interface Building Techniques 333

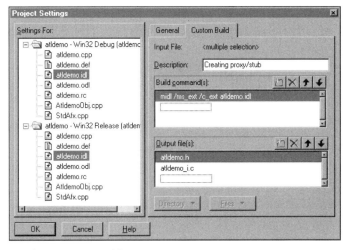

Figure 8.6 Setting the Custom Build steps.

8.4). If you are using the newest MIDL compiler, you can combine these files into a single file.

Listing 8.3 The ODL file.

```
// atldemo.odl : type library source for atldemo.dll
//

////////////
// NOTE - Make sure and edit the atldemo.idl file as well when you make
// changes to this file
////////////

// This file will be processed by the Make Type Library (mktyplib) tool to
// produce the type library (atldemo.tlb).

[
   uuid(BE3A4F61-F676-11CF-A7B2-444553540000),
   version(1.0),
   helpstring("atldemo 1.0 Type Library")
]
library ATLDEMOLib
{
   importlib("stdole32.tlb");

   [
      uuid(BE3A4F62-F676-11CF-A7B2-444553540000),
      dual,
      helpstring("IAtldemo Interface"),
   ]
   interface IAtldemo : IDispatch
   {
   // custom function
```

```
    [id(1)] HRESULT Beep();
    };
    [
        uuid(BE3A4F66-F676-11CF-A7B2-444553540000),
        helpstring("Atldemo Class")
    ]
    coclass Atldemo
    {
        [default] interface IAtldemo;
    };
};
```

Listing 8.4   The IDL file.

```
// atldemo.idl : IDL source for atldemo.dll
//

///////////////
// NOTE - Make sure and edit the atldemo.odl file as well when you make
// changes to this file
///////////////

// This file will be processed by the MIDL tool to
// produce the marshalling code.

    [
        object,
        uuid(BE3A4F62-F676-11CF-A7B2-444553540000),
        pointer_default(unique)
    ]
    interface IAtldemo : IDispatch
    {
        import "oaidl.idl";
        // our custom function(s)
        HRESULT Beep();
    }
```

After you modify the ODL and IDL files, it is a simple matter to add the **Beep** function to the header and CPP files. The function itself is trivial. You may add as many functions as you like. Of course, they can do something more useful than this one, too.

If you want to verify that the object works, you can use the simple demo program in Listing 8.5. This is a very simple dialog-based program. When you dismiss the dialog with the **OK** button, the code initializes the ActiveX system, creates an object, and uses it to create an instance of the class via its ProgID. (Note that I changed the ProgID from its default on the second ATL Wizard screen.)

To build the files that contain the object that wraps the ActiveX control, you simply use Class Wizard to add a new class. You can ask Class Wizard to add the new class based on a TypeLib and select the control you want to wrap. Class Wizard takes care of the rest, building a CPP and H file. It even adds it to the project. Of course, you still have to refer to the new H file in the source files where you plan to use the new class.

Listing 8.5 Using the ATL control.

```
// atluser.cpp : Defines the class behaviors for the application.
//
#include "stdafx.h"
#include "atluser.h"
#include "atluserDlg.h"
#include "atldemo.h"

#ifdef _DEBUG
#define new DEBUG_NEW
#undef THIS_FILE
static char THIS_FILE[] = __FILE__;
#endif

/////////////
// CAtluserApp

BEGIN_MESSAGE_MAP(CAtluserApp, CWinApp)
    //{{AFX_MSG_MAP(CAtluserApp)
    // NOTE - the ClassWizard will add and remove mapping macros here.
    //    DO NOT EDIT what you see in these blocks of generated code!
    //}}AFX_MSG
    ON_COMMAND(ID_HELP, CWinApp::OnHelp)
END_MESSAGE_MAP()

////////////////
// CAtluserApp construction

CAtluserApp::CAtluserApp()
{
    // TODO: add construction code here,
    // Place all significant initialization in InitInstance
}

////////////////
// The one and only CAtluserApp object

CAtluserApp theApp;

////////////////
// CAtluserApp initialization

BOOL CAtluserApp::InitInstance()
{
    // Standard initialization
```

```
    // If you are not using these features and wish to reduce the size
    // of your final executable, you should remove from the following
    // the specific initialization routines you do not need.

#ifdef _AFXDLL
    Enable3dControls();         // Call this when using MFC in a shared DLL
#else
    Enable3dControlsStatic();   // Call this when linking to MFC statically
#endif

    CAtluserDlg dlg;
    m_pMainWnd = &dlg;
    int nResponse = dlg.DoModal();
    if (nResponse == IDOK)
    {
       IAtldemo obj;
       AfxOleInit();
       obj.CreateDispatch("AtlDemo.AtlDemoObject");
       obj.Beep();
    }
    else if (nResponse == IDCANCEL)
    {
    }

    // Since the dialog has been closed, return FALSE so that we exit the
    //  application, rather than start the application's message pump.
    return FALSE;
}
```

Next Steps

There are several modifications you can attempt to help solidify your understanding of ATL. First, you can add a second interface function. Just follow the steps outlined in the *Customizing Interfaces* section. You might also try decreasing the code size using the steps from the *Decreasing Code Size* section.

If you really want a challenge, try adding an entirely different interface. You'll need to arrange for your object class to derive from another new class, and modify the COM map. Can you add a new object? That is similar to adding a new interface, except you'll create a new class, a new COM map, and you'll need to modify the object map.

Useful ATL Classes

There are several ATL classes you might find useful in your own code (even if you don't use ATL). You can find the code for these classes (and all of ATL) in the ATL source (ATLBASE.H, ATLCOM.H, ATLIMPL.CPP, and ATLUTIL.H). All of these files reside in the ordinary *include* directory.

One general-purpose class that ATL uses is **CRegKey**. This is a simple wrapper for a registry key. You can find its member functions in Table 8.2. Manipulating the registry is not overly difficult, but this wrapper makes it more C++-like, and provides a few handy helper functions that are not direct translations of the API.

Another class you might use is the **CComPtr** class. This template stores an **IUnknown** pointer and automatically handles calling **AddRef** and **Release** at the appropriate times. You can specify the type of the actual pointer as the template argument:

```
CComPtr<IDispatch> dispatchptr;
```

You can find the operations defined for **CComPtr** in Table 8.3. There is only one oddity in these functions. The reference operator faces a dilemma. If you want a reference to a pointer, you are probably passing the pointer to a function as an output parameter. Since the function you call won't know

Table 8.2 The CRegKey class.

Function	Description
Attach	Attach existing HKEY
Detach	Detach HKEY
Create	Create new key
Open	Open existing key
Close	Close key
SetValue	Set named value
QueryValue	Find named value
SetKeyValue	Set default key value
DeleteSubKey	Delete key
RecurseDeleteKey	Delete key and everything under it
DeleteValue	Delete a value

Table 8.3 CComPtr functions.

Function	Definition
operator T*	Casts pointer to template parameter type
operator int	Casts pointer to integer
operator *	Dereference pointer
operator &	Generate reference to pointer (see text)
operator ->	Dereference pointer
operator =	Assignment

this is a special **CComPtr**, the class can't correctly release the pointer before the caller uses the variable. Therefore, it always releases the current pointer and sets it to **NULL** before returning the reference. This works fine if the parameter is really an output parameter. However, if the function expects to find a non-**NULL** value in the parameter for input, all bets are off.

Look at these two fictitious functions:

```
void f1(IDispatch *&p)
   {
   p=fill_in_pointer();
   };

void f2(IDispatch *&p)
   {
   IDualZap zap;  // some interface
   if (FAILED(p->QueryInterface(IID_DualZap,&zap)) 
      p=fill_in_pointer();
   }
```

Now consider the following code:

```
CComPtr<IDispatch> p(disp_ptr);
f1(disp_ptr);   // OK, f1 uses as output param
f2(disp_ptr);   // Bad: original contents released first
```

In this example, the code releases the original pointer (**disp_ptr**) before calling **f1**. The **f1** function receives a reference to a **NULL** pointer. However, since **f1** doesn't attempt to use the pointer, that's no problem. It simply fills in the pointer and returns.

The **f2** function, on the other hand, tries to use the reference parameter passed into it. Since taking the reference of the **CComPtr** causes it to become **NULL**, there is no valid parameter for **f2** to examine. This is

Other Interface Building Techniques 339

insidious because everything compiles and appears to work fine. The **CComPtr** class behaves this way on purpose, but it can cause you problems if you are unsuspecting.

BASECTL: Another Approach

If you want a low-overhead, non-MFC control, but you don't want to get into so much detail, you might find the BASECTL sample from the ActiveX SDK useful. This is a bare-bones library similar to ATL (but not template-based). There are several skeletal controls all ready to go. You can modify them for your own purposes to get a control going quickly. BASECTL is technically a sample program, and therefore Microsoft doesn't support it. ATL, on the other hand, is not currently supported, but will one day ship with Microsoft's compiler and become a full-fledged, shipping product.

The overhead of this approach is low, although you lose the ability to use MFC. Still, for many controls—especially those without any user interface—that isn't much of a loss. Besides, a control that doesn't use MFC can be quite lean and not depend on a large DLL.

The key classes you need to work with from BASECTL are:

- **CUnknown.** All objects derive from this class and it helps support aggregation
- **CAutomationObject.** A generic automation object
- **COleControl.** Derived from CAutomationObject; This object implements a traditional ActiveX control
- **CPropertyPage.** An ActiveX property page

To create an ActiveX object, you'll derive a new object from **COleControl** and the class that contains your interface functions. If you support multiple interfaces, your control has to derive from them all.

In your derived class, you have to implement a few virtual functions (see Table 8.4). You also have to place information about your object in a global table (**g_ObjectInfo**). You can define any objects here by using the **CONTROLOBJECT**, **AUTOMATIONOBJECT** and **PROPERTYPAGE** macros. Then in the class header file, you'll use another macro to actually set the type (one of: **DEFINE_CONTROL_OBJECT**, **DEFINE_WINDOWLESS CONTROL**, **DEFINE_AUTOMATIONOBJECT**, or **DEFINE_PROPERTY PAGEOBJECT**). Finally, you need to place your TYPELIB's **LIBID** in the **g_pLibid** variable.

Table 8.4 BASECTL mandatory virtual functions.

Function	Description
OnDraw	Draw control
WindowProc	Window procedure (don't handle **WM_PAINT** here; use **OnDraw**)
LoadBinaryState	Load binary properties from an **IPersist** interface
LoadTextState	Load text from an **IPersistPropertyBag** interface
SaveBinaryState	Save binary properties
SaveTextState	Save text properties
RegisterClassData	Register window class information

In addition to the functions you must override, the framework provides many useful functions that you can override, if you want. For example, you can override **OnSetExtent** if you need to know when the control's size changes.

There are many functions you may call to help you perform common tasks, too. For instance, **GetAmbientProperty** and **GetAmbientFont** which do what you think they do. **PropertyChanged** will notify the client that a property has changed. You can call **ControlFromUnknown** to convert an **IUnknown** pointer to the corresponding **COleControl** pointer. You can find a complete list in the BASECTL README.TXT file.

Although BASECTL is an effective solution for ActiveX controls, it is only slightly easier than ATL. It is also not as flexible as ATL. That, combined with the lack of official support, make BASECTL a poor choice in most cases.

Summary

If you go back and count, you'll find at least five different methods to create ActiveX controls: straight C++, modified MFC, MFC Control Wizard, ATL, and BaseCtl. Which is best? What's the best tool? A hammer, a screwdriver, or a wrench? There isn't a single correct answer for everyone in every situation.

If you are developing applications for which you can easily deploy the MFC libraries, it is hard to beat the Control Wizard. It does so much for you and makes things much easier. However, if you have to send the entire control (including the MFC DLL) over a slow connection, you might consider using some of the other methods. ATL is probably the most flexible, but it is also the next to the most difficult technique to use. The most difficult is using straight C++, which you should avoid like the plague. When you use straight C++, you get to do all the work and you get absolutely no help. ATL, at least, will create your class factory, implement **IUnknown**, and do other mundane tasks with which you'd rather not deal.

As ActiveX grows in importance, you will see more tools that are capable of generating controls and components. Many of these will use C++, but some will not. Regardless, if you understand ActiveX fundamentals, you'll have no problem with these new tools. Advanced understanding of ActiveX can lead to better designs and easier debugging. So don't worry. Time spent learning the fundamentals now will pay off in the future.

The End?

No epilogue, I pray you,
For your play needs no excuse.
Never excuse.

—**A Midsummer's Night Dream**

WHO KNOWS WHAT THE FUTURE will hold? Over the long haul, nobody really knows. However, for the foreseeable future, it's clear that Microsoft will be a big part of that future. And, for good or ill, Microsoft wants ActiveX to succeed.

Why fight it? Overall, ActiveX is a very versatile protocol for working with binary objects. It can be as efficient as you like or as feature-rich as you need (although not always at the same time). With the proper tools (like the MFC Wizards in Chapter 6), ActiveX doesn't even have to be all that difficult.

Do you remember the imaginary scenario in Chapter 1? The example where you (disguised as a Herman Miller salesman) send me some flaming email? That future is not very far off. ActiveX (and technologies layered on top of ActiveX) will make it possible.

If you go out a bit further, you'll see even more changes. Imagine a workspace that allows you to plug in modules that you need to perform certain jobs. A word processor is a great example of that. As a business owner, I need a word processor that types letters, packing lists, and proposals. As an author, I need a word processor that handles huge documents, does indexing, and word counting. As a programmer, I need a word processor that handles inserting code snippets, graphics, and produces RTF for my help files.

Today, when you buy a word processor you get all of this and more. For example, I never use the features aimed at producing legal pleading papers (thank goodness). You wind up with a giant program that is hard to learn and use.

What if you had a general-purpose frame into which you could drop a universal text component? The text component would do basic text manipulation. Since I need indexing and style management compatible with a publishing program, I could drop in those modules (maybe from two different vendors). The text component might have a spell checker, that is horrible at spell checking computer-related documents, so I'd buy a computer-literate spell checker from someone else.

When programming, I might use the same text component for writing code. Then I'd use the compiler module and the help file module to compile, debug, and create help all in the same environment. We'd have the ultimate customizable programming environment.

Another example would be a high-end graphics program. You can easily imagine various graphics converters, filters, and drawing tools forming a mix and match environment. Of course, if you did it right, the same tools from the graphics program would drop right into the word processor and vice versa.

Will this come to pass? I think so. The obstacles are more legal and diplomatic than technological. If the industry can agree on how components integrate their functionality with a controlling frame and meaningfully share content, then this sort of application is right around the corner. Things like ActiveX controls approach this, but they still lack an easy way to share content. For example, how does the spell checker control cooperate with the frame that contains text?

The Future Of The Internet

Don't forget: The ActiveX controls in this book just scratch the surface of Microsoft's Internet strategy. There are server scripting tools that can allow Web servers to store preferences, tally votes, and run code either on the server or on the host.

Once there is some uniform way to provide active content, look for more plug-in tools that will extend Web pages. You can already build 3D Web sites, or include sophisticated presentation graphics. What will be next? Interactive games? Live stock quotes? Real time video from concerts?

The Future Of Java

Java has an unusual position in the PC world. It started the idea of active content on the Internet. While Java works well at those tasks for which it was explicitly designed, it falls short in areas where people have pushed it. Java is largely interpreted and often lacks sophisticated development tools that the C++ industry has spent years building. Java code can't easily communicate with other Java programs (or applets). It also can't easily communicate with its container (the Web browser).

Besides, many people already know how to program in C++ or some other standard language. If these languages can provide the same features as Java, then why learn Java and switch?

About the only compelling argument for Java today is its cross-platform nature. Java will run on nearly any kind of computer with any operating system: Windows PCs, Macs, Unix boxes, and more. Today, ActiveX is primarily a Windows phenomenon. Microsoft promises that ActiveX will move to other platforms rapidly, however. Only time will tell how successful these ActiveX ports will be. On the other hand, the basic ideas behind ActiveX are quite simple and similar to RPC. It is easy to imagine how other machines and operating systems could incorporate ActiveX technology.

Shortly before this was written, Microsoft released a beta-test version of Visual J++, a Java environment that works like Microsoft's Visual C++ environment. This certainly gives Java a world-class development environment (whether you like the environment or not, you have to admit that there's plenty of it). It also telegraphs an odd strategy for Microsoft: straddling the fence. It is clear that Microsoft wants ActiveX to be the long-term answer for active Web content. But Microsoft also realizes that for the immediate future, Java was there first. In particular, until ActiveX successfully demonstrates its ability to cross platforms seamlessly, Java will still have its proponents.

The Future Of Other Object Standards

When it comes to building reusable objects, ActiveX has plenty of competition. There are many competing standards that attempt to define binary object compatibility guidelines (for example, DSOM or CORBA). However, these standards have not gained widespread acceptance—at least, not in the Windows world.

Why these other standards can't gain a foothold isn't clear. Of course, Microsoft's full weight behind ActiveX hasn't hurt it any. Also, instead of one cohesive standard there are a half-dozen different "standards." This limits the possibility of any serious competition to ActiveX, because Microsoft doesn't need a lot of cooperation to set a standard.

The Future Of Windows

There's an old saying in the engineering world: I don't know what language engineers will be using to write programs in the year 2020, but I know they will call it FORTRAN. You could make the same observation about operating systems: I don't know what the desktop operating system will be in the year 2020, but I know it will be named Windows. Granted, it is possible that some brilliant company will find a way to break the Microsoft stranglehold on the desktop operating system market. However, how that would happen is far from clear (if you know, then put down this book, go out, and get rich).

For developers, this isn't necessarily a bad thing. Having an operating system that runs on the vast majority of computers makes things easier for us. There are fewer new things to learn, large markets for our software, greater protection on our investments (both time and money) in hardware, software, and code.

However, Windows is not set in stone. In the last decade, we've seen Windows move from a very sophisticated DOS shell, to an operating system that has more in common with Unix and the Macintosh (shudder) than it does with DOS. You can look for even more changes as Windows embraces object orientation.

The good news is that ActiveX provides a very flexible, extensible framework within which future Windows enhancements can work. If you know ActiveX, you already know how many new features work in a general sort of way. You only need learn the specifics. I expect new Windows technology to be ActiveX-based for the foreseeable future.

The Future Of Programming

Many nay-sayers tell me that C++ is a thing of the past. They say that soon, blissful programmers will drop little modules on forms and create wonderful applications in hours. That's probably true. But who is writing these modules? To get rid of the low-level programmers, you need a collection of perfect modules that are as efficient as possible, as well as a very efficient way to tie them together. You also need a set of basic modules from which you can do anything. That strikes me as unlikely, at least in our lifetime.

True, the market for high-tech C++ programmers may shrink—many programs are best written using high-level constructs. Many programs are not sensitive to efficiency. Still, there will always be room for some number of people who build the tools and modules that others use to create their programs.

How do you hedge your bets? Stick with C++ (I plan to). However, don't be too quick to dismiss tools like Visual Basic, Delphi, and the like. You don't have to use them, but you owe it to yourself to keep abreast of them. Many workaday programmers will be using these tools to generate the thousands of everyday programs that run the world. And since these languages can incorporate ActiveX controls and objects, they represent a huge market for C++ products. Besides, there will always be some programs that you must write using a system-level programming language like C++. Just be careful not to let the market shrink to where you no longer fit in it.

Another oddity I've noticed is that while Visual Basic programmers, for example, are eager to embrace components, C++ programmers tend to turn their noses up at them. Yet C++ programs can use ActiveX components and controls quite easily. Few people refuse to use the standard I/O library. Why shouldn't you use off-the-shelf components where they are available?

Where To Go?

Do you remember the movie, *The Graduate*? In that movie, there was a scene where some body told a young Dustin Hoffman the one-word secret to success: "plastics."

Imagine if you had invested in plastics before it exploded. What about buying Intel or Microsoft stock when you could afford it? Success in the computer business is not too different. If you guess the right place to be, you can be wildly successful. Witness all the fortunes made by oddballs who were staking out the Internet first. Microsoft itself can be accused of being at the right place (IBM) at the right time (pre-1980) with the right product (MSDOS, which they bought from another company).

If you guess wrong–well, that's another story. Look at the fortunes lost on sure things like OS/2, artificial intelligence, and even the PC Jr. So the trick is to guess the right technology and get there before anyone else.

I'd like to tell you that I know where the future lies. But the truth is, I haven't any more of a clue than anyone else. The trick here is to not get too stuck in one rut. If you know Java, learn ActiveX. If you know C++, try VB for a change. I know it is distasteful, but the different perspective will do you good. I'm not saying to drop C++ (or whatever you are currently using). I'm simply saying you can afford to broaden your point of view a bit. Programmers–like weight lifters–have to cross train to stay limber.

Magazines are a good way to stay current on trends. However, you have to be careful about editorial bias. Many magazines, for example, stayed committed to OS/2 long after the programming community at large had drifted away from it. Conferences are another good way to see what some group of people believe is the wave of the future.

In the end, nothing is better than simply talking to other people in the computer business. In the past, that meant going to user group meetings, conferences, and even job interviews. I've known people who go on interviews just to see what other companies are doing. Today, you need only log into the Internet.

There are many ways to interact with people over the net. Subscribe to a mailing list or participate in a Usenet group. Both are excellent ways to stay abreast of the industry trends in a real way. If you are like me, you find most Usenet groups a bit noisy. That's not a problem any more. Simply use one of the search services that index news groups (www.altavista.digital.com and www.dejanews.com come to mind).

End Of The Soapbox

Okay, that's all of the preaching for today. Whatever course you should take, you'll find ActiveX all along it. At least, that seems true for the foreseeable future.

Just as today's Windows bears only a passing resemblance to the older versions, there is no telling what ActiveX will look like in, say, five years. However, it is a good bet that ActiveX will still exist in five years, too. All that's left is to wish you good luck!

ActiveX Thesaurus And Glossary

ONE OF THE THINGS THAT makes learning ActiveX so much fun is that Microsoft scrambles up all the names every six months. If you find some of the jargon from other sources confusing, check out this list of ActiveX synonyms. Entries with an asterisk are the words this book usually uses to express a concept.

*ActiveX Component
An ActiveX server that provides one or more tables of function pointers (interfaces) that other programs can use to request services.

*ActiveX Control
A special class of ActiveX component that understands how to work like an ordinary Windows control. This type of component replaces older standards like Visual Basic Extensions (VBX). Notice that Microsoft currently calls almost

any ActiveX server a control, but I prefer to call them components. Controls specifically know how to interact with a window.

*ActiveX Object
Another word for ActiveX component.

*Advanced Template Library
A library, based on C++ templates, that allows you to create ActiveX interfaces in a simplified fashion. As this book was being written, the library was still in beta form.

*Ambient Property
A property that a container exposes to its controls.

*Asynchronous Moniker
A moniker that returns from a binding call before the bound object is completely ready. The object binding completes while program execution continues.

*ATL
The Advanced Template Library.

*Base Control
An example shipped with Visual C++ that you can use as a starting point for ActiveX controls.

*BSTR
A counted string such as used by Visual Basic.

CA
Certification Authority.

*CATID
A UUID that identifies a component category.

Certification Authority
A trusted entity that makes a statement (represented by an X.509 certificate) about the authenticity of another certificate.

CGI
Common Gateway Interface.

*Client
Any program that uses ActiveX components.

*CLSID
A UUID that identifies a class.

*COleControl
The MFC class that represents all OCX-style ActiveX controls. This class derives from **CWnd**.

COM
Component Object Model; older term for ActiveX.

COM Object
An ActiveX object.

Common Gateway Interface
The traditional way to activate web pages. This is a means for web pages to send data back to a host machine which can then select or generate a page on the fly.

Component Object Model
An older name for ActiveX. Usually, COM refers to OLE technology outside the scope of document linking and embedding.

Compound Documents
See Structured Storage System.

*Container
A program that can hold an ActiveX control or DocObject.

Cryptographic Digest
A one-way hash function that takes a variable-length input string and converts it to a fixed-length output string (called a cryptographic digest). This fixed-length string is similar to a checksum (albeit, a large checksum) for the file.

*CString
An MFC class that represents a string.

*CWnd
The class that MFC uses to represent all windows.

*Data Bound Property
A property that can request permission to change from its container and notify the container when a change takes place.

*Dispatch Interface
An IDispatch interface that translates **DISPID**s into method calls or property accesses.

*DISPID
An integer that identifies the function requested of a dispatch interface.

*DocObject
An ActiveX server that can supply a document to link or embed in a container. This is the same thing that OLE documents have always been.

*Enumerator
An ActiveX object that provides a way to walk through some list of items.

*Event
A message that a control sends to its container.

*Form View
An MFC view that uses a dialog template to simulate a form.

*GUID
Globally Unique Identifier. This is another name for a UUID.

*HTML
The markup language ("**H**ypertext **M**arkup **L**anguage") used to build Web pages.

*Interface
A table of function pointers. Clients make requests of an object by calling functions from an interface. An object may have more than one interface.

*IDL
Interface Description Language.

*IID
Interface Identifier. This is a UUID that identifies an interface.

*Interface Description Language
A script language that allows you to describe interfaces so that the IDL compiler can automatically create marshaling code. Newer versions of the IDL compiler can accept scripts that can also create type libraries.

Local Registration Authority
An intermediary between a publisher and a CA. The LRA can, for example, verify a publisher's credentials before sending them to the CA.

LRA
Local Registration Authority.

*Marshalling
A technique that allows programs in one process to transparently call interfaces that reside in another process. The processes need not be on the same machine.

*Method
A function that an ActiveX control exposes to its container.

*MFC
Microsoft Foundation Classes.

*Microsoft Foundation Classes
A C++ library designed to simplify many Windows programming tasks, including ActiveX programming.

*Moniker
An ActiveX object that encapsulates a data item's name, location, and the operations required to open it. For example, a moniker might contain a file name or a URL.

Object Application
A server.

OLE Control
An ActiveX control.

OLE Control Extension
An OCX or OLE Control.

OLE Automation
Scripting.

OCX
An ActiveX control.

*Object Description Language
A script that describes objects for the purpose of creating type libraries. Newer versions of the IDL compiler can accept a mixed IDL/ODL file so that you can maintain one single IDL file for both purposes.

*ODL
Object Description Language.

*Persistence
Any means of writing an object to some external data storage so that a program can later recreate the object with all of its internal state intact.

PKCS#7 Signed Data
A Public Key Certificate Standard #7 (PKCS#7) signed-data object encapsulates the information used to sign an file. It usually includes the signer's certificate, the root certificate, and the signer's public key.

*Property
A pseudo-variable that an ActiveX control allows containers to access. The property may correspond to a variable in the control, or may trigger a function call to set or retrieve the value.

*Property Sheet
A dialog page, typically used in a tabbed dialog, that allows users to read and set properties.

Protocol
Interface.

*Proxy
A function that works with a stub to transparently handle calls between processes. You can automatically generate proxies from an IDL script.

Recursion
See "recursion."

*Regedit
A program (first shipped with Windows 95) that allows you to manually view and manipulate the registry.

*Regedt32
A Windows NT version of REGEDIT.

*Registry
A system-wide database that contains configuration information in a hierarchical database.

*SAFEARRAY
An array type that ActiveX defines to facilitate sharing of array data between clients and servers.

*Scripting
The ability for a program to control objects from other programs without prior knowledge of those programs. This used to be known as OLE automation.

*Server
Any DLL or EXE that provides ActiveX Components. DLL servers are also known as InProc servers.

Software Publishing Certificate
A PKCS#7 signed-data object containing X.509 certificates, and public key signatures.

SPC
Software Publishing Certificate.

*Synchronous Moniker
A moniker that doesn't return from a binding call until the bound object is completely ready.

Trust Provider
The portion of Windows that decides whether or not a given file is trusted. This decision is based on the certificate associated with the file.

*Stock Events
Events that have a common meaning defined by ActiveX.

*Stock Property
A standard property. That is, a property whose meaning is predefined by ActiveX.

*Storage
A portion of the structured storage system that most resembles a directory. It may contain substorages or streams.

*Stream
A portion of the structured storage system that most resembles a file. Contrast with storage.

*Structured Storage System
A way for an ActiveX object to treat some form of storage (e.g., a file, or a database record) in a way that is conducive to saving objects.

*Stub
A function that works with a proxy to transparently handle calls between processes. You can automatically generate stubs from an IDL file.

*Test Container
A special program provided by the Microsoft Visual C++ environment for testing ActiveX controls. The container can alter properties, call methods, change ambient properties, monitor events, and perform other testing functions.

*Type Library
Data about the interfaces and types provided by an ActiveX component.

*URL
A Uniform Resource Locator. This is an address used to specify items (particularly Web pages). It consists of a data type, a server name, and a path.

*UUID
Universally Unique Identifier. This is a 128 bit number that you can generate so that they are unique. These numbers identify interfaces (IIDs), classes (CLSIDs), and categories (CATIDs). Sometimes UUIDs are known as GUIDs.

*VARIANT
A data structure that contains a union and a type field. Programs must use the type field to determine what portion of the union to read. ActiveX defines this structure to help facilitate data sharing between clients and servers.

VBX
Visual Basic Extension.

*VIEW
An MFC class responsible for displaying data and accepting input.

Visual Basic Extension
A packaged piece of code usable by Visual Basic and certain other 16-bit programming environments. Visual Basic Extensions (VBXs) were superseded by OCX controls.

WIN_CERTIFICATE
A Win32 data structure that contains either a PKCS#7 signed-data object or an X.509 certificate.

X.509 Certificate
A cryptographic certificate that contains a vendor's unique name and the vendor's public key.

Just Enough HTML

HTML (HYPERTEXT MARKUP LANGUAGE) is the *lingua franca* of the Web. Web content, from the simplest personal home page to a state-of-the art virtual reality extravaganza, uses HTML to define the appearance of the page.

Of course, HTML (by itself) isn't powerful enough to build virtual reality venues, but it is powerful enough to contain objects (such as ActiveX objects) that can do anything you can dream up.

There have been entire books written on how to create HTML, but in this appendix I want to show you enough HTML to get started and try a few things. You'll need to create some HTML to test your ActiveX creations on the Web.

If you are really interested in creating high-quality Web pages, stop! Your best bet is to get a tool that creates Web content automatically. For example, you can get the Internet Assistant for Microsoft Word (or PowerPoint or several other products), that allows you to layout Web pages without knowing much about HTML.

Still, if you want to do anything out of the ordinary, you'll need to know HTML, so you might as well dig right in and get started. Even the best tools won't do everything you need. It also isn't unusual to have to tweak automatically-generated HTML to get the results you want.

By the way, HTML started as a subset of SGML (the Standard Generalized Markup Language) designed to transfer documents between systems. If you know SGML, you might find you practically know HTML already.

The Basic Structure

HTML files are really just ASCII text files. By convention, they use the .HTML extension unless MS-DOS is involved, in which case, the .HTM extension is the standard.

Ordinary text in an HTML file appears as ordinary text in the produced document. What could be easier? The magic comes into play when you add tags to produce special formatting. Most tags come in pairs, so that they affect the text between them. For example, to indicate boldface, you'll use the **<B>** and **</B>** tags:

```
<B>This is bold text</B> This is not!
```

The starting tag has no slash, while the ending one does. In a few special cases, you can omit the ending tag, but usually you do need it. For instance, the above line needs the **</B>** tag so that the remaining text is not in bold. By the way, tags are not case sensitive. You could just as well use **** and **** in the above example.

Some tags take parameters which appear *inside* the angle brackets. Others are required by the HTML specification, but not required by common browsers. Like most other things involving computers, HTML is subject to some interpretation.

An HTML Document

An HTML document has several standard elements. Some of them are optional some of the time, but all of them are available if you want to use them. Here is the structure of a correctly-formatted HTML document:

```
<HTML>
<!-- A comment - these can go anywhere-->
<HEAD>
<!-- Header information (the page title, for example)-->
</HEAD>
<BODY>
<!-- Main text which consists of headings, paragraphs, and images-->
</BODY>
</HTML>
```

Notice that the entire content appears between the **<HTML>** and **</HTML>** tags. While this is officially correct, most browsers will display any file with a .HTM or .HTML extension as HTML, even if it doesn't contain this tag.

The first portion of the HTML document appears between the **<HEAD>** tags. This is for special information pertaining to the entire document. You can use the **<TITLE>** tag, for example, to set a title for your page. Keep it 64 characters or less if you expect it to be visible in its entirety.

Another tag that can appear in the **<HEAD>** section is the **<BASE>** tag. This tag has no closing tag; it appears by itself. You can use it to specify the address of the page. This is helpful if someone copies your page (to a local machine, for example). If someone tries to follow a link and the browser can't find it, it will search relative to the address specified in the **<BASE>** tag. Any time you need to specify a URL in a tag, you'll use the **HREF** parameter, as in:

```
<BASE HREF=http://www.coriolis.com/made_up.html>
```

It isn't strictly necessary, but some pages place an **<ADDRESS>** tag pair after the **</BODY>** tag. The intent of this tag is to place information about the page's authorship, revision date, and so forth at the bottom of the page. When you see a line at the bottom of the page that reads

```
Last modified: April 1, 1996. Send comments to webmaster@coriolis.com
```

that text is probably inside a pair of **<ADDRESS>** tags.

You can enter special characters by using an ampersand. This is especially important for the '<', '>', and '&' characters, as well as currency symbols and other non-ASCII characters. You can use a letter name followed by a semicolon (for example, **<** is the '<' character and **>** is the '>' character). Alternately, you can use the sequence **&#nnn;** where **nnn** is a decimal character code from the ISO Latin-1 character set. You can find a list of common key names in Table B.1. Key names, by the way, are one place where HTML is case-sensitive.

Inside The Body (With Apologies To Asimov)

Within the body of the document, the browser will wrap all normal words into one long paragraph—unless you tell it otherwise. This makes sense, because you can't know how wide the user's screen is. It would be a bad idea, but you could put one word on each line of your HTML source and the browser would take care of wrapping it into a paragraph.

When you want to start a new paragraph, use the **<P>** tag. Technically, you use this tag to start a paragraph, and the **</P>** tag to end it. However, very few people actually use the **</P>** tag since it is optional.

Sometimes, you just want a line break inside the same paragraph. Then you can use the **
** tag to start a new line. This tag has no corresponding ending tag. For example, to format an address, you might write:

Table B.1 Common key names.

Name	**Key**
amp	Ampersand (&)
copy	Copyright sign ©
gt	Greater than sign (>)
lt	Less than sign (<)
nbsp	Non breaking space
quot	Quotation mark (")
reg	Registered trademark ®
shy	Soft hyphen

```
Coriolis Group Books <BR>
7339 E. Acoma Drive #7<BR>
Scottsdale, AZ 85260<BR>
```

You can format text in a variety of ways. The best way is to use a logical formatting attribute. You tell the browser what you want to do, and it figures out how to represent that format. For example, if you tell the browser you want strong emphasis (using the **<STRONG>** tag), it will probably render the text in bold face. Table B.2 shows the common logical attributes and common ways that browsers render them. Notice that the browser may elect to show different items in different colors, or use a user-defined style, so don't count on the appearance of these items to be consistent. Naturally, all of these tags have a corresponding closing tag.

Sometimes you want more control over the appearance of your text. Then you can use the physical attribute tags shown in Table B.3. These allow you to specify exactly how the text should look.

Table B.2 Logical attributes.

Tag	Name	Use	Often rendered as...
<CITE>	Citation	References to books	Italic
<CODE>	Code	Source code	Monospaced
<DFN>	Definition	Definition of a word	Italic
<EM>	Emphasis	Special emphasis	Italic
<KBD>	Keyboard	Text the user should type (for example, in a procedure document)	Bold and monospaced
<SAMP>	Sample	Sample output	Monospaced
<STRONG>	Strong	Strong emphasis	Bold
<VAR>	Variable	Placeholder text	Italic

Table B.3 Physical attributes.

Tag	Name	Description
<B>	Bold	Heavy face text
<I>	Italic	Italic type face
<U>	Underline	Line drawn beneath text
<TT>	Teletype	Monospaced text

You can nest attributes. For example, if you wanted bold underlined text, you might use:

`Try <B><U>ActiveX</U></B>`

Be sure to place the closing tags in the reverse order of the starting tag. Otherwise, some browsers may get confused.

In addition to normal paragraphs, HTML can create paragraphs in six different styles for headings. The intent is for you to use these as headings for different sections of the document. In truth, you can use them for anything you like. You can also use them in any order. You don't have to use them at all. The tags are **<H1>** through **<H6>** (and, of course, the usual closing tags).

Often you'd like to place a line between sections of your documents. Printers call these lines *rules*. HTML allows you to use the **<HR>** tag (by itself) to insert a horizontal rule in the text. This is better than drawing a line with ASCII characters (or even a graphic), since you don't know how wide the user's screen is.

In addition to the header styles, HTML also provides the **<BLOCKQUOTE>** and **<PRE>** paragraph tags. The **<BLOCKQUOTE>** style sets off text in some way (usually by using indentation and italics). The **<PRE>** style implies that the text is preformatted. The browser does *not* wrap text in a **<PRE>**-style paragraph. It shows it exactly as it is in the HTML file. This is useful for source code. Usually, a **<PRE>** paragraph appears in monospaced type. You can specify the width of the text in characters by using the **WIDTH** parameter to the **<PRE>** tag. Don't forget the closing tags **</BLOCKQUOTE>** and **</PRE>**.

Images And Objects

Of course, the big selling point to the Web is graphics. The **<IMG>** tag is the ordinary way to insert a graphic in your document. However, the **<OBJECT>** tag (discussed in Chapter 6) will also insert graphics in a more general way. Since the **<OBJECT>** tag is new, however, most pages still use the **<IMG>** tag for simple graphics. Many browsers don't support **<OBJECT>** yet, and those that do may not support it completely.

Each **<IMG>** tag requires a **SRC** parameter to name the file that contains the image. This file name can be a full-blown URL, or just a file name if the file is in the same location as the Web page (or its base address). Since some browsers don't show graphics (or users will turn graphics off), it is a good idea to specify the **ALT** parameter, too. This parameter specifies some text to show in case the image does not display. Here's a typical image statement:

```
<IMG SRC="PIX1.GIF" ALT="The first picture">
```

Normally, an image acts like a single character in your text. If you don't want things to appear after your image, you'll need a **
** or **<P>** tag following it. You can also control the alignment of text around the image by using the **ALIGN** parameter. This parameter can take one of three values: **TOP**, **BOTTOM**, or **MIDDLE**. If you don't use an **ALIGN** parameter in your **<IMG>** tag, the text will line up with the bottom of the image.

Of course, you could also insert the same image with:

```
<OBJECT DATA="PIX1.GIF">
</OBJECT>
```

The **<OBJECT>** tag is more flexible because it can insert typed data (like a .GIF file) or an object (see Chapter 6). Table B.4 shows a summary of parameters the **<OBJECT>** tag accepts.

The **WIDTH** and **HEIGHT** parameters allow you to specify the desired size (which need not match the actual size). This allows you to scale up a small image (which transfers faster). You can specify sizes in pixels or in the units found in Table B.5. For example, to make an image 2 inches square, you would specify "2in" in both parameters.

Lists

HTML supports several types of lists. These are similar to paragraph styles. The most common types of lists use the **<LI>** tag to denote the beginning of a list element. To create a numbered list, use the **<OL>** ("ordered list") tag. For example:

```
<OL>
<LI> Item 1
<LI> Item 2
</OL>
```

Table B.4 Object tag parameters.

Parameter	Description
ID	Name of object
DECLARE	Don't create object until referenced
CODEBASE	Location to find object
DATA	Data to use with object (object may be implied by type)
TYPE	Type of data (if not implied by extension)
CODETYPE	Type of object
STANDBY	Message to display while loading
ALIGN	Alignment properties
HEIGHT	Height of object
WIDTH	Width of object
BORDER	Size of border (0=no border)
HSPACE	Horizontal space to leave around object
VSPACE	Vertical space to leave around object
USEMAP	Use an image map to create anchors
SHAPES	Use a client-side image map to create anchors
NAME	Name used in forms

Table B.5 Unit suffixes.

Suffix	Description
%	Percentage of display area
pt	Points (72 points==1 inch)
pi	Picas (6 picas==1 inch)
in	Inches
cm	Centimeters

produces

```
1. Item 1
2. Item 2
```

If you prefer a bulleted list, use the **<UL>** ("un-numbered list") tag. You can also get a more compact list by using **<MENU>** or **<DIR>**. Items in a menu list should not exceed one line of text. The **<DIR>** list items shouldn't exceed 20 characters so that the browser can form columns, if it has that capability.

There is another kind of list that HTML supports: the description list. This type of list uses text instead of a bullet and may be used for lexicons or encyclopedia-style entries. The **<DL>** tag starts the list. You begin each text "bullet" with the **<DT>** tag. After the text, place a **<DD>** tag (not a **</DT>** tag). Then follow with the text that goes with that pseudo-bullet. There is no **</DD>** tag; just start another **<DT>** entry or end with **</DL>**. Some browsers will attempt to place short text "bullets" on the same line as the other text if you specify the **COMPACT** parameter to the **<DL>** tag.

Hyperlinks

The H in HTML stands for hypertext, and the Web wouldn't be the same without links, would it? Each link has two parts: a presentation part (text or graphics) and an invisible portion (the *anchor* that specifies where to go).

The **<A>** tag inserts anchors. The presentation portion can be any mix of text or graphics that you like. This allows you to create very sophisticated links since you can use any text or HTML commands you like in the presentation. Here is a simple link:

```
To continue click <A HREF="http://www.coriolis.com/nextpage.htm">here</A>
```

When you click the word "here" the browser jumps to the correct URL. Usually, the browser will show the link word underlined (and possibly in a special color). Of course, you can use graphics as the presentation portion, too:

```
<A HREF="http://www.coriolis.com/p1.htm"><IMG SRC="clickme.gif"></A>
```

You can also use anchors to name a spot in your document. For example:

```
<A NAME="Summary">My Conclusions</A>
```

This line creates an anchor named "Summary". You can jump to it by using a '#' character in the **HREF** portion of another anchor tag. For example:

```
<A HREF="#Summary">Jump directly to summary</A>
```

or

```
<A HREF="http://www.coriolis.com/report.html#Summary">See summary</A>
```

The first example jumps to the Summary anchor on the same page. The second example jumps to a new page and finds the Summary anchor on that page.

Image Maps, Forms, And More

There is much more to HTML. For example, you can divide up a single graphic into multiple anchors or use a background graphic. You can use tables and multiple windows (frames). You can create forms and process them on your server, you can add sounds, scrolling marquees, and—well, you get the idea.

With each new browser release, there are new HTML features. One of the best ways to get information about HTML is from the Web itself. There are technical specifications, tutorials, and even software to help you create HTML. Look at **http://www.w3.org** for the latest specifications for HTML. After all, what better place to find information about the Web than on the Web?

What's On The CD-ROM

The companion CD-ROM is packed with megabytes of project code and examples to help you learn ActiveX development, as well as a few surprises!

You'll see specific, real-world examples of how to develop ActiveX controls with Visual C++ and other tools. There's also plenty of code that you can simply copy and paste into your own ActiveX development projects.

INDEX

A

AAWSound object, 76, 179
AAWSound.CPP, 99–101
AAWSOUND.H, 98–99
AboutBox, 190
Activate, 202
Active Internet Platform. *See* AIP.
ActiveX, 4, 7
   and C++, 30–31
   categories, 9
   client, 14
   compared with Java, 31–32
   competing standards, 346
   components, 14, 16–19, 351
   containers, 14
   controls, 8–9, 14, 178, 185, 351
   document object, 14
   macros, 70
   objects, 14–17, 352
   reserved name characters, 124
   server, 14
   template library, 320–25
ActiveX, and the Internet, 261–62
   asynchronous monikers, 298–302
   building the browser, 268–88
   code downloading, 303–7
   HTML, 184
   ICP components, 262
   ICP HTML control, 268–71
   non-dialog views, 288–98
   trust verification, 307–12
   URL monikers, 302–3
   Web browser, 263–68
ActiveX-enabled browser, 6
Add Function, 326
AddConnection, 204
AddRef, 23–26, 74, 327
Advanced Template Library. *See* ATL.
Advise, 150–51, 194–95
Aggregation, 17, 25–27, 106–8
   and ATL, 327–28
AIP, 3
   and ActiveX, 4
   components, 5–7
   and monikers, 10
   page view, 5
   security, 11

Algorithms, in classes, 318
ALIGN, 366
Alloc, 73, 111
Altair, 67
Ambient property, 187, 192, 352
Ambient property functions, 213
AmbientBackColor function, 223
amp (ampersand), 362
Angle brackets, 360
Another Version Controller. *See* AVC.
ANSI characters, command line, 81
Anti (moniker), 148–49
Application setup, 97
Apply, 202
appobject (type attribute), 59
App Wizard, 68, 95–96, 106, 268–87
Argument list, 160
Arguments, 53, 75–76, 121–22
   MakeCert, 310
   named, 160
   number of, 160
   optional, 160
   positional, 160
Array pointer, 156
ASCII characters, 362
ASCII file, 53
Asynchronous Monikers, 7, 9–10, 298–302, 352
atime, 123
ATL, 178, 316–20, 352
   and aggregation, 327–28
   classes, 337–39
   control, 331–36
   drawbacks of, 321–22
   features of, 320–21
   getting started with, 322–24
   and object maps, 324–25
   source, 337
ATL Wizard, 323
Atomic Monikers, 140
Attach, 337
Automatic events, 214
Automation, 102
Automation controller, 165, 169
Automation object, creating, 162
Automation server, 94
Automation-specific code, removing, 96
AutoTreatAs, 53, 57
AVC, 127–29

application, 130–40
    dialog box, 128
AVI, 6

B

<B>, 363
BackColor, 187–89
Backslash, 83
BackStyle, 189
Base class, 18, 269
Base control, 352
BASECTL, 339–40
    classes, 339
BASECTL virtual functions, 340
Beep, 331, 334
BeginRetrieval, 270
BEGIN_INTERFACE_MAP, 103
BEGIN_INTERFACE_PART, 103
Binary data, 39
Bind context, 300
Bindable properties, 188
Binding the moniker, 147
Binding time and efficiency, 170–71
BindToObject, 73, 148, 303
BindToStorage, 73, 148, 303
Bitmap, 173
Bitwise or, 297
<BLOCKQUOTE>, 364
Bold face text, 363
bool, 157
BORDER, 366
BorderColor, 189
BorderStyle, 189
BorderVisible, 189
BorderWidth, 189
Braces, 22
Breakpoint, 84
Browser. *See* Web browser.
Browsing, 6, 8
BSTR, 154, 352
    functions, 155
bstrVal, 157
Built-in types, 317
Bull control, 218–29
BULL.CPP, 228–29
byref, 157

C

C++, 31
    and ActiveX, 30–31
    constructor function, 153
    destructor function, 153
    and early binding, 170
    multiple inheritance, 93
    programmers, 31
    templates, 178, 316
CA, 352
CAB file, 304–6
Cabinet, 304
Cache (function), 201
Cache API, 8
Caching, 8
Cancel, 189
Cancel (ICP HTML control), 270
Caption, 189
cArgs, 160
Case-sensitive, 362
Categories, 204
Category ID, 204
CATID, 352
cbSize, 123
CCmdTarget, 94–96
CComConnectionPointContainerImpl, 329
CComModule, 321
CComObjectBase, 321
CComPtr functions, 338
CDocHeader, 284
CDocHeaders, 284
CDocInput, 284
CDocOutput, 284
Certification authority, 352
cfFormat, 172
CFormView, 268, 285–88
CGI, 11, 353
Characters, 362
CHECKIN, 128
CHECKOUT, 129
CHKTRUST utility, 311
CHTML class declaration, 271–84
CHTMLForm, 284
CHTMLForms, 284
<CITE>, 363
Class algorithm, 318
Class factory, 76, 96
Class factory object, 79
Class installation, 52–53
class keyword, 317
Class Wizard, 95–96, 106, 153, 162–65, 230, 288
Class Wizard-generated code, 168
CLASSFAC.CPP, 79–81
CLASSID, 183
Click, 189–90
Client, 14, 352
Client basics
    arguments to CoCreateInstance, 75
    IEnum pseudo interface, 74
    IMalloc interface, 73

Index 373

IShellFolder interface, 73–74
  overview, 70–71
  shell client excerpts, 71–73
Client site, 194
Client site interface, 194
Clipboard, 171
Clone, 74, 112–13, 121–23
Close, 194, 337
CLSCTX_ALL, 85
CLSID, 50, 106, 123, 352
CLSID (Class ID), 21
clsid:, 183
CLSIDFromProgID(), 51
cm (centimeters), 366
cNamedArgs, 160
coclass, 58, 61
CoCreateGuid, 21
CoCreateInstance, 24, 52, 74, 78, 85
  arguments, 75
<CODE>, 363
Code downloading, 303–7
Code reuse, 16–19
Code size, decreasing, 327
CODEBASE, 303, 366
Codebase values, 307
CODETYPE, 366
CoFreeUnusedLibraries, 92
CoGetClassObject, 78
CoGetMalloc, 72
CoInitialize, 71, 72
COleControl, 236–37, 353
COleFont, 284
Color property sheet, 226
COLORREF, 223
COM, 70, 353
Command line, ANSI characters, 81
Command-line options, SignCode, 311
Commit, 120–21, 126
Common Gateway Interface, 11, 353
CommonPrefixWith, 148
CompareIDs, 73
Component(s), 14, 351
  category, 352
  class, 58
  compared with controls, 14
  seeking, 307
Component Gallery, 22, 268, 270, 284, 289
Component Object Model, 70, 353
ComposeWith, 148
Composite moniker, 147–50
Compound documents, 357
Compound files, 127–29
Connectable objects, 150
Connection point containers, 329–30
Connection speed, Internet, 8

ConnectTemplate, 97
Constructor function, 153
Container, 14, 353
Containment, 17
ContextSensitiveHelp, 197–98
control (type attribute), 59
Control(s), 8, 14, 178, 185–86, 351
  counter, 229–36
  interfaces, 192
  key, 204
  and slow data links, 9
  subclassed, 236–43
  window, 255
Control Wizard, 205, 230, 243
CONTROLINFO, 198
Controls, compared with components, 14
copy (copyright sign), 362
Copy the array, 156
CopyTo (function), 120–21
CoRegisterClassObject, 76, 88
CoRegisterMallocSpy, 110
CoRevokeMallocSpy, 110
CoTreatAsClass(), 57
CoUninitialize, 71, 83
Count property, 256
Counter control, 229–36
Counter HTML, 236
CProgressCtrl, 243
Create, 237, 289, 337
Create an array, 156
CreateGenericComposite, 149
CreateInstance, 76
CreateStorage (function), 120
CreateStream (function), 120
CreateStreamOnHGlobal, 122
CreateURLMoniker, 302
CreateViewObject, 73
Credentials, 309
CRegKey class, 337
Cryptographic certificate, 358
Cryptographic digest, 353
Cryptography API, 11
CSimpleWin, 179
CString, 353
ctime, 123
Curly braces, 50, 61, 87
Currency symbols, 362
Custom control, countdown timer, 244–48
Custom control, subclassing, 243–57
Custom Interface, 322
Custom interfaces, 325–27
CWinApp, 69
CWnd, 236, 353
cyVal, 157

D

DAdvise, 174
Dashes, 22, 50, 56
DATA, 366
Data bound property, 187, 353
Data objects, 172
Data path property, 299
date (field), 157
DblClick, 190
dblVal, 157
Deactivate (function), 202
Debugger, 46
Debugging
    allocation, 110
    server, 84–85
Decimal character code, 362
DECLARE, 366
DECLARE_INTERFACE_MAP, 103
DECLARE_OLE_CREATE, 104
DEF file, 86
Default (property), 189
Default button, 187
Default values, 37, 49
delete function, 327
DeleteSubKey (function), 337
DeleteValue (function), 337
Delimiter character, 148–49
Derivation, 16
Design-time state, 191
Desktop folder, 71
Destroy, 156
DestroyElement (function), 120
Destructor function, 153
Detach (function), 337
Device-driver resource list, 39
<DFN>, 363
DialogParms, 129
Diamond directive file (DDF), 306
DidAlloc, 73
DidAlloc (function), 111
Dimensions, 156
DiscardCache, 201
Dispatch interface, 353
Dispatch map, 96, 99
Dispatch object, 167
DISPATCH_METHOD, 159
DISPATCH_PROPERTYGET, 159
DISPATCH_PROPERTYPUT, 159
DISPATCH_PROPERTYPUTREF, 159
DispGetParam, 160
DISPID, 153, 298, 354
dispinterface, 58
DisplayAsDefault, 187

DISPPARAMS structure, 160
DLL server, 89
    creating with AppWizard, 105
DLLCanUnloadNow, 84, 91–92
DLLGetClassObject, 84, 91
DllMain, 91, 327
DLLMAIN.CPP, 89–92
dllname (type attribute), 59
DllRegisterServer(), 56
DLLs, self-registering, 56
DllUnregisterServer(), 56
DocInput, 270
DoClick, 190
DocObject, 354
DocOutput, 270
Document-view architecture, 69
DoModal(), 40
DoNewElement, 270–71
DoPropExchange, 223, 255
DoSuperclassPaint, 237
Double-click function, 40
DoUpdateRegView(), 40
DoVerb, 194
Draw (function), 201
DrawStyle, 189
DrawWidth, 189
Dual interface, 171, 322, 331
DUnadvise, 174
dwAspect, 172
dwClsContext, 75
DWORD, 75, 87
dwStgFmt, 123

E

Early binding, 170
EditProperty, 202
80 Micro, 68
ElemNotification, 270
<EM>, 363
Embed flag, 82
Embed variable, 81
/Embedding, 84, 102–4
EnableAutomation, 96, 106
Enabled (property), 189
EnableModeless, 198
Encapsulation, 16
EndRetrieval, 271
END_INTERFACE_MAP, 104
END_INTERFACE_PART, 103
Enhanced metafile, 173
entry (type attribute), 59
Enum, 148

EnumAdvise, 194–95
EnumCache, 201
EnumConnectionPoints, 151
EnumConnections, 151
EnumDAdvise, 174
EnumElements, 124, 127
EnumElements (function), 120
Enumerate named values, 36
Enumeration, 74
    classes, 328–29
Enumerator, 71–74, 354
Enumerator interfaces, 113
EnumFormatEtc, 174
EnumObjects, 73, 149
EnumVerbs, 194
Equal sign, in key values, 38
Error (event), 190, 284
Error (ICP HTML control), 271
error 0x80040150, 83
Error function, 331
Error handling, 330–31
Error returns, 38
Error status, 20
Evaluate method, 153
Events, 188–90, 354
Event freezing, 192
Event-handling macros, 297
Exception handling, 327
Exclamation point, 148–49
EXE Automation Server, 94
EXEs, self-registering, 56
ExpandEnvironmentStrings(), 38
Extended controls, 188
Extensions, 360
ExternalAddRef, 94, 97, 106
ExternalQueryInterface, 94, 97, 106, 113
ExternalRelease, 94, 97, 106

F

Fibonocci enumerator, 114
Fibonacci, Leonardo, 114
Fibonacci numbers, 112
File (moniker), 148
File name formats, 147
FillColor, 189
FillStyle, 189
FinalConstruct, 328
FindConnectionPoint, 151
FindFullKey(), 40
Firing function, 213
fltVal, 157
Flush (function), 141
Font (property), 187, 189

ForeColor, 187, 189
Form view, 354
FORMATETC structure, 113, 172
Forward slash, 56
Frame controls, 191
Free (function), 73–74, 111
Free memory, 71–73, 92, 111, 122
Free Threading model, 30
Freeze (function), 201
FreezeEvents, 199
FTP, 7, 262
Function names, "Ex" in, 49
Function pointers, 22

G

GetAdvise, 201
GetAttributesOf, 73
GetBackColor, 223
GetBindCtx, 300
GetBindInfo, 301
GetCanonicalFormat, 174
GetClassID (function), 143–45, 301
GetClassInfo, 151
GetClientSite, 194
GetClipboardData, 194
GetColorSet, 201
GetConnectionInterface, 151
GetConnectionPointContainer, 151
GetContainer, 197
GetControlInfo, 199
GetCurFile (function), 143
GetCurMoniker, 301
GetData, 174
GetDataHere, 174
GetDescription, 331
GetDisplayName, 148
GetDisplayNameOf, 73
GetDisplayString, 203
GetDlgItem, 287
GetExtendedControl, 199
GetExtent, 194, 201
GetForeColor, 223
GetGUID, 331
GetHelpContext, 331
GetHelpFile, 331
GetIDsOfNames, 152, 164
GetLastError(), 38
GetLocaleID, 203
GetMiscStatus, 194
GetModuleHandle, 129
GetMoniker, 194, 197
GetObject, 149
GetObjectParam, 302

GetObjectStorage, 149
GetOptions (function), 75
GetPageContainer, 203
GetPageInfo, 202
GetPredefinedStrings, 203
GetPredefinedValue, 203
GetPriority, 301
GetRunningClass, 200
GetSite, 300
GetSize, 73, 111
GetSizeMax (function), 144
GetSource, 331
GetTimeOfLastChange, 148
GetTypeInfo (function), 152
GetTypeInfoCount (function), 152
GetTypeInforOfGuid, 152
GetUIObjectOf, 73
GetUserClassID, 194
GetUserType, 194
GetWindow, 197–98
GetWindowLong, 248
GIF, 6
Global classes, and code shrinkage, 327
Global memory, 141, 173
Globally Unique Identifier. *See* GUID.
Gopher, 7
Grab handles, 187
Graphics, 192, 364–65
Green, Wayne, 68
grfLocksSupported, 123
grfMode, 121–23
grfStateBits, 123
gt (greater than sign), 362
GUID, 21, 354

H

HandsOffStorage (function), 145
Hash function, 353
Hashing, 311
Hatching, 187
hBitmap, 173
HDC, 29, 243
HeapMinimize, 73, 111
HEIGHT, 366
Help (function), 202
helpcontext (type attribute), 59
helpfile (type attribute), 59
helpstring (type attribute), 59
hEnhMetaFile, 173
hGlobal, 173
hidden (type attribute), 59
High bit, 83
HKEY, 35

hMetaFilePict, 173
HRESULT, 20–21
HRESULT, and DLLs, 84
HSPACE, 366
HTM extension, 360
HTML, 183–84, 262, 354, 359
   case-sensitivity, 362
   control, 263
   counter, 236
   document, 360–62
   extension, 360
   files, 360
   ICP HTML control., 270, 285
   latest specifications, 368
   and Param tags, 187
   script generators, 217
HTTP, 262
Hyperlinks, 367–68
Hypertext Markup Language. *See* HTML.

I

<I>, 363
IAAWSound interface, 75
IAdviseSink, 194
IBindStatusCallback, 300–1
IClassFactory, 76
IClassFactory2, 76
Icon view, 196
IConnectionPoint, 151
IConnectionPointContainer, 151, 192
ICP components, 262
ICP HTML control, 268–71, 285
ID, 366
ID property, 236
IDataObject, 172–75, 192
IDispatch, 94, 152–71, 192, 321
IDispatch example, 165–66
IDispatch interface, 58
IDL, 85, 354
   file, 86–87, 334
   IDE, 85–86
IEnum, 111–19, 321
IEnum pseudo interface, 74, 112
IEnumFORMATETC, 113
IEnumIDList, 73
IEnumMoniker, 113
IEnumOLEVERB, 113
IEnumSTATDATA, 113
IEnumSTATSTG, 113
IEnumString, 113
IEnumUnknown, 113
IEnumVARIANT, 113
IErrorInfo interface, 331

IExplorer control, 262
IExternalConnection, 204
IExternalInterface, 192
IID. *See* Interface Identifier.
ILockBytes, 141–42
IMalloc, 71–74, 110–11
IMallocSpy, 110–11
<IMG>, 364
IMoniker, 147–50
IMPLEMENT_OLE_CREATE, 104
importlib, 58, 61
in (inches), 366
in (type attribute), 59
INF file, 304–6
INI files, 34
InitCache, 201
InitDialog, 82
InitFromData, 194
Initialization call, 71
InitInstance, 69, 101–3, 234
   EXE server, 81–82
InitNew (function), 144–45
InPlaceDeactivate, 197
Inproc DLLs, 50
InprocHandler32, 50, 53
InprocServer32, 50, 53
Insert object dialog, 51
Insertable, 51, 53
InsertReg(), 40
Intel-style format, 39
interface, 58, 61, 354
Interface Description Language. *See* IDL.
Interface functions, 31, 106
Interface Identifier, 21, 85, 354
Interface map, 96, 103, 106
Interface names, 16
Interface tables, 15
Interfaces, 14, 23–24, 53, 109–10
   customizing, 325–27
   IConnectionPoint, 150
   IConnectionPointContainer, 150–51
   IDataObject, 171–75
   IDispatch, 152–71
   IEnum, 111–19
   ILockBytes, 141–42
   IMalloc and IMallocSpy, 110–11
   IMoniker and IOleItemContainer, 147–50
   IPersistFile, IPersistStream, and IPersistStorage, 142–46
   IProvideClassInfo, 151–52
   IStorage and IStream, 119–41
   predefined and custom, 27
   tear-off, 330
INTERFACES key, 85
INTERFACE_AGGREGATE, 104

INTERFACE_PART, 104
Internal linking, 196
Internal variable, 186
InternalAddRef, 98
InternalQueryInterface, 98
InternalRelease, 98
Internet, 3, 75, 178, 345
Internet Assistant for Microsoft Word, 360
Internet Control Pack, 262, 268–71
Internet Explorer, 262
Internet Server API, 7, 10
Internet, and ActiveX, 261–62
   asynchronous monikers, 298–302
   building the browser, 268–88
   code downloading, 303–7
   ICP components, 262
   ICP HTML control, 268–71
   non-dialog views, 288–98
   trust verification, 307–12
   URL monikers, 302–3
   Web browser, 263–68
InternetOpen, 7
InternetOpenUrl, 7
InternetReadFile, 7
Intranet, 11
InvalidateRect, 224
Inverse, 148
Invoke (function), 152–53, 160
Invoke (method), 158
IOleAdviseHolder, 195
IOleCache, 200–1
IOleCache2, 192, 200–1
IOleClientSite, 196–97
IOleControl, 192, 198–99
IOleControlSite, 199
IOleInPlaceActiveObject, 192, 198
IOleInPlaceObject, 192, 197
IOleItemContainer, 147–50
IOleObject, 192–93
IOleObject interface, 194
IPerPropertyBrowsing, 192, 203
IPersist, 178, 190, 192
IPersistFile, 142–43
IPersistMoniker, 301
IPersistStorage, 144–45
IPersistStream, 143–44, 150
IPersistStreamInit, 143–44
IPropertyPage, 201–2
IPropertyPage2, 201–2
IPropertyPageSite, 203
IProvideClassInfo, 151–52, 192
IRunnableObject, 192, 200
ISAPI, 7, 10
IsDirty (function), 143–45, 301
IsEqual, 148

IShellFolder interface, 71–74
ISO Latin-1 character set, 362
IsPageDirty, 202
ISpecifyPropertyPages, 192, 203
IsRunning, 148–49, 200
IsSubclassedControl, 237
IsSystemMoniker, 148
IStorage, 119–41
IStream, 119–41
ISupportErrorInfo, 330
IsUpToDate, 194
Item (moniker), 148
IUnknown, 22–23, 27, 86, 97, 179, 185
iVal, 157
IViewObject, 192, 200–1
IViewObject2, 192, 200–1

J

Java, 32, 178
    future of, 345–46
JPEG, 6

K

<KBD>, 363
Key handle, 35
Key names, 362
Keyboard handling, 191
Keyboard mnemonics, 191
KeyDown, 190
KeyPress, 190
Keys, 34, 38–39
    default values, 38
    deleting using Windows 95, 38
    equal signs in, 38
KeyUp, 190

L

L prefix, 130
Language IDs, 59–60
Languages, 16
Late binding, 170
LayoutDone, 270
lcid (type attribute), 59
LCIDs, 60
Libraries
    template, 320–25
    not template-based, 339
    type, 28, 34, 57–63, 104
    See also ATL.
lindex, 172
Line break, HTML, 362

LIST, 129
Lists, 365–67
Load (function), 143–45, 301
LoadBinaryState, 340
LoadLibrary, 249
LoadTextState, 340
Local caching, 6, 8
Local registration authority, 354
LocaleID, 187
Locales, 60
localserver variable, 83
LocalServer32, 50, 53
Lock the array, 156
LockContainer, 149
LockInPlaceActivate, 199
LockRegion (function), 121, 141
LockRunning, 200
LockServer, 76, 92
Logical attributes, 363
lpszFileName, 173
LPUNKNOWN, 75
LPVOID, 75
LRA, 354
lt (less than sign), 362
lVal, 157

M

Macros, 60, 69–70, 95–96, 106
    aggregation, 328
    BEGIN_COM_MAP, 325
    event-handling, 297
    MFC, 103–4
    object map, 324
    to port code, 70
    PX_, 212, 224, 230
    SUCCEEDED and FAILED, 20
    VARIANT, 159
MAKE file, 86
MakeCert, 309
MakeCert, arguments, 310
MAKELANGID, 60
MapPropertyToPage, 203
Maps, 324–25
Marshalling, 28–30, 85, 355
Max, 317
MD5 hashing, 311
MDI interface (Multiple Document Interface), 88
Member functions, and nested classes, 97
Memory, 71–74, 122
    allocation, 72–73, 111
    as structured storage, 141
Memory handle, 142
MessageReflect, 187

Index 379

Metafile, 173, 200
Method(s), 188–90, 355
   adding, 163–64
METHOD_PROLOGUE, 104
METHOD_PROLOGUE macro, 97
MFC, 165, 177, 206, 316, 355
   adding code, 208–10
   adding events, 213–15
   adding methods, 212–13
   adding properties, 210–12
   adding property sheets, 215–16
   ambient properties, 212
   COleControl, 216
   Control Wizard, 206–8
   examples, 69
   generated files, examining, 216–17
   techniques, 94–104
   testing and using the control, 217–18
   window message reflection, 255–56
   aggregation, 106–8
MFC AppWizard, 54
MFC DLL server, 105–6
MFC EXE server, 94–98
Microsoft Corporation, 123, 343
   ActiveX object terminology, 14
   ATL, 178, 316
   browsing applications, 8
   and C++, 31
   connectable objects, 150
   EnumElements, 127-28
   OLE automation, 11
   self registration code, 92
   state bits, 120
   UUID, 21-22
Microsoft Foundation Class. *See* MFC.
Microsoft Interface Description
   Language (MIDL), 30, 85
Microsoft Internet Explorer, 262
Microsoft Visual C++, 22
Microsoft Web site, 262
Microsoft Windows, 3, 12, 33, 346–47
Microsoft Windows 95, 33, 38, 125
   and deleting keys, 38
   and RegDeleteKey(), 37
   registry editor, 35
   and subclassing, 243
   Word Pad, 50
Microsoft Windows NT, 33, 38
   and RegDeleteKey(), 37
   and REGEDIT, 35
   and Regedt32, 356
Microsoft Word, 88
MITS, 67
MKTYPLIB, 60, 321
Mnemonics, 187, 192

module, 58, 61
Monikers, 113, 147–48, 355
   asynchronous, 7, 9–10, 298–302, 352
   synchronous, 302, 357
   URL, 6, 9–10, 302–3
Motorola-style format, 39
Mouse click events, 189
MouseMove, 190
MouseUp, 190
Move (function), 202
MoveElementTo (function), 120
mtime, 123
Multiple inheritance, 93, 321
Multiple interfaces, 92–94
Multiple threads, 30
Multithreading, 94

N

NAME, 366
Name (property), 189
Named arguments, 160
nbsp (nonbreaking space), 362
Nested classes, 93, 95, 97
   and member functions, 97
Network connection speed, 8
Network proxy, 29
Neutral language, 60
new, 92, 327
New paragraph, HTML, 362
Next (function), 74, 112, 124
NNTP, 262
Non-dialog views, 288–98
NULL, 38
Null characters, 39
Null-terminated string, 39
NumMethods, 85

O

Object(s), 14–17, 352
   application, 355
   containment, 18
   creation, 16, 23–24
   functions, 14
   impersonating, 56–57
   maps, 324–25
   registering, 50–52
   tag, 183, 364
   tag parameters, 366
Object Description Language. *See* ODL.
<OBJECT> tag, 303
OCX, 178, 355
   extension, 304

OCX Control, 268
OCX-style ActiveX controls, 353
ODL, 59–62, 333–34, 355
OLE
    Automation, 11, 96, 106, 162, 355
    control, 269, 355
    Events, 164
    object viewer, 299
    objects, 50
    programming, 13
OLE32.DLL, 50
OleLoad (function), 146
OleSave, 146
OnAmbientPropertyChange, 199
OnBeginRetrieval, 284
OnClose, 194
OnControlInfoChanged, 199
OnCreate, 289
OnDataAvailable, 301
OnDataChange, 194
OnDblClick(), 40
OnDocWindowActivate, 198
OnDraw, 223, 236, 237, 340
OnEndRetrieval, 284
OnFileNew, 105
OnFocus, 199
OnFrameWindowActivate, 198
OnInitDialog, 46, 69, 82–83
OnLowResource, 301
OnMnemonic, 199
OnObjectAvailable, 301
OnOcmCommand, 237
OnOK, 69, 83
OnPaint, 69
OnPlay, 69
OnProgress, 301
OnReadyStateChange, 301
OnRename, 194
OnResetState, 255
OnSave, 194
OnSetExtent, 340
OnShowWindow, 197
OnStartBinding, 301
OnStatusChange, 203
OnStepChanged function, 224
OnStopBinding, 301
OnViewChange, 194
ON_EVENT, 297
ON_EVENT_RANGE, 297
ON_PROPNOTIFY, 297
ON_PROPNOTIFY_RANGE, 297
Open (function), 337
Open Software Foundation, 21, 86
OpenStorage, 120
OpenStream, 120
Operation flags, 159
Option character, 56
optional (type attribute), 59
Optional arguments, 160
out (type attribute), 59
Overwrite, 126

P

Page view, 5, 11
Paragraph, HTML, 362
Param tags, 187
Parent (property), 189
Parent window, 255
parray, 157
ParseDisplayName, 73, 148–49, 300
ParseDone, 270
pbool, 157
pbstrVal, 157
PCT (Private Communication Technology), 11
pcyVal, 157
pdate, 157
pdblVal, 157
pdispVal, 157
Persistence, 190, 355
PESIGMGR, 312
pfltVal, 157
Physical attributes, 363
pi (picas), 366
piVal, 157
PKCS#7 signed data, 355
Play (function), 75
plVal, 157
Pointer (moniker), 148
Polymorphic objects, 19
Polymorphism, 17–20
POP3, 262
Positional arguments, 160
PostAlloc, 111
PostDidAlloc, 111
PostFree, 111
PostGetSize, 111
PostHeapMinimize, 111
PostRealloc, 111
ppdispVal, 157
ppstgOpen, 121–22
ppunkVal, 157
ppv, 75
<PRE>, 364
PreAlloc, 111
PreCreateWindow, 237, 249, 297
PreDidAlloc, 111
PreFree, 111
PreGetSize, 111

Index

PreHeapMinimize, 111
PreRealloc function, 111
PRIMARYLANGID, 60
Profile information, 49
ProgID, 51, 53
　spaces in, 51
ProgIDFromCLSID(), 51
Programming, future of, 347
Progress bar control, 237
Properties, 186–90
Property, 163, 356
Property sets, 192
Property sheet, 225, 356
Protocol, 356
Proxies, 28–30, 87
Proxy, 356
ProxyStubCLSID32, 85
pscode, 157
pstg, 173
pstgPriority, 122
pstm, 173
pt (points), 366
ptd, 172
pThis, 97–98
public (type attribute), 59
Public Key Certificate Standard #7, 355
pUnkForRelease, 173
pUnkOuter, 75
punkVal, 157
pvarVal, 157
pwcsName, 121–23
PX_ exchange macros, 224

Q

QueryGetData, 174
QueryInterface, 23–24, 74, 92, 113, 327
QueryValue (function), 337
quot (quotation mark), 362

R

Radio Shack TRS80, 68
RCA 1802, 68
rclsid, 75
ReactivateAndUndo, 197
Read (function), 121
ReadAt, 141
ReadProfileInt, 234
ReadyState, 301
Readystate values, 302
Realloc, 73, 111
Recompose, 195
RecurseDeleteKey, 337

Recursion, 356
Reduce, 148
REFCLSID, 75
Reference count, 23–25
REFIID, 75
Refresh (method), 190
reg (registered trademark), 362
REG file, 83–84
RegCloseKey, 36
REGCLS_SINGLEUSE, 76
RegConnectRegistry, 36
RegCreateKeyEx(), 35–36
RegDeleteKey(), 36–37
RegDeleteValue(), 36, 49
REGDEMO, 38–49
REGDEMOVIEW.CPP, 40–46
REGDIALOG.CPP, 46–48
REGEDIT, 35, 53–55, 356
REGEDT32, 35, 356
RegEnumKeyEx, 36
RegEnumValue(), 36–37
RegFlushKey, 36
RegisterBindStatusCallback, 300
RegisterClassData, 340
Registration, components requiring, 52
Registry, 356
　data types, 39
　entries, 53, 167, 204
　as hierarchical database, 34
　-related calls, 35–36, 49
Registry, using to control ActiveX, 33, 34
　class installation, 52–53
　impersonating objects, 56–57
　INI files, 34–37
　oddities, 37–38
　REGDEMO, 38–49
　REGEDIT, 37–38, 53–55
　registering objects, 50–52
　self-registration, 55–56
　type libraries, 57–63
RegServer, 56
REGSVR32.EXE, 92
RegUnloadKey, 36
REG_BINARY, 48
REG_DWORD, 48
REG_SZ, 48
RelativePathTo, 148
Release, 23–26, 74, 327
ReleaseConnection, 204
Remote Procedure Calls (RPC), 86
Remote registry, 36
REMOVE, 129
RenameElement, 120
RequestDoc, 270, 284
RequestNewObjectLayout, 197

RequestSubmit, 270
reserved, 121–22
RESET, 242
Reset, 74, 112
Resize an array, 156
ResizeBorder, 198
Revert, 120–21
RGB value, 223
rgdispidNamedArgs, 160
rgvarg, 160–61
riid, 75
Root storages, 124
ROOT.CER, 309
RPCPROXY.H, 85
RPCRT4.LIB, 86
Run, 200
Runtime state, 191

S

SAFEARRAY, 154–56, 356
<SAMP>, 363
Save (function), 143–45, 301
SaveBinaryState, 340
SaveCompleted, 143–45, 301
SaveObject, 197
SaveTextState, 340
SCODE, 20–21, 157
Script language, 11
Scripting, 7, 10–11, 356
Security, 11
Security warning dialog, 313
Seek (function), 121
Selector class, 318
Self-registering servers, 52–53
Self-registration, 55–56, 179
Self-registration code, 92
Semicolon, 362
SendOnClose, 195
SendOnRename, 195
SendOnSave, 195
Serialize, 288
Server, 14, 357
Server (test)
    CLASSFAC.CPP, 79–81
    debugging, 84–85
    IDL file, 86–87
    IDL IDE, 85–86
    InitInstance, 81–82
    marshalling, 85–86
    OnInitDialog code, 82–83
    overview, 78
    REG file, 83–84
    SERVER.CPP, 78–79

Server design
    class factories, 76
    IAAWSound interface, 75
    overview, 74–76
    server usage, 76
Server, DLL, 89
Server, EXE, 88–89
SERVER.CPP, 78–79
SetAdvise, 201
SetClass, 120
SetClientSite, 146, 194
SetColorScheme, 194
SetContainedObject, 200
SetData, 174, 201
SetElementTimes, 120
SetExtent, 194
SetHostNames, 194
SetKeyValue, 337
SetModifiedFlag, 224
SetMoniker, 194
SetNameOf, 73
SetObjectRects, 197
SetObjects, 202
SetOptions, 75
SetPageSite, 202
SetRegistryKey, 234
SetSite, 300
SetSize, 121, 141
SetStateBits, 120
SetValue (function), 337
SetWindowLong, 248
SGML (Standard Generalized Markup
    Language), 360
SHA1 hashing, 311
SHAPES, 366
Sharing flags, 124
Shell client, 71–73
ShellExec(), 54
SHGetDesktopFolder, 71–74
ShGetMalloc, 72
Show (function), 202
ShowGrabHandles, 187
ShowHatching, 187
ShowObject, 197
ShowPropertyFrame, 199
shy (soft hyphen), 362
Signature block, 309, 312
SIGNCODE wizard, 309
SignCode, command-line options, 311
SimpleWin.cpp, 181–83
Single use argument, 76
Sink, 150–51
16-bit components, 50
Skip (function), 74, 112
Slash, 360

SMTP, 262
snbExclude, 122
Software Publishing Certificate, 357
Software, HTML, 368
Source code, 18
SPC, 357
spc file, 309
Square brackets, 54, 87
Standard ambient properties, 187
Standard Generalized Markup Language, 360
STANDBY, 366
Stat (function), 120–24, 141
STATDATA, 113
State bits, 120
Static object, 196
STATSTG, 113, 123
StatusUpdate, 298
STDMETHOD, 69–70
STDMETHODIMP, 70
STDMETHODIMP_, 69–70
STDMETHOD_, 70
Step, 223
StgCreateDocfile, arguments, 121
STGC_DANGEROUSLYCOMMITMERELYTO-DISKCACHE, 126
STGC_DEFAULT, 126
STGC_ONLYIFCURRENT, 126
STGC_OVERWRITE, 126
StgIsStorageFile, 127
STGMEDIUM union, 172–74
StgOpenStorage, arguments, 122
StgSetTimes, 127
Stock events, 357
Stock properties, 189, 357
Storage, 124–27, 357
Stream(s), 119–24, 357
    names, 124
    objects, 120
    and transactioning, 127
Strings, 48, 74
<STRONG>, 363
Structured storage system, 357
Stub, 28–30, 87, 357
Subclassed Control, 236–43, 250
Subclassing, 243–57
Subkeys, 34, 36
SUBLANGID, 60
Substorages, 124
Sun Microsystems, 32
SupportsMnemonics, 187
Synchronous binding, 298
Synchronous moniker, 302, 357
SysAllocString, 155
SysAllocStringByteLen, 155
SysAllocStringLen, 155

SysFreeString, 155
SysReAllocString, 155
SysReAllocStringByteLen, 155
SysReAllocStringLen, 155
SysStringLen, 155
System registry, 6
S_FALSE, 74
S_OK, 56, 74

T

Tables, 14
Tags, 360
TCONTROL header file, 248
TCP, 262
Tear-off interfaces, 330
Technical specifications, HTML, 368
Templates, 178, 316–20
    See also ATL.
Terminating zero, 38
Test client, 76–78
Test container, 357
Text (property), 189
32-bit binary, 48
32-bit number, 39
TimeOut, 271
TLB file, 28, 60
TLB library, 151
Traditional control interfaces, 191–204
Transacted storage, 146
Transactioning, 129
TransformCoords, 199
TranslateAccelerator, 198–203
TranslateColor, 223
TreatAs, 53, 57
Tree view, 40
Trust provider, 357
Trust verification, 307–12
<TT>, 363
Tutorials, HTML, 368
tymed, 172–73
tymed values, 172
type, 123, 366
Type attributes, 59
Type flag, 48
Type libraries, 28, 34, 57–58, 104
    creating, 60–63
    elements, 58
    location, 58–59
Typed data, 38
typedef, 58, 61
TypeLib, 58

U

<U>, 363
ucode, 130
UDP, 262
UIDeactivate, 197
UIDead, 187
Unadvise, 151, 194–95
Uncache, 201
Unexpanded references, 39
Unfreeze, 201
UNICODE, 81
Unicode characters, 124
Unicode constants, 130
Unicode names, 130
Unicode symbolic link, 39
Uniform Data Transfer, 171
Uniform Resource Locator. *See* URL.
Unit suffixes, 366
Universally Unique Identifier. *See* UUID.
UNKWN.IDL, 86
Unlock the array, 156
UnlockRegion (function), 121, 141
Unregistration, 55
UnregServer, 56
Update (function), 194
UpdateCache, 201
URL, 6, 8–9, 147, 270, 284, 299, 307, 358, 361
URL Monikers, 6, 9–10, 262, 302–3, 313
USEMAP, 366
User-defined classes, 317
UserMode, 187
UUID, 21-22, 61, 96, 352, 358
uuid (type attribute), 59
UUIDGEN, 21

V

Values, and type flag, 48
<VAR>, 363
vararg (type attribute), 59
VARIANT, 113, 154–58, 284, 328, 358
 data structure, 157
 macros, 159
 types, 158
VariantClear, 159
VariantCopy, 159
VariantCopyInd, 159
VariantInit, 159
VBX, 358
Verbs, object, 113
version (type attribute), 59
Version control system, 127
VersionIndependentProgId, 53

VIEW, 290, 358
VIEW.CPP file, 290–97
Virtual file system, 141
Visible (property), 189
Visual Basic, 165, 178
Visual Basic Scripting Edition, 11
Visual C++, 165, 297, 326
VSPACE, 366
vt, 157
VT_EMPTY, 160
VT_ERROR, 160

W

Web browser, 3, 177, 188, 263–68
 building, 268–88
 security settings, 309
Web page, 177, 185
 creating, 360
Whitespace, 22
WIDTH, 366
Win32, 38, 130
Win32 programming
 and function names, 49
Win32S, 50
Window (property), 189
WindowProc, 340
Windows HWND, 237
Windows Trust Verification Services, 11
WINERROR.H, 83
WinExec(), 53
WinInet, 6, 7
WinMain, 69
WINNT.H, 60
WinSock, 7
WinVerifyTrust, 312
WIN_CERTIFICATE, 358
WM_COMMAND, 69
WM_INITDIALOG, 69
WM_PAINT, 69
Word Pad, 50
World Wide Web, 3
Write (function), 121
WriteAt, 141
WriteClassStg, 146
WriteClassStm, 146
WriteProfileInt, 234
WTYPES.IDL, 86

X

X, in class name, 103
X.509 certificate, 352, 358

Bonus Chapter

http://www.coriolis.com

Want to learn how to do *fast* image processing over the World Wide Web? Here's a special preview chapter from *KickAss Java Programming,* another top-notch Coriolis book for programmers who like algorithms with attitude!

KickAss Java Programming is now available in book stores, or you can order directly from The Coriolis Group by calling 800-410-0192.

Order# ISBN 1-883577-99-3

Written by Java guru and programming "bad boy" Tonny Espeset, *KickAss Java Programming* shows you how to do blazingly-fast animations and image transfers on the Web, as well as use little-known Java features that make your programs super-efficient.

Chapter 1	Easy Animation
Chapter 2	Playing with Sounds
Chapter 3	Image Processing in Java
Chapter 4	Rendering 2D Animations
Chapter 5	Entering the Third Dimension
Chapter 6	Real 3D in Java
Chapter 7	Adding Realism
Chapter 8	Scrolling Text
Chapter 9	Navigation
Chapter 10	Optimization
Chapter 11	Easy Animation
Appendix A	The Image Processor and Other Classes

Image Processing in Java

One of the biggest problems with the Internet today is that it's much too slow to give users any true sensations of multimedia. Even static images can make users twist in agony as they wait for them to load. Luckily, however, there are ways around this problem, especially after the birth of Java. In this chapter, you'll learn to manipulate an existing image with advanced image processing techniques. By using these techniques, you can generate a whole set of images that look completely different from the original, even if they're all based on just one image. This way, you can build exciting scenes without having to load large images. By basing a set of images on a single image like this, you can dramatically reduce the amount of information that must be sent over the Internet, and speed up the multimedia display on the user's screen.

Using image processing tools is also an excellent way of generating cool animations without the time penalty of having to load each frame separately. By passing an image through various image processing filters with changing parameters, you can render some pretty interesting

Have you ever wanted to carve your face in stone, blow up your worst enemies, or make aliens out of models? Well, with image processing, here's your big chance!

animations. Some of the filters discussed in this chapter are actually so heavily optimized that you can use them real-time, even without the Just in Time compiler (JIT).

> **TIP** **Just in Time Compiling**
> All the image-processing filters discussed in this chapter are real CPU-hungry beasts, even though they're optimized. This is because an image contains tens of thousands of pixels, all of which must be filtered separately. On top of that, since Java is an interpreted language, it's still rather slow. This is because Java programs are not compiled into machine-specific code for the CPU to execute directly, but into so-called bytecode, a format that must be interpreted prior to execution by the Java Virtual Machine built into your Java-enabled browser or the AppletViewer. The problem is, interpreting bytecode is a rather slow process, and to improve performance the Just in Time compiler translates the bytecode into machine-specific code before the program is executed. A performance boost of ten to twenty times is not unusual, and you still have the benefit of platform independence. Neat!

If you want to get right into action and start using these filters in some real applets, you can skip this chapter. But if you want some deeper understanding of the inner workings of them, read on.

Getting to Know Your RGB

First of all, let's take a look at how an image is represented in Java. Basically, it's a two-dimensional array of pixels, where the top-left pixel is located at coordinate (0,0) and the bottom-right pixel is located at coordinate (imageWidth -1, imageHeight -1), as shown in Figure 1.

As you can see in Figure 1, computers tend to stick to a coordinate system where the y coordinate grows downward. This is the opposite of what is normally used in the world of mathematics.

Each pixel has its own color value represented by three bytes. One byte stores the red intensity, the next stores the green intensity, and the last

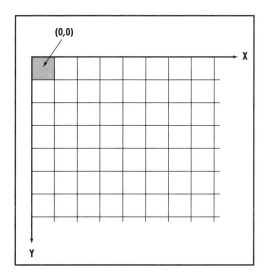

FIGURE

The computer's coordinate system.

stores the blue intensity. These bytes are all packed in one integer, so to access a pixel you only have to change one value instead of three separate values. In addition to the red, green, and blue components, a pixel also has an alpha channel with transparency information. This channel is also described by a byte, and is integrated into the same integer as the red, green, and blue components.

TIP The RGB Color Model

The RGB color model is the most commonly used model when dealing with CRT (cathode ray tube) devices like your monitor or television set. If you use a magnifying glass and take a close look at your TV screen, you'll see it's composed of a large number of red, green, and blue dots. Each of these dots is fluorescent and emits light when hit by electrons from the electron gun inside the TV. These three colors are so close to each other that they're perceived by your eye as being one color. By combining them in different ways, you can display almost all colors the eye can tell apart. Red and green become yellow; blue and green become cyan;

while red, green, and blue become white—and so on. If you're unfamiliar with this way of describing colors, experiment a little with the palette tool in a paint program like Paint for Windows 95.

Since Java stores each red, green, and blue component as a byte, each component may represent 256 different intensities of the corresponding color. This means you can play with more than 16.7 million colors. This is often referred to as true-color, since it's more colors than the human eye can distinguish. The really neat thing is you don't have to worry about how many colors users are actually able to display on their systems. Java takes care of converting the true-color image to a suitable format before displaying it. The quality of the conversion varies a bit on different platforms, but it's usually more than adequate. Later on, you'll learn how to bypass Java's image-displaying routine by manually printing each pixel to get better image quality.

In addition to the red, green, and blue information, each pixel has transparency information referred to as the *alpha channel*. This can be very useful if you want non-rectangular images. You'll see how to make interesting effects with the alpha channel later. If a pixel has an alpha value of 0, it's completely transparent; if its value is 255, the pixel is opaque. Any values in between will make the pixel partially transparent. Unfortunately, current versions of Java don't support true transparency. A pixel can, in reality, only be visible or invisible when sent to the screen, but by using dithering techniques, Java simulates transparency, as shown in Figure 2.

The image in Figure 2 was generated using Java. In the middle it's completely transparent, and toward the borders it becomes more and more solid. But as you can see from the magnified image, the transparency is fake.

TIP Some Words About Hexadecimal

Computers are most fond of number systems based on two, and if computers ruled the world, you'd find yourself programming with endless sequences of 0s and 1s. Fortunately, they don't—at least not yet—but sometimes it comes in handy

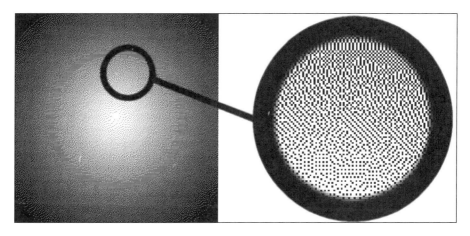

FIGURE 2

Java only simulates transparency.

speaking in numbers they do understand best. The most popular alternative number format is hexadecimal, which is based on the number 16 rather than 10. When you count from 0 to 256 in hexadecimal you get the following number sequence: 0, 1, 2, 3, 4, 5, 6, 7, 8, 9, A, B ,C ,D, E, F, 10, 11, 12... F9, FA, FB, FC, FD, FE, FF, 100. As you see, you can write down all numbers from 0 to 255 using only two digits. This is a great advantage in our case, because this happens to be all the values one byte can hold, and recall that each color component in a true-color image is represented by exactly one byte. This will help you write colors as numbers in a tidy and easy-to-read manner. In Java, the compiler knows that a number is hexadecimal if it begins with 0x. So the number 255 would be written as 0xFF in hexadecimal.

The color components discussed are organized as an integer, as shown in the following code line:

```
0xAARRGGBB
```

To extract the red, green, and blue components plus the Alpha channel value from an integer **rgb**, you can use the following code snippet:

```
Byte Alpha = (rgb&0xff000000)>>24;
Byte Red = (rgb&0xff0000)>>16;
Byte Green = (rgb&0xff00)>>8;
Byte Blue = rgb&0xff;
```

The Creation Of A New Image

Now let's use what you've learned so far to generate an image. The first thing you need to do is make an array of integers corresponding to the size of the new image. If the image is going to have the proportions 200x100, you would have to make an array of 20,000 integers as shown in the following code snippet:

```
Int imageWidth=200;
Int imageHeight=100;
int pixels[] = new int[imageWidth * imageHeight];
```

This array has to be one dimensional, even though it might have been easier to access individual pixels by passing x and y coordinates to a 2D array. But by knowing the width of the image, you can easily calculate the pixel's correct offset from its x and y coordinates like this:

```
pixels[y * imageWidth + x]=newColor;
```

Mostly you would want to access the pixels in the same order as they are represented in the array though, so this one-dimensional way of storing the colors usually works just fine.

Once you've filled the array with color values in the 0xAARRGGBB format we discussed earlier, it's time to create the image, as shown in the following code line:

```
Image myimage=createImage(new MemoryImageSource(imageWidth, imageHeight, pixels, 0, imageWidth));
```

Java then translates the true-color representation of the image to a format suitable for the display. This image is then passed to the **drawImage** method, and voilá! Sit back and admire your first step toward generating mind-blowing animations with Java. The code is shown in Listing 1, while the output is shown in Figure 3.

Listing 1 Creating an image from a true-color source.

```java
import java.awt.*;
import java.awt.image.*;

public class createimage extends java.applet.Applet {

    Image myimage;

    public void init() {

        int imageWidth=size().width;
        int imageHeight=size().height;

        int pixels[] = new int[imageWidth*imageHeight];

        int index=0;
        for (int y = 0; y < imageHeight; y++)
        {
            int red=(y * 255) / (imageHeight - 1);
            int green=255-(y * 255) / (imageHeight - 1);
            for (int x = 0; x < imageWidth; x++)
            {
                int alpha=(x * 255) / (imageWidth - 1);
                int blue=(x * 255) / (imageWidth - 1);
                pixels[index++] = (alpha<<24) | (red<<16) |
                  (green<<8) | blue;
            }
        }
        myimage=createImage(new MemoryImageSource(imageWidth,
          imageHeight, pixels, 0, imageWidth));
    }


    public void paint(Graphics g){
        g.drawImage(myimage, 0, 0, this);
    }
}
```

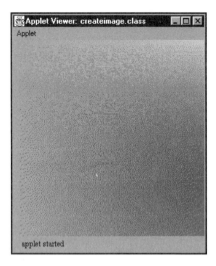

FIGURE 3

The output from Listing 1.

Reading Pixels From An Image

Making images from scratch is interesting, but manipulating already-existing pictures is much more fun. Imagine running an explode effect on the image of Bill Gates; that's far more visually catchy than blowing up some old fractal image! What you need is a way of reading the color values of each pixel in an existing image, manipulating it, and then saving it.

First you'll have to grab all the pixels in the image and put them in an array of integers, where each integer describes the color value of one pixel. This format is the same one you used to create the new image earlier. There are three simple steps to manipulate an existing image:

1. Convert the image into an array of integers, where each integer holds the value of one pixel in the ARGB (alpha, red, green, and blue) format.

2. Manipulate the pixel array, a process often referred to as *filtering*. The changes won't be visible in the image, since you're now working on the image duplicate.

3. To make your changes visible in the image, first you have to delete it and then re-create it using the updated pixel array.

We've already covered step 3 (how to create a new image) and the basics of step 2 (how to access the different pixel elements), so let's go one step further and take a look at how to make Java expose the pixels in an image.

First we'll use **getImage** to load the image we want to change, but, as you might know, Java will not finish loading the image immediately after the **getImage** function is called. This is usually an advantage, since images can be loaded in separate threads as the program continues its execution, but this isn't what we have in mind for now. You'll need to wait for all the pixels to be loaded before you can start manipulating the image. To do this, a **MediaTracker** object is added to watch the loading process, as shown in the following code snippet:

```
int ID=0;
MediaTracker tracker = new MediaTracker(this);
Image joe=getImage(getCodeBase(), "joe.gif");
tracker.addImage(joe, ID);
try {
     tracker.waitForID(ID);
} catch (InterruptedException e);
```

This code snippet starts to load the requested image "joe.gif," and makes sure all pixels are received before continuing. This might seem like a lot of code just to load one image, but the good news is you can add several images to the same **MediaTracker** using **.addImage**, and then tell it to make sure all images with the same ID are loaded with **.waitForID**.

Now it's safe to read the height and width of the image, and allocate the pixel array to hold the image duplicate, as shown in the following code snippet:

```
imageWidth=joe.getWidth(this);
imageHeight=joe.getHeight(this);
int pixels[] = new int[imageWidth*imageHeight];
```

The next thing you need to do is grab hold of the image's pixels and put them in an array of integers. For this, we'll use the class with the promising name **PixelGrabber**, shown in the following code snippet:

```
PixelGrabber pg = new PixelGrabber(joe, 0, 0, imageWidth, imageHeight,
  pixels, 0, imageWidth);
try {
    pg.grabPixels();
} catch (InterruptedException e);
```

There. Now you have access to all the pixels in the image, they're now located in the array **pixels[],** and it's about time to do some real image processing. The first and most simple filter you can use is **negative**, which simply inverts each color component in the image, as shown in the following code snippet:

```
invertedRed=255-currentRed;
invertedGreen=255-currentGreen;
invertedBlue=255-currentBlue;
```

To optimize this further, **exclusive or** can be used. As you might recall, an **exclusive or** (^) with one will always result in the negated bit value: 1 **xor** 1=0, 0 **xor** 1=1. We'll take advantage of this negating effect and invert both the red, green, and blue components all at once. We'll leave the alpha channel alone, and the inner loop of this filter will simply contain the following code line:

```
pixels[index]=pixels[index]^0xffffff;
```

Since your filters will have to deal with tens of thousands of pixels in one session, it's very important to thoroughly optimize their inner loop. Many of the optimizing techniques covered in this chapter will work very well in other circumstances too, so it's worth your while to spend a little extra time examining them now. For a real-world example again, take a look at this source code. It is shown in Listing 2. The output is shown in Figure 4.

Listing 2 Inverting an image.
```
import java.awt.*;
import java.awt.image.*;

public class filterimage extends java.applet.Applet {

    Image joe,invertedjoe;
```

```java
    int imageWidth, imageHeight;

    public void init() {

        MediaTracker tracker = new MediaTracker(this);
        joe=getImage(getCodeBase(), "joe.gif");
        tracker.addImage(joe, 0);

        try {
            tracker.waitForID(0);
        } catch (InterruptedException e);

        imageWidth=joe.getWidth(this);
        imageHeight=joe.getHeight(this);

        int pixels[] = new int[imageWidth*imageHeight];

        PixelGrabber pg = new PixelGrabber(joe, 0, 0, imageWidth,
          imageHeight, pixels, 0, imageWidth);
        try {
            pg.grabPixels();
        } catch (InterruptedException e);

        for (int index=0;index<imageWidth*imageHeight;index++)
            pixels[index]=pixels[index]^0xffffff;

        invertedjoe=createImage(new MemoryImageSource(imageWidth,
          imageHeight, pixels, 0, imageWidth));
    }
    public void paint(Graphics g){
        g.drawImage(joe, 0, 0, this);
        g.drawImage(invertedjoe, imageWidth, 0, this);
    }
}
```

Building The Image Processing Class

You now have all the basic information you need to start building the image processing class; **ImageProcessor**. First you'll need to implement the constructor, which is used to accept an image as input, and then use **PixelGrabber** to make the image's pixels accessible to all image filters we're going to implement. The constructor will simply make sure all the image's pixels are finished loading and extract the pixel information into the pixel

FIGURE 4

The output from Listing 2.

array, as we discussed earlier in this chapter. In fact, the only new code here are the lines that extract the width and the height fields of the image, shown in the following code snippet:

```
width=picture.getWidth(this);
height=picture.getHeight(this);
```

The midpoint of the image will also come in handy. It's therefore calculated and stored as (**centerX**, **centerY**), shown in the following code snippet:

```
centerX=Math.round(width/2);
centerY=Math.round(height/2);
```

One other field worth mentioning is **bgColor**. It describes the color that any non-defined pixel will be replaced with after it's been processed by a filter. If you rotate the image 45 degrees, for example, there will be large parts of the new image that are undefined, and by default this area will be replaced by 0's, which is the initial value of **bgColor**. In other words, it'll appear transparent (recall that 0 in the ARGB format will give "transparent black"). This is shown in Figure 5.

Here are the first lines of the **ImageProcessor** class, along with its constructor, shown in the following code snippet:

FIGURE 5

The wave filter, among others, leaves undefined areas that are filled with bgColor.

```
class ImageProcessor extends java.applet.Applet
{
    int width;
    int height;
    int centerX;
    int centerY;
    int[] pixels,snapshotPixels;
    int bgColor=0;

    ImageProcessor(Image picture)
    {
        //First make sure the image is fully loaded
        waitForImage(picture);

        //Get the width and height of the image
        width=picture.getWidth(this);
        height=picture.getHeight(this);
        centerX=Math.round(width/2);
        centerY=Math.round(height/2);

        //Allocate buffer to hold the image's pixels
        pixels = new int[width * height];
```

```
        //Grab pixels
        PixelGrabber pg = new PixelGrabber(picture, 0, 0, width,
          height, pixels, 0, width);
        try {
            pg.grabPixels();
        } catch (InterruptedException e);
    }
}
```

The routine that makes sure all pixels in an image are loaded will come in handy later, and it is therefore itself implemented as a method, as shown in the following code snippet:

```
void waitForImage(Image picture)
{
    //Make sure the image is fully loaded
    MediaTracker tracker = new MediaTracker(this);
    tracker.addImage(picture, 0);
    try {
        tracker.waitForID(0);
    } catch (InterruptedException e);
}
```

The constructor makes an array of integers in the ARGB format from the image, a perfect format for the filters you're about to implement. But to put the image back on the screen, this format is not very suitable. What you need is a method that takes the ARGB array and generates an image out of it again. This is real easy, as you've already seen, and can be accomplished by the following code snippet:

```
Image createImage()
{
  return createImage(new MemoryImageSource(width, height, pixels, 0,
    width));
}
```

Now you have all the overhead you need to put in a filter. Let's take a look at how much code you need to implement the negative filter shown earlier, shown in the following code snippet:

```
void invert()
{
    for (int index=0;index<width*height;index++)
        pixels[index]=pixels[index]^0xffffff;
}
```

Amazing, just one line of code! It seems that the overhead took much of the load off the filter itself, which means you can now concentrate on making good filters instead of dealing with a lot of nitty gritty details.

Let's take a look at how a complete negating filter program would look when using the **ImageProcessor** class, compared to the one described earlier. This is shown in Listing 3.

Listing 3 Inverting an image using ImageProcessor.
```
import java.awt.*;
import java.awt.image.*;

public class filterimage extends java.applet.Applet {

    Image joe,invertedjoe;
    ImageProcessor joeP;

    public void init() {
        joe=getImage(getCodeBase(), "joe.gif");
        joeIP=new ImageProcessor(joe);
        joeIP.invert();
        invertedjoe=joeIP. createImage();
    }


    public void paint(Graphics g){
        g.drawImage(joe, 0, 0, this);
        g.drawImage(invertedjoe, joeP.width, 0, this);
    }
}
```

As you can see, you get very compact and easy-to-read code. This is starting to look like a good idea! Now it's about time to put in some more sophisticated filters.

No More Colors!

Tired of all those colors? Probably not, but a filter for converting a color image to gray can sometimes come in handy. Say you want a row of icons that are gray until the user points at one. What you do is load all the color icons and convert them to gray while keeping the originals. This saves valuable downloading time, since you won't have to bother downloading the gray versions of the icons. Plus, you're spared the tedious process of using an image processing program to make them yourself. The class **ImageProcessor** has all you need!

A color-to-gray filter is very simple. Just take each color component and find the light intensity it represents. Blue, for example, is not as bright as green, and should therefore contribute less to the final gray intensity. Each color component is given a "weight," according to how bright it is compared to the others (red weight=3, green weight=4, blue weight=2). In this filter, you'll use integer weights, since the computer handles integers faster than floating point values. Although this isn't 100-percent exact, it's more than good enough in most cases.

First, you need to extract the red, green, and blue components from the image, as you learned earlier. This is shown in the following code snippet:

```
int c=pixels[index];
int r=(c&0xff0000)>>16;
int g=(c&0xff00)>>8;
int b=c&0xff;
```

Next, you calculate the correct gray intensity, based on each color component's weight, as shown in the following code line:

```
int gray=(r*3+g*4+b*2)/9;
```

You must divide by nine because all the weights sum up to nine, and the valid gray values range from 0 to 255.

To save the correct gray value, you simply put the gray value into all color components as shown in the following code line:

```
pixels[index]=(c&0xff000000)+(gray<<16)+(gray<<8)+gray;
```

Notice that we've also preserved the alpha channel with the following code line:

```
(c&0xff000000)
```

This part simply masks out the current alpha channel before the red, green, and blue color components are added, a trick you'll use in most filters to keep the alpha channel unchanged.

Now you only need to add a small loop to make sure all pixels are processed, and you have a complete gray filter, as shown in the following code snippet:

```
void gray()
{
    for (int index=0;index<width*height;index++)
    {
        int c=pixels[index];
        int r=(c&0xff0000)>>16;
        int g=(c&0xff00)>>8;
        int b=c&0xff;
        int gray=(r*3+g*4+b*2)/9;   //calculate the right gray value
          //based on r, g and b intensities
        pixels[index]=(c&0xff000000)+(gray<<16)+(gray<<8)+gray;
    }
}
```

Wild Colors

Even though a filter that converts a color image to gray can be useful, it's much more fun to add some colors! The **pseudoColors** filter uses a simple approach to give your image sharp colors and hard contrasts. The filter takes a seed for the random generator as a parameter, and by changing this seed the image will be painted in many different colors—quite handy for getting some attention.

The core of this filter looks much like the **invert** filter's, as shown in the following code snippet:

```
for (int index=0;index<width*height;index++)
{
```

```
        int c=pixels[index];
        pixels[index]=(c&0xff000000)+((random+c)&0xffffff);
    }
}
```

The **random** variable holds a random integer value that is simply added to the color of all pixels. This gives pretty wild and unsuspected results! The complete filter looks like the following code snippet:

```
void pseudoColors(long seed)
{
  Random rnd=new Random();
    rnd.setSeed(seed);
    int random=rnd.nextInt();

    for (int index=0;index<width*height;index++)
    {
        int c=pixels[index];
        pixels[index]=(c&0xff000000)+((random+c)&0xffffff);
    }
}
```

Brighten Up!

Another filter that's great to use in conjunction with user interfaces is **brightness**, which simply makes an image brighter or darker according to a **percent** parameter. You could make a navigation icon brighten up as the user points at one, and fade it out when the mouse pointer leaves its domain. Again, you'll only need to load one image per icon. The subsequent frames you need for the animation can be generated quite simply by using this **brightness** filter from the **ImageProcessor** class with varying parameters.

The formula to use is very simple. Given the **r**, **g**, and **b** components of a pixel and the **percent** of brightness to apply, the core of the filter will look like the following code snippet:

```
r=Math.min(255,(r*percent)/100);
g=Math.min(255,(g*percent)/100);
b=Math.min(255,(b*percent)/100);
```

Pretty straightforward. The only thing you have to keep in mind is to make sure the value of each component never exceeds 255. For this purpose, the

Math.min method comes in handy. **Math.min** simply returns the smallest value of the new calculated brightness and 255. Notice also that since only integer values are used, performance is increased when the new brightness value is calculated by multiplying the color component with **percent** *first*, *then* it's divided by 100. This makes sure the result is accurate even without the use of floating point numbers. Consider a formula like that shown in the following code line:

```
r=Math.min(255,(r/100)*percent);
```

This formula would not work properly, even if—mathematically speaking—it does exactly the same thing as the previous line:

```
r=Math.min(255,(r*percent)/100);
```

This is because (r/100) will be handled as an integer and therefore won't respond well to a **percent** value like 40, which would give the integer result of 0 instead of the correct floating point value 0.4.

So why not just use floating point variables exclusively to avoid all this confusion? As mentioned, the reason is performance. Integer values are handled far faster by the CPU than floating point values. Although this difference does not seem too great in standard interpreted Java, the introduction of the Just in Time compiler will make sure the difference is more than noticeable. It's therefore important to make an effort to keep all algorithms based on integers, without loss of quality.

To sum things up, the following code snippet shows the complete **brightness** filter:

```
void brightness(int percent)
{
   for (int index=0;index<width*height;index++)
   {
       int c=pixels[index];
       int r=(c&0xff0000)>>16;
       int g=(c&0xff00)>>8;
       int b=c&0xff;

       r=Math.min(255,(r*percent)/100);
```

```
        g=Math.min(255,(g*percent)/100);
        b=Math.min(255,(b*percent)/100);

        pixels[index]=(c&0xff000000)+(r<<16)+(g<<8)+b;
    }
}
```

Using **brightness** is a fine way of making images appear different, but what if you changed the brightness of each red, green, and blue component separately? This could be used for some stunning visual effects, like a picture of your face slowly turning red, then green, and suddenly yellow.

By using simple method overloading, you can build another filter called **brightness**, which this time takes three parameters instead of one. The filter is otherwise an exact copy of the previous one, but you'll have to calculate each color component using the corresponding percent value, like the following code snippet:

```
void brightness(int percentR,int percentG,int percentB)
{
    for (int index=0;index<width*height;index++)
    {
        int c=pixels[index];
        int r=(c&0xff0000)>>16;
        int g=(c&0xff00)>>8;
        int b=c&0xff;

        r=Math.min(255,(r*percentR)/100);
        g=Math.min(255,(g*percentG)/100);
        b=Math.min(255,(b*percentB)/100);

        pixels[index]=(c&0xff000000)+(r<<16)+(g<<8)+b;
    }
}
```

So why not discard the previous filter and just use this one instead? By using the same value for **percentR**, **percentG**, and **percentB**, you get the exact same results as before. Well, this approach is almost a matter of taste, but I like to make this library as accessible as possible for you, the programmer. If you just want to change the overall brightness of the image, why should you be forced into typing more parameters than you have to? Let the computer struggle a little more instead. Programming is time consuming enough as it is.

Making Some Noise

While you're into the concept of changing the brightness of an image, why not take it a step further and invent a white-noise filter. This filter will simply add some noise to your image by increasing the brightness of each pixel randomly.

While this might sound like a stupid idea for still images, it can give some funky results when applied to your animation. Imagine a TV screen on your web page with a lot of noise, suddenly the image of your face, dog, girlfriend, or whatever appears slowly. This filter can also be combined successfully with some others, like **emboss**. By combining it with this particular filter, you get a nice sand-like effect, as shown in Figure 6.

This filter is almost identical to **brightness**, but this time the brightness scalar is chosen randomly for each pixel, as shown in the following code line:

```
int RandomBrightness=(int)(rnd.nextFloat()*percent)+100;
```

FIGURE 6

The noise filter.

The **percent** variable is used to control how much noise is to be added. The complete source code for the **noise** filter is given in the following code snippet:

```
void noise(float percent)
{
    Random rnd=new Random();

    for (int index=0;index<width*height;index++)
    {
        int c=pixels[index];
        int r=(c&0xff0000)>>16;
        int g=(c&0xff00)>>8;
        int b=c&0xff;

        int RandomBrightness=(int)(rnd.nextFloat()*percent)+100;

        r=Math.min((r*RandomBrightness)/100,255);
        g=Math.min((g*RandomBrightness)/100,255);
        b=Math.min((b*RandomBrightness)/100,255);

        pixels[index]=(c&0xff000000)+(r<<16)+(g<<8)+b;
    }
}
```

Make A 3D Button

Another filter that comes to mind while we're darkening and brightening the colors in an image, is **button**, a very handy filter that makes a 3D button out of an image. Often you want to make some icons for users to push while navigating your Web site, and those icons will definitely look much more pushable if they have the familiar 3D-button look. What's more, if you use this filter, users will actually be able to see the button being pushed down when they hit it, as shown in Figure 7. This is more than just a fancy effect; it's important to give users some feedback to tell them the program actually registered their action, especially if the actual response to the click is somewhat slow because of data being computed or loaded.

The benefits of using this filter instead of manually creating the buttons should be apparent. First of all, you'll never again have to bother making those 3D borders manually, a time-consuming and boring job—especially if you want the border to be partially transparent, like the **button** filter

FIGURE 7

The button filter.

makes it. And you only need to download one icon to generate both states of your button. This saves downloading time, which will definitely keep the user happy.

The implementation of this filter is simple. Given an intensity and border size, the filter is supposed to shade the border according to an imaginary light source placed above and left of the screen. For each color component on the left and top side of the border, a simple formula is used as shown in the following code snippet:

```
r=Math.max(Math.min(r+intensity,255),0);
g=Math.max(Math.min(g+intensity,255),0);
b=Math.max(Math.min(b+intensity,255),0);
```

If **intensity** is positive, this part of the border will appear brighter. For the bottom and right border, the same formula is used, but this time **intensity** is subtracted, as shown in the following code snippet:

```
r=Math.min(Math.max(r-intensity,0),255);
g=Math.min(Math.max(g-intensity,0),255);
b=Math.min(Math.max(b-intensity,0),255);
```

KickAss Java Programming

If the button is supposed to be pushed, all you need to do is change the sign of **intensity**. This is done automatically if the parameter **pushed** is true.

Before you take a look at the source code, here's a little tip: Sometimes you don't want the border to look so sharp. This can easily be avoided by creating the button using a little loop similar to the one shown in the following code snippet:

```
for (int i=0;i<8;i++)
        iconIP.button(i,20,false);
```

The code is pretty fast, so don't be afraid to call it several times. Now for further details, take a look at the source code, shown in Listing 4.

Listing 4 Code for the Button Class.
```
void button(int borderSize,int intensity, boolean pushed)
{
    if (pushed) intensity=-intensity;

    //Draw top and bottom border
    for (int y=0;y<borderSize;y++)
        for (int x=0;x<width-y;x++)
        {
            //Draw top border
            int c=pixels[x+y*width];
            int r=(c&0xff0000)>>16;
            int g=(c&0xff00)>>8;
            int b=c&0xff;

            r=Math.max(Math.min(r+intensity,255),0);
            g=Math.max(Math.min(g+intensity,255),0);
            b=Math.max(Math.min(b+intensity,255),0);

            pixels[x+y*width]=(c&0xff000000)+(r<<16)+(g<<8)+b;

            //Draw bottom border
            c=pixels[width-x-1+(height-y-1)*width];
            r=(c&0xff0000)>>16;
            g=(c&0xff00)>>8;
            b=c&0xff;

            r=Math.min(Math.max(r-intensity,0),255);
            g=Math.min(Math.max(g-intensity,0),255);
            b=Math.min(Math.max(b-intensity,0),255);
```

```
            pixels[width-x-1+(height-y-
                1)*width]=(c&0xff000000)+(r<<16)+(g<<8)+b;
        }

        //Draw side borders
        for (int x=0;x<borderSize;x++)
        for (int y=borderSize;y<height-x;y++)
        {
            //Draw left border
            int c=pixels[x+y*width];
            int r=(c&0xff0000)>>16;
            int g=(c&0xff00)>>8;
            int b=c&0xff;

            r=Math.max(Math.min(r+intensity,255),0);
            g=Math.max(Math.min(g+intensity,255),0);
            b=Math.max(Math.min(b+intensity,255),0);

            pixels[x+y*width]=(c&0xff000000)+(r<<16)+(g<<8)+b;

            //Draw right border
            c=pixels[width-x-1+(y-(borderSize-x))*width];
            r=(c&0xff0000)>>16;
            g=(c&0xff00)>>8;
            b=c&0xff;

            r=Math.min(Math.max(r-intensity,0),255);
            g=Math.min(Math.max(g-intensity,0),255);
            b=Math.min(Math.max(b-intensity,0),255);

            pixels[width-x-1+(y-(borderSize-x))*width]=
                    (c&0xff000000)+(r<<16)+(g<<8)+b;

        }
}
```

Catch The Waves

The **horizontalWave** and **verticalWave** filters are very simple, yet extremely effective when it comes to animation, especially if used together and without resetting the image for each frame rendered. Using these filters will lead to wonderful and unpredictable results, as shown in Figure 8.

To get the proper wave effect, you simply move each line up and down or left to right in a sinus pattern, with a given amplitude and frequency, as shown in Figure 9.

FIGURE 8

Combining horizontal and vertical waves.

First we'll make a duplicate of the pixel array to be sure we have a clean source image to move the pixels from at all times, undisturbed by the filter itself. This is shown in the following code snippet:

```
int[] sourcePixels=pixels;
pixels = new int[width * height];
```

The parameters passed to this filter is **nWaves**, **percent**, and **offset**. The **nWaves** parameter is the number of waves you want in the image. The **percent** parameter is the amplitude of the wave, given in percent of the image's width (**horizontalWave**) or height (**verticalWave**). We describe the amplitude like this because the same settings will give the same results independent of the image's size. The last parameter, **offset**, describes the wave's position. If **offset** varies from 0 to 100, the wave has moved exactly one wavelength.

I won't waste any space describing these simple filters in more detail, but you'll learn how to use them to create strange and wild animations later on. First, you might want to take a look at how these filters are implemented. The code is shown in Listing 5.

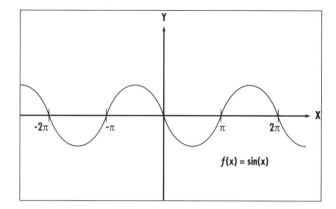

FIGURE 9

The sinus function as a wave maker.

Listing 5 Implementing the filters.
```
void horizontalWave(double nWaves,double percent,double offset)
{
  //Duplicate image
  int[] sourcePixels=pixels;
  pixels = new int[width * height];

  double waveFrequency=(nWaves*Math.PI*2.0)/height;
  double waveOffset=(offset*nWaves*Math.PI*2.0)/100.0;
  double radius=(width*percent)/100.0;

  int index=0;
  for (int y=0;y<height;y++)
  {
      int xOffset=(int)Math.round(Math.sin(
        y*waveFrequency+waveOffset)*radius);
      for (int x=0;x<width;x++)
      {
          if (xOffset>=0&&xOffset<width)
            pixels[index++]=sourcePixels[xOffset+width*y];
          else
            pixels[index++]=bgColor;
          xOffset++;
      }
  }
}
void verticalWave(double nWaves,double percent,double offset)
```

```
{
  //Duplicate image
  int[] sourcePixels=pixels;
  pixels = new int[width * height];

  double waveFrequency=(nWaves*Math.PI*2.0)/height;
  double waveOffset=(offset*nWaves*Math.PI*2.0)/100.0;
  double radius=(width*percent)/100.0;

  int index=0;
  for (int x=0;x<width;x++)
  {
      int yOffset=(int)Math.round(Math.sin(
        x*waveFrequency+waveOffset)*radius);
      for (int y=0;y<height;y++)
      {
          if (yOffset>=0&&yOffset<height)
            pixels[width*y+x]=sourcePixels[width*yOffset+x];
          else
            pixels[width*y+x]=bgColor;
          yOffset++;
      }
  }
}
```

Underwater Waves

Let's go one step further and experiment some more with waves. Although simple, waves are very appealing when used in animations, and when used right they can create some very impressive and unexpected effects.

Waves are often associated with water, so why not make a more "watery" wave? How can we reproduce the feeling of an image laying in water with waves above?

One simple approach is to duplicate the image line by line, but distort the source line in a wave-like fashion, as shown in Figure 10.

You can use a simple sinus function to generate the wave, much like you did in the previous example. This filter is actually pretty straightforward, but one major optimization technique is utilized. The filter is working by moving horizontal lines about, and, as you know, the image is stored in the pixel array as horizontal lines. These two facts mean that if we could just

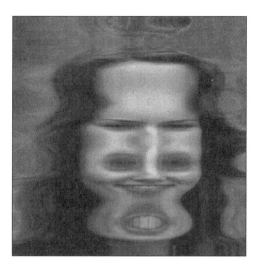

FIGURE 10

The verticalWave3D filter.

find a way to copy a whole line fast from one place to another, astonishing performance could be gained. This way you would only need to care about moving each line's y coordinate. And you're in luck. Java has a built-in method for moving data from one array to another at lightning speed, called **System.arraycopy**. **System.arraycopy** will actually make this filter so fast it can even be used to create real-time animations, without any Just in Time compiling!

All kinds of filters for moving horizontal lines can be generated fast using the method shown in the following code line:

```
System.arraycopy(sourcePixels,y1*widthpixels,y2*width,width);
```

In this code line, **y1** points to the line to be copied, and **y2** points to the destination line.

Unfortunately, this method only works with horizontal lines, so with this watery filter you'll only get fast processing on vertical waves. Horizontal waves will be as slow as ever. For further details, Listing 6 shows the source code to these filters.

Listing 6 Code for the horizontal-wave filters.

```java
void verticalWave3D(double nWaves,double percent, double offset)
{
    //Duplicate image
    int[] sourcePixels=pixels;
    pixels = new int[width * height];

    double angleRadians=(offset*3.6)/(180.0/Math.PI);

    double angleStep=((Math.PI*2)*nWaves)/height;
    double amplitude=(percent*height/2)/100.0;

    int y=0;
    for (int offset1=0;offset1<width*height;offset1+=width)
    {
        int offset2=(Math.max(Math.min((int)(
                (Math.cos(angleRadians)*amplitude+y)  ),height-
                1),0))*width;
        y++;
        System.arraycopy(sourcePixels,offset2,pixels,offset1,width);
        angleRadians+=angleStep;
    }
}

void horizontalWave3D(double nWaves,double percent, double offset)
{
    //Duplicate image
    int[] sourcePixels=pixels;
    pixels = new int[width * height];

    double angleRadians=(offset*3.6)/(180.0/Math.PI);

    double angleStep=((Math.PI*2)*nWaves)/width;
    double amplitude=(percent*height/2)/100.0;

    for (int x=0;x<width;x++)
    {
        int xOffset=Math.max(Math.min((int)(
            (Math.cos(angleRadians)*amplitude+x)  ),width-1),0);
        for (int yOffset=0;yOffset<width*height;yOffset+=width)
            pixels[x+yOffset]=sourcePixels[xOffset+yOffset];
            angleRadians+=angleStep;
    }
}
```

The Art Of Line Art

So far the images have been left pretty much intact, but to fool users into believing they're being fed all new images instead of just manipulated ones, something more drastic has to be done, namely **lineArt**. The **lineArt** filter changes the image into a very computer-inspired version. This filter is great for fancy special effects, especially animated ones. Color images turn into beautiful line drawings in a matter of milliseconds. The filter is demonstrated in Figure 11.

How is this magic edge detection done? First, you need to scan each line from left to right. The only thing you have to care about is how much each color component changes in intensity from pixel to pixel. If a color changes from black to white, this difference is big and therefore the contrast is sharp, so a line is detected and plotted. In essence, what you have is a contrast detector. High contrasts will cause the corresponding pixel in the filtered image to appear bright, low contrasts will hardly show at all. But make sure you choose good source images; high-quality true-color JPEGs work best. A horizontal line-art scan is demonstrated in Figure 12.

Once you've scanned the image, horizontally, you have to scan it, using the same algorithms, vertically as well. The reason is that horizontal scanning

FIGURE 11

The lineArt filter.

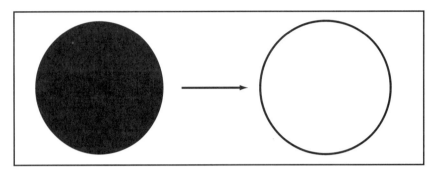

FIGURE 12

The result of a horizontal line-art scan.

only deals with horizontal edges. The new vertical scan results are simply added to the horizontal ones. The result is shown in Figure 13.

The contrasts in an image are seldom so easily detectable as black and white, so a scalar value is multiplied with the color component intensity change. This helps make even small contrasts visible as a line, but since some images already have very high contrasts, this scalar value is given by the parameter **intensity** so you'll be able to tune the **lineArt** function to suit your image best. Interesting results can also be gained if you change this parameter over time in an animation.

Now, let's take a look at how this filter can be implemented. As usual, performance is important, and the most obvious optimization is to detect all edges in just one pass. So, instead of first detecting all horizontal edges and then all vertical edges, you would benefit from detecting both horizontal and vertical edges at the same time.

To be able to detect the current contrast of a pixel, we need to know a little about two of its neighbors, namely the pixel directly on top of it and the pixel to its left. The left pixel is needed for the horizontal scan, while the pixel on top is used for the vertical scan. If **index** varies from **width** to **width*height**, the color components you need can be read with the code shown in the following snippet:

```
//Read pixel to the left
int c=sourcePixels[index-1];
```

```
int r1=(c&0xff0000)>>16;
int g1=(c&0xff00)>>8;
int b1=c&0xff;

//Read pixel above
c=sourcePixels[index-width];
int r2=(c&0xff0000)>>16;
int g2=(c&0xff00)>>8;
int b2=c&0xff;

//Read current pixel
c=sourcePixels[index];
int r=(c&0xff0000)>>16;
int g=(c&0xff00)>>8;
int b=c&0xff;
```

Now you have all the information you need to calculate the brightness of the new pixel, as shown in the following code snippet:

```
r=Math.min((Math.abs(r2-r)+Math.abs(r1-r))*intensity,255);
g=Math.min((Math.abs(g2-g)+Math.abs(g1-g))*intensity,255);
b=Math.min((Math.abs(b2-b)+Math.abs(b1-b))*intensity,255);
```

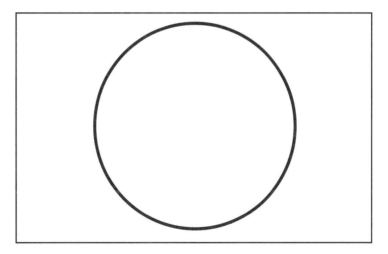

FIGURE 13

The result of both a horizontal and vertical line-art scan.

Even though these lines might look like a mess, it's all very simple. For the red color component, the contrast between the current pixel and its neighbor above is given by the following code line:

```
Math.abs(r2-r)
```

The contrast to the left neighbor is given by the following code line:

```
Math.abs(r1-r)
```

If you wonder what **Math.abs** has to do with it, this method simply removes any negative sign the result **r2-r** and **r1-r** might get, to make sure it's always positive.

These two contrast values are then added together to make sure both the vertical and the horizontal scan is considered. Finally, this value is multiplied with the **intensity** scalar to make it more visible. At last, **Math.min** is used to make sure the new value never exceeds the maximum byte value, which is 255.

Since the **index** variable is initialized with **width** and not 0 for the main loop, the first line of the image will not be affected at all. This is a side effect of the optimization, and to deal with it you can simply put the color defined by **bgColor** in the first line of the image, as shown in the following code line:

```
for (int index=0;index<width;index++) pixels[index]=bgColor;
```

The complete source for this filter is shown in Listing 7.

Listing 7 Source code for the filter.
```
void lineArt(int intensity)
{
    //Duplicate image
    int[] sourcePixels=pixels;
    pixels = new int[width * height];

    //The first line is undefined, give it the color of bgColor
    for (int index=0;index<width;index++) pixels[index]=bgColor;
```

```
for (int index=width;index<width*height;index++)
{
        //Read pixel to the left
        int c=sourcePixels[index-1];
        int r1=(c&0xff0000)>>16;
        int g1=(c&0xff00)>>8;
        int b1=c&0xff;

        //Read pixel above
        c=sourcePixels[index-width];
        int r2=(c&0xff0000)>>16;
        int g2=(c&0xff00)>>8;
        int b2=c&0xff;

        //Read current pixel
        c=sourcePixels[index];
        int r=(c&0xff0000)>>16;
        int g=(c&0xff00)>>8;
        int b=c&0xff;

        r=Math.min((Math.abs(r2-r)+Math.abs(r1-r))*intensity,255);
        g=Math.min((Math.abs(g2-g)+Math.abs(g1-g))*intensity,255);
        b=Math.min((Math.abs(b2-b)+Math.abs(b1-b))*intensity,255);

        pixels[index]=(c&0xff000000)+(r<<16)+(g<<8)+b;
    }
}
```

Back To The Stone Age

Often you need a background image for your applet, but the sad truth is that background pictures are large and nasty creatures with an unwillingness to download quickly, and inevitably make the user wait a small eternity before anything happens on the screen. Instead, you can use a boring, blank background—or you can generate cool backgrounds using this emboss filter on a scaled version of a small downloaded picture. This effect gives any picture a wild 3D look, as shown in Figure 14, and makes it more neutral so it won't hurt the eyes.

The **emboss** filter is actually not much different from the **lineArt** filter described earlier. In fact, it's much simpler because you'll only have to scan the pixels once.

FIGURE 14

The emboss filter.

Think of the image as a mountain. Each pixel represents its own height, and the brighter it is, the higher it's located. When imaginary light is cast, the uphills facing the light are lit up, and the downhills facing away are shaded. What you have to do is simulate a light ray by scanning the source pixels in the direction it's moving. When the "light" moves uphill, the color in the destination image is brightened by the height change from the previous pixel. When the "light" moves downhill, the destination's color is darkened instead. This is shown in Figure 15.

The implementation is pretty simple: If a color component goes from light to dark in the scan direction, the difference in intensity is subtracted from the matching background color component, which is given by the **red**, **green**, and **blue** parameters. If the red component changes from 128 to 100, then 28 is subtracted from the background red component and saved back into the filtered image. If the opposite is the case, the difference is added instead.

If the light is located to the left, a left-to-right scanline algorithm is used. If the light source is above the image, a top-to-bottom scanline algorithm fits best. But changing the scan direction like this is troublesome and could easily cause the code to become rather lengthy. Instead, always scan left to

FIGURE 15

Think of the image as a mountain like this.

right, but change which of the neighbors of the source pixel is to be considered. This neighbor is described by an offset, **light**, determined by the following code line:

```
int light=(int)(Math.round(Math.sin(angleRadians))*
  width)+(int)(Math.round(Math.cos(angleRadians)));
```

The **angleRadians** describes the angle of the incoming light, but only angles divisible by 45 are valid. The reason is that each source pixel only has eight neighbors, and 360 degrees divided by 8 is 45 degrees.

Another thing worth mentioning is that all border pixels are undefined. For example, if the light comes from the left, the first pixel is to be compared to its left neighbor. The problem is that pixels at the left border don't have left neighbors. The same goes for the other borders, if all light angles are to be considered. You must, therefore, draw a solid border around the embossed picture to get rid of potential strange effects in this area.

The full source code is shown in Listing 8.

Listing 8   The emboss method.

```
void emboss(double angle,double power,int red,int green, int blue)
{
    //Duplicate image
    int[] sourcePixels=pixels;
    pixels = new int[width * height];

    double angleRadians=angle/(180.0/Math.PI);
    int light=(int)(Math.round(Math.sin(angleRadians))*
       width)+(int)(Math.round(Math.cos(angleRadians)));

    for (int index=width+1;index<width*height-width-1;index++)
    {
        //Read current pixel
        int c=sourcePixels[index];
        int r1=(c&0xff0000)>>16;
        int g1=(c&0xff00)>>8;
        int b1=c&0xff;

        //Read pixel in the direction given by angle
        c=sourcePixels[index-light];
        int r2=(c&0xff0000)>>16;
        int g2=(c&0xff00)>>8;
        int b2=c&0xff;

        int r=Math.min(Math.max(red+(int)((r2-r1)*power),0),255);
        int g=Math.min(Math.max(green+(int)((g2-g1)*power),0),255);
        int b=Math.min(Math.max(blue+(int)((b2-b1)*power),0),255);

        pixels[index]=(c&0xff000000)+(r<<16)+(g<<8)+b;
    }

    //Borders are undefined, fill with specified color
    int color=(red<<16)+(green<<8)+blue;
    for (int index=0;index<width;index++)
    {
        pixels[index]=(sourcePixels[index]&0xff000000)+color;
        pixels[width*height-index-1]=(sourcePixels[width*height-index-
           1]&0xff000000)+color;
    }
    for (int index=0;index<width*height;index+=width)
    {
```

```
            pixels[index]=(sourcePixels[index]&0xff000000)+color;
            pixels[index+width-1]=(sourcePixels[index+width-
               1]&0xff000000)+color;
    }
}
```

Getting Blurry

Background images are fine if you want to spice up your Java applet, but often they have a tendency to take center stage. There are several ways to make your background images more anonymous, but one of the most effective is using the **blur** filter, shown in Figure 16.

A pixel is smoothed by finding the average color of all pixels surrounding it within a given distance. The larger the distance, the more blurred the pixel will seem. To optimize this, you can consider all pixels within a surrounding square, rather than a surrounding circle.

So, how do you find the average color of an area? Easy. Simply add all intensities for each red, green, and blue color component, then divide these three sums by the number of components considered. The resulting values are your average colors.

FIGURE 16

The blur filter.

Since even the lowest form of blur would have an average color value of 9 pixels (all neighbors of the source pixel plus the source pixel itself), the blurring process can be rather lengthy. For an image with the dimension 320x200 pixels, 576,000 pixels would have to be considered (320x200x9 pixels=576,000). For the next level of blur, you'd have to take 4,096,000 pixels into consideration (320x200x16 pixels=4,096,000)!

For further details about the implementation, take a look at the source code in Listing 9.

Listing 9 The blur method.

```
void blur(int power)
{
    //Duplicate image
    int[] sourcePixels=pixels;
    pixels = new int[width * height];

    int index=0;
    for (int y=0;y<height;y++)
        for (int x=0;x<width;x++)
        {
            int red=0, green=0, blue=0,nColors=0;
            for (int dy=-power+y;dy<=power+y;dy++)
                for (int dx=-power+x;dx<=power+x;dx++)
                    if ((dx>=0)&&(dx<width)&&(dy>=0)&&(dy<height))
                    {
                        int c=sourcePixels[dx+dy*width];
                        red+=(c&0xff0000)>>16;
                        green+=(c&0xff00)>>8;
                        blue+=c&0xff;
                        nColors++;
                    }
            red/=nColors;
            green/=nColors;
            blue/=nColors;
                pixels[index]=(sourcePixels[index]&0xff000000)+
                    (red<<16)+(green<<8)+blue;
                index++;
        }
}
```

Rotate

Rotating an image is often useful, both when it comes to animations and for representing static images. Unfortunately, the process of rotating an image around an arbitrary angle is rather time consuming and often inaccurate.

The most straightforward method is to scan through each pixel in the source image, rotate it around the center, and put it back into the destination image.

Although this method may sound perfect at first glance, you'll discover it leaves you with a rotated image full of small holes. This is because of small computing errors that make some pixels overlap and, hence, leave empty space.

One approach to solving this problem is to make all computations exceptionally accurate—fine if you happen to have a supercomputer nearby. If not, you'll be happy to know there's another solution.

The trick is to *rotate the source coordinates instead of the destination coordinates*—a very important point to remember when dealing with computer graphics. In fact, I think I'll say it once more—slowly this time: The trick is to rotate the source coordinates instead of the destination coordinates. In fact, this is a trick you can use successfully with many other filters. Even games like Doom use this backward-rendering technology to make the graphics more fluid and accurate.

To explain this further, let's take a look at how a simple duplication of an image works. First you need to have a source and a destination image. In pseudo-code, it would look something like the following code snippet:

```
for (int dY=0;dY<height;dY++)
    for (int dX=0;dX<height;dX++)
    {
        sX=dX;
        sY=dY;
        destinationImage(dX,dY)=sourceImage(sX,sY)
    }
```

Remember that pseudo-code means this code snippet would actually generate a syntax error in Java; it's only readable by humans, so don't try this at home kids. The destination point (**dX,dY**) travels from left to right, down and left to right again until all pixels in the image are covered. In this case, the source point (**sX,sY**), is a duplicate of the destination point, and the resulting image would be an exact copy of the source image.

So, what happens if you mess a little with the source point, like in this slightly changed version of the code snippet shown earlier? The revised code is shown in the following code snippet. The result is shown in Figure 17.

```
for (int dY=0;dY<height;dY++)
    for (int dX=0;dX<height;dX++)
    {
        sX=dX/2;
        sY=dY;
        destinationImage(dX,dY)=sourceImage(sX,sY)
    }
```

Because the source point now only moves half a pixel to the right while the destination point moves one pixel, the image will appear stretched horizontally by a factor of two.

Now it's about time to apply some more interesting modifiers to the source coordinate. A point (**dX,dY**) can be rotated by an arbitrary angle **a**, around

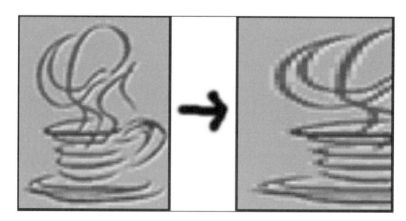

FIGURE 17

Stretching of the image by manipulating the source point while copying it.

the mathematical center point (0,0) with the formula shown in the following code snippet:

```
sX=dX*cos(a) - dY*sin(a);
sY=dY*cos(a) + dX*sin(a);
```

But, of course, the middle of your image is not located at coordinate (0,0). This point is, as you know, located in the upper-left corner of the image. Since you probably don't want to rotate the image around its corner, but rather around its center, all points passed to these functions must temporarily be moved to make sure the point (0,0) is the center of the image while it's rotated. This can easily be done by subtracting **centerX** from **dX** and **centerY** from **dY**, because, as you recall, (**centerX**, **centerY**) is the center point of the image as defined in the **ImageProcessor** class. A more general formula to rotate an image around its center is shown in the following code snippet:

```
sX=(dX-centerX)*cos(a) - (dY-centerY)*sin(a);
sY=(dY-centerY)*cos(a) + (dX-centerX)*sin(a);
```

Of course, this code could be optimized by making **dX** go from **-centerX** to **centerX** and **dY** go from **-centerY** to **centerY** in the first place, instead of subtracting **centerX** and **centerY** all the time.

The last thing you have to do is translate the source coordinates back to where they came from by adding **centerX** and **centerY** again, because in your image's coordinate system (**centerX,centerY**) is the center of the image rather than (0,0). This is shown in the following code snippet:

```
sX=((dX-centerX)*cos(a) - (dY-centerY)*sin(a)) + centerX;
sY=((dY-centerY)*cos(a) + (dX-centerX)*sin(a)) + centerY;
```

TIP Degrees and Radians

Most of us are pretty familiar with the concept of degrees. If a man with a mean expression in his face comes walking toward you in a dark alley and asks what an image will look like if you rotate it 180 degrees, you can simply answer, "Easy! The image will appear upside down and mirrored," and he'll go away smiling. But what if he uses another unit for describing angles, and asks what happens if he rotates the image 1.57 radians? Ouch! It's hardly intuitive that he means 90 degrees, and you could end up being seriously hurt. As you might have suspected, the reason for me bringing this up is because Java happens to love radians, and this is the format you have to deal with. It's hardly intuitive, but luckily the translation of degrees to radians is simple: 360 degrees equals 6.28 radians, or Pi*2 radians to be exact. A simple formula can therefore be implemented to make sure you can work with degrees all the way, and just translate to radians when you have to: radians=degrees/(180.0/Math.PI). Now you never have to worry about radians again.

An operation like rotating an image around an arbitrary angle is very computation intensive, so you'll need to optimize it as much as possible. The first thing to do is eliminate the computation of one cosine and one sinus for each pixel. Even though these operations seem innocent enough, they use a vast number of CPU cycles each. What you can do is simply calculate these values outside the main loop and put the results into some temporary variables, as shown in the following code snippet:

```
double ca=Math.cos(angleRadians);
double sa=Math.sin(angleRadians);
```

The idea of putting pre-calculated values into temporary variables or lookup tables, to save time later, is perhaps the number one optimizing technique.

Now you're ready to implement the filter. Well, almost. First a couple of words about clipping: It might seem natural to expand the image if you rotate it, say, 45 degrees, but instead its corners are clipped. This is because if it really did expand, successive calls to **rotate** while rendering an animation without resetting the image would cause the image to grow into enormous proportions. This is shown in Figure 18.

FIGURE 18

Clipping of a rotated image.

Let's take a look at the final piece of code, shown in the following snippet:

```
void rotate(double angle)
{
  //Duplicate image
  int[] sourcePixels=pixels;
  pixels = new int[width * height];

  //Convert from degrees to radians and calculate cos and sin of angle
  //Negate the angle to make sure the rotation is clockwise
  double angleRadians=-angle/(180.0/Math.PI);
  double ca=Math.cos(angleRadians);
  double sa=Math.sin(angleRadians);

  int index=0;
  for (int y=-centerY;y<centerY;y++)
      for (int x=-centerX;x<centerX;x++)
      {
          int xs=(int)(x*ca-y*sa)+centerX;
          int ys=(int)(y*ca+x*sa)+centerY;
          if (xs>=0&&xs<width&&ys>=0&&ys<height)
            pixels[index++]=sourcePixels[width*ys+xs];
          else
            pixels[index++]=bgColor;
      }
}
```

FIGURE 19

The spiral filter.

Spiral Fun

Now that you've entered the world of rotating, you can achieve some very interesting effects. In the previous example, all pixels were rotated around the center at the same angle, but imagine what happens if you rotate the source coordinates at different angles, according to certain rules!

The first rule that comes to mind is to rotate the source coordinate according to the destination coordinate's distance from the center. This way, pixels in the center would be rotated zero degrees, and as the pixels become farther away from the center, they would be rotated more and more, up to a given maximum. This leads to a nice spiral effect which is just perfect for animation, as shown in Figure 19.

For this **spiral** filter, you can recycle the core from **rotate**. The only thing you have to add is a formula for calculating the distance from a given point. Good old Pythagoras, whose idea is illustrated in Figure 20, figured out that the distance **d** from the center coordinate (0,0) to a point at coordinate (**x,y**) is given by the rather important formula shown in the following code line:

```
double d=Math.sqrt(x*x+y*y);
```

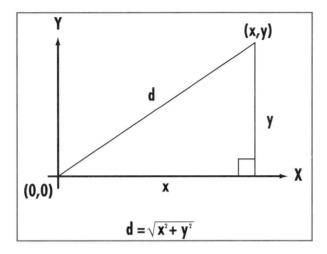

FIGURE 20

Pythagorean theorem.

That is about all the magic you need for this filter. To get the correct rotation angle based on this distance, you must multiply it by a scalar **scale**, which is calculated from the maximum **angle** parameter as shown in the following code snippet:

```
double angleRadians=-angle/(180.0/Math.PI);
double maxDist=Math.sqrt(width*width+height*height);
double scale=angleRadians/maxDist;
```

Now the angle **a** is given by the following code lines:

```
a=Math.sqrt(x*x+y*y)*scale;
```

As you might see by now, the inner loop of this filter includes the calculation of one cosine, one sinus, and one square root per pixel. This means the filter will be rather CPU hungry, so use with care. The code is shown in Listing 10.

Listing 10 The spiral function.

```
void spiral(double angle)
{
  //Duplicate image
```

```
        int[] sourcePixels=pixels;
        pixels = new int[width * height];

        double angleRadians=-angle/(180.0/Math.PI);
        double maxDist=Math.sqrt(width*width+height*height);
        double scale=angleRadians/maxDist;

        int index=0;
        for (int y=-centerY;y<centerY;y++)
            for (int x=-centerX;x<centerX;x++)
            {
                double a=Math.sqrt(x*x+y*y)*scale;
                double ca=Math.cos(a);
                double sa=Math.sin(a);

                int xs=(int)(x*ca-y*sa)+centerX;
                int ys=(int)(y*ca+x*sa)+centerY;
                if (xs>=0&&xs<width&&ys>=0&&ys<height)
                    pixels[index++]=sourcePixels[width*ys+xs];
                else
                    pixels[index++]=bgColor;
            }
    }
```

Digital Ripples

Let's take the idea of rotating one step further and make a ripple effect. Again, you can recycle the previous **spiral** example, which contains most of the elements you'll need.

This filter will try to simulate the circular waves that appear and move away from the center when a droplet hits the surface of water. This effect is really not as hard to achieve as you might think. All you need to do is rotate the source pixels in a sinus fashion around the center, according to the destination pixels' distance from the center. This is shown in Figures 21 and 22.

The only change you'll have to make from the **spiral** filter is to pass the scaled distance into a sinus function, instead of using it directly as an angle, as shown in the following code lines:

```
double a=Math.sin(Math.sqrt(x*x+y*y)*scale+offset)*angleRadians;
```

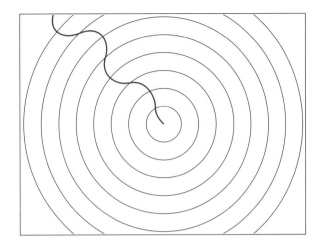

FIGURE 21

The pixels follow this path in a ripple effect.

FIGURE 22

The ripple filter.

Recall that the **spiral** version of the same line is the following code line:

```
double a=Math.sqrt(x*x+y*y)*scale;
```

So, two new variables are added: **offset** and **angleRadians**. The **angleRadians** variable is the amplitude of the waves, and is calculated from the **percent** parameter. A **percent** value of 100 will cause a maximum "wave rotation" of 360 degrees. In this case, it'll hardly look like a ripple filter, but exaggerated values like this often yield interesting results. The **offset** variable ranges from 0 to 100, and if this is changed from 0 to 100 in an animation, the wave will move exactly one wavelength.

In addition to these changes, the **scale** value is also changed to make sure you get the number of waves you requested with the **nWaves** parameter, as shown in the following code snippet:

```
double maxDist=Math.sqrt(width*width+height*height);
double scale=(Math.PI*2.0*nWaves)/maxDist;
```

As you can see, it's pretty easy to incorporate new effects using the **rotate** filter as a basis. Experiment more on your own; real neat effects are still unexplored.

Listing 11 shows the complete source code for the **ripple** filter.

Listing 11 The ripple filter.
```
void ripple(double nWaves,double percent,double offset)
{
  //Duplicate image
  int[] sourcePixels=pixels;
  pixels = new int[width * height];

  double angleRadians=(Math.PI*2.0*percent)/100.0;
  double maxDist=Math.sqrt(width*width+height*height);
  double scale=(Math.PI*2.0*nWaves)/maxDist;
  offset=(offset*Math.PI*2.0)/100.0;

  int index=0;
  for (int y=-centerY;y<centerY;y++)
      for (int x=-centerX;x<centerX;x++)
      {
          double a=Math.sin(Math.sqrt(x*x+y*y)*scale+offset)*
                      angleRadians;
          double ca=Math.cos(a);
          double sa=Math.sin(a);
```

```
            int xs=(int)(x*ca-y*sa)+centerX;
            int ys=(int)(y*ca+x*sa)+centerY;
            if (xs>=0&&xs<width&&ys>=0&&ys<height)
              pixels[index++]=sourcePixels[width*ys+xs];
            else
              pixels[index++]=bgColor;
      }
}
```

Explode!

Now it's time to do some even more drastic things to your poor defenseless image: Let's blow it up! This can lead to some interesting results when used in an animation, as I'm sure you can imagine.

But how does a picture behave when it's blown up? One approach is to put a virtual bomb somewhere in the picture, and simulate what happens when it goes off. We'll put our bomb in the middle of the screen, as shown in Figure 23.

Each pixel is then given a random speed toward the screen, the speed is greatest closest to the bomb.

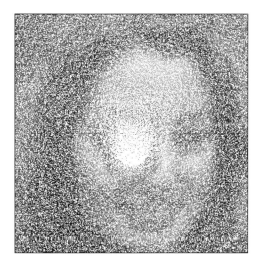

FIGURE 23

The explode filter.

When the speed of a pixel is found, it can simply be multiplied with the elapsed time from blastoff, and you get the new position of the pixel. To optimize the explosion filter, each pixel is only blown towards the screen, not to left and right or up and down. But of course, the perspective comes into play, so when the pixels are projected onto the flat screen from a virtual 3D space, the pixels are moved in all directions anyway, and you get a nice 3D effect. In addition to this, gravity is also considered, so the pixels will eventually be drawn downwards.

> **TIP** **Z-Buffering**
> When painting 3D worlds, some of the biggest problems concern finding out what's visible and what's not. One approach is to calculate how far from the camera each object is, and then paint them from back to front. This works fine a lot of the time, but what do you do if an object passes through another object, like a nail through a plank? What do you paint first, the nail or the plank? Whatever you do, the result could be wrong because the nail could actually be visible both in front of the plank and behind it. To deal with this, you can use a rendering technique called *z-buffering*. In addition to the image pixel array, an additional array of z—or depth—values are created for the image. This array can be used to remember the actual depth of each pixel plotted. The simple rule to follow when you're going to plot a pixel is: If the previous pixel was farther away according to its z-buffer value, then plot the new pixel and preserve the depth of it in the z-buffer array.

After the perspective projection, which is covered more thoroughly later in the 3D chapters, is applied to a pixel, it's placed onto the image—if there's no pixel in front of it at that position.

As mentioned, each pixel has its own random speed. For an image of 640x480 pixels, this sums up to 307,200 random values—a considerable amount if you're allocating memory for an array to save these values into. But here's where you can use a neat trick, because the random numbers generated by Java are not true random numbers. They're calculated using a seed as an input. This seed is fed to a function which spits out a pseudo random number. Usually the seed value is incremented automatically after each random number is retrieved, to make sure you always get a seemingly random number, but you can also set it to make sure the exact same sequence of random numbers is returned each time. This is what you can do in the explode filter, so you don't have to allocate memory to hold all the random speed values. Just use the random number generator as a virtual array of random values. The only thing you have to remember is to set the seed with **setSeed** before you start reading from this "array". Keep this trick in mind; it's quite handy when you need a vast number of random array elements to build a scene. Entire landscapes could be "stored" like this.

Take a look at the source for all details about the explode filter. The code is shown in Listing 12.

Listing 12 The code for the explode filter.

```java
void explode(double time)
{
    //Duplicate image
    int[] sourcePixels=pixels;
    pixels = new int[width * height];
    int[] zBuffer = new int[width * height];
    Random rnd=new Random();
    //Make sure the same sequence of random numbers are returned for
       each call to explode
    rnd.setSeed(0);

    int index=0;
    //This is the y value added because of gravity
    double yOffset=((time+1.0)*(time*1.0))/10.0;

    for (int y=-centerY;y<centerY;y++)
        for (int x=-centerX;x<centerX;x++)
        {
            int c=sourcePixels[index];
            if ((c&0xff000000)!=0)
            {
                //Calculate distance from center, or the 'bomb'
                double d=Math.sqrt(x*x+y*y);
                //Pixel's z, or depth, value
                double z=(rnd.nextDouble()+1)*time/d;
```

```java
            //Calculate x and y destination, add perspective
            int xd=(int)(x*z+x)+centerX;
            int yd=(int)((y+yOffset)*z+y)+centerY;
        //Calculate the pixels offset in the pixels array
            int offset=xd+yd*width;
            if (xd>=0&&xd<width&&yd>=0&&yd<height)
            //Check to see if another pixel blocks this
                if (zBuffer[offset]<=z)
                {
                    //The pixel is unblocked, plot and update z,
                   //or depth, value
                    pixels[offset]=c;
                    zBuffer[offset]=(int)z;
                }
        }
        index++;
    }
}
```

You Already Smelled The Coffee.
Now Move On To The Hard Stuff...

Web Informant will get you there.

Developing successful applications for the Web is what you really like to do. You like your information straight. You want it bold and to the point.

Web Informant Magazine is the only source you need, offering nuts and bolts programming solutions, specific coding techniques, actual code and downloadable files—no gimmicks, trends or fluff.

It's a powerful source of information, and it's the only source of information challenging enough to keep you on the edge. It's tough. It's Java®, Perl, JavaScript, HTML, and VRML. It's unexplored territory, and you like it that way.

Web Informant will get you there.

You can get there from here. To order, and recieve a free bonus issue call 1.800.88.INFORM or 916.686.6610. FAX: 916.686.8497. Ask for offer #COR8000

To get there via a direct link to our *test drive* page:
HTTP://WWW.INFORMANT.COM/WI/WITEST.HTM

FREE ISSUE! YES! I want to sharpen my Web development skills. Sign me up to receive one free issue of *Web Informant*, The Complete Monthly Guide to Web Development. If I choose to subscribe, I'll get 11 additional BIG issues (12 in all) for the super low price of $49.95.* That's a savings of 30% off the single-copy price. If I don't, I'll simply write "cancel" on the invoice and owe nothing, with no further obligation on my part.

Name _____
Company _____
Address _____
City/State/Zip _____
(City/Province/Postal Code)
Country _____ Phone _____
FAX _____
E-Mail _____

*International rates: $54.95/year to Canada, $74.95/year to Mexico, $79.95/year to all other countries. **COR 8000**

Informant Communications Group ■ 10519 E Stockton Blvd ■ Ste 142 Elk Grove, CA 95624-9704

VBScript & ActiveX Wizardry

Uses clear, understandable language to teach you the latest special effects for creating eye-popping Web pages.

Only $39.99

Call 800-410-0192

Fax 602-483-0193

Outside U.S. 602-483-0192

If you're tired of the same old drab, static, text-only Web pages, use Visual Basic Script and ActiveX Wizardry to make your Web pages perform impressive tricks. You'll learn to create frames, animate graphics and text banners, play music or sound effects, create data entry forms, obtain and validate data from users, and use exciting new ActiveX controls. All the techniques are demonstrated with real-life projects that you can modify and incorporate into your own Web pages.

CORIOLIS GROUP BOOKS

http://www.coriolis.com

VISUAL DEVELOPER magazine

Give Yourself the Visual Edge

Don't Lose Your Competitve Edge Act Now!

1 Year $21.95
(6 issues)

2 Years $37.95
(12 issues)

($53.95 Canada; $73.95 Elsewhere)
Please allow 4-6 weeks for delivery
All disk orders must be pre-paid

The first magazine dedicated to the Visual Revolution

Join Jeff Duntemann and his crew of master authors for a tour of the visual software development universe. Peter Aitken, Al Williams, Ray Konopka, David Gerrold, Michael Covington, Tom Campbell, and all your favorites share their insights into rapid application design and programming, software component development, and content creation for the desktop, client/server, and online worlds. The whole visual world will be yours, six times per year: Windows 95 and NT, Multimedia, VRML, Java, HTML, Delphi, VC++, VB, and more. *Seeing is succeeding!*

1-800-410-0192

See *Visual Developer* on the Web! http://www.coriolis.com

7339 East Acoma Dr. Suite 7 • Scottsdale, Arizona 85260

WEB • CGI • JAVA • VB • VC++ • DELPHI • SOFTWARE COMPONENTS

Where have you been?

Stop wandering the Web and point your browser to http://www.coriolis.com. Here you'll find dozens of programming resources, books, and magazines that you can use to develop Web and Intranet apps, databases, games and more. In fact, we'll send you a FREE issue of Visual Developer Magazine just for stopping by and telling us what you think. Experience the world of software development with Coriolis Interactive. It's where you need to be.

Where You Need to be.

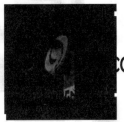

CORIOLIS GROUP

Coriolis Interactive

http//www.coriolis.com

Get A Jump On Java
Visit the Coriolis Group's NEW Java Web site!

Visual Developer Online
The only magazine dedicated to the visual revolution. Read an article, grab a back issue, or review the Editorial Calendar to see what's to come.

Developer's Connection
Jump into the "Developer's Connection", where you can stay up to date on hot topics, current articles, and the latest software, and browse the Developer's Club books and software.

Order A Book
Purchase a book online and save up to 20% off your total order. All orders are secure!

Search The Site
Know what you want but can't find it? Search the site quickly and easily.

News Flash
A quick peek at what's HOT on the Coriolis Web site and the Internet.

And The Winner Is...
Take a peek at the winners who won cool Coriolis products just visiting the Web site.

Books & Software
Look through Coriolis' vast selection of books with topics ranging from the Internet to game programming. Browse through descriptions, tables of contents, sample chapters, and even view the front cover before you buy. Secure online ordering is **now** available.

What's Free
Grab the goods for free...including a free copy of Visual Developer, plus read about the upcoming give aways available just for browsing our site.

What's An Idea!
Do you have a cool topic that is not being addressed? Maybe an emerging technology that has not been tapped into? Check here if you want to write for the Coriolis Group.